# Social Services Disrupted

# NEW HORIZONS IN SOCIAL POLICY

**Series Editors:** Patricia Kennett and Misa Izuhara, *University of Bristol, UK*

The New Horizons in Social Policy series captures contemporary issues and debates in social policy and encourages critical, innovative and thought-provoking approaches to understanding and explaining current trends and developments in the field. With its emphasis on original contributions from established and emerging researchers on a diverse range of topics, books in the series are essential reading for keeping up to date with the latest research and developments in the area.

Titles in the series include:

# Social Services Disrupted

Changes, Challenges and Policy Implications for Europe in Times of Austerity

*Edited by*

## Flavia Martinelli

*Professor of Policies and Strategies for Territorial Cohesion, Department of Architecture and Territory, Mediterranea University of Reggio Calabria, Italy*

## Anneli Anttonen

*Professor of Social Policy, Faculty of Social Sciences, University of Tampere, Finland*

## Margitta Mätzke

*Professor of Politics and Social Policy, Institute of Politics and Social Policy, Johannes Kepler University Linz, Austria*

NEW HORIZONS IN SOCIAL POLICY

Cheltenham, UK • Northampton, MA, USA

Published by
Edward Elgar Publishing Limited
The Lypiatts
15 Lansdown Road
Cheltenham
Glos GL50 2JA
UK

Edward Elgar Publishing, Inc.
William Pratt House
9 Dewey Court
Northampton
Massachusetts 01060
USA


A catalogue record for this book
is available from the British Library

Library of Congress Control Number: 2017941895


This book is available electronically in the **Elgar**online
Social and Political Science subject collection
DOI 10.4337/9781786432117

ISBN 978 1 78643 210 0 (cased)
ISBN 978 1 78643 211 7 (eBook)

Typeset by Servis Filmsetting Ltd, Stockport, Cheshire
Printed and bound in Great Britain by TJ International Ltd, Padstow

# Contents

*v*

# Figures and tables

## FIGURES

## TABLES

# Contributors

**Sofia Adam** is an independent researcher in the field of social and solidarity economy. She currently works as Project Coordinator at the Heinrich Boell Foundation, Greece.

**Anneli Anttonen** is Professor of Social Policy at the Faculty of Social Sciences, University of Tampere, Finland.

**Angela Bagnato** has worked as Post-doctoral Research Fellow at the Department of Architecture and Territory, University of Reggio Calabria, Italy.

**Stefania Barillà** has worked as Post-doctoral Research Fellow at the Department of Architecture and Territory, University of Reggio Calabria, Italy.

**Anikó Bernát** works at the TARKI Social Research Institute, Budapest, Hungary.

**Ingo Bode** is Professor of Social Policy, Society and Organizations at the Institute of Social Work and Social Welfare of the University of Kassel, Germany.

**Peter Brokking** is Research Engineer and Programme Director at the Department of Urban Planning and Environment, KTH-Royal Institute of Technology, Stockholm, Sweden.

**Blanca Deusdad** is Senior Lecturer of Social Work at the Department of Anthropology, Rovira i Virgili University, Tarragona, Spain.

**Danielle Dierckx** is Professor of Urban and Social Policies at the University of Antwerp and is affiliated to the Research Center on Inequality, Poverty, Social Exclusion and the City (OASeS), Antwerp, Belgium.

**Robert Fluder** is Professor of Social Policy, Bern University of Applied Sciences, Division of Social Work, Switzerland.

**Laurent Fraisse** is Associate Researcher at the Interdisciplinarity Laboratory of Economic Sociology, Conservatoire National des Arts et Métiers, Paris, France.

**Marisol García** is Professor of Urban Sociology at the Department of Sociology of the University of Barcelona, Spain.

**José Luis Gómez-Barroso** is Associate Professor of Applied Economics at UNED-National Distance Education University, Spain.

**Erika Gubrium** is Associate Professor at the Faculty of Social Sciences, Oslo and Akershus University College, Oslo, Norway.

**Liisa Häikiö** is Professor of Social Policy and Vice-Dean at the Faculty of Social Sciences, University of Tampere, Finland.

**Ivan Harsløf** is Associate Professor and Vice-Dean for Research at the Faculty of Social Sciences, Oslo and Akershus University College of Applied Sciences, Norway.

**Jana Havlíková** is a Researcher at the Research Institute for Labour and Social Affairs, Prague, Czech Republic.

**Jana Javornik** is Associate Professor of Social Policy and Director of the Noon Centre for Equality & Diversity at the University of East London, UK.

**Outi Jolanki** is Research Manager at the University of Tampere, Finland and Senior Researcher at the University of Jyväskylä, Finland.

**Olli Karsio** is a Researcher at the Faculty of Social Sciences, University of Tampere, Finland.

**Marcus Knutagård** is a Researcher and Senior Lecturer at the School of Social Work, Lund University, Sweden.

**Teppo Kröger** is Professor of Social and Public Policy at the Department of Social Sciences and Philosophy of the University of Jyväskylä, Finland.

**Kateřina Kubalčíková** is Assistant Professor at the Department of Social Policy and Social Work, Masaryk University Brno and Researcher at the Research Institute of Labour and Social Affairs, Prague, Czech Republic.

**Bettina Leibetseder** is Researcher at SORA, Vienna, and Privatdozent at the Institute of Politics and Social Policy of the Johannes Kepler University in Linz, Austria.

**Sagit Lev** is a doctoral student at Bar Ilan University, Israel.

**Raquel Marbán-Flores** is Assistant Professor of Economics at the Complutense University of Madrid, Spain.

**Flavia Martinelli** is Professor of Policies and Strategies for Territorial Cohesion at the Department of Architecture and Territory, Mediterranea University of Reggio Calabria, Italy.

**Rosa Mas Giralt** is a Post-doctoral Teaching Fellow and Researcher at the University of Leeds, United Kingdom.

**Margitta Mätzke** is Professor of Politics and Social Policy at the Institute of Politics and Social Policy, Johannes Kepler University, Linz, Austria.

**Andreas Novy** is Professor at the Institute of Multi-Level Governance and Development of the Vienna University of Economics and Business, Vienna, Austria.

**Einar Øverbye** is Professor at the Faculty of Social Sciences of the Oslo and Akershus University College, Oslo, Norway.

**Charles Pace** is Senior Lecturer (now Visiting) at the Department of Social Policy and Social Work, University of Malta, Malta.

**Peter Raeymaeckers** is Assistant Professor at the Master of Social Work of the University of Antwerp and is affiliated to the Research Center of Inequality, Poverty, Social Exclusion and the City (OASeS), Antwerp, Belgium.

**Stefania Sabatinelli** is Assistant Professor of Economic Sociology at the Department of Architecture and Urban Studies, Polytechnic of Milan, Italy.

**Antonella Sarlo** is Associate Professor of Urban Planning at the Department of Architecture and Territory, University of Reggio Calabria, Italy.

**Michela Semprebon** is Post-doctoral Research Fellow at the Unesco Chair on the Social and Spatial Inclusion of International Migrants of the IUAV University, Venice, Italy.

**Gábor Szüdi** is Assistant Professor at the University of Economics in Bratislava, Slovakia and a Research Associate at the Centre for Social Innovation, Vienna, Austria.

**Jaroslava Szüdi** is Assistant Professor at the University of Economics in Bratislava, Slovakia.

**Signy Irene Vabo** is Professor of Political Science at the University of Oslo, Norway.

**Dina Vaiou** is Professor of Urban Analysis and Gender Studies at the Department of Urban and Regional Planning, National Technical University of Athens, Greece.

**Sue Vella** is Senior Lecturer at the Department of Social Policy and Social Work, University of Malta, Malta.

**Zsuzsanna Vercseg** works at the Tempus Public Foundation, Budapest, Hungary.

**Serena Vicari Haddock** is Senior Associate Professor of Urban Sociology at the Department of Sociology and Social Research of the University of Milano-Bicocca, Italy.

**Carla Weinzierl** works at the Institute of Multi-Level Governance and Development, Vienna University of Economics and Business, Austria.

**Florian Wukovitsch** has worked at the Institute of Multi-Level Governance and Development, Vienna University of Economics and Business, Austria.

# Acknowledgements

This volume conveys the main findings of the COST Action IS1102 *SO.S. COHESION – Social services, welfare states and places: the restructuring of social services in Europe and its impact on social and territorial cohesion and governance*, which ran from 21 November 2011 to 30 April 2016. The Action was coordinated by Flavia Martinelli at the Mediterranea University of Reggio Calabria and involved 24 countries, over 40 research and university institutions and about 90 researchers and scholars in Europe.

In addition to the hard copy edition, the volume is published as an open access electronic book – fully available to the broader public and freely downloadable on Edward Elgar Publishing's website and in main libraries – thanks to a dissemination grant from the COST Association, which we gratefully hereby acknowledge. We take the opportunity here to enthusiastically endorse the COST (European Cooperation in Science and Technology) programme for its key role in supporting the circulation and development of knowledge in Europe and beyond – in general and with specific regard to our Action. Despite the fact that many of us were already engaged in comparative studies, in the course of the Action we still all learned a whole lot more about the diversity of national, regional and local service systems within Europe and gained an enriched perspective on the challenges facing Europe in this field. Special thanks must go to the COST Administrative and Scientific officers who accompanied our Action, Leo Guilfoyle, Andreas Obermaier and Rossella Magli, for their invaluable help in making it a success.

We also wish to express our gratitude to all the participants in the Action, including those who did not directly contribute to this book, for their generous and lively engagement in the Action's activities and for sharing their work; the content of this volume is largely based on the collective capital gathered in the course of the Action in the form of working papers and presentations. We also gratefully acknowledge and thank the discussants that attended our final conference in Reggio Calabria and the anonymous reviewers – two per chapter – who generously accepted to read the contributions to this volume, provided invaluable comments, and thus greatly helped improve its contents, albeit the final responsibility obviously rests with the authors. Special thanks go to Patricia Kennett and Misa Izuhara, the editors of the 'New Horizons in Social Policy' Series, who positively reviewed our book proposal and gave us precious advice, as well as to Alex Pettifer, Victoria Raven and Emily Mew at the UK Editorial Office of Edward Elgar, for their great support in the process of producing this book.

Last, but not least, we wish to thank the grant holder institution, the Mediterranea University of Reggio Calabria, in the persons of the Rector and his staff, the Rector's Delegate and the Administrative officer at the International relations office, and especially the research team and the grant management staff at the Department of Architecture and Territory, for their unsparing support throughout the course of the Action.

The editors and the contributors

COST (European Cooperation in Science and Technology) is a pan-European intergovernmental framework. Its mission is to enable break-through scientific and technological developments leading to new concepts and products and thereby contribute to strengthening Europe's research and innovation capacities. www.cost.eu

This publication is based upon work from COST Action IS1102, supported by COST (European Cooperation in Science and Technology).

EUROPEAN COOPERATION
IN SCIENCE AND TECHNOLOGY

COST is supported by EU Framework Programme Horizon 2020

COST Action IS1102
**SO.S. COHESION**
Social Services, Welfare States and Places
http://www.cost-is1102-cohesion.unirc.it

And we're in the middle of a 'perfect storm'. These days, government social services are being bad-mouthed and de-funded. The non-profit world is looking more and more like the for-profit world. The growing gap between rich and poor makes most of us very anxious about where we stand.

(Arlie Hochschild in an interview for *AlterNet*, August 2012)

# Introduction

## Flavia Martinelli, Anneli Anttonen and Margitta Mätzke

Publicly provided in-kind social services are a key component of the welfare state in most of Europe, albeit their development trajectories, coverage and legal status still vary considerably among countries. The way such services are provided and made available to people bears significantly on social and territorial cohesion, on the gender balance and, ultimately, on the wealth of any society. On the other hand, while much is discussed and written about social policy and welfare systems, social services are somewhat neglected. Although they have progressively gained a stronger foothold in national legislations and social policy agendas, their status remains weaker compared to health or education services. Moreover, because of the austerity measures brought about by the 2008 financial crisis, they have been the primary object of cuts and reorganisation.

And yet, from a social capital and social investment perspective social services should earn much more attention. Cuts in the social service systems have, in fact, very severe consequences on older people and people with disabilities, as well as on households – women – with small children or living in poverty, i.e. on people whose labour market position is weak. The public provision of in-kind services, more than monetary transfers and benefits, represents a social investment that not only generates welfare, social inclusion and jobs, but also reduces future social risks. The theoretical debate on social policy and welfare states needs thus to be enriched by comparatively informed research on the restructuring of social services. This is also a field where national, regional and local variations are large and greater empirical evidence is needed.

The aim of this book is to revive the discussion on publicly funded social services and their changes, with a focus on care services (for small children, older persons and other people that are not self-sufficient) and services that enhance the social inclusion of vulnerable groups (immigrants, minorities, recipients of social assistance, homeless people). It addresses the changes that have affected the organisation and supply of publicly supported social services in Europe over the last thirty years. The restructuring of welfare

*1*

states that started in the late 1980s throughout Europe has profoundly affected the governance of social services, possibly more than other welfare provisions. There have been changes in the 'vertical' division of responsibility among different government levels, as well as in the 'horizontal' division of responsibility among service providers – the state, the family, the market and the community. There have been changes in the way social services are financed, organised and produced, with the introduction of 'market mechanisms' in the management of services and in the selection of providers, as well as in access parameters (e.g. with the introduction of user fees). All such changes were aimed at reducing public expenditures, while at the same time democratising governance, improving the quality of services and increasing the satisfaction of users. In the last few years, the intensification of old and new social risks, together with the financial crisis of 2008, have added further stress on the capability and/or willingness of welfare states to support social services, albeit with different intensities and outcomes, depending on countries and their welfare state traditions and trajectories.

The book conveys the main findings of the COST Action IS1102 *SO.S. COHESION – Social services, welfare states and places: the restructuring of social services in Europe and its impact on social and territorial cohesion and governance*, which was operational from 21 November 2011 to 30 April 2016. The Action involved 24 countries, over 40 research and university institutions and close to 90 among researchers and scholars, about half of whom were early stage researchers (for more information see the Action website at http://www.cost-is1102-cohesion.unirc.it and the COST website at http://www.cost.eu/COST_Actions/isch/IS1102). The aim of the Action was to share and critically compare research on the restructuring of social services in Europe over the last thirty years – but with a focus on the period after the financial crisis of 2008 – and on the social impacts of these changes, from five key perspectives:

1.  *Cost/quality effectiveness.* Did changes in the organisation of social services bring about the expected reduction in public expenditures, increase in users' choice and satisfaction, as well as improved quality of services?
2.  *Democratic governance.* Did the vertical re-scaling of authority among different government levels and the horizontal re-mix of responsibility among different suppliers bring about increased citizen participation and empowerment, greater democracy in decision-making processes, improved subsidiarity and optimised cooperation among actors?
3.  *Social and territorial cohesion.* Did the restructuring maintain or improve universal access, i.e. access to social services for all, regardless

of origin, income, gender and place, while ensuring diversified and customised services?

4. *Labour market of care and social work.* What are the consequences of the restructuring of social services on the training, skills and/or contractual conditions of social service workers?

5. *Gender.* How has the restructuring of social services affected the social position of women, in terms of access to the labour market, quality of employment, gender divisions of labour in the household?

As already mentioned, our COST Action focused especially on care services (for early childhood, older people, people with disabilities) and services for the inclusion of other vulnerable groups (immigrants, recipients of social assistance, minorities such as Roma, as well as homeless people). Among these services, however, care for older people has moved centre stage. This is partly because, while early childhood education and care is generally on the rise in most European countries, also as a consequence of the Barcelona targets, services for older people – and many other vulnerable groups – are bearing the brunt of the recent restructuring.

The book is based primarily on the information and empirical evidence gathered in the course of the COST Action on the restructuring of these services in different places. The core of the Action was the comparison of national and regional trajectories, as well as of 'case studies' on changes in the provision of services in specific places (cities and regions), mostly of a qualitative and evaluative nature (review of research and documents, interviews of privileged witnesses, field work, etc.), but often backed by statistical data. These country and regional reports and these case studies were drafted and discussed in the course of the Action and some of them were later published in different forms. Throughout the book they are referred to as CAPs (COST Action Papers or Presentations) and their full references are spelled out in the bibliography of each chapter.

They confirm that in Europe there is a great variety in social service and care provision models. However, this diversity, while a challenge for comparative purposes, also proves to be an asset. A major strength of the book is that no 'single' case study is presented, whereas all chapters engage in some form of 'transversal reading' across places, service fields and/or policy tools, from a given perspective or focusing on a particular theme, while sharing a common conceptual and analytical framework. Although it cannot be considered a strict 'comparative' methodology, this 'transversal reading' approach contributes to highlight differences and similarities in restructuring trends across places. It also contributes to identify the main issues and implications of the restructuring of social services and the key challenges for an inclusive Europe.

The book includes 19 chapters, grouped in five parts. Part I includes three chapters which contribute to set the general context and conceptual framework. Chapter 1 provides an overview of the debates on social services as a key, but very specific, component of both the service sector and the welfare state, stressing the need for a time- and space-sensitive approach to understand the great variety of national and regional restructuring trajectories. The author then proceeds to 'unpack' the main trends involved in the restructuring of social services and identifies a number of key analytical dimensions. Chapter 2 addresses EU policy discourses, strategies and regulations concerning the organisation of social services in Europe, stressing the ambiguous position of social services within the EU regulatory and strategic framework and highlighting the unsolved tension between competition policy and social policy. The authors also draw attention to some inadequacies of the EU Cohesion policy to redress imbalances in this domain, despite its ambitious inclusive goals. Chapter 3 addresses the policy 'conceptions' underlying the designs of social service systems, by examining their core commitments (priorities) and target orientations. Priorities vary between emancipatory and disciplining commitments, whereas targets can concern individuals, communities or polities. The approach, illustrated through three case studies, contributes to a clearer understanding of institutional designs, beyond political rhetoric.

Part II addresses the transformations of the governance of social services and includes five chapters. Chapter 4 retraces the overall evolution of social service systems in post-industrial Europe, highlighting its 'success' aspects (expansion, institutionalisation, professionalisation), but also its 'tragic' loopholes and limitations (incompleteness, selectivity, inequality of access, residualism). It also emphasises how recent changes in the governance of social services, such as re-privatisation, competition among providers, and the growing role of for-profit providers, are bringing about a 'disorganisation' in social service systems. Chapter 5 addresses the 'vertical' division of authority concerning social services within the state, stressing the re-scaling processes that have occurred in the last decades, both upward (towards the EU) and downward (towards the local scale). Based on a number of COST Action case studies from several European countries, the authors highlight the dangers of the devolution rhetoric, especially when social services are concerned, since in many instances the decentralisation of responsibility has involved a devolution of austerity and has led to growing territorial differences, reduced accountability and an unsustainable burden for local authorities and communities. Chapter 6 is somewhat complementary to the previous chapter, as it addresses changes in the 'horizontal' division of responsibility among the state, the market, the third sector and the family. Drawing on case studies from the Action in several European countries, the authors identify the main 'directions' of this 're-mix' – marketisation, re-familialisation and re-communitarisation – stressing how such trends can be formal or informal, passive or active. Chapter 7 explores how the 'activation turn' in social policy has affected the horizontal division of responsibility at the local level in the case of social assistance services in four European countries. Drawing on evidence from the Action, the authors highlight how the new forms of collaboration now encouraged among different providers at the local level are highly discretionary and hence depend not so much on the national institutional framework, but rather on the initiative of local actors, allowing for enhanced territorial differences. There is also a 'creaming of the crop' effect that leads to prioritising the less needy recipients. Chapter 8, the last chapter in this part of the book, explores the gender implications of recent changes in care provisions for early childhood and older people in two quite different European countries: Spain and the UK. The chapter highlights how in both countries the financial crisis has negatively affected the relative progress towards gender equality and is reinforcing the traditional gendered division of labour. It also shows how different policy tools – parental leave, in-kind services and cash benefits – have differentiated impacts.

Part III of the book focuses on recent trajectories in the public provision of services for older people. It includes four chapters. Chapter 9 offers an overview of the evolution of these services, as observed in the course of the Action in several European countries, according to five 'dimensions' or dichotomies: centralisation/decentralisation; direct provision/outsourcing; health/care; home-based care/institutional care; formal/informal care. The authors identify striking similarities in a number of trends, although they also highlight that impacts are conditioned by the specific national regulatory traditions. Chapter 10 focuses on the Nordic countries and the process of 'marketisation' they are experiencing, especially Finland and Sweden. The authors stress how the introduction of market logics in the public provision of services for older people and the opening up to for-profit providers is significantly changing, 'from within', the Nordic model, especially in what concerns the role of the state and the position of users (now 'customers'), although social impacts are still tempered by the long tradition of universalism characteristic of these countries. Chapter 11 addresses the de-institutionalisation strategy implemented in two Transition countries: the Czech Republic and Slovakia. In presenting two very different local case studies, the authors highlight how despite very similar national strategies – based on decentralisation and 'ageing in place' – the actual implementation of de-institutionalisation beyond discourses and legislation is contingent on regional and local capabilities, both financial and institutional. They also underscore that, despite more or less successful de-institutionalisation processes, users' preferences for institutional care remain high. Chapter 12 also addresses de-institutionalisation processes, but in three Mediterranean countries. Here too, the authors stress the gap between de-institutionalisation strategies and actual implementation, showing how the ineffectual implementation of home-based care for older people, while institutional care does not follow the growth in demand, ends up favouring a 're-familisation' of care.

Part IV of the book groups four chapters that address the socially innovative potential of local initiatives in the domain of social services. Chapter 13 focuses on the ambivalence – the 'Janus face' – of the concept of social innovation. The authors stress the different meanings given to this notion in the literature – ranging from a more radical view that emphasises the societal transformative potential of local initiatives to a more mainstream view that stresses the potential of such initiatives to fill the gaps left by the retrenchment of the welfare state – and test this ambivalence in four case studies in Europe. Chapter 14 compares two socially innovative local initiatives for the inclusion of Roma, in Austria and Hungary. In this case both initiatives exhibit empowering and transformative potential, but the authors stress the importance of multilevel governance for the sustainability of such innovative experiences. Chapter 15 addresses the role of local initiatives for the social inclusion of immigrants in two originally very different systems: Italy and the UK. The authors show that a convergence is occurring in the way both national governments are addressing the growing immigration flows, as both national governments are maintaining a firm grip over 'immigration' policies (entry), whereas 'immigrant' policies (services for their social inclusion) are decentralised at the local level. Here, third sector initiatives are increasingly filling the void of retrenching public services. Chapter 16 addresses the impact of market-oriented reforms, the financial crisis of 2008 and the ensuing austerity measures on housing and neighbourhood services. By examining a number of case studies, the authors highlight how socially innovative local initiatives are attempting to contrast the growing social exclusion generated by these trends, filling the void left by the state. They also stress the differentiated social innovation potential of such initiatives and the need for multilevel responsibility.

The last section of the book includes three chapters, where the editors present their shared interpretation of the restructuring of social services in the last thirty years, drawing on the wealth of empirical evidence gathered and compared in the course of the Action and in the book. They point out key trends and impacts, challenges and dilemmas, especially focusing on the policy implications of such findings.

Before concluding this brief presentation, we wish to stress that the book is intended for both the academic and the policy-making, practitioners' and also users' circles. On the one hand, it will be a very useful reading for students and scholars in the fields of comparative social policy and welfare systems, urban and regional studies, sustainable development and cohesion policy; on the other, it will be a key tool for policy-makers, civil servants, civil society and users' organisers, as well as service providers at local, national and EU levels, since there is an urgent need for new comparative knowledge on European care, services and welfare systems. In fact, although theoretically and scientifically informed, the book contents and policy outlooks have a very pragmatic nature and are written in a language accessible to all, including non-academic operators, who in everyday practice aim at providing better services for their target groups, struggling with complex management and coordination problems. The open access formula, thanks to the COST Association, will maximise dissemination to this non-academic audience, which does not always have access to university libraries and cannot afford the price of academic books.

# PART I

# Context and Concepts

# 1. Social services, welfare states and places: an overview

**Flavia Martinelli**

## INTRODUCTION

Social services – publicly funded social services – have come a long way in Europe. From a family concern, charitable endeavour or employment-related benefit, in the span of a century they have been to a large extent taken over by the state and have become – at least in principle – a right extended to all citizens. This remarkable progress was part and parcel of the construction of national welfare states, although it occurred with different timings and intensities across countries and service fields. Compared to other forms of welfare provision (such as social insurance schemes) and other well established social services (such as education and health), however, many care services and services for the social inclusion of vulnerable groups have not been fully developed and still have a weak social status. Moreover, many of these services have experienced relevant changes over the last three decades and are threatened by the austerity measures implemented throughout Europe as a consequence of national fiscal difficulties and the financial crisis of 2008.

In this chapter I review the theoretical and conceptual discussion that informed the COST Action IS1102 *SO.S. COHESION – Social services, welfare states and places* and I put forward the building blocks of our analytical approach. In the first section I position our topic – social services and their restructuring – within the contemporary debates on the service economy, the welfare state, social and territorial cohesion, as well as the post-Keynesian restructuring, highlighting their specificities and key social and economic implications. In the second section I stress the importance of a time- and space-sensitive approach to analysing changes and I review the concepts of welfare 'regimes' and 'models'. In the third section I 'unpack' the main restructuring trends discussed in the literature, highlighting their features and implications as well as a number of key conceptual tools. In the light of this overview, I conclude posing a number of questions as to what we can learn from the national and regional trajectories and case studies examined in the course of our COST Action and critically summarised in this book and what the possible policy lessons could be, questions which I will then resume in the concluding chapter of the book.

# 1. THE FOCUS: POSITIONING SOCIAL SERVICES IN THE CURRENT DEBATES

Social services lie at the crossroads of several scholarly debates: the debate on the 'service economy' and the tension between 'producer' and 'reproductive' services; the debate on the welfare state, its components and 'models'; the debate about universalism and social and territorial cohesion.

## Social Services Within the Service Sector

In the second half of the twentieth century, employment in the service sector surpassed that in the industrial sector in all advanced economies of the Western world, heralding the advent of the so-called 'post-industrial' society. However, the service sector includes a very heterogeneous set of activities (Martinelli, 1991; Martinelli and Gadrey, 2000), comprising both services supporting *production* (called 'producer' or 'business' services) and services supporting *reproduction* (of the labour force, of citizenship, of institutions and culture, and of the general conditions of accumulation). The latter include services such as health, education and other social services, but also activities related to government and public administration, membership organisations, culture and leisure institutions. In the scholarly debate that developed in the late 1970s and 1980s around services, a sort of disciplinary division of labour occurred between economists, who focused on producer services and their role in fostering innovation and competitiveness, and sociologists and political scientists, who focused on reproductive services – social services especially – and their role in ensuring welfare, citizenship and social justice, a dichotomy that somehow endorsed the hypothesis that social services are not productive. As I will stress later, this assumption is unfounded and social services do perform a key economic role.

Defining/delimiting social services is tricky. There are broad and narrow definitions (see EC, 2010; Eurostat, 2011; BEPA, 2011; Sirovátka and Greve, 2014). In the broad definition, social services encompass not only the great variety of services provided to support the welfare and the social inclusion of people – care for small children, older people and people with disabilities, social assistance services, employment and training services, services for the inclusion of disadvantaged groups – but also education and health services, social housing and even social activities such as sport and leisure. The narrow definition includes only services for the care, protection and inclusion of children and minors, older people, people with mental or physical disabilities, substance abusers, and other vulnerable groups (minorities, immigrants, etc.). But even with services in the narrow definition, there is still an issue of boundaries, as in many instances there are overlaps among different services (such as with education in the case of childcare or with health services in the case of care for older people). In this book, we adopt the narrow definition of social services and we especially focus on the social component of *care services* (for small children and older people) and *services for the social inclusion of vulnerable groups* (such as recipients of social assistance, immigrants and minorities), with the addition of *housing*.

A key dimension of social services is their *public* character. Public or publicly supported social services have registered a spectacular growth in the second half of the twentieth century in all European countries. By taking charge of many such services, the state contributed to the de-familisation and de-commodification (Esping-Andersen, 1990) of activities previously provided within the family or purchased in the market and to the transformation of charitable activities in social rights. All these processes represented a major vector of the *social citizenship* principle and were characterising features of the so-called 'Keynesian' welfare state (see next section in this chapter).

However, in contrast to the widespread belief that social services are a mere redistributive tool to ensure social justice, hence a cost that has now become unsustainable, I contend that publicly funded social services perform a key economic role and actively support development. First, as stressed by Swyngedouw and Jessop (2005; see also Jessop, 1999), public social services contribute to lower the cost of reproduction of the labour force, thereby sustaining the accumulation process. By providing free or affordable education and training, health care, childcare, housing, etc. the state increases the purchasing power of workers, indirectly subsidising employers. Secondly, public social services perform a Keynesian role, since by providing jobs and salaries, they support domestic demand for goods and services (see also EC, 2010). This countercyclical role and its potential to stabilise or relaunch the economy in a time of crisis have recently been stressed by the European Economic and Social Committee (EESC, 2014). Third, public social services represent a 'social investment'. The view that social services should be considered 'productive' was first put forward by Alva and Gunnar Myrdal in the 1930s and was re-launched at the end of the 1990s with the EU 'social investment strategy' (Hemerijck, 2012). It argues that social policy should not be considered a cost but an investment which contributes to lower future costs by making people better skilled and more productive.

This double role of social services – contributing to social justice *and* to accumulation – makes it all the more important to understand change trends, their drivers and their impacts.

## Social Services Within the Welfare State

It is important to position – and distinguish – social services vis-à-vis the welfare state and social policy, as these services are part and parcel of both, while being very specific.

All welfare systems, although with different proportions and features, are made of two main components: (1) a *social insurance system*, based on more or less compulsory contributions from employers and workers against the risks of work and life (sickness and accidents, old age, unemployment), originally targeted to workers and their families and later extended to other categories; and (2) *social policies*, mostly financed through general taxation, which address a broader spectrum of social needs – sometimes called 'new' social risks (see Harsløf and Ulmestig, 2013, for a discussion) – from the care of children, older people and people with disabilities to the reconciliation of work and family, from (re)training and job placement to the protection and integration of vulnerable groups.

Another key distinction must be made between: (a) *monetary* transfers or *cash* benefits to individuals and/or households; and (b) *in-kind* benefits or services. Although these two forms of public support roughly – but not always – correspond to the two components introduced above, in the literature these differences are not always sufficiently stressed (see Jensen, 2008). In fact, the entity and articulation – within any welfare system – of the social insurance and social policy components, on the one hand, and of the cash transfers and in-kind social services, on the other, are (or should be) key parameters in the classification of welfare models, since the grouping of countries in these typologies strongly depends on which components of the welfare state are considered.

Although conceptually clear, in practice the boundaries between cash transfers and in-kind services[1] are often blurred, as the two forms of support are substitutable and complementary: older people may get old age pensions or targeted cash allowances and/or in-kind care services, whether at home or in specialised institutions; support for childcare can be provided either through childcare vouchers to purchase services in the market and/or through public day care services. What must be stressed, however, is that cash transfers and in-kind services obey two very different logics and have very different impacts (see Martinelli, Chapter 19, in this volume). The former support the purchasing power of households in the market; the latter presume the public organisation and/or co-ordination of the actual production of services.

**Social Services, Universalism and Territorial Cohesion**

As a key component of the welfare state, social services are a major tool for social inclusion and territorial cohesion. Their capacity to achieve both these aims hinges on the degree of *universalism* their provision affords.

As stressed by Anttonen et al. (2012), universalism is a 'deeply normative concept' (p.1), closely aligned with both the social democracy and social liberalism traditions, that was central to the construction of the post-WW2 welfare state in many countries, most particularly in the Nordic countries, but to a certain extent also in the UK (Anttonen and Sipilä, 2012). It promoted equality and solidarity across social classes, breaking away from the paternalistic and stigmatising poverty relief measures of the time. It is the basis of the principle of social citizenship (Marshall, 1950) and the characterising feature of the Nordic welfare model (Esping-Andersen, 1990), which inspired many post-WW2 Western welfare states, albeit with different degrees of determination and institutionalisation. Besides being an ideal and a characterising attribute of the Nordic model, universalism is also an administrative principle (Anttonen et al., 2012), which significantly affects policy designs (see Mätzke et al., in this volume). But it remains a highly fuzzy and contested concept.

In the 1980s and 1990s, universalism came under criticism, from both the feminist movement (Williams, 1992), which denounced its male-biased and paternalistic stance, and other social movements, which stressed the 'difference-blind' approach of many social policies and services (Anttonen et al., 2012, p.9), especially in what concerned minorities and other disadvantaged groups (see also Weinzierl et al., in this volume). These 'new' social movements, which replaced the traditional class-based movements (Martinelli, 2010), called for recognition of diversity, user-centred approaches, as well as users' choice and empowerment. Their claims contributed to a re-discussion of the notion of universalism (Häikiö and Hvinden, 2012), lessening some of its initial rigidities and further articulating its meaning.

In defining access, for example, a major discussion involved the tension between universalism and selectivism (Anttonen and Sipilä, 2012; see also Thompson and Hogget, 1996), but it has become accepted that there can still be universalism in providing services to groups defined by their position in the human life cycle, such as for instance *all* children aged 0–3 or *all* older people. It is also understood that, within these categories, there can be positive discrimination or selectivism, i.e. in favour of users in greater need via for instance means-tested programmes, as well as particularism, i.e. tailoring services to particular needs or cultural frameworks, and that these specifications not only can overcome the apparently irreconcilable tension between universalism and diversity, but can also be a way to make universalism more effective (Vabø and Szebehely, 2012).

Taking into account the discussion above, the notion of 'universalistic social services' I adopt here implies equal access for all persons characterised by a given need, to the same level of good quality (and affordable) service, independently of gender, ethnicity, *income*, or *place*.[2] The last two dimensions are especially crucial for ensuring *social inclusion* and *territorial cohesion*. But while the socially inclusive impact of more or less universalistic service systems across social classes or income groups has always been at the core of social policy debates, the territorial aspect has been somewhat neglected or left implicit. And yet, territorial disparities in the supply of social services – either among different regions, or between urban and rural areas – exist in every country, even Nordic ones (Trydegård and Thorslund, 2001), albeit with different intensities. They are a major vector of social exclusion, which profoundly undermines the principle of universal social citizenship, however defined within each national boundary. Why such territorial disparities exist and persist depends on many structural and institutional factors. As I will stress in the next sections, they especially depend on national economic development and welfare state trajectories, but also on the 'vertical division of authority' within the state in what concerns the responsibility for social services.

**The Restructuring of Social Services: Modernisation and Social Innovation**

Within the welfare state and among social services in the broad sense, the services we address in this book – care services and services for the social inclusion of vulnerable groups – have remained somewhat the 'Cinderella', compared to more established social insurance provisions or to education and health services. In fact, with the possible exception of some Nordic countries, their recognition as a social right and their development as universalistic public services occurred much later and to a much lesser extent. This already 'weak' status has been in many instances further undermined by the restructuring of the last thirty years.

This restructuring – often referred to as 'modernisation' (Huber et al., 2006) – started in the 1980s, with the end of the 'golden age' of growth and welfare state expansion, as a consequence of several transformative pressures (see Starke, 2006 for a review; Ferrera, 2008; Bode, 2009). On the one hand, there were bottom-up (demand side) pressures, coming from social movements and users' claims for greater recognition, better choice, more customised services, and, generally, more democratic and accountable governance systems, in contrast to the existing bureaucratic and stand-ardised public services; on the other hand, there were top-down (supply side) pressures, essentially related to the first signs of a fiscal crisis of national states (OECD, 1981), with consequent attempts at curbing public expenditures and increasing the efficiency of welfare spending. These two types of pressures found an odd convergence in the post-Keynesian (and EU-sponsored) discourses and strategies of *subsidiarity* and *liberalisation*, heralding a season of multifaceted processes of change, often referred to as the 'neo-liberal turn' (Crouch et al., 2001).

Although bottom-up claims undoubtedly played a role, it is my con-tention that it is mostly top-down strategies – i.e. engineered by national governments and the EU – that have driven the restructuring of social ser-vices in the last three decades, especially after the completion of the Single European Market and the establishment of the European Union in 1992. Alongside the introduction of new market-inspired management princi-ples in the organisation of public services and a re-scaling of government authority, generally away from central state responsibility and towards both the EU and the local level (Sellers and Lidstrom, 2007; Keating, 2009), a liberalisation of the 'market' of social services has taken place, with the entry of new suppliers – both profit and non-profit – alongside or in substitution of state-provided services (Ascoli and Ranci, 2002; Schmid, 2003; Carmel and Harlock, 2008). The onset of the financial crisis in 2008 has then exacerbated social needs, while placing further pressures on public spending and determining, in many countries, dramatic cuts in the public support of social services, through various mechanisms. (On restructuring trends, see the third section in this chapter.)

Parallel to the above top-down restructuring processes, the last thirty years have also witnessed a blossoming of bottom-up initiatives at the local level, which aimed either at improving the way social services were supplied or at providing services in instances where they were not supplied or had been curtailed. These local collective initiatives – characterised by practices of users' participation, co-production and social economy – have been studied in the context of *social innovation theory* (Moulaert et al., 2005; 2010; 2013; Nicholls et al., 2015; Brandsen et al., 2016). The subject has become quite fashionable in the last ten years, even more so after the financial crisis of 2008, and significant expectations are being attached to 'socially innovative' initiatives as a means to reduce public outlays and involve communities in the provision of social services (Murray et al., 2010; Mulgan, 2012). However, several scholars have also highlighted how, while socially innovative local initiatives can contribute to give voice to, and empower, social groups that are excluded from certain services and decision-making processes, they cannot and should not compensate for a retrenching welfare state (Martinelli et al., 2010; Martinelli, 2012a).

## 2.   A TIME- AND SPACE-SENSITIVE APPROACH

Having positioned social services within the current debates, I can now start unfolding the analytical approach proposed in this chapter. The restructuring of social services has taken place with different timings, intensity and features across countries and service fields, yielding different results depending on how context-specific structural, institutional and sociocultural factors have conditioned change trajectories. Therefore, to investigate changes in the organisation and supply of social services in Europe in the last thirty years, it is necessary to deploy a *time-* and *space-sensitive* approach, which involves taking on board the notions of welfare *regimes* (over time) and welfare *models* (across space), as well as the notion of *path-dependency*.

Two main welfare 'regimes' or periods and five main welfare 'families' or models are considered. These are not new or original. I here summarise the main features of a number of ideal types from the literature for purely heuristic purposes, i.e. as tools to help us understand patterns of change over time and differences across space. In fact, being a relevant component of the welfare state, social services were established in given periods and in given forms, depending on places; and these specificities have conditioned subsequent processes of change. In other words, restructuring trajectories are path-dependent, whereby apparently similar processes can yield different outcomes depending on the starting configuration.

### The *Time* Dimension and Welfare *Regimes*

In the second half of the twentieth century two main periods are generally identified in what concerns the *role of the state* and the *forms of state intervention*: (1) the period of the *Keynesian (welfare) state*, which for some countries started with the great depression, but is generally positioned between 1945 and 1980; (2) the period of the post-Keynesian or *neo-liberal (welfare) state*, which started in the early 1980s and still persists. These periods are also referred to as 'eras', 'phases' or 'waves' (Hemerijck, 2012). I prefer to call them *regimes*,[3] since they are characterised by distinct and interrelated sets of ideologies, discourses and principles about the role of the state, different policy objectives, strategies and tools, as well as different actors (see also Jenson, 2012).

The *Keynesian regime* (1945–80) was characterised by the dominance of the nation state on all internal and external affairs, a state which heavily intervened in both the economy – featuring the so-called 'developmental' state (Dickens, 1998), with robust policies in support of accumulation (commercial, industrial, regional policies), as well as direct ownership of productive activities and infrastructure – and in society – featuring the modern 'welfare' state, with more or less extended social protection measures and publicly provided social services.

The Keynesian state intervention was couched in a 'nation-strengthening' strategy, aimed at supporting (a balanced) national growth and at reducing internal social and geographical[4] inequalities. The role of the state was to support but also steer the market, through investment in strategic sectors. Intervention in the social domain had both redistributive and developmental aims, since social security and social services contributed to lowering the cost of the reproduction of labour, hence indirectly supporting accumulation (Jessop, 1999; Swyngedouw and Jessop, 2005). This was the 'golden' period of welfare state expansion, when social protection, from a private or charity affair, became a 'right' (Jenson, 2012). Although heavily oriented towards supporting the 'male breadwinner' model, the Keynesian welfare state held – in principle – a universalistic approach, i.e. aimed at providing free public services for all, albeit to different extents and with different temporalities depending on countries. This approach was based on a class compromise and a social pact between the two main collective actors of that time: capital (represented by national corporate champions) and labour (represented by national unions), with the state acting as mediator. The state itself was typically Weberian, i.e. a hierarchical bureaucracy, with formalised accountability processes (Jenson, 2012).

The *neo-liberal regime* (1980s onward) set in after the first major post-WW2 economic crisis of the mid-1970s, the slowdown of growth rates and the incipient fiscal difficulties of Western states. With the Reagan and Thatcher administrations in the 1980s, neoclassical economics resurfaced and supply-side policies gained consensus, finding a concrete political outlet in what has come to be called the 'neo-liberal' paradigm (Hemerijck, 2012). In this new phase, the market was viewed as the best allocation mechanism and the state as an encumbrance to the free working of the market. Liberalisation, deregulation and privatisation became the key principles guiding the restructuring and retrenchment of state intervention, in all domains.

By the end of the 1980s, the new paradigm had become hegemonic throughout the Western capitalist world. A major driver of its diffusion in Europe was the acceleration of European integration following the Single European Act of 1986 and the completion of the Single European market by 1992, i.e. the removal of all barriers to the free circulation of people, capital, goods and services. The Treaty of Maastricht in 1992 and the requirements established to join the European Monetary Union in 1998 further strengthened the neo-liberal principles, undermining the sovereignty of the national state in several economic policy areas and enforcing a number of corollaries of the market liberalisation strategy, such as the privatisation of many state-owned activities and infrastructures, now viewed as unfair competition (Schiek, 2013).

In what concerns the welfare state, the 1990s witnessed major changes in social policy and in the public supply of social services, as documented in a now quite large body of literature (see, among many others, Crouch et al., 2001; Huber and Stephens, 2001; Ascoli and Ranci, 2002; Taylor-Gooby, 2004). Ensuring social protection to (almost) all was deemed no longer feasible. Universal entitlements were considered an unsustainable burden on the public budget and the need to increase the responsibility of individuals and families was asserted. In the domain of unemployment and poverty an 'activation' strategy was deployed, attempting to steer social assistance towards employability. In the domain of in-kind social services, the imperatives of liberalisation and competition gained ground, reinforced by the growing financial difficulties of many a state: new public management practices were introduced as well as outsourcing to private providers; the service 'market' was liberalised, allowing the entry of private providers – both profit and non-profit – in services that in many nations had been an exclusive state monopoly; competition among providers and free choice principles were adopted. In some countries, greater responsibilities were given to local administrations, deemed the best level for efficient governance.

The periodisation above is obviously not as clear-cut as described. The shift from one regime to the other was differently timed, depending on countries and regions. In some 'latecomer' Southern European countries and regions, for example, a number of universalistic welfare state measures were actually introduced in the 1980s and 1990s, i.e. *during* the neo-liberal phase, albeit many of these measures were not adequately funded (León and Pavolini, 2014).

Starting in the early 2000s, a possible third phase, inspired by the *'social investment' approach* – i.e. a new set of principles made explicit in the Lisbon Council of 2000 – has been identified by a number of scholars (Morel et al., 2012; Hemerijck, 2012), although it would only apply to the welfare domain, rather than to state intervention in general. The new approach, which found political legitimacy in a series of European documents and directives (see Goméz-Barroso et al., in this volume), allegedly marks a setback of the neo-liberal paradigm and the return of social policy onto governments' agendas, albeit in a very different form, compared to the previous Keynesian approach (Hemerijck, 2012). It reverses the neo-liberal idea that social policy is unproductive, arguing that it represents an investment, and hence a productive factor. It also recovers a key role for the state in lessening the ('new') social risks brought about by structural and social changes, addressing needs from a 'life course' perspective and stressing the necessity to start investing very early in the life course of citizens, in order to create a more competitive work force. At the same time, it maintains the goal of changing the welfare state from a passive benefit system to an 'activating' mechanism geared to 'capacity building' and it confirms the need for mobilising individual and family responsibilities.

Whether the social investment approach can be considered a fully-fledged regime remains questionable. As stressed by Morel et al. (2012), the social investment is a 'perspective', still in search of political consensus, rather than a settled paradigm. Jenson (2012) notes that the strengths – and weaknesses – of the approach lie precisely in its ambiguity, which makes it acceptable to many parties, but also makes it rather indeterminate. Moreover, it should be noted that, despite its rhetoric, the social investment strategy does not really apply to groups such as older and other vulnerable people, except, perhaps, in terms of delaying care costs.

The *financial crisis of 2008* and its aftershocks certainly represent a major (turning) moment in the evolution of Western welfare, although it may not necessarily mark the beginning of a new regime. Its impact in Europe has been significant, but diversified. Almost everywhere it has dampened the social investment approach and legitimised a relapse into, and an aggravation of, neo-liberal recipes. As such it has affected existing trajectories, sometimes by accelerating ongoing trends, other times interrupting set courses. In some countries, its effects have been dramatic, notably in a number of Southern European nations where drastic cuts in public spending and social services have curtailed even long-established basic services such as health care (Petmesidou and Guillén, 2014). But important cuts in the public support of social services have been observed also in other countries such as the UK or some Nordic countries (Brennan et al., 2012). Two main effects seem to emerge, as also witnessed in our COST Action: first, a generalised slowdown and more selective application of the social investment strategy, privileging social services that have more potential for capacity building and growth (e.g. early childcare or 'active' labour market services); secondly, a new cleavage between the North and the South of Europe, after a period of *relative* convergence in the form and extent of public social services (see Martinelli, Chapter 19, in this volume).

## The *Space* Dimension: Welfare *Models* and the *Multiscalarity* of Governance

The chapters in this book investigate changes across several European countries and, in some cases, different regions of the same country. The *spatial* is thus a very relevant analytical dimension, calling for a *space-sensitive* approach, which in turn involves taking into account both *place* and *scale*. In fact, national and regional trajectories are strongly conditioned by *place*-specific factors – i.e. the socio-economic and institutional context of any given place – and the geometry of the state – i.e. the articulation of authority among different government *scales*.

In what concerns *place*, the first systematic attempt to pin down and classify the diversity of welfare state forms across Western countries was carried out by Esping-Andersen in his *Three Worlds of Welfare Capitalism* (1990). In that seminal work, he identified three basic models:[5] (a) the *Social democratic* or *Scandinavian* model; (b) the *Liberal* or *Anglo-Saxon* model; and (c) the *Conservative/Corporatist* or *Continental* model. Since this first taxonomy, the debate has evolved,[6] different groupings have been proposed, and two additional models have been identified: (d) the *Familistic* or *Mediterranean* model; and (e) the *Transition* or *Central-Eastern European* model.

I do not intend here to address the *methodenstreit* surrounding the nature and validity of such taxonomies.[7] The grouping of countries is strongly contingent upon *which* components of the welfare state (social insurance, social policies) and forms of support (cash transfers, in-kind benefits) are actually considered; moreover, these groups/models are generally well represented by one exemplary country, whereas most of the others do not so perfectly fit the one single model and are often borderline or 'shape-shifters'. Nonetheless, it is useful to sketch these models as 'ideal types' and loosely categorise countries in such welfare 'families'[8] as a heuristic device to better contextualise changes and understand differences among nations and regions.

The description of the five 'families' that follows is a synthetic blend of several representations and discussions (Ferrera, 1996; Anttonen and Sipilä, 1996; Arts and Gelissen, 2002; Bambra, 2005; Kazepov, 2008; Jenson, 2012; Schieck, 2013).[9] The main taxonomic parameters retained here are the extent of public support, the proportion between cash benefits and in-kind services, the universalistic vs. contributory blend, the providers mix (state, market, community, family), the ideology about women and their position in the labour market, and the type of industrial relations.

In the *Liberal* or *Anglo-Saxon* family (represented first and foremost by the United States, but also by the UK and Ireland in Europe),[10] the state had generally a weak role, relying significantly on the market, whereas social risks were individualised and relieved especially through means-tested cash transfers. The inclusion of women in the labour market was not actively encouraged (e.g. through the public provision of childcare). The model was also characterised by rather adversarial industrial relations.

In the *Social democratic* or *Nordic* family (represented by Sweden especially, but generally extended to Iceland, Norway, Finland and Denmark) social risks were afforded through the (quasi universalistic) provision of in-kind public services, and women were strongly encouraged to participate in the labour market. There was also significant cooperation among social partners (trade unions and employers' organisations) in the organisation of welfare.

The *Corporatist* or *Continental* family (Germany *in primis*, but also Austria, Belgium, the Netherlands and sometimes France[11]), was strongly reliant on contribution-financed and state-regulated social insurance schemes (the so-called 'Bismarckian' model), i.e. strongly anchored to the employment status (of 'male breadwinners' and their families), whereas women's employment was not encouraged. It was also characterised by cooperative industrial relations, with sector- and/or nation-wide collective bargaining. The role of community organisations – mutualistic, philanthropic, religious – was also very strong in providing in-kind social services as a 'collective solidarity actor' (Jenson, 2012), often with public support.

The *Familistic* or *Mediterranean* family (Italy,[12] Spain, Portugal, Greece, with the possible addition of Malta, Cyprus and Israel; see Gal, 2010 for a discussion on this) was added later to the taxonomy. It was first conceptualised by Ferrera (1996) and further elaborated by others (see Gal, 2010 for a review). It was characterised by a distinct mix of features:[13] relatively recent democratisation and industrialisation, weak state traditions (with relatively inefficient – often clientelistic – bureaucracies), a 'Bismarckian' model of social insurance, a historically residual role of the state in social assistance and only recent public engagement in developing modern welfare provisions (Ferrera, 1996). In fact, countries in this family are 'latecomers' in what concerns the public provision of universalistic social services, many of which were introduced during the neo-liberal phase in the 1980s and 1990s, albeit often underfunded (Da Roit and Sabatinelli, 2013; León and Pavolini, 2014; Petmesidou and Guillén, 2014). But the most distinctive feature of the model was the strong reliance on the family as main provider of care services (Leitner, 2003).

The *Transition* or *Central and Eastern European* family (Poland, Slovakia, Czech Republic, Hungary, Romania), was also conceptualised later. This is the least homogeneous family[14] and it groups countries that, beyond their diversity, have common roots in their former socialist and authoritarian welfare institutions. These institutions have undergone a rapid transformation in the wake of the transition to a market economy and accession to the EU, which has put strong pressures on the decentralisation, de-institutionalisation and marketisation of social services (Koldinská and Tomeš, 2004; Fenger, 2007; Hacker, 2009).

As will become clear throughout the book, these models – especially the first three, which were defined with reference to the 'Keynesian' welfare regime – have profoundly changed over the last thirty years. But it remains useful to keep them in mind as 'starting' configurations, to better appreciate changes and differences.

The spatial dimension of our analysis is not limited to place; it also addresses *scale*. A key feature of welfare systems, which strongly conditioned their trajectories, is the *geometry of the state*, i.e. the role of, and the relations among, different *scales of government*, notably, between the central state and the local administrations. On this aspect too, there is a rich debate (see Bennett, 1993; Goldsmith, 1996; Kazepov, 2008; Rauch, 2008). As I shall stress in the next section the *'vertical' division of authority* among different levels of the state – central, meso- and local – in what concerns the regulation, the funding, the planning and the provision of social services, as well as the degree and tradition of local governments' autonomy, significantly affects both the features and the impacts of the restructuring of social services.

**Path-dependency and Restructuring Trajectories**

The *time* and *space* analytical dimensions just described merge in the notion of *path-dependency*. This concept is particularly useful when addressing structural and institutional changes (Martinelli and Novy, 2013; CAP Martinelli and Sarlo, 2014), even more so in the case of social services. As many chapters in this book will show, national, regional and local restructuring trajectories in the last three decades have been strongly conditioned by the timing of reforms and the pre-existing institutional contexts. In other words, the way national, regional and/or local service systems have been transformed has been dependent on *when* the neo-liberal restructuring started and *which* geometry of the state, welfare institutions, socioeconomic structure and actors, as well as sociocultural norms characterised each context. As stressed by Jenson (2012, p. 62), changes are promoted by specific actors (organised interest groups, political forces, international think tanks, etc.), but they are 'grafted' onto specific welfare systems, which are, in turn, 'historically located and rooted'.

Path-dependency also explains why apparently similar strategies may have yielded very different results, depending on the context they were

implemented in. For example, the introduction of outsourcing, de-institutionalisation or cash allowances has had very different impacts in systems
characterised by a strong tradition of universalism and direct public provision of services (see for instance Anttonen and Karsio, in this volume;
CAP Jensen and Fersch, 2013), compared to systems characterised by a
historically residual role of the state or an authoritarian state tradition (see
Kröger and Bagnato; Kubalčíková et al., in this volume).

There can also be instances of 'path-breaking', although these are more
rare and difficult. One such moment has certainly been the implementation of the Single European market and the enforcement of liberalisation in 1992; another has been the precipitation of the financial crisis in
2008, which in many places – including a number of Nordic countries –
interrupted set courses and/or precipitated abrupt changes. It remains to
be seen, however, whether such shocks have been absorbed in force of the
resilience of existing institutions or have set entirely new courses.

## 3.   UNPACKING THE RESTRUCTURING OF SOCIAL
##       SERVICES: MAIN TRENDS AND KEY ISSUES

Having underscored the importance of a time- and space-sensitive
approach, I now turn to the chief focus of this book and 'unpack' the
main features and key analytical dimensions of the restructuring of social
services, as they are discussed in the literature.

Several concepts have been mobilised to address the changes that
occurred in social policy – and in the organisation of social services – since
the 1980s, albeit their meaning and definition often overlap. The most
used term is *restructuring*, which does not point to any specific direction,
but implies structural changes in the way the welfare state and its social
services components are organised. *Reform* (Taylor-Gooby, 2004; Bahle,
2008) and *recalibration* (Ferrera et al., 2000) are also used, similarly imply-
ing a general remodelling of the welfare state as a response to structural
changes and the emergence of new social risks. Another term, often used
in EU documents, is *modernisation*, which gives a positive ring to processes
aiming at making the provision of services less bureaucratic, more efficient
and innovative (Newman, 2001; Cochrane, 2004; Newman et al., 2008).
More normatively charged is the concept of *retrenchment* (Pierson, 1994;
Clayton and Pontusson, 1998; Starke, 2006), which implies a reduction in
the support provided by the state to certain social policies and services.
Then, of course, there are more clear-cut terms – which also specifically
apply to public social service – such as *privatisation*, which refers to the
growing (re-)involvement of private providers, be they the family, the

market or the community (Leibetseider et al., in this volume), and *marketisation*, which implies a shift towards a market logic and market providers (Brennan et al., 2012; Anttonen and Meagher, 2013; Anttonen and Karsio, in this volume).

## Main Processes and Directions of Change

Out of this literature, I have identified and mapped three broad interconnected *processes* and *directions* of change since the 1980s: (1) changes in the *extent* and *form* of *public support* to social services, generally featuring what I call a *disengagement of the state*; (2) changes in the *'vertical' division of responsibility* for social services, i.e. a *re-scaling of authority* among different levels of government, generally *away from the central state*; and (3) changes in what I call the *'horizontal' division of responsibility* among public and private providers of social services, in the direction of a more *diversified providers mix*. Each of these main trends was driven by several interrelated, transformative pressures – structural, institutional and ideological (Jensen, 2011) – acting on both the demand and the supply side of social services (see Table 1.1). They, in turn, involve different, often overlapping, sub-processes and features.

### Changes in the extent and form of public support towards a 'disengagement' of the state

In this first 'family' of changes three main concurrent processes can be grouped: (a) a relative *contraction* in the *amount* of publicly supported in-kind services; (b) the *outsourcing* of production to private suppliers; (c) a shift to, or preference for, *cash transfers* in lieu of in-kind services.

In what concerns the reduction in the *extent* of public support to in-kind services, it should be stressed that this process might have occurred without a decrease in overall public social spending. Indeed, as shown by a number of studies (Huber and Stephens, 2001; Castles, 2005; OECD, 2008), the curbing of public social expenditures sought by many a government in the 1980s and 1990s did not really succeed and in many countries the actual overall amount of social spending reached unprecedented peaks in the late 1990s and early 2000s, as a consequence of the tremendous growth of social needs. But even if overall social spending and, more specifically, the absolute amount of resources allocated to in-kind social services may not have changed, in many countries and service fields there has been a *relative* contraction. In fact, as a consequence of structural and socio-cultural changes such as ageing, intensified migration flows, greater female activity rates and more numerous single-parent families, increased unemployment and poverty, there has been a dramatic growth in *needs* and *users* of social

*Table 1.1*   *The main drivers of the restructuring of social services over the last thirty years*

| Demand side | Supply side |
| --- | --- |
| ***Structural trends*** | ***Structural trends*** |
| *Demographic changes* | *Economic changes* |
| ● Ageing of the population (→ increased needs for care services, health services, LTC services) | ● Low growth rates → shrinking tax base (introduction of cost-reducing reforms) |
| ● Intensification of migration flows (→ increased needs for inclusion/ integration services) | *The financial crisis and its aftershocks (since 2008)\** |
| *Economic changes* | ● Fiscal crisis of the state → intensification of austerity measures (cuts in public expenditures and/or reduction in social service coverage) |
| ● Technical change (→ need for (re) training services) | |
| ● De-industrialisation (growth in unemployment) | ● Focus on short-term strategies rather than long-term sustainability |
| ● 'Dualisation' and 'precarisation' of the labour market as a consequence of 'tertiarisation' and labour market 'deregulation' (increase in low-wage and 'precarious' jobs; increase in poverty and related social risks) | ***Institutional and political changes*** |
| | *Changes in government structures* |
| | ● Upward re-scaling and EU regulation → liberalisation of service markets (outsourcing, privatisation of social services) |
| ● Financialisation of real-estate (→ increased needs for affordable housing) | ● Downward re-scaling: decentralisation/devolution of authority → national 'de-responsibilisation', emergence of 'local' welfare systems and increase in territorial differentiation |
| *Sociocultural changes* | |
| ● Growing female participation in the labour market and new family structures (dual earner, single parent → increased needs for childcare, care for older people and people with disabilities) | |
| | *Ideological and political changes* |
| ● Changes in inter-generational relations | ● New (social) policy ideologies, discourses and strategies (neo-liberalism; 'caring liberalism'; social investment) |
| ● Recognition/emergence of new risks and needs (→ services for the (re) integration and protection of people with disabilities, substance abusers, victims of violence, children and youth at risk, etc.) | ● Changes in political elites/ parties/coalitions |
| | *Changes in collective actors and pressure groups* |
| *The financial crisis and its aftershocks (since 2008)\** | ● Pressures from private for-profit and non-profit operators to enter the 'market' of social services |
| ● Precipitation of structural contradictions and further worsening of social risks: unemployment and | |

*Table 1.1*    (continued)

| Demand side | Supply side |
|---|---|
| poverty, social exclusion, territorial inequality (→ enlargement of social needs) | |

**Institutional and political changes**

*Changes in collective actors and pressure groups*
- Weakening of historical mass organisations (trade unions) and increased social fragmentation (→ lower organised resistance to restructuring)
- 'New' social movements and claims (women's movements; movements for the recognition of diversity; users' movements for greater choice)
- Proliferation of community and bottom-up (socially innovative) initiatives from users and civil society

*Note:*    * The financial crisis of 2008 is not a driver on its own, as it was the abrupt manifestation of existing structural trends and contradictions, but it has been separated here to stress its specific impacts in accelerating or changing social service reform trajectories.

*Source:*    Author's compilation.

services, while public support has been unable/unwilling to keep pace with the growth of demands. The relative contraction has occurred through different, often concurrent, mechanisms: introducing *greater selectivity in access*, through for instance the tightening of eligibility criteria; increasing *users' co-payments* through the introduction of means-tested procedures and users' fees; *reducing the 'intensity' of services per user* by cutting the length or depth of the services provided to individual users. Some of these mechanisms had already been introduced in the 1990s, but the financial crisis of 2008 and its aftershocks have determined a further stress on the spending capacity of governments and, in some countries, even a contraction of expenditures in absolute terms (especially in Mediterranean ones, but also in the UK and some Nordic countries) (Saraceno, 2013). In these countries, many in-kind public services, and even cash-transfers, have been curtailed or altogether discontinued, as is well illustrated in a number of chapters of this volume (Kröger and Bagnato; Deusdad, Javornik et al.; Häikiö et al.; Mas Giralt and Sarlo).

There have been changes also in the *form* of public support, with a generalised *disengagement* of the state from the *direct public provision* of in-kind services. This type of disengagement includes two main processes, both of which have been justified with the aim of introducing competition among providers and granting greater choice to users. In many cases, however, it was a pragmatic way to shed operational responsibilities and reduce direct costs. The first process involves *outsourcing* (also referred to as *subcontracting* or *externalisation*), whereby the state entrusts the actual production of public social services to private suppliers (for-profit or non-profit) but still finances them (entirely or partly). In this case, private providers are more or less regulated and accredited by the state and might be selected on the basis of bidding procedures (competitive tenders). The second process involves a shift to, or a preference for, *cash benefits*, instead of in-kind services (Ungerson, 2004), in the form of allowances or vouchers more or less targeted or earmarked to purchasing specific services on the private market. In both instances, the extent of public support, at least in principle, may not change, but new providers step in. As such, these two forms of state disengagement also fall under the rubric of the 'horizontal' reorganisation of responsibility for social services, addressed in the third family of changes below.

### Changes in the 'vertical' division of authority towards a 'hollowing' of the national state

Until the 1970s, most European countries – with the notable exceptions of Germany and Switzerland – were characterised by a strong centralisation of authority at the national level. Since then, there has been a generalised *re-scaling of authority*, first downward towards the regional or local scales, and later upward towards the EU (Hooghe and Marks, 2001), a process that has 'hollowed' the central state sovereignty in a number of policy domains and has strongly affected social services (see Table 1.1).

In what concerns the *downward re-scaling*, also called 'vertical subsidiarity' (Kazepov, 2010), in many countries the last quarter of the twentieth century has witnessed – with different timings and intensity – an administrative *decentralisation* process (later called *devolution*), whereby a number of policy responsibilities, including social policy and/or services, were transferred from the central to lower scales of government (Sellers and Lidstrom, 2007), although not always accompanied by a parallel devolution of resources and/or tax levying authority. In some countries, it was the 'meso-' tier that was privileged, such as with the establishment of *regional governments* in Italy or *autonomous communities* in Spain, but the lower level of government authority, the *municipality, township* or *commune* (which in most countries already had responsibilities for social services) was also concerned. This process was partly the result of bottom-up 'regionalist' or 'localist' claims for greater autonomy, but was also fuelled by the EU discourses about 'subsidiarity' and a 'Europe of regions', which sponsored the normative assumption that administrative decentralisation meant greater administrative efficiency and democracy (Andreotti et al., 2012).

In the vertical division of authority, the *local/municipal* level is indeed particularly important, since in most countries this is the level directly in charge of organising and delivering social services (Wollmann et al., 2010). The process by which it came to hold this responsibility, however, varies greatly. As is the case for welfare models, also local governments are involved in a 'typology' debate, with different attempts at grouping nations in function of one parameter or other (Goldsmith, 1996; Bennett, 1993). In this debate, the 'Northern' or 'Scandinavian' group (but also the UK), characterised by a longstanding 'functional' autonomy of local governments, albeit strongly regulated by the central state, is contrasted with the 'Franco' or 'Napoleonic' group (France, but also Belgium and sometimes Italy), historically characterised by a strong centralisation of authority, or with the 'Continental/Central European' group (Germany, the Netherlands, Switzerland), characterised by a more or less complex/ efficient co-governance among different government tiers, or yet with the 'Southern' group (Italy again, Spain, Portugal) where, after the decentralisation process of the 1980s, regions and municipalities now enjoy a significant legal and political autonomy, which does not necessarily correspond to a real 'functional' autonomy (Goldsmith, 1996, p. 189).

This is to say that here too path-dependency counts and affects the way local governments operate. And, in fact, understanding the 'vertical' division of responsibility among government levels in static terms is not sufficient, as administrative capabilities are not established by decree. The current – quite complex – geometries of authority observed across European states are the result of processes that were embodied in, and/or grafted onto, pre-existing institutional configurations and administrative traditions and have, hence, produced different results. A case in point is Italy, where a common administrative structure – very centralised until the 1970s and later strongly decentralised – has yielded very different social service systems, depending on local government traditions and cultures (Costa, 2009; Pavolini, 2015).

This said, in contrast to the assumption that decentralised authority means more democratic and efficient governance *per se*, many authors argue that decentralising responsibility for social services in a context of economic crisis has been a strategy implemented by national governments to 'avoid blame' and shift the unpleasant task of managing austerity to the local level (Keating, 1998; Rodríguez-Pose and Ezcurra, 2010; Bonoli, 2012; León et al., 2015; see Sabatinelli and Semprebon, in this volume).

It should also be noted that, although decentralisation has been the prevailing trend, in some policy domains and functions, the state has maintained *centralised control* and there are even cases of *re-centralisation* of authority. Many cash transfer provisions linked to national social insurance systems, for instance, have remained firmly managed at the central level, albeit often through regional and local offices, in the same way as in many countries 'core' regulatory aspects concerning social services (standards, entitlements, access or accreditation) have also remained centrally defined. In some countries and services there are also instances of (re)centralisation (Wollmann et al., 2010), either via the (re)introduction of central control over some services, such as is the case of child care in Germany (CAP Mätzke, 2012) or via the enforcement of centrally decreed austerity measures in the funding of social services, such as in the UK (Lowndes and Pratchett, 2012; CAP Yeandle, 2014).

In what concerns *upward re-scaling*, with the completion of the Single European market and the signing of the Treaty of Maastricht in 1992, the EU has come to hold supra-national power in many economic policy domains that were once the prerogative of national governments: commercial policy, industrial policy, regional policy and, for the Eurozone, even monetary policy. As stressed by Scharpf (2002), European integration has 'succeeded beyond expectation' in economic terms, but not so well in social policy terms (p. 648), creating 'a fundamental asymmetry between policies promoting market efficiencies and those promoting social protection and equality' (p. 665). In fact, while member states have been progressively legally constrained – through 'hard' law' – by EU directives that enforced market integration, liberalisation and competition, the harmonisation of welfare systems and the establishment of a common social policy framework were prevented by the great diversity that existed, not only in terms of national capacity to pay for social transfers and services, but also 'in normative aspirations and institutional structures' (p. 645), not to mention issues of domestic political consensus. Hence the choice to regulate social policies through 'soft' law mechanisms (i.e. the 'open method of coordination') and 'voluntary' tools (i.e. performance indicators, benchmarking, peer reviewing, etc.), the effectiveness of which is undermined by their very voluntary nature.

And yet, the 'hard' rules imposed by the *economic* agenda of the EU have had a much more far-reaching impact on social services than the 'soft' tools in the domain of *social* policy. Many highly regulated and/or formerly state-operated services (from banking, to transportation and telecommunication, including social services) were severely affected by EU rules on market liberalisation, which viewed them as unfair competition and supported processes of privatisation and/or opening to private suppliers. Although in the mid-2000s, following the *White paper on services of general interest* of 2004, an important discussion developed about the specificities of 'social' services within services 'of general economic interest' (EC, 2006; 2007; 2010), which acknowledged the welfare dimension and inclusive role of social services (EC, 2007, pp. 5–7) and provided some margins to national and local governments for preserving the public provision of social services (see Gómez-Barroso et al., in this volume), many member states have moved from direct provision of in-kind services to outsourcing and/or cash transfers (see next section below).

This said, what is missing in the debate on government decentralisation and vertical subsidiarity in the domain of social services is a clear identification of *'who' does 'what'*. As I shall argue later, the way the different *functions* involved in the production and delivery of social services – regulation, financing, planning, implementation – are attributed to the different tiers of the state profoundly affects their capacity to respond to needs.

### Changes in the 'horizontal' division of responsibility towards a diversified service providers' 'mix'

A final set of changes concerns what is generally referred to as the 'welfare mix' (Evers and Wintersberger, 1990; Evers, 2005; Jenson, 2012), i.e. the relative contribution of the four main parties involved in the production of social services: the state, the family, the market (for-profit providers), and the community or third sector (non-profit organisations), which constitute the so-called 'providers diamond' (Jenson, 2015). The re-shuffling of responsibilities among these providers also goes under the name of 'horizontal subsidiarity' (Kazepov, 2008; 2010), 'welfare pluralism' (Abrahamson, 1995) or 'new welfare governance' (Klenk and Pavolini, 2015), and has been labelled 're-mix' in the chapter by Leibetseder et al. (in this volume).

The division of labour between the state and other providers was always considered a key factor in the literature about – and classifications of – both welfare *regimes* and welfare *models* (see section 2 in this chapter). In Esping-Andersen's analysis (1990), the main distinction was between the state, on the one hand, and market and family on the other, and the main trends observed in the period of the construction of the Keynesian welfare state were 'de-familisation' and 'de-commodification', meaning that the state was taking over responsibilities traditionally carried out within the family (especially care) or purchased in the market (by the richer classes). These processes were most prominent in the Nordic countries, which became the 'ideal-type' of the universalistic, social democratic welfare state model, i.e. a model that ensured access by all its citizens to the same (high) quality public services, independently of origin, gender, income or place. The other welfare models were somewhat described 'against' this ideal type.

Other authors, however, considered also a fourth provider, alternatively referred to as the third sector, the non-profit sector, the non-governmental sector, the civil society, or the community (Evers, 1995; Bode and Brandsen 2014; Jenson, 2015). This is certainly not a 'new' provider, as philanthropic or charitable organisations and mutual aid associations or cooperatives provided social assistance and services to the poor and/or to specific communities already in the nineteenth century (Martinelli, 2010). In some countries (e.g. Germany) they have remained a pillar of (public) social services, whereas in other countries (e.g. Nordic countries, but also France and Italy) they were progressively replaced by the state. They are now (re)gaining attention in conjunction with the development of the debate on the social economy (Nyssens, 2006) and social innovation (Moulaert et al., 2010; Evers and Ewert, 2015; Jenson, 2015).

The specificity of this fourth type of provider is that it includes private *organisations*, hence suppliers with some degree of formal organisational structure, that are *non-profit*, hence having a 'social' mission and generally working for a 'community' of users, be it a neighbourhood (e.g. residents' associations), a category of workers or users (e.g. mutual aid associations or targeted support association), or a membership group (e.g. cooperatives). They thus generally have a local nature, but they may also belong to quite large 'umbrella' organisations or networks, on a national and even international level. In the current debates, these different organisations are generally lumped together, but there are profound differences within the category that need to be stressed, the main one being the difference between *voluntary* and *non-profit* organisations. Voluntary organisations do not pay their workers and generally do not ask fees or payments from their users. Non-profit organisations, even if they do not distribute profits, do hire and pay their workforce and hence need a steady flow of resources, either from the state or from users, to function. They also operate in the market, albeit not for a profit, and must often compete with for-profit providers (e.g. in competitive biddings for outsourced public services). A few chapters in this book will highlight these ambiguities and weaknesses of the third sector as provider of services (see Bode; Leibetseider et al.; Anttonen and Karsio).

All this said, the providers' mix that was in place at the height of the Keynesian regime in every country or region – whatever its configuration – began to change in the 1980s and 1990s, when the neo-liberal paradigm set in. The key trend in this 're-shuffling' of the welfare mix has been a disengagement of the state, as described earlier. All three forms of such disengagement – contraction of public support, outsourcing to private providers, and shift to cash transfers – have involved an increased role of the other providers. Whether it was the family, the market or the third sector depended on the specific configuration of the welfare system and the restructuring strategies implemented. In fact, some of these changes were explicitly engineered by the state, such as with the outsourcing of public services or the shift to cash transfers; other changes came about 'by default' (Saraceno and Keck, 2010), i.e. as a spontaneous adjustment to the contraction or insufficient growth of public services (Da Roit and Sabatinelli, 2013; see also the chapters by Kröger and Bagnato; Deusdad, Lev et al., in this volume).

In the case of outsourcing, both market and third sector providers have benefited, depending on central and local government strategies. As shown by Anttonen and Karsio (in this volume), even among Nordic countries there are differences, depending on whether private companies were allowed – or found it convenient – to enter the public service market. In Italy, legislation on outsourcing especially favoured the third sector (social cooperatives) (Bifulco and Vitale, 2006). In the case of cash transfers, in the form of allowances or vouchers to purchase services in the private market, the effects on the providers' mix depend again on context, regulation and generosity of monetary transfers. In principle, cash transfers are supposed to enhance users' choice and, especially in the case of care activities, to give women the freedom to choose between caring in person for children or other non-self-sufficient persons (while receiving an allowance) and purchasing services in the market. But, in reality, this choice is constrained by many factors. In contexts characterised by unemployment and poverty and/or where fees charged by private providers are too high, women will tend to care in person for needy family members. In places where an informal market of privately hired caregivers has developed, in the absence of employment regulation enforcement (such as in some Mediterranean countries), cash transfers can contribute to reproducing the black market of immigrant care workers (Van Hooren, 2012; Williams and Brennan, 2012). In some places where the economic crisis has worsened unemployment and poverty, cash allowances often become a source of income for the whole household. In any case, cash-transfers generally involve either a 're-commodification' or a 're-familisation' process (Da Roit and Sabatinelli, 2013).

A major consequence of the horizontal re-shuffling of responsibilities among service providers has been an increase in *complexity* and, in some cases, a *fragmentation* of responsibility. Both involve higher transaction costs, while requiring greater *coordination* mechanisms, which are not always ensured. Moreover, complexity may become *'disorganisation'*

(Bode, 2006; see also Chapter 4, in this volume), hence reducing the quality and the reach of services. And it often reduces *transparency*, as information is not readily available to the most vulnerable groups, thereby limiting accessibility. But, as was the case for the vertical reorganisation of authority, in order to better understand the consequences of the new horizontal division of responsibility, one must look at *'who does what'*, as I will explain in the coming section.

### The Main Functions Involved in Public Social Service Systems

The features and impacts of the restructuring of social services depend very much on 'who does what'. In the organisation, production and delivery of public social services, I identify four key *functions*: (a) regulation; (b) funding; (c) coordination, planning and monitoring; (d) production and delivery. A first division of responsibility for these functions occurs in 'vertical' terms, i.e. among the different tiers of the state. The diagram proposed in Table 1.2 – with an example from Italy – can be a useful tool to summarise and chart the role of the different government levels in the different functions, for any given social service, at any one time or place. But clearly identifying 'who does what' in 'horizontal' terms, i.e. among the different parties of the providers' mix, is also relevant when it comes to the actual production and delivery function.

The *regulation* function generally pertains to the state. It defines rights and duties, service standards, entitlement and access criteria, procedures

*Table 1.2   The 'vertical division of authority' within the state: the case of early childhood care services in Italy\**

| Functions | EU | Central government | Regional government | Municipality |
|---|---|---|---|---|
| Regulation | (X) | (X) | X | (X) |
| Funding | | (X) | X | X |
| Coordination, planning & monitoring | | | X | (X) |
| Production & delivery | | | | X |

*Note:*   \* The vertical division of responsibility described here refers to the period from 2001, when almost exclusive regulatory authority over social services was devolved to Regional governments, to the end of 2016. In the course of 2017 the Italian Parliament enacted legislation transfering early childhood education and care services from the domain of social services to that of education, a transfer that may alter the present vertical division of authority among the different tiers of the state.

*Source:*   Author's compilation.

for the production, accreditation, delivery and monitoring of social services, etc. Most importantly, it defines which level of government does what and which suppliers are authorised to provide services. We have already addressed the indirect regulatory role of the EU in social policy – through its agendas and 'soft' law instruments – and its rather stronger influence in what concerns social services as economic activities. But since social policy is still by and large a national prerogative, it is at this level that regulation still has the greatest impact: how much is defined at the national level – especially in what concerns service standards and eligibility – has fundamental consequences on the *universalistic* dimension of social services. The more nationally regulated are social services, the more uniform the supply and coverage is likely to be across places; in contrast, when the regulatory function is decentralised, territorial differences in quality and access are inevitable, especially when there are differences in economic development levels and administrative traditions. In Italy, for example, the regulatory role of the central state in the domain of social services was weak to start with, but the 2001 constitutional reform has granted full regulatory autonomy to the regional governments, thereby enhancing the already quite high regional differentiation in service systems (Costa, 2009; Pavolini, 2015). Strong (national) regulation is even more necessary when private providers are involved – e.g. in the case of outsourcing – in order to guarantee minimum requirements in terms of service standards, access, training and contractual conditions for workers. This said, the lower levels of government can – and do – concur in the regulation function, especially in what concerns regulating the actual production of services.

*Funding* is another key function, since the amount and provenance of financial resources affect both the quantity and the quality of services. This is still an eminently public function, although co-payments and co-production (from users, the family and the community) are increasingly called upon. A great variety of configurations is possible, though. At one extreme of an ideal-typical spectrum can be found a hypothetically fully centralised system where resources are levied at the national level (through fully centralised taxation) and territorially allocated according to given parameters (population, needs, etc.). At the other extreme can be found a hypothetically fully decentralised system where regions and/or municipalities have complete fiscal autonomy and hence levy their own resources and fund their own services. In the former case, the central state can perform an important redistributive role, i.e. ensure that places have the resources necessary to provide social services independently of their tax base. In the latter case, the amount and quality of services would depend exclusively on the wealth of places. In reality, most countries have mixed systems and the central state retains some redistributive power. But regardless of the system, the degree of the central state's redistributive power – together with the degree of national regulatory power – strongly affect the universal character of social services (see the next section in this chapter).

The *coordinating, planning and monitoring* function involves the actual organisation of social services, i.e. making choices and implementing procedures to assess needs, allocate funding to specific services and territories, attribute tasks to specific actors, and monitor the supply. This function too is still eminently a state prerogative and is generally shared among different government levels, although the bulk is generally carried out at the lower echelons (the regional and/or the local levels). In some cases, the meso-level acts as the chief planning tier (for instance the Regional governments in Italy); in many other cases, the planning of services is directly entrusted to the lower level (e.g. municipalities or districts).

The actual *production and delivery* of social services is the final task in the system. This function is necessarily carried out at the local level, i.e. at the municipal or districts level, since social services require proximity to their users. It is in this function that the state – in those countries where it had stepped in[15] – has most 'disengaged': from direct – and often sole – provider, it has evolved into a 'commissioner' of social services (Diamond and Liddle, 2012), in the case of outsourcing, or an 'enabler' of market mechanisms, in the case of cash-transfers. In the first instance, the state retains its role of coordinator, in the second it abdicates this role to the market. There is of course also the instance of insufficient development or actual retrenchment of public social services, in which case production is carried out by the family, the market or the third sector 'by default'. Either way, it is in this function that the 'horizontal' division of responsibility is most relevant, as the family, third sector and for-profit providers are increasingly (re)entering the production of services, alongside, on behalf, or in substitution of the state.

In conclusion, key issues in the vertical division of authority – which bear on the *universalistic* dimension of social services – are the degree of national control over regulation and funding (i.e. redistribution) and whether the division of authority and responsibility is clearly defined. As some of the chapters of this volume will show, the restructuring of social services has seen in many cases a devolution of authority without a parallel devolution of funding capabilities (Sabatinelli and Semprebon) and a complexification – if not a blurring – of both the vertical division of authority between the different tiers of the state and the horizontal division of responsibility among providers (Bode; Leibetseder et al.), which has determined fragmentation, disorganisation, lack of transparency and reduction of accountability in the organisation of the service supply.

### Key Issues in the Vertical and Horizontal Division of Responsibilities

'Who does what' – and which functions are retained by the state, at which level and to what extent – is not just an idle academic concern, since it directly affects a number of key aspects involved in the public support of social services.

A first key aspect is that of *universalism*. As stressed in section 1 of this chapter, this was the pillar of the Keynesian welfare state and the basis of the notion of social citizenship. Even in its 'softer' version, i.e. allowing for positive selectivism and particularism, it implies the basic right for people to have access to good quality and affordable services, independently of origin, religion, gender, income or place. From the discussion above, it clearly appears that the capability to ensure both social inclusion and territorial cohesion hinges directly on how much the *central* state retains control over the regulation and funding of social services, ensuring a redistribution of resources in favour of the poorest and/or neediest social groups and territories. Irrespective of systems and traditions in the vertical division of authority among different levels of the state, it is still the national government – at present – that can ensure the necessary redistributive mechanisms. The challenge is then how to conjugate universalism with choice.

Another key aspect that depends on central state regulation is how much the new division of responsibility among the family, the market and the third sector is *formalised*, i.e. 'above board', transparent and accountable. When outsourcing and cash transfers – but also privately produced social services – are not regulated, i.e. are not subject to formal rules and monitoring, informal, 'grey' or outright 'black' market activities can develop, involving exploitative labour relations, lack of professional training and/ or neglect or abuse of vulnerable users. For example, when cash transfers are provided it makes a great difference whether they are earmarked, i.e. they can only be spent to purchase services from accredited – formal – suppliers (as is the case, e.g. in Denmark; CAP Jensen and Fersch, 2013), or they are not monitored at all, allowing for the purchase of 'informal' services from hired caregivers, often immigrant women (as is the case, e.g. in Italy; see Van Hooren, 2010; CAP Martinelli, 2012b). The same applies to third sector service providers, which can be highly regulated and integrated into the public system (as for instance in Germany) or informally set up to meet social needs not covered or regulated by the state (as for instance in Greece; see Häikiö et al., in this volume). It also makes a difference for family carers, who in some countries are formally recognised and financially supported. In other words, the more regulated and monitored are the different policy tools, the more formalised and accountable they are, also in terms of quality of service for the user and working conditions for the providers.

A final issue concerns the role of *local initiatives* in triggering and up-scaling *social innovation* in the production and delivery of social services. In the diversified panorama of national, regional and local processes of change examined in the course of the Action, several innovative local initiatives have been analysed, some integrated in publicly funded (experimental) social policy programmes, but most of them of a spontaneous nature trying to address ignored social needs, new needs or needs determined by cuts in public services. They have generally involved multiple local actors, such as the civil society, non-governmental organisations, public authorities, and sometimes also private companies. Four chapters in this volume are dedicated to the analysis of some of these local initiatives (Häikiö et al.; Weinzierl et al.; Mas Giralt and Sarlo; Brokking et al.). They raise major analytical and normative questions, related to the actual socially innovative impact of such initiatives. According to the more emancipatory conception of social innovation (Moulaert et al., 2005; 2010; see also Mätzke et al., in this volume), socially innovative initiatives must empower users, transform social relations among actors involved and bring about some form of durable social progress, beyond the individual or the community. In many of the observed initiatives, however, these outcomes were not attained. Local action merely substituted for an absent public provision of (satisfactory) services, did not involve/challenged the overall system, and remained confined at the local level, with limited societal impact and sustainability over time.

## 4. CONCLUDING QUESTIONS

Against the above background, the chapters that follow in this book have all explored the directions, features and specificities of changes in the public provision of social services in different places and service fields. They have all investigated the impacts of changes from one or more among the five 'perspectives' mobilised in the course of our COST Action (see *Memorandum of Understanding*, 2011): (i) cost efficiency and user satisfaction; (ii) democratic governance; (iii) social and territorial cohesion; (iv) labour market of care and social work; (v) gender. They have all addressed one or more of the following questions:

- What were the prevailing changes at work in any given place or service in the last decades and in which direction? Were there any detectable new trends compared to those identified here?

- How has the financial crisis of 2008 and its aftershocks affected restructuring trajectories? Are there continuities or discontinuities with regard to the pre-existing neo-liberal restructuring processes?
- Has the 'social investment strategy' affected in any way the ongoing restructuring?
- Are there differences in processes and directions among service fields?
- How have these processes been influenced by pre-existing welfare systems and other context-specific factors? In other words, how has path-dependency played out in national and regional trajectories?
- Is there convergence or divergence among national and regional trajectories in Europe? With respect to which features?
- What are the effects of such changes, especially in what concerns the satisfaction of needs, users' choice and empowerment, democratic governance, social and territorial cohesion, the conditions of social work, gender?
- What are the implications and challenges of these trends in terms of social policy?

These are rather ambitious questions, which this book does not claim to answer in any definite and exhaustive way, especially given the great variety of contexts and services. But despite this variety, as the editors will stress in the last part of the volume, all chapters have contributed some tesserae towards a better understanding of what is happening to social services in Europe, calling attention to a number of social consequences and policy challenges.

## NOTES

1. I am aware that the expression 'in-kind services' is redundant, as services can only be in kind. But I will continue using it to stress the distinction with 'cash benefits'.
2. In this acceptation, universalism does not mean undifferentiated supply, nor does it preclude the possibility of choice.
3. I am aware that since the book by Esping-Andersen (1990), the term 'regime' is generally used to characterise what I call, instead, welfare state 'models' or 'families' (see next section). My terminology is more in tune with Jane Jenson's notion of 'citizenship regimes', which refers to the same periodisation (2012).
4. From this point of view also called 'spatial Keynesianism' (Martin and Sunley, 1997; Brenner, 2003).
5. Although he used the term 'regime'.
6. See the special issue of the *Journal of European Social Policy* in the occasion of the 25th anniversary of the book.
7. See the entertaining contribution by Baldwin (1996) on the matter, although in his article he mostly disputes the existence of a 'European' welfare state model.

8. The term 'family' of countries is used by Castles (1993) and Gal (2010).
9. The first three stylise 'Keynesian' models, i.e. welfare systems that took shape before the neo-liberal turn, whereas the last two are hybrids, as they formed or were identified in the 1990s.
10. In fact, the UK is not fully consistent with this model, as this country was the first in Europe to introduce a universalistic – 'Beveridgean' – social insurance and health system after WW2.
11. France is a 'shape-shifter' country, since on some counts it resembles the Liberal model (because of its generous cash transfers), whereas on others it is closer to the Nordic model (because of a number of universalistic public services).
12. Italy is a borderline country because of its strong territorial differentiation: the Northern regions are closer to the Corporatist/Continental family, whereas the Southern regions are fully Mediterranean.
13. Some authors (Guillén and León, 2011) stress similarities with the corporatist model, but also a key difference (highlighted by Saraceno and Keck, 2010) – i.e. the fact that in the corporatist welfare states the family is 'supported', whereas in the Southern European ones it is 'unsupported'.
14. Some authors even question the existence of such a family and place the different countries in other groups (see Fenger, 2007 for a discussion on this).
15. In 'Continental' countries, such as Germany, where the role of the Third sector has remained important, this trend is less conspicuous, although forms of 'disengagement' of the state are still observed (Bode, in this volume).

# REFERENCES

Abrahamson, P. (1995), 'Welfare pluralism: towards a new consensus for a European social policy?', *Current Politics and Economics of Europe*, **5** (1), 29–42.
Andreotti, A., E. Mingione and E. Polizzi (2012), 'Local welfare systems: a challenge for social cohesion', *Urban Studies*, **49** (9), 1925–40.
Anttonen, A. and G. Meagher (2013), 'Mapping marketisation: concepts and goals', in G. Meagher and M. Szebehely (eds), *Marketization in Nordic Eldercare: A Research Report on Legislation, Oversight, Extent and Consequences*, Stockholm: Stockholm University, pp. 13–22.
Anttonen, A. and J. Sipilä (1996), 'European social care services: is it possible to identify models?', *Journal of European Social Policy*, **6** (2), 87–100.
Anttonen, A. and J. Sipilä (2012), 'Universalism in the British and Scandinavian social policy debates', in A. Anttonen, L. Häikiö and K. Stéfansson (eds), *Welfare State, Universalism and Diversity*, Cheltenham, UK and Northampton, MA, USA: Edward Elgar Publishing, pp. 16–41.
Anttonen, A., L. Häikiö, K. Stéfansson and J. Sipilä (2012), 'Universalism and the challenge of diversity', in A. Anttonen, L. Häikiö and K. Stéfansson (eds), *Welfare State, Universalism and Diversity*, Cheltenham, UK and Northampton, MA, USA: Edward Elgar Publishing, pp. 1–15.
Arts, W. and J. Gelissen (2002), 'Three worlds of welfare or more? A state-of-the-art report', *Journal of European Social Policy*, **12** (2), 137–58.
Ascoli, U. and C. Ranci (eds) (2002), *Dilemmas of the Welfare Mix. The New Structure of Welfare in an Era of Privatization*, New York: Springer-Verlag.
Bahle, T. (2008) 'The state and social services in Britain, France and Germany since the 1980s. Reform and growth in a period of welfare state crisis', *European Societies*, **10** (1), 25–47.

Baldwin, P. (1996), 'Can we define a European welfare state model?', in B. Greve (ed.), *Comparative Welfare Systems*, New York: St Martin's Press, pp. 29–44.

Bambra, C. (2005), 'Cash versus services: "Worlds of Welfare" and the decommodification of transfers and health care services', *Journal of Social Policy*, **34** (2), 195–213.

Bennett, R.J. (1993), 'European local government systems', in R.J. Bennett (ed.), *Local Government in the New Europe*, London, UK and New York, USA: Belhaven Press, pp. 28–47.

BEPA – Bureau of European Policy Advisers (2011), *Empowering People, Driving Change. Social Innovation in the European Union*, Luxembourg: Publications Office of the European Union.

Bifulco, L. and T. Vitale (2006), 'Contracting for welfare services in Italy', *Journal of Social Policy*, **35** (3), 495–513.

Bode, I. (2006), 'Disorganized welfare mixes: voluntary agencies and new governance regimes in Western Europe', *Journal of European Social Policy*, **16** (4), 346–59.

Bode, I. (2009), 'On the road to welfare markets: institutional, organizational, and cultural dynamics of a new European welfare state settlement', in J. Powell and J. Hendricks (eds), *The Welfare State in Post-Industrial Society*, New York: Springer-Verlag, pp. 161–77.

Bode, I. and T. Brandsen (2014), 'State–Third sector partnerships. A short overview of key issues in the debate', *Public Management Review*, **16** (8), 1055–66.

Bonoli, G. (2012), 'Blame avoidance and credit claiming revisited', in G. Bonoli and D. Natali (eds), *The Politics of the New Welfare State*, Oxford: Oxford University Press, pp. 93–110.

Brandsen, T., A. Evers, S. Cattacin and A. Zimmer (eds) (2016), *Social Innovations in the Urban Context*, London: Springer Open.

Brennan, D., B. Cass, S. Himmelweit and M. Szebehely (2012), 'The marketisation of care: rationales and consequences in Nordic and liberal care regimes', *Journal of European Social Policy*, **22** (4), 377–91.

Brenner, N. (2003), '"Glocalization" as a state spatial strategy: urban entrepreneurialism and the new politics of uneven development in Western Europe', in J. Peck and H. Wai-chung Yeung (eds), *Remaking the Global Economy. Economic-Geographical Perspectives*, London: Sage, pp. 197–215.

Carmel, E. and J. Harlock (2008), 'Instituting the "third sector" as a governable terrain: partnership, procurement and performance in the UK', *Policy & Politics*, **36** (2), 155–71.

Castles, F.G. (1993), 'Introduction', in F.G. Castles (ed.), *Families of Nations*, Dartmouth: Aldershot, pp. xiii–xxiii.

Castles, F.G. (2005), 'Social expenditures in the 1990s: data and determinants', *Policy & Politics*, **33** (3), 411–30.

Clayton, R. and J. Pontusson (1998), 'Welfare state retrenchment revisited. Entitlement cuts, public sector restructuring, and inegalitarian trends in advanced capitalist societies', *World Politics*, **51** (1), 67–98.

Cochrane, A. (2004), 'Modernisation, managerialism and the culture wars: the reshaping of the local welfare state in England', *Local Government Studies*, **30** (4), 481–96.

COST Action IS1102 (2011), *Memorandum of Understanding*, Brussels: COST Secretariat, accessed in December 2016 at http://www.cost.eu/COST_Actions/isch/IS1102.

Costa, G. (ed.) (2009), *La solidarietà frammentata*, Milan: Bruno Mondadori.

Crouch, C., K. Eder and D. Tambini (eds) (2001), *Citizenship, Markets and the State*, Oxford: Oxford University Press.

Da Roit, B. and S. Sabatinelli (2013), 'Nothing on the move or just going private? Understanding the freeze on child- and eldercare policies and the development of care markets in Italy', *Social Politics: International Studies in Gender, State and Society*, **20** (3), 430–53.

Diamond, P. and R. Liddle (2012), 'Aftershock: the post-crisis social investment welfare state in Europe', in N. Morel, B. Palier and J. Palme (eds), *Towards a Social Investment Welfare State? Ideas, Policies and Challenges*, Bristol: Policy Press, pp. 285–308.

Dickens, P. (1998), *Global Shifts*, 3rd edn, London: Guilford Press.

EC-European Commission (2006), *Implementing the Community Lisbon programme: Social Services of General Interest in the European Union*, COM (2006) 177 final, Brussels.

EC-European Commission (2007), *Services of General Interest, Including Social Services of General Interest: a New European Commitment*, COM (2007) 724 final, Brussels.

EC-European Commission (2010), *Second Biennial Report on Social Services of General Interest. Commission Staff Working Document*, SEC (2010) 1284 final, Brussels.

EESC-European Economic and Social Committee (2014), 'Opinion of the European Economic and Social Committee on "The impact of social investment on employment and public budgets"', *Official Journal of the European Union*, C 226, 21–7.

Esping-Andersen, G. (1990), *The Three Worlds of Welfare Capitalism*, Princeton: Princeton University Press.

Eurostat (2011), *ESSPROS Manual – The European System of integrated Social PROtection Statistics*, Luxembourg: Publications Office of the European Union.

Evers, A. (1995), 'Part of the welfare mix: the third sector as an intermediate area', *International Journal of Voluntary and Nonprofit Organizations*, **6** (2), 159–82.

Evers, A. (2005), 'Mixed welfare systems and hybrid organisations. Changes in the governance and provision of social services', *International Journal of Public Administration*, **28** (9–10), 737–48.

Evers, A. and B. Ewert (2015), 'Social innovation for social cohesion', in A. Nicholls, J. Simon and M. Gabriel (eds), *New Frontiers in Social Innovation Research*, New York: Palgrave Macmillan, pp. 107–28.

Evers, A. and H. Wintersberger (eds) (1990), *Shifts in the Welfare Mix. Their Impact on Work, Social Services and Welfare Policies*, Frankfurt am Mein, Germany and New York, USA: Campus Westfield.

Fenger, H.J.M. (2007), 'Welfare regimes in Central and Eastern Europe: incorporating post-Communist countries in a welfare regime typology', *Contemporary Issues and Ideas in Social Sciences*, **3** (2), 1–30.

Ferrera, M. (1996), 'The "Southern model" of welfare in social Europe', *Journal of European Social Policy*, **6** (1), 17–37.

Ferrera, M. (2008), 'The European welfare state: golden achievements, silver prospects', *West European Politics*, **31** (1–2), 82–107.

Ferrera, M., A. Hemerijck and M. Rhodes (2000), 'Recasting European welfare states for the 21st century', *European Review*, **8** (3), 427–46.

Gal, J. (2010), 'Exploring the extended family of Mediterranean welfare states', in M. Ajzenstadt and J. Gal (eds), *Children, Gender and Families in Mediterranean Welfare States*, Dordrecht: Springer, pp. 77–101.

Goldsmith, M. (1996), 'Normative theories of local governments: a European comparison', in D. King and G. Stoker (eds), *Rethinking Local Democracy*, London: Macmillan, pp. 174–92.

Guillén, A.M. and M. Léon (2011), 'Introduction', in A.M. Guillén and M. Léon (eds), *The Spanish Welfare State in European Context*, Farnham, UK and Burlington, USA: Ashgate, pp. 1–16.

Hacker, B. (2009), 'Hybridization instead of clustering. Transformation processes of welfare policies in Central and Eastern Europe', *Social Policy & Administration*, **43** (2), 152–69.

Häikiö, L. and B. Hvinden (2012), 'Finding the way between universalism and diversity: a challenge to the Nordic model', in A. Anttonen, L. Häikiö and K. Stéfansson (eds), *Welfare State, Universalism and Diversity*, Cheltenham, UK and Northampton, MA, USA: Edward Elgar Publishing, pp. 69–89.

Harsløf, I. and R. Ulmestig (2013), 'Introduction', in I. Harsløf and R. Ulmestig (eds), *Changing Social Risks and Social Policy Responses in the Nordic Welfare States*, Basingstoke: Palgrave Macmillan, pp. 1–24.

Hemerijck, A. (2012), 'Two or three waves of welfare state transformation?', in N. Morel, B. Palier and J. Palme (eds), *Towards a Social Investment Welfare State?*, Bristol: Policy Press, pp. 33–60.

Hooghe, L. and G. Marks (2001), *Multi-level Governance and European Integration*, Lanham: Rowman & Littlefield.

Huber, E. and J.D. Stephens (2001), *Development and Crisis of the Welfare State: Parties and Policies in Global Markets*, Chicago: University of Chicago Press.

Huber, M., M. Maucher and B. Sak (2006), *Study on Social and Health Services of General Interest in the European Union. Final Synthesis Report*, Report prepared for DG Employment, Social Affairs and Equal Opportunities, Brussels: DG EMPL/E/4VC/2006/0131.

Jensen, C. (2008), 'Worlds of welfare services and transfers', *Journal of European Social Policy*, **18** (2), 151–62.

Jensen, C. (2011), 'Determinants of welfare service provision after the Golden Age', *International Journal of Social Welfare*, **20** (2), 125–34.

Jensen, P.H. and B. Fersch (2013), 'Local variations and preferences in the organization of elder care: the Danish case', unpublished paper presented at the COST Action IS1102 Workshop, University of Iceland, Reykjavik, 3–7 June.

Jenson, J. (2012), 'Redesigning citizenship regimes after neo-liberalism: moving towards social investment', in N. Morel, B. Palier and J. Palme (eds), *Towards a Social Investment Welfare State?*, Bristol: Policy Press, pp. 61–87.

Jenson, J. (2015), 'Social innovation. Redesigning the welfare diamond', in A. Nichols, J. Simon and M. Gabriel (eds), *New Frontiers in Social Innovation*, Basingstoke: Palgrave Macmillan, pp. 89–106.

Jessop, B. (1999), 'The changing governance of welfare: recent trends in its primary functions, scale and modes of coordination', *Social Policy & Administration*, **33** (4), 348–59.

Kazepov, Y. (2008), 'The subsidiarization of social policies: actors, processes and impacts', *European Societies*, **10** (2), 247–73.

Kazepov, Y. (ed.) (2010), *Rescaling Social Policies towards Multilevel Governance in Europe*, Avebury: Ashgate.

Keating, M. (1998), *The New Regionalism in Western Europe: Territorial Restructuring and Political Change*, Cheltenham, UK and Northampton, MA, USA: Edward Elgar Publishing.

Keating, M. (2009) 'Social citizenship, solidarity and welfare in regionalized and plurinational states', *Citizenship Studies*, **13** (5), 501–13.

Klenk, T. and E. Pavolini (eds) (2015), *Restructuring Welfare Governance. Marketization, Managerialism and Welfare State Professionalism*, Cheltenham, UK and Northampton, MA, USA: Edward Elgar Publishing.

Koldinská, K. and I. Tomeš (2004), 'Social services in accession countries', *Social Work and Society, International Online Journal*, **2** (1), 110–17.

Leitner, S. (2003), 'Varieties of familialism: the caring function of the family in comparative perspective', *European Societies*, **5** (4), 353–75.

León, M. and E. Pavolini (2014), '"Social investment" or back to "familism": the impact of the economic crisis on family and care policies in Italy and Spain', *South European Society and Politics*, **19** (3), 353–69.

León, M., E. Pavolini and A.M. Guillén (2015), 'Welfare rescaling in Italy and Spain: political strategies to deal with harsh austerity', *European Journal of Social Security*, **17** (2), 182–201.

Lowndes, V. and L. Pratchett (2012), 'Local governance under the Coalition government: austerity, localism and the Big Society', *Local Government Studies*, **38** (1), 21–40.

Marshall, T.H. (1950), *Citizenship and Social Class*, London: Pluto Press.

Martin, R. and P. Sunley (1997), 'The post-Keynesian state and the space economy', in R. Lee and J. Wills (eds), *Geographies of Economies*, London: Arnold, pp. 278–89.

Martinelli, F. (1991), 'A demand-oriented approach to understanding producer services', in P.W. Daniels and F. Moulaert (eds), *The Changing Geography of Advanced Producer Services*, London: Belhaven Press, pp. 15–29.

Martinelli, F. (2010), 'Historical roots of social change: philosophies and movements', in F. Moulaert, F. Martinelli, E. Swyngedouw and S. Gonzalez (eds), *Can Neighbourhoods Save the City? Community Development and Social Innovation*, Oxford and New York: Routledge, pp. 17–48.

Martinelli, F. (2012a), 'Social innovation or social exclusion? Innovating social services in the context of a retrenching welfare state', in H.-W. Franz, J. Hochgerner and J. Howaldt (eds), *Challenge Social Innovation. Potentials for Business, Social Entrepreneurship, Welfare and Civil Society*, Berlin: Springer, pp. 169–80.

Martinelli, F. (2012b), 'Current organisational framework of care services for older people – Italy', unpublished paper presented at the COST Action IS1102 Workshop, Rovira i Virgili University, Tarragona, 17–19 October.

Martinelli, F. and J. Gadrey (2000), *L'economia dei Servizi*, Bologna: Il Mulino.

Martinelli, F. and A. Novy (2013), 'Urban and regional trajectories between path-dependency and path-shaping. Structures, institutions, discourses and agency in contemporary capitalism', in F. Martinelli, F. Moulaert and A. Novy (eds), *Urban and Regional Development Trajectories in Contemporary Capitalism*, Oxford, UK and New York, USA: Routledge.

Martinelli, F. and A. Sarlo (2014), 'Early childhood services and territorial cohesion. A comparative analysis of supply trajectories in the Emilia Romagna and Calabria regions of Italy', *COST Action IS1102 Working Papers*, no. 6, accessed at http://www.cost-is1102-cohesion.unirc.it/docs/working-papers/wg2. italy-childcare-martinelli-and-sarlo.pdf?v=3.

Martinelli, F., F. Moulaert and S. Gonzalez (2010), 'Creatively designing urban futures: a transversal analysis of socially innovative case studies', in F. Moulaert, F. Martinelli, E. Swyngedouw and S. Gonzalez (eds), *Can Neighbourhoods Save the City? Community Development and Social Innovation*, Oxford, UK and New York, USA: Routledge, pp. 198–218.

Mätzke, M. (2012), 'Current organisational framework of childcare services – Germany', unpublished paper presented at the COST Action IS1102 Workshop, Rovira i Virgili University, Tarragona, 17–19 October.

Morel, N., B. Palier and J. Palme (2012), 'Beyond the welfare state as we knew it?', in N. Morel, B. Palier and J. Palme (eds), *Towards a Social Investment Welfare State?*, Bristol: Policy Press, pp. 1–32.

Moulaert, F., F. Martinelli F. and E. Swyngedouw (eds) (2005), *Social Innovation in the Governance of Urban Communities: A Multidisciplinary Perspective*, special issue of *Urban Studies*, **42** (11).

Moulaert, F., D. MacCallum, A. Mehmood and A. Hamdouch (eds) (2013), *The International Handbook on Social Innovation: Collective Action, Social Learning and Transdisciplinary Research*, Cheltenham, UK and Northampton, MA, USA: Edward Elgar Publishing.

Moulaert, F., F. Martinelli, E. Swyngedouw and S. Gonzalez (eds) (2010), *Can Neighbourhoods Save the City? Community Development and Social Innovation*, Oxford, UK and New York, USA: Routledge.

Mulgan, G. (2012), 'Social innovation theories: can theory catch up with practices?', in F. Hans-Werner, J. Hochgerner and J. Howaldt (eds), *Challenge Social Innovation. Potentials for Business, Entrepreneurship, Welfare and Civil Society*, New York: Springer Verlag, pp. 19–43.

Murray, R., J. Caulier-Grice and J. Mulgan (2010), *The Open Book of Social Innovation*, London: The Young Foundation.

Newman, J. (2001), *Modernising Governance: New Labour, Policy and Society*, London: Sage.

Newman, J., C. Glendenning and M. Hughes (2008), 'Beyond modernisation? Social care and the transformation of welfare governance', *Journal of Social Policy*, **37** (4), 531–57.

Nicholls, A., J. Simon and M. Gabriel (eds) (2015), *New Frontiers in Social Innovation Research*, New York: Palgrave Macmillan.

Nyssens, M. (2006), *Social Enterprise at the Crossroads of Market, Public Policies and Civil Society*, London: Routledge.

OECD (1981), *The Welfare State in Crisis*, Paris: OECD.

OECD (2008), *Growing Unequal*, Paris: OECD.

Pavolini, E. (2015), 'How many Italian welfare systems are there?', in U. Ascoli and E. Pavolini (eds), *The Italian Welfare State in a European Perspective*, Bristol: Policy Press, pp. 283–301.

Petmesidou, M. and A.M. Guillén (2014), 'Can the welfare state as we know it survive? A view from the crisis-ridden South European periphery, *South European Society and Politics*, **19** (3), 295–307.

Pierson, P. (1994), *Dismantling the Welfare State? Reagan, Thatcher, and the Politics of Retrenchment*, Cambridge: Cambridge University Press.

Rauch, D. (2008), 'Central versus local service regulation. Accounting for diverging old age care developments in Sweden and Denmark, 1980–2000', *Social Policy & Administration*, **42** (3), 267–87.

Rodríguez-Pose, A. and R. Ezcurra (2010), 'Does decentralization matter for regional disparities? A cross-country analysis', *Journal of Economic Geography*, **10** (5), 619–44.

Saraceno, C. (2013), 'Three concurrent crises in welfare states in an increasingly asymmetrical European Union', *Stato e Mercato*, no. 3, 339–58.

Saraceno, C. and W. Keck (2010), 'Can we identify intergenerational policy regimes in Europe?', *European Societies*, **12** (5), 675–96.

Scharpf, F. (2002), 'The European social model: coping with the challenges of diversity', *Journal of Common Market Studies*, **40** (4), 645–70.

Schiek, D. (2013), 'The EU's socio-economic model(s) and the crisi(e)s – Any perspective?', in D. Schiek (ed.), *The EU Economic and Social Model in the Global Crisis*, Farnham: Ashgate, pp. 1–22.

Schmid, H. (2003), 'Rethinking the policy of contracting out social services to non-governmental organizations. Lessons and dilemmas', *Public Management Review*, **5** (3), 307–23.

Sellers, J.M. and A. Lidstrom (2007), 'Decentralization, local government, and the welfare state', *Governance: An International Journal of Policy, Administration and Institutions*, **20** (4), 609–32.

Sirovátka, T. and B. Greve (2014), 'Social services and the public sector', in B. Greve and T. Sirovátka (eds), *Innovation in Social Services. The Public–Private Mix in Service Provision, Fiscal Policy and Employment*, Aldershot: Ashgate, pp. 9–20.

Starke, P. (2006), 'The politics of welfare state retrenchment: a literature review', *Social Policy and Administration*, **40** (1), 104–20.

Swyngedouw, E. and B. Jessop (2005), 'Regulation, reproduction and governance', *WP2 Discussion Papers*, DEMOLOGOS – Development Models and Logics of Socio-economic Organisation in Space, FP6 – Specific Targeted Project, Contract CIT2-CT-2004-505462, Newcastle, GURU.

Taylor-Gooby, P. (ed.) (2004), *New Risks, New Welfare: The Transformation of the European Welfare State*, Oxford: Oxford University Press.

Thompson, S. and T. Hogget (1996), 'Universalism, selectivism and particularism. Towards a post-modern social policy', *Critical Social Policy*, **46** (16), 21–43.

Trydegård, G.B. and M. Thorslund (2001), 'Inequality in the welfare state? Local variation in care of the elderly the case of Sweden', *International Journal of Social Welfare*, **10** (3), 174–84.

Ungerson, C. (2004), 'Whose empowerment and independence? A cross-national perspective on "cash-for-care" schemes', *Ageing and Society*, **24** (2), 189–212.

Vabø, M. and M. Szebehely (2012), 'A caring state for all older people', in A. Anttonen, L. Häikiö and K. Stéfansson (eds), *Welfare State, Universalism and Diversity*, Cheltenham, UK and Northampton, MA, USA: Edward Elgar Publishing, pp. 121–43.

Van Hooren, F. (2010), 'When families need immigrants: the exceptional position of migrant domestic workers and care assistants in Italian immigration policy', *Bulletin of Italian Politics*, **2** (2), 21–38.

Van Hooren, F.J. (2012), 'Varieties of migrant care work: comparing patterns of migrant labour in social care', *Journal of European Social Policy*, **22** (2) 133–47.

Williams, F. (1992), 'Somewhere over the rainbow: universality and diversity in social policy', *Social Policy Review*, **4**, 200–19.

Williams, F. and D. Brennan (2012), 'Care, markets and migration in a globalising world. Introduction to the special issue', *Journal of European Social Policy*, **22** (4), 355–62.

Wollmann, H., I. Koprić and G. Marcou (eds) (2010), *The Provision of Public Services in Europe: Between State, Local Government and Market*, Cheltenham, UK and Northampton, MA, USA: Edward Elgar Publishing.

Yeandle, S. (2014), 'Reconfiguring services for older people living at home in Leeds, UK: how have services changed?', unpublished paper presented at the COST Action IS1102 Workshop, University of Tampere, Tampere, 2–6 June; now published as Yeandle, S. (2016), 'From provider to enabler of care? Reconfiguring local authority support for older people and carers in Leeds, 2008 to 2013', *Journal of Social Service Research*, **42** (2), 218–32.

# 2. The European Union policy framework for social services: agendas, regulations and discourses

**José Luis Gómez-Barroso, Stefania Barillà and Ivan Harsløf***

## INTRODUCTION

This chapter aims at assessing the EU's emergent policy framework – the agendas, regulations and discourses – concerning social services within the larger field of social protection. As discussed in Chapter 1, social services stand out as a contested and changing policy area in discussions about the architecture of the welfare state. Some countries adhere to a liberal welfare model where public social service provision is considered a paternalistic market interference. In others of more conservative orientation, it is feared as a potential threat to the social fabric of the family and local community. And even in countries with traditions of comprehensive and service-intensive welfare provisions, current debates revolve around the most appropriate level of government responsibility, mostly favouring decentralised social services designed and delivered by local authorities. These deep-seated differences in views and traditions complicate any supra-national regulation, and indeed, the European Union (EU), encompassing representatives of several different welfare models, has taken a somewhat ambivalent stance on the role of social services in a more integrated Europe.

This has been one of the reasons why, for half a century, social services were not explicitly included in the roadmap to an integrated European Union. The other main reason is that the European Economic Community was designed to create a level playing field to facilitate economic activity, and the social dimension was incorporated primarily to prevent unfair competition. Thus, although the European social charter signed in Turin by the member states of the Council of Europe on October 1961 established that 'everyone has the right to benefit from social welfare services' (Council of Europe, 1961, Article 14), the nearly contemporary Treaty of

Rome made no reference to social services, and neither did the subsequent treaties. In 2012, the Charter of Fundamental Rights of the EU recovered an article incorporated in the 2004 failed project for a European constitution, recognising the entitlement to social services 'providing protection in cases such as maternity, illness, industrial accidents, dependency or old age, and in the case of loss of employment' as well as the 'right to social and housing assistance so as to ensure a decent existence for all those who lack sufficient resources' (Articles 34.1 and 34.3).

Regardless of the lack of references to social services in the Treaties, a number of non-binding forms of legislation were issued prior to 2000 on particular areas of social policy, together with – or as a result of – some valuable work behind the scenes that was done in agencies, observatories and networks. Since the early 2000s, a growing acknowledgment of social services occurred. It went hand in hand with the diffusion of the 'Social investment' approach sponsored by a number of scholars and think tanks in the late 1990s (Hemerijck, 2012). This approach considers social services not solely as a welfare 'right' for the individual, but also as a productive enterprise for society. At the same time, but not necessarily in tune with the above processes, a regulatory frame has been taking shape for social services, in the course of the implementation of the Single European Market. Over the past ten years, the content and specificities of the so-called 'social services of general interest' have been addressed by 'soft law' documents and rules have been established concerning the application of competition policy to public service providers and about the public funding of social services.

However, the growing acknowledgement of social services by the EU remains, as stressed earlier, ambivalent. After almost 60 years of work towards European integration, social services continue to be regarded mainly as a national affair. Indeed, the consolidated Treaty on the functioning of the EU clearly characterises the role of the Union as only complementary to national social policy (EC, 2012b, Article 153.1). This ambivalence notwithstanding, it is possible to refer to a European social policy framework that includes – albeit not always consistently – social services. To be more precise, it is possible to find a tangled set of policies with goals that are broadly related to social inclusion, by means also of the provision of social services, made of an even more tangled set of recommendations, actions, tools and budgets that have at least a potential impact on the local provision of social services.

In this chapter, the complex social policy framework and regulation established at the EU level is reviewed and critically assessed, with particular attention to its implications for social services. The review was carried out in the course of the COST Action IS1102 *SO.S. COHESION – Social services, welfare states and places*, to better understand the policy context of changes observed in the Action case studies. An account of the evolution of the EU general social policy agenda from 2000 to date (section 1) is followed by a review of the EU regulation of social services of general interest (section 2). Subsequently, the discourses and ideological tenets underlying the EU stance on social services are discussed (section 3), while some concluding remarks are made in section 4.

The main argument put forward is that, beyond the very ambitious discourses and goals set out in its documents, an ambivalent stance and a number of structural tensions permeate the EU social policy framework and especially the initiatives more specifically geared to social services. Among these tensions can be mentioned the gap between the very ambitious goals and the actual financial means; the tension between the attempt to set up a European regulatory framework and national sovereignty in the social domain; and the contradiction between competition policy applied to services and the right to welfare involved in social services. These unsolved tensions are the result of compromises between different approaches, goals and interests, which have yielded a very complex, often redundant set of guidelines, actions and funding schemes.

## 1. THE EU SOCIAL POLICY STRATEGIES, FUNDS AND TOOLS IN THE NEW MILLENNIUM

Arguably, the first formal commitment towards a more unified European social policy occurred in 2000 when, as a way of addressing the social dimension of the Lisbon strategy, the EU and its member states agreed on a European *Social policy agenda*, which was later integrated into the *Europe 2020* strategy.

### The Lisbon Strategy and Europe 2020

In what concerns social policy, three main phases can be identified in the Lisbon strategy (Agh, 2010).

The *Lisbon I period* (2000–2004) was set out in the European Council of Lisbon in 2000, featuring a very ambitious ten-year reform programme. The goal was to 'become the most competitive and dynamic knowledge-based economy, capable of sustainable economic growth with more and better jobs and greater social cohesion' (EC, 2000, p. 2). This involved – among other things – 'modernising the European social model, investing in people and combating social exclusion' (EC, 2000, p. 5). This became the pillar of the 'new' European *Social policy agenda* and marked a shift from the previous sector-focused approach to a more integrated perspective (Decaro, 2011, p. 36). A key principle of the new agenda was the viewing of 'social policy as a productive factor' (EC, 2000, p. 5), in line with the 'social investment' approach sponsored by the EU in the late 1990s (Hemerijck, 2012). To implement the strategy, the European Council assumed a prominent coordinating role, introducing new governance tools: the 'Open method of coordination' as a means for spreading best practices without enforcing regulation; the annual 'Spring European Council' for monitoring progresses; and the 'Broad guidelines for economic policies'.

The *Lisbon II period* (2005–2008), which was set out in the mid-term review of the Spring council of 2005, inaugurated the 'renewed' *Social policy agenda*. Following the recommendations of the Kok report, the agenda was re-focused on growth and employment, while more responsibilities were given to member states. 'Integrated guidelines for growth and jobs' were adopted and a 'Community Lisbon programme' was drafted, which for the first time introduced regulatory measures, some financial instruments, and specific proposals for policy development, while, at the same time, member states had to prepare a 'National reform programme', adapting the Lisbon strategy to their national context.

The *Lisbon III period* (2008–2010) was launched at the Spring council of 2008 with only minor adjustments, focusing on implementation (Butković and Samardžija, 2010) and further stressing that social policy was cross-cutting and multidimensional, covering a wide range of domains, from labour market policies to education, health, immigration and intercultural dialogue (EC, 2008a, p. 3). It also emphasised the need to connect the Lisbon strategy with the financial resources available for the European *Cohesion policy*, an important change in strategy that we shall address later in this section.

The Lisbon strategy and its Social policy agenda were re-examined at the end of the decade. As acknowledged in the document *Europe 2020: A Strategy for European Union Growth (2010–2020)*, the EU faced intensified challenges, coming from further globalisation, climate change and demographic evolution, as well as from the aftershocks of the 2008 financial crisis. Its economic recovery needed to be supported by a number of reforms to guarantee a sustainable development in the coming decade (EC, 2014).

*Europe 2020* explicitly placed social policy at the core of the EU new growth strategy (EC, 2013c), which was articulated in three priorities, five objectives (associated with precisely quantified 'headline targets'), and seven 'flagship initiatives'. Growth had to be 'smart', 'sustainable', but also 'inclusive'. The latter priority was articulated in two objectives – 'Education' and 'Fight against poverty' – and two flagship initiatives –

the 'Agenda for new skills and jobs' and the 'European platform against poverty and for social inclusion'. A number of monitoring and coordinating tools were also established (EC, 2013c): the 'European semester', a new institutional process providing member states with *ex-ante* guidance and the 'Annual growth survey', while the 'Open method of coordination' was reconfirmed for steering structural reforms.

Compared to the Lisbon strategy, the goals of *Europe 2020* were more articulated and somewhat less high-sounding. Moreover, social inclusion now figured more prominently. The 'Social investment' approach was strengthened, as well as the tools to monitor and guide member states. On the other hand, although more cautious, goals remained rather ambitious (Lundvall and Lorenz, 2012, p. 334).

### The EU Policy Toolkit for Social Services in the Frame of Europe 2020

With the launch of *Europe 2020*, all EU funds and programmes were now to comply with the new strategy. Of particular importance were the changes introduced in the European Structural and Investment Funds, the main financing tool of the European Cohesion policy. The two EC Directorates general (DGs) most directly involved in funding and implementing social policy were DG-EMPL (Employment, social affairs and inclusion) and DG-REGIO (Regional and urban policy).

*DG-EMPL* is entrusted with all matters in the domains of employment, social affairs and social inclusion (EC, 2013d, p. 4). More specifically it is responsible for: (1) *social investment* activities (active inclusion and social innovation, investing in children, housing, active ageing, social services of general interest); (2) *social protection* activities (poverty and social exclusion, health care, long-term care, pensions). It is also responsible for the *European social fund (ESF)*, one of the European Structural and Investment Funds, specifically targeted to improving the employment opportunities and standard of living for workers in the internal market (Article 162 of the TFEU – Treaty on the Functioning of the European Union) and to strengthening the EU economic, social and territorial cohesion (Art. 174 TFEU). With Europe 2020, the activities of DG-EMPL have been significantly re-oriented towards increasing social inclusion, also through the provision of social services. Its two main tools are the 'European platform against poverty and social exclusion' and the 'Social investment package'.

The *European platform* is one of the seven flagship initiatives of the Europe 2020 strategy, designed to help EU countries reach the very ambitious headline target of lifting 20 million people out of poverty and social exclusion. It features five areas of action (EC, 2010b; 2015), two of which are directly relevant for social services: (a) *delivering actions to fight poverty and exclusion across the policy spectrum*, among which the 'Social protection and access to essential services' action explicitly addresses services, especially long-term care and active ageing, as well as social innovation; (b) *making EU funding deliver on the social inclusion and social cohesion objectives of Europe 2020*, among which the 'Developing an evidence-based approach to social innovations and reform' action also addresses social services. The European platform is also responsible for three coordination tools: (1) the 'European semester' for monitoring the structural reforms of member states; (2) the 'Scoreboard' for keeping track of the progress towards the poverty targets; (3) the 'Annual convention of the European platform against poverty and social exclusion' as an opportunity for dialogue between policy-makers and non-governmental stakeholders.

The *Social investment package* re-pledges the EC commitment to link social expenditure to the economic goals of growth, employment and productivity and it outlines the reforms necessary to secure more adequate and sustainable social policies (EC, 2014). The key policy recommendations include: (1) a 'simplification' of services in order to improve their efficiency; (2) institutional reforms and, in particular, 'deinstitutionalisation', i.e. a transition from institutional to community-based care; (3) the 'modernisation' of social policies (such as activation measures or personalised approaches); (4) innovation as an essential element of social investment.

*DG-REGIO* is responsible for implementing the so-called European *Cohesion policy*, established after the Single European Act of 1986 in order to strengthen the economic, social and territorial cohesion of the EU and reduce regional disparities within and between member states. Its programmes are financed mainly through the *European regional development fund (ERDF)* and the *Cohesion fund (CF)* (EC, 2013e, p. 3), albeit the *European social fund* (ESF) also contributes significantly and some resources can be pooled from the other two European investment and structural funds: the *European agricultural fund for rural development* (EAFRD) and the *European maritime and fisheries fund* (EMFF).

The EU Cohesion policy is implemented through multi-annual investment programmes, with management procedures shared among the EC, member states, and regional and local authorities. Since its onset in 1989, there have been five programming periods. The current one covers the years 2014–20, which coincide with the last seven years of the Europe 2020 strategy. In fact, this new round of the EU Cohesion policy introduces a very relevant social dimension: four of its 11 'thematic objectives' are dedicated to the 'inclusive growth' priority (see Table 2.1). Moreover, for the first time, a minimum of 23 per cent of the European social fund is earmarked for the implementation of Cohesion policy.

*Table 2.1*  *EU Cohesion policy 2014–20: priorities, thematic objectives and European structural and investment funds*

| 3 Priorities | SMART | | | | SUSTAINABLE | | | INCLUSIVE | | | |
|---|---|---|---|---|---|---|---|---|---|---|---|
| 11 Thematic objectives | 1 | 2 | 3 | 4 | 5 | 6 | 7 | 8 | 9 | 10 | 11 |
| 5 European structural & investment funds | Research & innovation | Information & communication technology | Competitiveness of SMEs | Low-carbon economy | Combating climate change | Environment & resource efficiency | Sustainable transport | Employment & mobility | Social inclusion | Better education & training | Better public administration |
| ESF | x | x | x | x | | | | X | X | X | X |
| ERDF | X | X | X | X | x | x | x | x | x | x | x |
| CF | | | | X | | | X | | | | X |
| EAFRD | x | x | x | x | x | x | | x | x | x | |
| EMFF | | | X | | | X | | X | | | |

*Source:* Authors' compilation.

Of the four thematic objectives attached to the 'Inclusive growth' priority, the one on *Social inclusion* has direct relevance for social services. Its 'lines of action' include:

- enhancing access to affordable, sustainable and high-quality services, including health care and 'social services of general interest', also in rural areas (this line can draw upon resources from ESF, ERDF, EAFRD);
- investing in health care and social infrastructure (ERDF);
- promoting the transition from institutional to community-based services (ERDF);
- supporting social enterprises (ESF, ERDF).

This thematic objective also includes five 'areas of action' (see Figure 2.1), among which the most directly relevant for social services are, again, 'Social inclusion' and 'Transition from institutional to community-based care'. Within the first, the key policy recommendations mirror those of the Social Investment Package: simplification of services, public administration reforms to enhance access to affordable, sustainable and high-quality

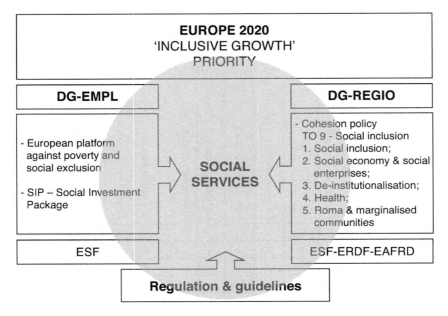

*Source:*　Authors' compilation.

*Figure 2.1　Current EU funds and tools concerning social services*

services, modernising social services, innovation. In the second, initiatives aim at transferring resources, workforce and users (children, older people, people with disabilities) from institutional to community- and family-based care. In this area, strong emphasis is placed on the notion that EU financial support to deinstitutionalisation must be temporary, as new care systems must become self-sustained.

**A Complex, Redundant and Sometimes Unfriendly Policy Framework**

The EU social policy agenda has come a long way since the Lisbon council, in several respects. Despite the financial crisis, the notion of social investment has resisted and social inclusion has become an explicit priority of the Europe 2020 strategy, now integrated in the EU Cohesion policy. While the autonomy of member states in social policy has been preserved, it is now more firmly cast in a European framework, with 'soft' governance and coordination tools and some funding, through Cohesion policy. In particular, the open method of coordination is emphasised in many social policy areas.

On the other hand, the current policy framework and tools – especially in what concerns social services – appear convoluted, redundant and often confusing. To make everything fit in and to integrate everything with everything else, a very complex policy architecture has been devised, based on a multitude of objectives, priorities, flagship initiatives, thematic objectives, guidelines, lines of action, areas of action, platforms, packages, and so on and so forth, which risks discouraging and disorienting, rather than accompanying and supporting the average stakeholder. Moreover, tensions remain – unsolved – between goals and resources: while the Europe 2020 social goals remain very ambitious, the resources mobilised (essentially the ESF and part of the ERDF) to support the less developed member states and regions are rather limited. In addition, while Cohesion policy provides resources for 'investment' in social infrastructure, the resources needed to 'operate' social services must come from member states, an option not always viable in times of austerity.

As will be argued later, the above described social policy framework is the result of a compromise between different approaches and interests, whereby very different goals, but also a number of enduring ambiguities – and even contradictions – coexist. Among these, the tension between liberalising services as economic activities, on the one hand, and keeping the universal character of social services, on the other, will be the focus of the next section.

## 2. THE REGULATION OF SOCIAL SERVICES OF GENERAL INTEREST (SSGI): STATE AID AND PUBLIC PROCUREMENT RULES

### The Emergence and Ambiguity of the SSGI Concept Within Services of General Interest (SGI)

The term 'Services of general economic interest' (SGEI) was first introduced in Article 86(2) of the 1957 Treaty of Rome. It was an entirely new concept that was not recognised in any language of the original member states or in the scientific literature (Bauby, 2011). However, it was not until the strategies of privatisation, liberalisation and integration into the single market gained momentum during the 1990s that the concept was actually developed (Gómez-Barroso and Marbán-Flores, 2013). At the time, it was broadly accepted that those strategies needed to be accompanied by programmes to foster social and political integration; therefore, accessible and affordable services of general interest (SGI) became an important part of these efforts (Clifton et al., 2005).

As a consequence, the Commission dedicated a first Communication to the SGI (EC, 1996), wherein the SGEI were basically defined as a subset of SGI services: 'market services which the member states subject to specific public service obligations by virtue of a general interest criterion' (EC, 1996, p. 2). No reference was made to social services. It was in the *Green paper on SGI* (EC, 2003, p. 5) that it was recognised that 'the reality of services of general interest, which include services of both general economic and non-economic interest [. . .], covers a broad range of different types of activities, from certain activities in the large network industries to health, education and social services'. A year later, the *White paper on SGI* introduced the expression 'social services of general interest' (SSGI), stressing that they should 'have a specific role to play as an integral part of the European model of society' (EC, 2004, p. 16), albeit they remained under the responsibility of individual member states.

The message was reasserted in the *European social agenda* (EC, 2005b). Thus, 'to identify and recognise the specific characteristics of SSGI and to clarify the framework in which they operate' became a 'policy development initiative' for the Lisbon programme (EC, 2005a). The initiative took form with a first communication, in 2006, devoted to SSGI (EC, 2006). The White paper had already clarified that 'while there is some interest in further clarification of the situation of organisations providing social services under community law and in protecting the non-economic services of general interest as part of the European social model, there is broad agreement that the community should not be given additional powers in the area of non-economic services' (EC, 2004, p. 24). In the same way, the 2006 communication was limited to a finer definition of SSGI (health services were excluded from the list) and to clarify the conditions 'for the application of certain community rules' (EC, 2006, p. 6).

The Commission further refined its position on SSGI in 2007 (EC, 2007) and has since published three biennial reports (EC, 2008b; 2010c; 2013f). As the 2013 report acknowledges, the issue that 'has dominated the scene for at least the last decade' is the application of EU general rules on state aid, internal market and public procurement to social services. Indeed, accompanying the communication of 2007, two 'Frequently asked questions (FAQ)' documents on the application of state aid and public procurement rules were published. Three years later, in December 2010, both FAQ documents were updated and combined as a *Guide* (EC, 2010d). Following the adoption of a communication that set out the Commission's approach to SGI in a comprehensive manner (EC, 2011), the Commission updated the *Guide* in February 2013 (EC, 2013g).

The documents issued by the Commission not only made the rules of application clear, but also justified why rules were needed and welcomed.

The third biennial report stated that 'in recent years, several public authorities and civil society organisations representing service users and providers have claimed that the EU rules create unnecessary difficulties'. Rejecting such views, the Commission argued that EU rules took into account the specific characteristics of social services and that, 'if the public authorities apply them correctly, these rules can help them organise and finance high-quality cost-effective social services in a transparent manner' (EC, 2013f, p. 4).

**State Aid Rules**

The 2011 *Almunia package* consisted of four documents, setting out the conditions under which state aid in the form of public service compensation was compatible with the Treaty on the Functioning of the European Union (TFEU). The rules apply whenever public authorities in member states (be they national, regional or local) finance SGEI. They therefore apply to social services of an economic nature. The notion of 'economic nature' is a source of uncertainty. The criterion marking the economic character of the activity is not related to the status of the service provider, or to the nature of the service itself. Indeed, this is the first of a number of subsequent questions that should be answered to define a framework applicable to social services.

a)   *Do public services have an economic nature?* Any activity consisting of offering goods and/or services in a given market is an economic activity as defined by the competition rules. The fact that the activity in question is termed 'social' or is carried out by a non-profit operator is not in itself sufficient to avoid classification as an economic activity. In spite of this general rule, certain activities of a purely social nature have been determined to be non-economic. Examples are the management of compulsory insurance schemes pursuing an exclusively social objective, functioning under the principle of solidarity, and offering insurance benefits independently of contributions, or the provision of public education financed by the public budget and carrying out a State task. Anyway, in many instances the application of this key notion can only rely on a case by case analysis and will remain a relative 'source of uncertainty' (Baquero Cruz, 2013, p. 309).

b)   *Is public funding always regarded as state aid?* State funding for the provision of social services of an economic nature is not regarded as state aid, provided that four conditions – 'the Altmark criteria' – are met: (1) the beneficiary of a state funding mechanism must be formally entrusted with the provision of an SGEI, the obligations of which must be clearly defined; (2) the parameters for calculating the compensation must be established beforehand in an objective and transparent manner; (3) the compensation cannot exceed what is necessary to cover all or part of the costs incurred in the discharge of the SGEI, taking into account a reasonable profit; (4) where the beneficiary is not chosen pursuant to a public procurement procedure, the compensation granted must be determined on the basis of an analysis of the costs that a typical 'well-run' undertaking would have incurred.

c)  *Is state aid compatible with the internal market?* Public service compensation that constitutes state aid can yet be compatible with the internal market and the Commission does not need to be notified. Indeed, this is the general rule for social services. The 2011 Decision (EC, 2012c) exempts providers from prior notification, regardless of the level of financing, for all services 'meeting social needs as regards health and long-term care, childcare, access to and reintegration into the labour market, social housing and the care and social inclusion of vulnerable groups'. This list is exhaustive. However, the last sentence allows the flexibility to include various services for those groups in society 'that need them the most, in accordance with the variety of needs and preferences of users that may result from different geographical, social or cultural situations among the member states'.

Of course, compatibility does not mean absolute freedom. While public authorities do not have to notify the Commission of their financing of social services, they must nevertheless establish a clear and precise act of entrustment and ensure that the service provider does not receive any overcompensation.

**Public Procurement Rules**

On the other hand, in its *Charter of fundamental rights* (EC, 2012a, p. 18), the Commission also stated that 'all too often, public authorities assume that by complying with state aid rules they have ensured the legality of their financing arrangements'. When organising and financing social services, public authorities must not only identify the amount of finance, but also address other questions. Who will provide the service: the public authority itself or an external provider? If an external provider, how will it be selected? It is in this context that public procurement rules come into play.

In the end, social services are barely affected by the rules laid down in the directives in force, considering that 'given the importance of the cultural context and the sensitivity of these services, member states should be given wide discretion to organise the choice of the service providers in the way they consider most appropriate' (European Parliament and Council, 2014, p. 7). Nevertheless, public authorities must always comply with the treaty principles of transparency, equal treatment and non-discrimination, mutual recognition and proportionality. In particular, this means that the authority in charge must: (1) adequately advertise its intention to outsource the provision of the social service and to conclude a public service contract with an external provider; and (2) deal in a non-discriminatory and impartial way with all the providers that have shown an interest in such a contract.

Thus, the EU public procurement rules apply only when a public authority decides to outsource the provision of a service to an external provider that the public authority pays to provide. They do not apply when the public authority grants licences or authorisations to all service providers that meet the conditions laid down for the provision of services beforehand.

## 3. DISCOURSES AND IDEOLOGIES UNDERLYING THE CURRENT EU STRATEGIES FOR SOCIAL SERVICES

The above-described redundancies and ambiguities in current policy tools and regulations concerning social services are paralleling ambiguities on the discursive level. EU discourses on social policy reflect the 'changing interests of changing coalitions of actors in the general intergovernmental bargaining process . . . [of which the] product represents a *discursive* settlement of conflict' (Barbier, 2011, p. 12; emphasis in original). While in the early 2000s the EU was dominated by left-leaning governments, right-wing governments are now in the overwhelming majority (The Economist, 7 June 2011). This change, which is a result of both the entrance of new member states with a more conservative or neo-liberal orientation and political shifts in the old ones, has been reflected in the post-Lisbon casting of strategies for social services.

As discussed earlier, the Lisbon council established important new intergovernmental bargaining arenas, in particular with the introduction of the Open method of coordination tool in the field of social protection and the cross-European social benchmarking/target-setting. Arguably, the Lisbon strategy marked a policy shift in the EU position on social services (Daly, 2006). Such services were now assigned a central role in easing the post-industrial transformation that European countries faced. As stressed by Hantrais (2004, p. 193):

> At the heart of the 2000 social policy agenda was the modernisation of the European social model, which had the overall aim of strengthening the role of social protection as an effective tool for the management of change [. . .] Modernisation and improvement of social protection were central components in the response to the advent of the knowledge economy and to changing social and family structures.

While social services had previously been regarded merely as policies to alleviate negative externalities caused by market failures, the Lisbon strategy underscored the positive externalities. This new orientation manifested itself in the setting of targets related to alleviating critical social problems, and to the volume of specific social services to be provided by member countries. For example, the policy documents produced in the wake of the 2002 Barcelona council (extending the targets established in Lisbon from six to 20) linked the provision of childcare services to the achievement of a number of broader societal goals. These included fighting school drop-out, countering the intergenerational transmission of social inequalities, mobilising (female) labour, promoting gender equality and even strengthening European fertility (EC, 2013a, pp. 4-6).

Moreover, by setting ambitious targets for employment rates, with the intention 'to realise Europe's full employment potential' (EC, 2000, p. 15), the European Union took an important step towards endorsing a social model in which social services played an integral part. Prominent social scientists were commissioned to sketch the underlying rationale. They argued that to create good quality jobs and a suitable productive labour force to fill them, it was necessary to regard welfare state expenditure on social and educational services as 'investments' (Esping-Andersen et al., 2002). Furthermore, by placing employment promotion high on the agenda, a welfare model close to the Beveridge ideal was embraced, in contrast to a North American-style neo-liberal model (Korpi and Palme, 2003).

Thus, by speaking simultaneously to economic and social concerns, the social investment perspective epitomises Barbier's 'discursive settlement of conflict' (2011, p. 12) between neo-liberal and social democratic ideals inherent in the way the Lisbon strategy evolved throughout the 2000s. This decade saw the mobilisation of a series of parallel concepts such as 'flexicurity', 'social entrepreneurship' and 'social innovation' that shared this dual ideological orientation. Hence, this new vocabulary, and the sets of actions that such ideas prompted, took what Offe (2003, p. 440) has characterised as a century-old 'European way' of handling conflict and diversity through institutionalisation, to a new level.

In the transition from the Lisbon strategy to the Europe 2020 and Social investment package strategies, while the conceptual framework has remained the same, it is now more specific in what concerns the methodology to achieve the objectives (Budd, 2013, p. 287). The Package aims at 'redirecting member states' policies, where needed' (EC, 2013b, pp. 3–4), by linking the Europe 2020 targets with the relevant EU funds. As mentioned earlier, in the 2014–20 period, the Commission proposes to set aside at least 23 per cent of the European social fund for activities that align with the social investment perspective, while the European regional development fund should complement such social investment by funding social service infrastructure. In this way, by strengthening the dimension of 'aid conditionality' (Van Gerven et al., 2014), a change in the mode of governance is observed; the 'soft' law mechanisms of recommendations and policy learning are significantly hardened.

In particular, the Platform against poverty is meant to provide new impetus to the promotion of better social services. The Commission argues that among poverty's multiple dimensions there is 'inadequate access to basic services' (EC, 2010b, p. 6) and calls for greater efficiency through service consolidation and better delivery, together with the mobilisation of a greater set of actors and instruments. A number of social services are emphasised as essential in alleviating poverty: childcare (the Commission mentions both 'quality childcare' and 'affordable childcare'), educational services, employment services, health services and care services for older people, and even publicly provided basic financial services (EC, 2010b, pp. 4–5, 11). Partly overlapping with the mentioned services, a number of critical policy areas are highlighted, including education, social care, housing, health, reconciliation and family policies (EC, 2010a, p. 5). Because people living in rural areas in Europe are disproportionally affected by poverty, the Commission also calls for an up-scaling of social service infrastructure in these areas (EC, 2010a, pp. 13–14). In this manner the Commission recognises the critical role of social services in achieving *territorial* cohesion, a perspective that social scientist have already pointed out (Kolberg and Esping-Andersen, 1991).

The social investment strategy put forward in the Platform outlines the reforms needed to secure more adequate and sustainable social policies by investing in people's skills and capabilities, by improving performance and devising more efficient and effective inclusion strategies and social budgets. As welfare systems face demographic change and financial crises, they need to modernise social policies and the way in which they are financed. Importantly, the Commission argues that providing welfare through services, rather than cash transfers, may be more conducive to the investment perspective (EC, 2013b, p. 10). This may be interpreted as an appreciation of the social democratic service-intensive welfare model. And yet the Commission's recommendations in other respects align more with what has been labelled the liberal welfare state model (Esping-Andersen, 1990).

This alignment concerns the debate on 'targeting' versus 'universalism', which goes to the heart of the political economy of the welfare state. While acknowledging that 'both universalism and selectivity need to be used in an intelligent way' (EC, 2013b, p. 9), the Commission takes quite a strong stance in encouraging member states to better target the provision of cash benefits and social services, in order to increase efficiency and effectiveness (EC, 2013b, pp. 3, 5, 9). In favouring selectivity, the Commission approximates the neo-liberal-type model for allocating welfare (Esping-Andersen, 1990).

Also, when discussing non-public sources of welfare, the Commission touches upon ideological questions fundamental to the welfare state. When it recommends that private enterprises provide more social services to their employees and governments further rely on third-sector involvement in welfare production and delivery (EC, 2013b, pp. 5–6) it endorses again a neo-liberal agenda rather than a social democratic one. The Commission also calls for more support to private businesses that promote social inclusion (the so-called 'social entrepreneurship'). Furthermore, it encourages member states to make use of financial arrangements whereby private investors are allowed to finance social programmes in return for the opportunity to receive some economic rewards (the so-called 'social impact bonds') (EC, 2013b, pp. 18–19). It also points to 'activation' measures (that is, measures that entail some kind of formalised activity in which the benefit claimant participates) as a prime tool for transforming social expenditures into investments. Furthermore, it emphasises conditionality and temporary rather than permanent benefits (EC, 2013b, pp. 3, 8–9). At a first glance, activation, as a supply-side measure in the active labour market policy toolbox, resonated well with the social democratic ideology. Yet the implied extension of activation as a measure to deal with not only the unemployed but with all benefit and service claimants, and the emphasis on conditionality, brings the Commission's recommendations closer to neo-liberal positions, as do also the Commission's call for more 'incentives to work' (EC, 2013b, pp. 5, 10, 12).

Likely reflecting a 'discursive settlement of conflict' – that is, a necessary compromise meant to accommodate the different welfare models coexisting in Europe – some underlying dilemmas remain in the new strategy documents. This is observed in the call for more conditionality (EC, 2013b, pp. 3, 8–9) and monitoring (EC, 2013b, p. 5) on the one hand, and a call for simplified procedures (EC, 2013b, pp. 3, 9) on the other. Indeed, imposing monitoring and conditionality necessitates a large legal and administrative apparatus that renders procedures quite complicated, to the extent that clients find themselves sanctioned for violating conditions of which they were not aware (Kvist and Harsløf, 2014). Likewise, the call for more individualised social services may be challenging to realise if it is to be implemented under a regime of more top-down control. Perhaps, as Peña-Casas (2011, p. 162) observes, emphasising individualisation more than anything ushers in a new and more individualised approach to social problems: social services will be provided with the purpose of ensuring that individuals can anticipate and manage change.

## 4. CONCLUDING REMARKS

The construction of the European Union is proving to be a long and complex journey. One of the many milestones along the way was reached at the turn of the new millennium, when it seemed that the conditions for a leap forward were in place. The Union seemed able to move forward both externally, by shifting its borders to the east, and internally, by building up a more cohesive entity.

However, the impetus soon lost momentum. It may be that there was no clear idea of how to orchestrate the implementation of the strategy, or the words did not represent real intentions. After only four years, in the mid-term review of the Lisbon strategy it was already clear that the European project would basically keep travelling essentially on economic rails. To make matters worse for the progress of a social Europe, a financial crisis arose. The term 'crisis' is a reduction of the causes and consequences of the economic crash that began in 2007. The aftermath of the crisis had and continues to have a significant impact on the social well-being of millions of European citizens, as the response of European institutions has far more to do with macroeconomic orthodoxy than with taking care of social circumstances. Austerity is putting pressure on social services in the domestic context and the European Union puts indirect pressure, via fiscal policy and European Monetary Union criteria, especially on the most crisis-ridden countries.

This does not mean that the notion of a European social policy has been abandoned. Some of it has remained, and has even been perfected. The Europe 2020 strategy maintains social policy as a priority, and has integrated it with the growth and competitiveness goals of the EU social and territorial cohesion policy. Indeed, social services have a more prominent position in the current strategy. Moreover, a relevant part of the structural and investment funds to pursue social policy goals has been earmarked, marking a slight change in the mode of governance towards 'harder' law mechanisms.

Yet the actual shape of the European social policy model has two important problems. The first and main one concerns credibility and trust. The past 15 years have been a period of big words and small achievements. There is no reason to believe that the political momentum is now stronger. The second problem lies in organisation and planning. The social policy framework, tools and regulations – especially in what concerns social services – are extremely redundant and unnecessarily complex. As this chapter has tried to show, there are an ever-increasing number of objectives, priorities, initiatives, actions, tools and so on, that make the policy framework almost impenetrable in terms of understanding and access, let alone implementation, to the average stakeholder, whether public or private. Moreover, a tension remains between goals and resources. While the EU cohesion policy provides resources for social infrastructure 'investments', the resources needed to operate social services and inclusive measures must come from member states, thereby requiring a firm commitment from the latter to support an expansive – albeit reformed – system of social services. Unfortunately, this does not seem to be happening. Tensions also remain between considering social services as 'economic' activities – subject to competition principles – or considering them as 'social' activities, as the contradictory regulation shows.

It is clear that so much diversity, within and across the different areas of social services in Europe, makes it difficult to devise and apply common rules. However, the gap between strict common rules and procedural rules could accommodate an ample set of actions, such as the establishment of minimum thresholds or social coverage parameters, genuine and clear guidelines for the allocation of funds, or basic regulations to address the uncertainties that actors in the social services experience. In contrast, if the soft regulatory approach persists and most of the effort is left to member states, a multiple-speed social Europe might become a permanent feature. The analyses of strategies, tools and discourses in this chapter suggest that a neo-liberal ideology is still permeating the post-Lisbon social policy directions – even if some elements of the social democratic model have been reintegrated. Ultimately, prioritising the economic-financial Europe over the social-political Europe might mean that social inequalities will continue to exist and possibly grow.

## NOTE

*   This chapter is the joint product of a close collaboration among all three authors. However, the Introduction should be attributed to José Luis Gómez-Barroso and Ivan Harsløf, section 1 to Stefania Barillà, section 2 to José Luis Gómez-Barroso, and section 3 to Ivan Harsløf. The conclusions are obviously shared.

# REFERENCES

Agh, A. (2010), 'The Europe 2020 strategy: a new vision for the EU', in H. Butković and V. Samardžija (eds), *From the Lisbon Strategy to Europe 2020*, Institute for International Relations – IMO, Zagreb and 'EU i' in cooperation with the Delegation of the European Union to the Republic of Croatia, accessed at: www. zagreb.hr/euzg/eu_publikacije/From_the_lisbon_strategy_to_europe_2020.pdf.

Baquero Cruz, J. (2013), 'Social services of general interest and the State aid rules', in U. Neergaard, E. Szyszczak, J.W. van de Gronden and M. Krajewski (eds), *Social Services of General Interest in the EU*, The Hague: T.M.C. Asser Press–Springer, pp. 287–313.

Barbier, J.-C. (2011), *Changes in Political Discourse from the Lisbon Strategy to Europe 2020: Tracing the Fate of 'Social Policy'*, Brussels: ETUI.

Bauby, P. (2011), 'From Rome to Lisbon: SGIs in primary law', in E. Szyszczak, J. Davies, M. Andenæs and T. Bekkedal (eds), *Developments in Services of General Interest*, The Hague: T.M.C. Asser Press–Springer, pp. 19–36.

Budd, L. (2013), 'Europe 2020: a strategy in search of a regional policy rationale?', *Policy Studies*, **34** (3), 274–90.

Butković, H. and V. Samardžija (2010), 'From the Lisbon Strategy to Europe 2020. An introduction', in H. Butković and V. Samardžija (eds), *From the Lisbon Strategy to Europe 2020*, Institute for International Relations – IMO, Zagreb and 'EU i' in cooperation with the Delegation of the European Union to the Republic of Croatia, accessed at: www.zagreb.hr/euzg/eu_publikacije/From_the_lisbon_strategy_to_europe_2020.pdf.

Clifton, J., F. Comín and D. Díaz Fuentes (2005), 'Empowering Europe's citizens? Towards a charter for services of general interest', *Public Management Review*, **7** (3), 417–43.

Council of Europe (1961), *European Social Charter*, Turin, 18 October, CETS No. 035.

Daly, M. (2006), 'EU social policy after Lisbon', *Journal of Common Market Studies*, **44** (3), 461–81.

Decaro, M. (2011), 'La strategia di Lisbona 2000–2010', in M. Decaro (ed.), *Dalla Strategia di Lisbona a Europa 2020. Fra governance e government dell'Unione europea*, Collana Intangibili, Fondazione Adriano Olivetti, Roma, accessed at: www.fondazioneadrianolivetti.it/_images/pubblicazioni/collana/120111100032Str ategia%20di%20Lisbona.pdf.

EC (1996), *Services of General Interest in Europe*, Brussels: Communication from the Commission, COM(96)443 final.

EC (2000), *Social Policy Agenda*, Brussels: Communication from the Commission to the Council, the European Parliament, the Economic and Social Committee and the Committee of the Regions, COM(2000)379 final.

EC (2003), *Green Paper on Services of General Interest*, Brussels: Communication from the Commission, COM(2003)270 final.

EC (2004), *White Paper on Services of General Interest*, Brussels: Communication from the Commission, COM(2004)374 final.

EC (2005a), *Annex to the Communication from the Commission to the Council and the European Parliament – Common Actions for Growth and Employment: The Community Lisbon Programme*, Brussels: Commission Staff Working Document, SEC(2005)981 final.

EC (2005b), *The Social Agenda*, Brussels: Communication from the Commission, COM(2005)33 final.

EC (2006), *Implementing the Community Lisbon Programme: Social Services of General Interest in the European Union*, Brussels: Communication from the Commission, COM(2006)177 final.

EC (2007), *Services of General Interest, including Social Services of General Interest: A New European Commitment*, Brussels: Communication from the Commission, COM(2007)725 final.

EC (2008a), *Renewed Social Agenda: Opportunities, Access and Solidarity in 21st Century Europe*, Brussels: Communication from the Commission to the Council, the European Parliament, the Economic and Social Committee and the Committee of the Regions, COM(2008)412 final.

EC (2008b), *Biennial Report on Social Services of General Interest*, Brussels: Commission Staff Working Document, SEC(2008)2179 final.

EC (2010a), *The European Platform against Poverty and Social Exclusion: a European Framework for Social and Territorial Cohesion*, Brussels: Communication from the Commission to the European Parliament, the Council, the European Economic and Social Committee and the Committee of the Regions, COM(2010)758 final.

EC (2010b), *List of Key Initiatives. Accompanying Document to the Communication from the Commission to the European Parliament, the Council, the European Economic and Social Committee and the Committee of the Regions. The European Platform Against Poverty and Social Exclusion: A European Framework for Social and Territorial Cohesion COM(2010) 758 final*, Brussels: Commission Staff Working Paper, SEC(2010)1564 final.

EC (2010c), *Second Biennial Report on Social Services of General Interest*, Brussels: Commission Staff Working Document, SEC(2010)1284 final.

EC (2010d), *Guide to the Application of the European Union Rules on State Aid, Public Procurement and the Internal Market to Services of General Economic Interest, and in Particular to Social Services of General Interest*, Brussels: Commission Staff Working Document, SEC(2010)1545 final.

EC (2011), *A Quality Framework for Services of General Interest in Europe*, Brussels: Communication from the Commission, COM(2011)900 final.

EC (2012a), *Charter of Fundamental Rights of the European Union*, Official Journal of the European Union, 26 October 2012 (2012/C 326/02).

EC (2012b), *Consolidated Version of the Treaty on the Functioning of the European Union*, Official Journal of the European Union, 26 October 2012 (2012/C 326/47).

EC (2012c), *Commission Decision, of 20 December 2011, on the Application of Article 106(2) of the Treaty on the Functioning of the European Union to State Aid in the Form of Public Service Compensation Granted to Certain Undertakings Entrusted with the Operation of Services of General Economic Interest*, Official Journal L7, 11.01.2012.

EC (2013a), *Barcelona Objectives: The Development of Childcare Facilities for Young Children in Europe with a View to Sustainable and Inclusive Growth*, Luxembourg: Publications Office of the European Union.

EC (2013b), *Towards Social Investment for Growth and Cohesion, including Implementing the European Social Fund 2014–2020*, Brussels: Communication from the Commission to the European Parliament, the Council, the European Economic and Social Committee and the Committee of the Regions, COM(2013)83 final.

EC (2013c), *Strengthening the Social Dimension of the Economic and Monetary Union*, Brussels: Communication from the Commission to the European Parliament and the Council, COM(2013)690 final.

EC (2013d), 'Annual Activity Report – Employment, Social Affairs and Inclusion', accessed at: ec.europa.eu/atwork/synthesis/aar/doc/empl_aar_2013.pdf.

EC (2013e), 'Annual Activity Report – DG Regional and Urban Policy', accessed at: ec.europa.eu/atwork/synthesis/aar/doc/regio_aar_2013.pdf.

EC (2013f), *Third Biennial Report on Social Services of General Interest*, Brussels: Commission Staff Working Document, SWD(2013)40 final.

EC (2013g), *Guide to the Application of the European Union Rules on State Aid, Public Procurement and the Internal Market to Services of General Economic Interest, and in Particular to Social Services of General Interest*, Brussels: Commission Staff Working Document, SWD(2013)53 final.

EC (2014), 'Europe 2020: a Strategy for European Union Growth', accessed at: eur-lex.europa.eu/legal-content/EN/TXT/HTML/?uri=URISERV:em0028&from =CS.

EC (2015), 'European Platform against Poverty and Social Exclusion', accessed at: ec.europa.eu/social/main.jsp?catId=961.

Esping-Andersen, G. (1990), *The Three Worlds of Welfare Capitalism*, Cambridge: Polity Press.

Esping-Andersen, G., D. Gallie, A. Hemerijck and J. Myles (eds) (2002), *Why We Need a New Welfare State*, Oxford: Oxford University Press.

European Parliament and Council (2014), Directive 2014/24/EU of 26 February 2014 on public procurement and repealing Directive 2004/18/EC, Official Journal L 94, 28.3.2014.

Gómez-Barroso, J.L. and R. Marbán-Flores (2013), 'Basic financial services: a new service of general economic interest?', *Journal of European Social Policy*, **23** (3), 314–21.

Hantrais, L. (2004), *Family Policy Matters: Responding to Family Change in Europe*, Bristol: Policy Press.

Hemerijck, A. (2012), 'Two or three waves of welfare state transformation?', in N. Morel, B. Palier and J. Palme (eds), *Towards a Social Investment Welfare State? Ideas, Policies and Challenges*, Bristol: Policy Press.

Kolberg, J.-E. and G. Esping-Andersen (1991), 'Welfare states and employment regimes', in J.-E. Kolberg (ed.), *The Welfare State as Employer*, New York: M.E. Sharpe.

Korpi, W. and J. Palme (2003), 'New politics and class politics in the context of austerity and globalization: welfare state regress in 18 countries, 1975–95', *American Political Science Review*, **97** (3), 425–46.

Kvist, J. and I. Harsløf (2014), 'Workfare with welfare revisited: instigating dual tracks for insiders and outsiders', in I. Lødemel and A. Moreira (eds), *Activation or Workfare? Governance and the Neo-liberal Convergence*, Oxford: Oxford University Press.

Lundvall, B.-A. and E. Lorenz (2012), 'From the Lisbon Strategy to Europe 2020', in N. Morel, B. Palier and J. Palme (eds), *Towards a Social Investment Welfare State? Ideas, Policies and Challenges*, Bristol: Policy Press.

Offe, C. (2003), 'The European model of "social" capitalism: can it survive European integration?' *The Journal of Political Philosophy*, **11** (4), 437–69.

Peña-Casas, R. (2011), 'Europe 2020 and the fight against poverty and social exclusion: fooled into marriage?', in D. Natali and B. Vanhercke (eds), *Social Developments in the European Union 2011*, Brussels: ETUI, pp. 159–85.

The Economist (2011), 'Left out: fewer and fewer European countries are run by left-leaning governments', *The Economist*, 7 June.

Van Gerven, M., B. Vantercke and S. Gürocak (2014), 'Policy learning, aid conditionality or domestic politics? The Europeanization of Dutch and Spanish activation policies through the European Social Fund', *Journal of European Public Policy*, **21** (4), 509–27.

# 3. Public policy conceptions: priorities of social service provision in Europe

**Margitta Mätzke, Anneli Anttonen, Peter Brokking and Jana Javornik**

## INTRODUCTION

There is great diversity in social service arrangements across countries. Some offer broadly accessible social services for their citizens, while in others social transfers and social services are fragmented and not available to everyone. Some care services are targeted or conditional, and therefore selective, while others are universally available. Policy reforms may open social services for new groups or new purposes, but they may also push social care and welfare production back into the realm of informal support and charity. They may try out new forms of organisation and governance and draw, for instance, on the private sector, users' co-production or social movement support. Such institutional features shape the extent and the ways in which citizens access care services; they affect their well-being and ways of life. They have a part in defining what role public policies play in societies and how states relate to their subjects. The design of social services is in that sense *normatively consequential,* and this chapter seeks to identify their overall character and conceptual underpinnings. It explores the core ambitions and policy goals underlying social service designs and identifies differences in normative commitments across policy fields and countries and over time.

The chapter distinguishes ideal-typical *policy conceptions*, which capture the goals and priorities informing the design of social service institutions. While they reveal a lot of ambiguity in their moral underpinnings, policy conceptions help us to see diverse goals and normative commitments that may leave their marks on the design of social policies. Because the institutional designs are normatively consequential, policy conceptions are in turn *institutionally consequential;* they suggest typical features of institutional design and not others. Institutional design and moral underpinnings are interdependent. This allows us to relate social service institutions to their normative background and evaluative dimensions. Against this back-drop, we explore the direction of institutional change in social services. This allows us to identify differences between the rhetoric surrounding social services and their actual institutional design and to assess the insti-tutional and normative coherence of policy innovation.

The next section introduces two evaluative dimensions that capture the diversity of public policy conceptions particularly well: *priorities and core commitments* and the *main orientation and targets* of public policy engage-ment in social service fields. Section 2 lays out the details of institutional design that allow us to draw conclusions about policy conceptions. Because public policy conceptions are institutionally consequential, three cases of social service developments are reviewed in section 3 in light of their underlying policy conceptions. This allows us to learn something about the (in-)consistency between policy conceptions underlying social service innovation and potential bones of contention in reform processes; it can be read as an interpretation of directions of policy change. As this inter-pretation is based on the analysis of institutional development, and not on political rhetoric or declarations of intent, it will necessarily be tentative about stipulating a coherent strategy and 'logic' of social services develop-ment. Section 4 concludes by commenting on the relationship between policy ideas and institutional change and the status of policy conceptions.

## 1.  POLICY CONCEPTIONS, CAPTURING THE CHARACTER OF SOCIAL SERVICE DESIGNS

'Traditional' informal care arrangements are often contrasted with a 'modern' system of social care in the public realm. But it is hard to under-stand private, for-profit forms of care services within a framework of this distinction, because the distinction collapses all forms of social care outside the private home of the family into one big category of 'modern-ised care arrangements'. It would suggest, for instance, that current trends of de-institutionalisation of care for the elderly entail 're-traditionalisa-tion' of care – a problematic interpretation. Likewise, only analysing the generosity of resources allocated for social service infrastructures does not adequately capture the significant characteristics of social service arrange-ments. These examples demonstrate that many of the customary distinc-tions of political commentary are somewhat difficult to use for describing and evaluating institutional arrangements in the field of social services, because the evaluative dimensions are not very clear.

Both practitioners and policy analysts are interested in questions like whose interests and whose decisions should take centre stage when thinking about social service design. This can be individuals or social groups – the notion that many in the social policy community intuitively embrace – but it can also be organisations or policy-making elites. This is the question about *principal outlook* and *core commitments* of social policy: is it *utilitarian* at its core in that it enlists individuals and social groups in the pursuit of goals (such as economic efficiency or a certain social order) that are not necessarily their own, or is social policy *emancipatory* in the sense that individuals are free to develop their own definitions of the means and ends of social policy – or at the very least allowed to participate in the definition of goals and priorities? This question has a longstanding tradition in the social policy community, and it is relatively straightforward as a question for evaluating institutional design. There is a second evaluative dimension of social service design, which concerns the question of who – or what – the (re-)designers of social services have in mind in their policy initiatives: is the perception and outlook on social services an *individualist* or a *collectivist orientation*? Who (or what kind of social unit) is the primary addressee of social policies? Including this analytical element adds relevant information because institutional changes affect this latter dimension independently of the first. The question of individualism or collectivism is more than a facet of the tension between emancipatory and utilitarian orientations.

There are, thus, two principal questions that help explore the function and the impact of social policy: does it discipline, or does it support? Is it collectivist or individualist in orientation? Together they constitute an evaluative metric that allows us to gauge the character of policy design and evaluate its conceptual and normative underpinnings. Let us have a closer look at the two dimensions.

**Principal Outlook and Core Commitments: Emancipatory or Utilitarian?**

The position of social policy as first and foremost supporting social groups and individuals in their pursuit of happiness is at the core of the social policy community's shared commitments, among researchers and practitioners alike. We find the idea of social policy as emancipatory and in that sense 'progressive' in T.H. Marshall (1950), who conceptualised social rights as citizenship rights and established progress in the qualitative aspects associated with social rights as one of the principal obligations of the welfare state. The primary purpose of social policy, Marshall says, is to secure living standards that will allow even the poor their fair share in their countries' socio-cultural heritage. In the development of social policy and the growth of qualitative equality, he expected 'the amelioration of the working classes' to go on 'steadily, if slowly, till, by occupation, at least, every man is a gentleman' (Marshall, 1950, p. 4f.). This notion of 'amelioration', of qualitative enhancement of individuals' fate and social conditions over time, is what George Steinmetz would later call a 'Whig narrative of social progress' (Steinmetz, 1993, p. 31), an image according to which welfare state development is a facet of social progress and sociopolitical modernisation of societies.

Steinmetz himself is critical of the perspective, and points to observations and interpretations about the regulatory and disciplinary aspects of social policy. A large body of research has described the roots of social policy in government activities that seek to police deviant behaviour (Higgins, 1980; Piven and Cloward, 1971). Welfare state scholars have also uncovered the incentive character and the educational ambitions of the big cash transfer schemes, in which conditionality rewards certain ways of life while putting others at a disadvantage (Mätzke, 2011). There are some arguments that consider attempts at regulating individual conduct to be increasingly important in current social policy approaches, because, informed by the activation paradigm, they place emphasis on individual responsibility (Evers, 2008). Historically the tradition of social discipline has been most pronounced in poverty policies (Leibfried and Tennstedt, 1985) and social work. Here the connotations with controlling deviant behaviour and instructing marginalised groups are most pronounced, and the perception of social policy as educational and even disciplinary is strongest. In modern social insurance systems and social service arrangements there is little by way of outright coercion that could require people to use certain social services (Anttonen and Sipilä, 1996). Still, the close historical and current connection with social work and looking after marginalised groups accounts for a legacy of social discipline in many contemporary social service fields. Social services and their expansion, therefore, do not automatically amount to an emancipatory agenda.

### The Targets of Social Policy Intervention: Individualist or Collectivist Orientations?

The second dimension along which policy conceptions vary captures the distinction between individualist and collectivist approaches to state intervention and public policy. It is an independent contrast in that emancipation does not imply an individualist approach to public policies, just as not all collectivist public policy conceptions would prioritise order and discipline. The two dimensions cut across each other. 'Individualism' would entail conceiving of patterns of interests and social problems strictly through the eyes of individuals (Spicker, 2013). A corollary of this view is that individuals' capacity to act and decide becomes important both on the conceptual and on the practical level (Spicker, 2013, p. 32). This may mean different things, however. It may entail an obligation of public policy to invest in enabling and empowering policies, a public policy conception quite far removed from the notions of minimalist government with which the individualist outlook tends to be associated most of the time (Spicker, 2013, pp. 195–200), but it may also imply an emphasis on employability, labour market activation, and workfarist educational measures, which are associated with the 'individual responsibility' – public policy ideal. In the case of active labour market policies, the dividing line between empowerment and social discipline tends to be blurry in any case, and on the individual level it is often difficult to distinguish enabling from tutelary policies (Goldberg, 2001, p. 304), and to set those apart from educational and disciplinary measures. The individualistic point of reference, therefore, can assume both flavours, that of an emancipatory public policy agenda, and that of educational and disciplinary intervention.

Communities of various description form alternative addressees of policy. Conceptualisations of social class as one of the principal units of collective identities and preferences are legion in the welfare state literature: Esping-Andersen (1990) refers to individual autonomy when introducing his concept of de-commodification, but he insists that this is not only about workers' welfare, but also about the working class movement's power. So, he has social groups in mind when thinking about de-commodification (Orloff, 1993, p. 311), and emancipation is not primarily individual advancement and empowerment but class emancipation (Goldberg, 2001, p. 305). In many social service fields the central collective unit is the family, both as welfare provider and policy target. Patricia Strach (2007) shows how even in the United States, where individualism is entrenched in political ideas, 'the family is an essential part of day-to-day politics'. It is used to accomplish political goals and appears in policy debates not only as a normative ideal to be defended, but also as a criterion of eligibility to social transfers and services and an administrator that takes goods and services and distributes them among the family members (Strach, 2006, p. 152f.). This too is social policy, taking a collectivist reference point. So does the subsidiarity principle, which plays such a central role in ideas about social services. The subsidiarity principle has evolved into a major justification for third sector involvement and new forms of self-help and bottom-up initiatives (Sachße, 2000, pp. 208–11). The point of reference for such forms of welfare production is various forms of social groups, recognising their shared interests, yet at the same time recognising and defending those interests as *particularist* ones.

State and society as reference points for public policy conceptions are also a 'collectivist' perspective. The 'whig narrative of the welfare state'

(Steinmetz, 1993) – of political development as growth of social justice and security – is an example of an 'ameliorationist' macro-perspective; it echoes Marshall's idea of civilisatory progress, and it is widespread among social policy researchers. It is also possible to conceive of the collectivist outlook on society in a utilitarian and disciplinary vein. Social groups can mobilise and rebel, or they can acquiesce. And public policies can create the incentives that encourage certain behaviours and militate against others (Mätzke, 2011). In that sense, we speak of public policy conceptions in which the macro-polity is reference point and beneficiary of certain public policies. Many public policies have such instrumentalist traits (Mätzke and Ostner, 2010). Mary Daly (2004, p.146f.) points out the utilitarian aspects of the social investment strategy, or one can observe them also in the expectations formulated about the family's functions in a newly developing discourse about family failures and parenting support (Ostner, 2011).

**A Map of Possibilities**

Regardless of whether public policies refer to individuals or collectives, they walk a fine line between support and emancipation, on the one hand, and discipline and control on the other. Often, we find both combined in the design of public policies and social services, and thus we should more adequately speak of a continuum and a field of tension in which different policies and institutions lay different emphases on one motif or the other (e.g. Javornik, 2014). The cross-section of the two dimensions yields a map of policy conceptions that can be used for describing and evaluating core commitments and main targets of policy designs. It presents *an institutional picture*, showing six ideal-typical constellations of commitments and targets (see Figure 3.1). Social service arrangements or institutional developments in countries or social service fields can be thought as occupying various positions in the field of tension defined by these ideal types. Amelioration and emancipation can pertain to individual advancement and empowerment, to that of social groups, and it can also assume the meaning of political development as social progress. Likewise, it can be individuals that are the focus of attention of educational endeavours, it can be social groups that are the target of attempts at co-optation and control, and it can be the polity itself, social stability, the maintenance of (a certain) social order, or even an active pursuit of some macro-political destiny that social reformers have in mind when designing and redesigning public policies.

# 2. OBSERVING INSTITUTIONAL DETAILS TO IDENTIFY POLICY CONCEPTIONS

There are broad areas of overlap among the public policy conceptions. Discipline and support have often co-existed in the design of social policies. Yet, however close the connection between support and discipline or individualism and collectivism may be, *they are not the same.* They are rooted in very different ideas of politics and society, and this is consequential: it affects not only the way in which policy-makers talk about and justify their policy choices, but more importantly also the way in which social service schemes are designed. *Because* policy conceptions have institutional consequences, they are also competing, at least to a certain extent – they suggest *certain* institutional features for policies and not others. And because this is so, in turn, it becomes possible to identify differences of emphasis in the design of social policy arrangements, as informed by different policy conceptions. It becomes possible to use the map of policy conceptions (in Figure 3.1) to characterise, position and evaluate public policies and social service arrangements and trends in policy development. And it becomes possible to study strategies and policy programmes, instances of policy innovation and processes of institutional change and to locate these on the map of possibilities.

CORE COMMITMENTS

|  | *Amelioration and liberty*<br>*( Emancipatory commitments )* | *Order and discipline*<br>*( Utilitarian goals )* |
|---|---|---|
| *Individuals* | (I)<br>Emancipation:<br>providing support in individual<br>advancement and empowerment | (II)<br>Regulation of individual conduct:<br>securing acceptable and<br>productive behaviour |
| *Social groups* | (III)<br>Emancipation:<br>mobilisation, empowerment and<br>participation of social groups | (IV)<br>Class politics as co-optation:<br>utilisation of social groups and families<br>as co-producers of welfare |
| *State & society* | (V)<br>Political development:<br>growth in social justice and equality<br>(the 'Whig-narrative' of the W.S.) | (VI)<br>Social order and political stability:<br>quiescence and behaviour of groups<br>and individuals as resource |

(MAIN TARGETS)

*Source:* Authors' elaboration.

*Figure 3.1 Policy conceptions: commitments and targets in social service design*

There is a range of features of institutional design that allow us to relate institutional development to the evaluative metric of policy conceptions and thus learn something about core commitments and targets of social policy design. In the case of social services, they all in one way or another regulate who can and who must use social services, i.e. different aspects of access and service quality. One can distinguish two perspectives from which to examine these aspects.

**The Supply Perspective**

Here access is a function of availability of social services, and availability, in turn, has a quantitative, a qualitative and a procedural side. It looks at social services from the perspective of the providers of social services, analyses their number, a range of qualitative aspects of their services, and the way they are regulated. Specifically, we can distinguish the following design features of social services:

1.  *The quantitative dimension of availability of social services*
    Overall coverage, i.e. the question regarding whether or not there is enough supply of social services (enough places in childcare facilities or enough care workers who could provide care services for older people, for instance) is one aspect of this dimension. The other one pertains to the spatial distribution of supply and the question of whether or not there is a social service infrastructure everywhere, such that access does not depend on where one lives.

2.  *The qualitative aspects of social service infrastructures*
    Qualitative aspects comprise the range of services offered, their quality and the professionalism of the staff providing the services. It also includes more strongly politicised questions of diversity. Is there a variety of different service providers, some of them, for instance, church affiliated, some others representing particular positions on the role and function of the service (such as pedagogical conceptions in the case of childcare or innovative housing arrangements for older people)?

3.  *The procedural side of social service regulation*
    Social service regulation can, more benignly, take the form of cooperation in order to coordinate and improve the supply of social services. Routines for monitoring quality are often part of such efforts. However, it can also take the form of very detailed substantive instructions and rules of conduct for providers, and this would then point to a more pronouncedly disciplinary outlook on social service design.

**The Demand Perspective**

Here access is considered from the perspective of users of social services, and it can be universalistic or selective. Selectivity, in this demand perspective, is a function of personal characteristics of users, who may be entitled or required to use certain social services, such that selectivity regulates take-up and use.

1. *Selectivity as targeting*
   Beyond the obvious fact that only people in need can and will use social services, users are further selected by membership in a vulnerable group, or individual demonstrated need.

2. *Selectivity as conditionality*
   People can only use social services if they fulfil special preconditions, such as membership in certain privileged groups or prior contributions.

3. *Mandatory use of certain social services*
   The entire population can be required to participate in social services such as primary schools or certain public health interventions. Specific groups can be required to participate in services such as activation and workfare activities.

Looking at the principal outlook of social service design as depicted in Figure 3.1, we see that not every one of the design features just outlined speaks to all policy conceptions. Instead, the institutional features of social service design allow for clear conclusions about some of the core commitments, while remaining neutral with regard to others. Specifically, individual advancement (I, in Figure 3.1) will be especially fostered by quantitative availability of social services that are good quality, and it will benefit from procedures coordinating and monitoring that supply. It may also benefit from targeting, depending on the specific design of needs testing, but conditionality or coercion would definitely impair an agenda of individual advancement. Mandatory use and certain types of targeting definitely suggest commitment to a more disciplinary approach to care services (II, in Figure 3.1), which would also go along with detailed requirements that the providers of social services have to fulfil. Recognition and empowerment of social groups (III, in Figure 3.1) would first and foremost benefit from diversity in the supply of services. From the perspective of users, the criterion of providing social services only for the members of certain groups in society is ambiguous: it can be an act of recognition, and as such empowering, but more often than not differential access to social benefits is part of a 'socially selectivist' approach to social policy that is geared toward co-optation, acquiescence and social order (IV, in Figure 3.1), much more than recognition and emancipation. By the same token, the criterion of mandatory use is not entirely clear in and of itself. It can be part of an agenda that is authoritarian in its essence (VI, in Figure 3.1), seeking to control the population by incorporating people in a tight set of state-controlled activities and organisations. In that case, it is combined with equally rigid and tightly monitored requirements for providers. But it can also merely indicate the intention to provide minimum standards for everyone on an obligatory basis in certain important substantive fields, such as education or public health. In that case, mandatory participation would be part of an agenda of social progressivism, without much of the coercive elements that characterise the disciplinary approach (V, in Figure 3.1). Mandatory use for the entire population presupposes that services are available for everybody, but it is of very little significance in the care service fields that focus on vulnerable groups and people in need. Here we find services targeted at particular groups (such as migrants or people who are long-term unemployed), and here mandatory use is strongly connected to the intention to exert some measure of control (II or IV, in Figure 3.1).

Policy conceptions as depicted in Figure 3.1 can offer interpretations of the features of institutional design that we find in social service institutions. They may point to conceptual inconsistencies within institutional arrangements or reform agendas, but they may also help us understand the general direction of social service development. At the same time, public policy conceptions are associated, as we have seen, with typical features of institutional design, which allows us to rely not entirely on the discourse and political rhetoric, but to some extent to draw on institutional realities and policies that are enacted and implemented when assessing the character and general direction of policy change.

## 3.   PUTTING PUBLIC POLICY CONCEPTIONS TO THE TEST IN THREE ILLUSTRATIVE EXAMPLES

This section considers three instances of social service development in three countries and three substantively very different examples. The goal is to demonstrate how public policy conceptions are manifest and play themselves out in very diverse settings. We will first explore the character of institutional arrangements and institutional development in the three instances and then (in the concluding section) see what we can learn about public policy conceptions and the relationship between policy orientations and institutional details.

## Recent Developments in Care for Older People in Finland

The main benefit systems for the care for older people in Finland are support for informal care (the ICA – Informal care allowance), home help services (integrated health and social care) and residential care services. Recent policy debates have revolved around the agenda of 'putting home first', with the two trends this entails toward informalisation and marketisation. The national government, the Ministry of Social Affairs and Health and the local authorities all strongly favour *ageing in place* (an EU policy objective) and thus care at home. 'The home' has become a benchmark and most important norm for good care in all circumstances (Häikiö et al., 2011).

In the home care sector the government's 'putting home first' agenda means that older people should have the right to stay at home as long as possible. Against this backdrop, it is noteworthy that home care services have *declined* over the last 20 years. Coverage of publicly funded services supporting care at home has declined from over 30 per cent (of people aged 75 and over) to 20 per cent, despite the fact that home care is rhetorically so strongly emphasised. Only people needing a great amount of help are entitled to these services. The home help service was also reorganised: if in the 1980s municipal home helpers often stayed 3–4 hours with one client, today typically one home helper visits 12–17 households, often staying only 10–15 minutes with one client, although care needs are on average much more extensive. Due to the decline of (professional) home help services, the importance of informal help is on the rise. An estimated 300 000 people (at least) give regular help to adults, with only 30 000, 10 per cent, covered by the informal care allowance (ICA). The informal care allowance was expanded, and keeps growing, to promote the government's home care agenda. ICA is granted to a person in need of care, but paid to informal caregivers accepted by the municipality (obligations are defined in care and service plans). Informalisation is thus a major consequence of the ageing in place policy. In part it explicitly stipulates that relatives and the elderly themselves assume greater responsibility; in part it is also an unintended process, where the lack of resources forces relatives and the elderly to take more responsibility than they would like to do. Older people receive most of the help they need from their close relatives, despite the fairly comprehensive public eldercare system in Finland. Still, when asked, older people in Finland prefer public services as a primary source of help (Van Aerschot, 2014).

In the residential sector 'putting home first' entails reducing the volume of traditional residential care, while expanding a new sector of intensive service housing (ISH). Residential care in these new institutions is supposed to resemble care given at home. Traditional institutional care is regarded to be too expensive, too hospital-like and even humiliating: 'so in intensive service housing it is in a way the person's home, so you decorate it with your own stuff; you have your peace and it is remarkably cosier than in a nursing home.' Living in ISH units is very much described by the word of 'home' (Anttonen and Karsio, 2016). The policy agenda is effective in that traditional institutional care in old age homes and long-term care wards (hospitals) is strongly declining and intensive service housing is accordingly growing, while the total volume (or coverage) of residential care has remained the same. The actual change is not as radical as one would expect, however. Often nursing homes are changed into ISH facilities, with the facilities remaining exactly the same. As one informant says (Anttonen and Karsio, 2016), the change is cosmetic; now older people have a room of their own, they do not need to share a room, and they are not moved from one room to another. Otherwise conditions are very much the same in that in most units residents' freedom of movement is strictly controlled, and residents do not, for instance, have keys to their own rooms. The medical model is dominating in spite of the ideology of 'home'. De-institutionalisation, therefore, is a contradictory aim: institutions are now different, but they are still institutions, and the transition from traditional nursing home care toward ISH care means re-institutionalisation, rather than de-institutionalisation (Anttonen and Karsio, 2016).

Another major policy development is marketisation. The idea behind marketisation is freedom of choice and it stipulates that citizens (residents) should have a right to choose the service provider (public, for-profit, non-profit and so on). This is thought to improve the quality of services and lower costs. In the field of care for older people marketisation is especially pronounced, with nearly half of ISH provided by for-profit providers. In particular the new ISH sector has turned out to be one of the major conduits of marketisation, as clients in these units are paying for all services separately: rent, meals, medication, cleaning, care and so on. Privacy and cosiness are accompanied by more extensive financial responsibilities, and it is also easier to create markets for all these functions when users have to pay for each of them separately. In a traditional old age home only one fee was paid, it was income-related, but it covered nearly all elements of living and caring.

Public sector dominance has been left behind in Finnish eldercare in favour of a welfare mix with a preference for welfare markets. The preference for putting the home first is informed by ideas about autonomy, independence and self-determination. There is nowadays less talk about social rights and more talk about individualisation, choice and voice (Häikiö et al., 2011). The actual situation is different though. With people living longer, memory disorders increase along with frailty and chronic disease, and there are more older people who have no resources to use choice and voice, but need other people's help. Living in intensive service housing units may be like living at home, but most residents are not able to manage their financial or practical things due to frailty and illnesses. It is therefore not possible to make out a general direction of policy change. Availability of professional domestic care services has declined, if anything, while informal care with its potential quality deficits is on the rise. This has led to increased inequalities: there are great differences between people who have resources and those whose resources are very limited (Van Aerschot, 2014); some older people have better access to services than others. Thus, overall the system might empower some people and impose stricter boundaries on others.

### Childcare Development in the UK

The UK appears to be a generous spender on childcare and early education. In 2011, government expenditure represented 1.1 per cent of GDP (including preschool), which was above the OECD average of 0.8 per cent (OECD, 2016). However, the UK's current approach of allocating provision is proving too expensive, too complex, inefficient and unsustainable and provides a low baseline of provision compared to other countries. This results in a shortage of supply, prohibitively high costs for parents and wide regional variation (London and the South East offer the most expensive under-5 childcare), which negatively affects women's employment (see Deusdad, Javornik et al., in this volume for more details).

Where is the problem? The UK combines part-time universal free places with demand-led funding through the tax and benefit systems for both preschool and school age children. Parents are reimbursed through the tax and benefit systems for childcare purchased in an open market, where fees are set by providers to maximise profitability (Javornik and Ingold, 2015). They can receive financial help; other subsidies go directly to childcare providers. Retrospective reimbursement through the tax and benefits system is inefficient and a deterrent for many families, and an array of actors operating across sectors and funding mechanisms add to high costs.

Childcare has been a growing concern for the British welfare state and an increasingly frequent object of its social policy since 1998, when the entitlement to the universal early-years provision was introduced by the Labour Government in the National Childcare Strategy (Lloyd, 2015). This marks a historically significant shift in UK childcare policy, providing universal childcare for 3- and 4-year-olds (equating to 15 hours of care per week for 38 weeks a year). This was intended to be gradually extended to the most disadvantaged 2-year-olds from 2008, together with 'wrap-around' care for school-age children through Extended schools and tax relief on employer-provided childcare vouchers (Javornik and Ingold, 2015). By January 2010 almost all eligible 4-year-olds (98 per cent) and the vast majority of eligible 3-year-olds (92 per cent) in England were included in free early years provision, provided through a variety of settings.

Since then the UK has changed two governments and introduced a number of significant policy changes that mark a fundamental reorientation in its policy outlook. Most recent are the 2014 Children and Families Act and the 2016 Childcare Act, which both continue this evolution.

The Coalition Government (2010–15) committed to implementing Labour's proposed changes to ensure that higher rate taxpayers did not disproportionately benefit, and in 2013 announced its intention to double to 40 per cent the share of 2-year-olds qualifying for the Early years entitlement. Following the 2010 Comprehensive spending review, however, there were cutbacks. The maximum limit for childcare costs under Working tax credit was reduced from 80 per cent to 70 per cent, and from 2011 funding provided under the Extended schools programme was brought within overall schools funding, meaning no specific amount was earmarked for extended services, with schools deciding locally on what should be offered.

In 2013, the Coalition announced plans for a new tax-free replacement for the existing employer-provided voucher system. Families would receive 20 per cent of yearly childcare costs, up to 10 000 GBP per child; to be eligible both parents need to be in work, each earning less than 150 000 GBP per year and not receiving support for childcare costs from tax credits or Universal credit (HM Treasury, 2014). However, this scheme is now scheduled to be introduced in autumn 2017, rather than 2015, and will actually leave some parents worse off. Increased subsidies may raise already prohibitively costly childcare, with the cuts made to the Sure start centres (with more closures planned) significantly affecting the most disadvantaged children. Most families with children under 3 years old wishing to use childcare will still be reliant on either self-payment, employer-provided vouchers or the new tax-free childcare scheme. This is problematic, as childcare in the UK is among the most expensive in the world: the cost of a part-time nursery place for a child aged under 2 had increased by 33 per cent and, for the first time, childcare costs broke the 6000 GBP-a-year barrier, averaging 115.45 GBP a week across Britain; this represents a rise of 5.1 per cent in a single year.

From 2016, the childcare costs covered under Universal credit were planned to increase to cover 85 per cent of eligible childcare (HM Treasury, 2014), going some way to addressing the criticisms made. However, tax-free childcare is subject to the cap on social spending, and it is not clear how this will be financed over time. Moreover, eligibility linked to being in work suggests that the government sees childcare largely as a support strategy for employed parents. But for parents in education, training, seeking a job or starting a business, having quality childcare in place is essential before they can undertake these activities. If the government is assuming equal economic participation of parents and non-parents, of both men and women, then limiting access to childcare intensifies a segregation between employed and unemployed parents, and parents with uneven working patterns, such as those with shift work or zero-hours contracts. Framing the policy in this way also ignores children's needs, disrupts children's daily lives (as parents move in and out of work) and puts high pressure on parents.

As part of its plan to get more people into work, the Conservative Government (2015 onwards) forged ahead with a pre-election pledge to double the current 15 hours per week of free childcare to 30 hours for working parents. We could look at the doubling of the free childcare entitlement as a step towards universal childcare, through the policy's emphasis on improving access. But the policy's aims seem paradoxical. The 2016 Childcare Act did not extend eligibility to all parents; in its current form, it introduced a 'duty to secure 30 hours free childcare available for working parents'. If the government's focus is indeed on child development and well-being, as argued, then not extending access to more free childcare to all children, but only those whose parents are 'working', suggests that quality childcare is not seen as an essential public service (Javornik, 2014). At the same time repositioning childcare as an educational programme 'for the poorest' could be a barrier to a progressive childcare system.

**Accommodation for Asylum Seekers in Sweden**

In the wake of the war in the Syrian Arabic Republic and conflicts in other parts of the world, the growing flow of migrants requires vast emergency response capacities in transit countries and challenges institutions and organisations in receiving countries. In Sweden, the Migration agency coordinates support to asylum seekers and considers the applications from people who seek asylum. In 2015, the number of applicants for asylum doubled from 81 000 in 2014 to 163 000 in 2015. For unaccompanied children, the number was five times as great as the previous year, i.e. 35400 in 2015 compared to 7000 in 2014 (Migrationsverket, 2016).

When refugees apply for asylum in Sweden, the Migration agency will assess their application in accordance with the Aliens Act, which specifies the rules for granting asylum. While awaiting the decision, asylum seekers can work, apply for financial support and receive emergency health and dental care. Minors have the same rights as all other children in Sweden, which involves school and health/dental care. The Migration agency offers temporary accommodation to asylum seekers while their application is in process. In the first days, refugees are offered so-called arrival accommodation, which is run by the Migration agency or contracted private providers. After registration of the application, asylum seekers are moved to accommodation centres for asylum seekers, which can be anywhere in Sweden. Asylum seekers can also choose to arrange their own accommodation, e.g. with friends or relatives. When receiving a positive decision and a residence permit from the Migration agency, people with a refugee status can move to any place in Sweden. The Swedish public employment service together with the municipal authorities offers support in finding a job and accommodation as part of a so-called introduction plan. At this stage, the new residents receive one offer, or they can find accommodation on their own.

In terms of *availability*, accommodation is available for all asylum seekers. However, due to the high numbers of applicants for asylum, an extraordinary situation arose in 2015, where the Migration agency was not able to guarantee accommodation to all. To meet the increased needs temporary solutions for arrival accommodations are established in collaboration with other authorities, e.g. in schools, military facilities or tent camps. There is also a lack of places in accommodation centres for asylum seekers, and therefore the Migration agency sets up contracts with private providers through public procurements. Asylum seekers with income or their own means have to pay for accommodation and subsistence, but for those without means, the Migration agency pays for the accommodation and provides a daily allowance to cover costs for subsistence. Regarding the *quality* of the accommodation centres for asylum seekers, the Migration agency applies a set of requirements in the procurement of new private facilities concerning aspects such as the minimum area per resident, furniture, laundry and showers, fire protection and travel time to the reception unit of the Migration agency. These requirements are updated prior to a new procurement, and due to the exceptionally high needs for new facilities the required quality standards were gradually lowered. For arrival accommodations, where incoming asylum seekers stay for about one week, the quality standards are generally lower in particular in the newly established temporary facilities. Representatives from the Migration agency visit all facilities regularly to monitor that the contracted accommodations meet the stated requirements. The Migration agency's ambition is to offer equal service to all asylum seekers. Nevertheless, there is *territorial varia-tion*, since the majority of asylum seekers today arrive from Denmark to the Scania region. As a consequence, the arrival accommodation in this region is burdened with large numbers of new asylum seekers. For the accommodation centres for asylum seekers the Migration agency depends on available facilities and a proportionally high number of facilities are located outside the main cities where property prices are lower than in the Stockholm region.

The mission of the Migration agency is to offer accommodation to all asylum seekers, but vulnerable groups with special needs (such as LGBTQ persons, unaccompanied minors, elderly, pregnant women and single parents with small children) will be offered accommodation to meet special needs. For unaccompanied minors there are special regulations, which in accordance with the UN convention on the Rights of the child means that the Migrations agency assigns the minor to a municipality that arranges accommodation. Also families with small children are prioritised in situ-ations where there is a lack of facilities. Hence, there is a certain level of targeting to provide appropriate accommodation to each person.

Although the Migration agency has the overall responsibility for the provision of accommodation to asylum seekers, the agency depends on collaboration with other authorities and private service providers. In par-ticular, Sweden's 290 municipalities are important partners, for example when establishing new facilities. For the accommodation and care of unaccompanied minors and the resettlement of persons that have received a residence permit, the Migration agency writes contracts with munici-palities, which specify the number of refugees the municipality will receive. Municipalities are reimbursed for a part of the costs for the reception of refugees. Also regional health care authorities are compensated by the state.

## 4. CONCLUSION: STUDYING DEEDS, NOT WORDS

It comes as no surprise that policies included in this analysis address sub-stantively different themes in the three cases: policy debates about care for older people in Finland revolve around 'ageing in place' and the implica-tions of that strategy for the home care and residential care sectors. The task of securing self-determination and possibilities to make choices about their lives, when beneficiaries of care services often lack the cognitive resources to make such choices is one of the central challenges in those policy debates. The central challenge in the UK childcare is financing an extremely expensive childcare system in such a way that service is accessible, affordable and of quality. The main policy challenge is inequality of access and conditionality of entitlement to free provision. The provision of accommodation for asylum seekers in Sweden faces the task of securing quality and installing special services targeted at particularly vulnerable groups of asylum seekers under conditions of exceptionally high case loads. The large numbers of refugees in 2015 posed formidable administrative challenges; a central concern under the circumstances was quality control, but it is noteworthy in the face of converse debates about the refugee crisis in Europe, that the approach to housing asylum seekers remained voluntarist, focused on practical tasks, rather than the aspect of policing migrants' behaviour, and no discourse about restricting access to the labour market or controlling asylum seekers' mobility while their application for political asylum is processed took centre stage.

Social services solved different problems in the three instances, and so the policy challenges differed, ranging from logistics tasks, as they were conceived, with regard to housing asylum seekers in Sweden, to financing and subsidisation modes in the case of UK childcare, to de-institutionalisation, marketisation and informalisation in the case of services for older people in Finland. These all seem far removed from the epic question of emancipation versus social discipline. It turns out, however, that all these fact-bound issues, *because* of some of their institutional details, speak to that large question. Even if the overt practical questions dominate discourse in the different policy fields, some of their institutional details also confront the overarching themes around the epic question: the capacity for self-determination and autonomy at old age is no precondition for access to care services, but a (citizenship-based) privilege. Access to affordable childcare should not be conditional, but obligatory. Housing services for asylum seekers are not holding facilities or 'hotspots' for groups awaiting deportation, but part of a set of services promoting integration. These are topics of great significance for the question of amelioration or order, that litmus test for social policy design. They become manifest in the wake of choices and developments concerning institutional details.

Political rhetoric often strays far from these institutional realities. Insistence on de-institutionalisation as a vehicle of greater autonomy and dignity at old age betrays the needs and capabilities of many care recipients, so that we have a discourse about autonomy and institutional developments toward constrained ranges of choice. Sometimes that disconnect is unintended, austerity driven, and without any conceptual thought given to the gap between rhetoric and reality. Sometimes, though, we get the impression that there is little motivation among the participants of policy debates to correct these errors and to dispose of the myths.

This is why we have sought to examine institutional manifestations – decisions and trends – to learn something about the character of social service development and accept deeds, rather than words, as testimony. Politically, examining deeds, not words, reflects a certain wariness of political discourses that all too often belie institutional realities. Conceptually it 'turns on its feet' a lot of social constructivist theorising about the role of ideas as explanations of policy development: policy conceptions have been construed as mental frames, channelling attention toward certain problems and not others (Surel, 2000), as frames shaping agenda-setting (Béland, 2005), as cultural lineages shaping identities and by that token preferences (Kahl, 2005), as policy paradigms shaping notions of the feasible and the appropriate (Hall, 1993), or as focal points forging agreement. In all these conceptualisations, causal pathways (Goldstein and Keohane, 1993) run from ideas to policy. Examining institutional development to learn something about policy conceptions, as we did in this chapter, turns this around and studies deeds to learn about ideas, examines policy designs to learn about mind-sets and conceives of concepts as sediments of institutional choices. Our conclusions about policy conceptions and social service developments are tentative, but applying this approach did allow us to avoid the sense of unreality that sometimes troubles the study of discourse and political rhetoric.

# REFERENCES

Anttonen, A. and O. Karsio (2016), 'Eldercare service redesign in Finland: deinstitutionalization of long-term care', *Journal of Social Service Research*, **42** (2), 151–66.

Anttonen, A. and J. Sipilä (1996), 'European social care services: it it possible to identify models?', *Journal of European Social Policy*, **6** (2), 87–100.

Béland, D. (2005), 'Ideas and social policy: an institutionalist perspective', *Social Policy & Administration*, **39** (1), 1–18.

Daly, M. (2004), 'Changing conceptions of family and gender relations in European welfare states and the third way', in J. Lewis and R. Surrender (eds), *Welfare State Change. Towards a Third Way?*, Oxford, UK and New York, USA: Oxford University Press, pp. 135–54.

Esping-Andersen, G. (1990), *The Three Worlds of Welfare Capitalism*, Princeton: Princeton University Press.

Evers, A. (2008), 'Investiv und aktivierend oder ökonomistisch und bevormundend? Zur Auseinandersetzung mit einer neuen Generation von Sozialpolitiken', in A. Evers and R.G. Heinze (eds), *Sozialpolitik: Ökonomisierung und Entgrenzung*, Wiesbaden: VS-Verlag für Sozialwissenschaften, pp. 229–50.

Goldberg, C.A. (2001), 'Social citizenship and a reconstructed Tocqueville', *American Sociological Review*, **66** (2), 289–315.

Goldstein, J. and R.O. Keohane (1993), 'Ideas and foreign policy: an analytical framework', in J. Goldstein and R.O. Keohane (eds), *Ideas and Foreign Policy: Beliefs, Institutions, and Political Change*, Ithaca, USA and London, UK: Cornell University Press, pp. 3–30.

Häikiö, L., L. van Aerschot and A. Anttonen (2011), 'Vastuullinen ja valitseva kansalainen: vanhushoivapolitiikan uusi suunta', *Yhteiskuntapolitiikka*, **76** (3), 239–49.

Hall, P.A. (1993), 'Policy paradigms, social learning, and the state. The case of economic policymaking in Britain', *Comparative Politics*, **25** (3), 275–96.

Higgins, J. (1980), 'Social control theories of social policy', *Journal of Social Policy*, **9** (1), 1–23.

HM Treasury (2014), *Budget 2014 (HC1104)*, London: House of Commons.

Javornik, J. (2014), 'Measuring state de-familialism: contesting post-socialist exceptionalism', *Journal of European Social Policy*, **24** (3), 240–57.

Javornik, Jana and Jo Ingold (2015), 'A childcare system fit for the future?', in L. Foster, A. Brunton, C. Deeming and T. Haux (eds), *In Defence of Welfare 2*, Bristol: Policy Press, pp. 75–8.

Kahl, S. (2005), 'The religious roots of modern poverty policy: Catholic, Lutheran, and reformed Protestant traditions compared', *European Journal of Sociology*, **46** (1), 91–126.

Leibfried, S. and F. Tennstedt (1985), 'Armenpolitik und Arbeiterpolitik. Zur Entwicklung und Krise der traditionellen Sozialpolitik der Verteilungsformen', in S. Leibfried and F. Tennstedt (eds), *Die Politik der Armut und die Spaltung des Sozialstaats*, Frankfurt am Mein: Suhrkamp Taschenbuch Wissenschaft, pp. 64–92.

Lloyd, Eva (2015), 'Early childhood education and care policy in England under the Coalition Government', *London Review of Education*, **13** (2), 144–56.

Marshall, T.H. (1950), *Citizenship and Social Class*, London: Pluto Press.

Mätzke, M. (2011), 'Staatsbürger als Wirtschaftssubjekte und als demografische Ressource. Die Ziele staatlicher Akteure in der Sozialpolitik', *Leviathan*, **39** (3), 385–406.

Mätzke, M. and I. Ostner (2010), 'Introduction: change and continuity in recent family policies', *Journal of European Social Policy*, **20** (5), 387–98.

Migrationsverket (2016), 'Nästan 163000 människor sökte asyl i Sverige 2015', *Nyheter*, 1 January, accessed 8 January 2016 at https://www.migrationsverket.se/Om-Migrationsverket/Nyhetsarkiv/Nyhetsarkiv-2016/2016-01-01-Nastan-163-000-manniskor-sokte-asyl-i-Sverige-2015.html.

OECD (2016), *OECD Family Database*, accessed 8 August 2016 at www.oecd.org/social/family/database.htm.

Orloff, A.S. (1993), 'Gender and the social rights of citizenship: the comparative analysis of gender relations and welfare states', *American Sociological Review*, **58** (3), 303–28.

Ostner, I. (2011), 'Care – eine Schlüsselkategorie sozialwissenschaftlicher Forschung?', in A. Evers, R.G. Heinze and T. Olk (eds), *Handbuch Soziale Dienste*, Wiesbaden: VS Verlag für Sozialwissenschaften/Springer Fachmedien, pp. 461–81.

Piven, F.F. and R.A. Cloward (1971), *Regulating the Poor: The Functions of Public Welfare*, New York: Vintage Books.

Sachße, C. (2000), 'Subsidiarität: Leitmaxime deutscher Wohlfahrtsstaatlichkeit', in S. Lessenich (ed.), *Wohlfahrtsstaatliche Grundbegriffe. Historische und aktuelle Diskurse*, Frankfurt am Main, New York: Campus Verlag, pp. 191–212.

Spicker, P. (2013), *Reclaiming Individualism. Perspectives on Public Policy*, Bristol: The Policy Press.

Steinmetz, G. (1993), *Regulating the Social. The Welfare State and Local Politics in Imperial Germany*, Princeton: Princeton University Press.

Strach, P. (2006), 'The politics of family', *Polity*, **38** (2), 151–73.

Strach, P. (2007), *All in the Family. The Private Roots of American Public Policy*, Stanford: Stanford University Press.

Surel, Y. (2000), 'The role of cognitive and normative frames in policy-making', *Journal of European Public Policy*, **7** (4), 495–512.

Van Aerschot, L. (2014), 'Vanhusten hoiva ja eriarvoisuus. Sosiaalisen ja taloudellisen taustan yhteys avun saamiseen ja palvelujen käyttöön' ['Care of older people and inequality: how socio-economic background is related to receiving care and using services'], *Acta Universitatis Tamperensis 1971*, Tampere: Tampere University Press.

# PART II

# The Transformation of Governance

# 4. Social services in post-industrial Europe: an incomplete success story and its tragic moments

**Ingo Bode**

## INTRODUCTION

This chapter provides a general reading of recent European developments in social service provision with a focus on *cross-country commonalities*, beyond the many international differences the other contributions to this book will bring to the fore. Basically, the analysis sets out the main thread of the story that can be written about the evolving social service sector for a period covering the last two or three decades, with particular attention to governance issues. It reveals that there are inconsistencies in this story that chime with the ambiguity prominent in European politics (see Gómez-Barroso et al., in this volume; CAP Barillà et al., 2016). On the one hand, social services have (more or less) become an institutionalised feature of European welfare states over the last decades, with a robust extension of service supply in mere quantitative terms, at least until the outbreak of the financial crisis in 2008. In the light of contemporary expectations held by key professions, dominant political forces and major sections of the wider public, Europe has thus witnessed a *success story*. On the other hand, as this institutionalisation proves selective in various respects, this success story has always been, and continues to be, *incomplete*. The social service sector exhibits loopholes and limitations, and there are tragic moments in its recent history as major promises have not been kept, and 'organised' social service provision has often become subject to what can be labelled 'disorganisation' (see below).

The next section will elaborate on the conceptual and methodological framework of the analysis. Thereafter, the institutionalisation of social services throughout Europe will be depicted, based on a short data review that covers its five major 'families of welfare states'. The third section will illuminate the selective character of this movement and discuss in which ways the aforementioned success story has remained incomplete. The conclusion will briefly elaborate on implications of the evidence.

## 1. METHODOLOGICAL AND CONCEPTUAL FRAMEWORK

The following analysis is based on the broad literature dealing with the evolving landscape of social service provision in Europe; on comparative research the author of this chapter has undertaken in recent years (Aiken and Bode, 2009; Bode et al., 2013; Breimo et al., 2016); and on findings from various contributions to the COST Action *SO.S. COHESION – Social services, welfare states and places*. Regarding terminological issues, the notion of the *social service sector* is used throughout to give a label to various areas of organised and publicly (co-)funded support to human beings, including social work and personal care but not health and education (see Martinelli, Chapter 1, in this volume). Inspecting this broad area, the focus has to be 'functionalist' to some extent; given that, within Europe, concepts concerning the character of available services, policy approaches, involved professions and providers, and so on, vary considerably from one country to another, the chapter concentrates on how social support is (re)arranged for key target groups: children and their parents, vulnerable and marginalised adults, including citizens with disabilities and care-dependent older people.

Drawing upon statistics as well as case-study evidence presented throughout the wider literature, the analysis is based on generic *research categories* for assessing the development of major social service areas. These categories include: quantitative developments in these areas; legal provisions relevant to both entitlements and institutional responsibilities; the typical organisational set-up of service provision; the mode of coordination governing actual service delivery; and, regarding current reform agendas, key elements of policy discourse. With regard to the aforementioned non-statistical research categories, the data analysis was inspired by qualitative methods applied to comparative policy studies (Mahoney, 2007; Mangen, 2013); basically, the endeavour consisted of finding common denominators for different manifestations of similar institutional phenomena. In what follows, insights from this analysis cannot be substantiated by detailed evidence at any instance; only some examples from key areas of social service provision will be given throughout in order to illustrate general observations.

Concerning its international perspective, the analysis covers those (five) varieties the wider literature distinguishes when it comes to the comparison of families of welfare states (Castles and Obinger, 2008; Martinelli, Chapter 1, this volume), that is, the Nordic or Social democratic, the Southern or Familistic, the Eastern or Transition, the Anglo-Saxon or Liberal and the Continental, or Corporatist, models. While this chapter cannot embark on a systematic comparative assessment, it looks at common features and trends concerning all (or the majority) of these models. Results of the review were refined by reiterated discussions among those experts who met in COST Action meetings and contributed to clarifying encultured readings engrained in national concepts and data (concerning the related epistemological approach, see Bode et al., 2013).

## 2.  A SUCCESS STORY: THE EVOLVING SOCIAL SERVICE SECTOR ACROSS EUROPE

For many decades now, European societies have accepted that they should ensure some kind of 'organised' social support to citizens who do not or cannot (yet) conform to what is considered to be 'normal' in a human being's life. This is a basic insight of earlier scholarship (Kahn, 1973; Kaufmann, 1980; Anttonen and Sipilä, 1996) and recent international assessments (Stoy, 2014; Greve and Sirovátka, 2014). Social intervention is expected to accompany key episodes in each citizen's life course, particularly so during early childhood and old age; it also occurs with critical situations in that life course such as endangered childhood, homelessness, disability, or chronic frailty. As some services address ever greater sections of the population, one can even state that there is a trans-European tendency towards their 'normalisation' (Giraud et al., 2014, for the case of home care). Thus, although such interventions are subject to distinctive legal frameworks, professions and organisations, social services have become – more or less – *institutionalised* throughout Europe.

To some extent, this evolution is an expression of the transition to a *post-industrial settlement* (Esping-Andersen, 1999; Bonoli, 2007; Hendricks and Powell, 2009; Mai-Klose and Moreno-Fuentes, 2013). The latter is not so much post-industrial in the literal sense, as the ascending service economy is heavily industrialised in itself, and many countries have maintained classical blue-collar industries or even redeveloped some. Nonetheless, major cornerstones of European societies exhibit a *post-*industrial character that differs from the ('Fordist') past ending in the 1980s (at the latest). Until then, and across most parts of Europe, major institutional and sociocultural frameworks had been informed by concepts related to 'big industry', on the one hand, and to (male) industrial work on the other. This connected with 'collectivistic patterns' in the organisation of employment, welfare and life courses. True, during this era, collectivities other than families, clans and neighbourhoods begun to take over practical responsibilities for social support activities for *some* groups of citizens or *some* situations – whereas, prior to that, the onus for that was lying almost exclusively with private networks (related to kinship or local acquaintance). However, the expansion, normalisation and (partial) professionalisation of organised activities gained momentum only after the end of this (Fordist) era. In post-industrial times, expectations regarding such formalised social support do not cease to grow (Ferragina and Seeleib-Kaiser, 2015, for the case of family services), although political responses to them do vary.

Against this background, the formation of the social service sector in Europe can be considered a *success story*. This also materialises in the fact that supranational bodies in the EU have made the development of the sector a *transnational policy issue* (see Gómez-Barroso et al., in this volume; CAP Barillà et al., 2016). Sought after are European service markets and social programmes that enable all citizens to take gainful employment, including those who previously carried the onus for taking care of the aforementioned target groups privately (women in most cases). The mantra consists of making social services more widespread in fields such as child daycare, services for older people, and work integration, including for people with disabilities (Polacek et al., 2011; Mills et al., 2014; Bouget et al., 2015) – notwithstanding that European institutions can hardly interfere with national legislation. This concern has been at the core of the recent 'social investment' agenda, but also of commitments to ensure social inclusion in ever more fragmented societies (Bothfeld and Rouault, 2015; Van Kersbergen et al., 2014; Marlier et al., 2007). At the same time, European institutions promote distinctive reform models that pertain to the *governance* of the social service sector; for instance, there are strong voices in favour of exposing non-profit and public undertakings to markets and helping private business access the sector. This ambition shines through various plans of EU institutions to make all sorts of providers deliver 'services of general interest' (Barbier, 2015).

To be sure, the development of the social service sector in Europe has remained *highly diverse*, featuring strong discrepancies between countries and targeted populations. The differences that Anttonen and Sipilä (1996) once figured out in their seminal paper on childcare and services addressing older people have persisted in most respects. As shown by statistical evidence, some countries exhibit high levels of service provision for both the young and the old, others are stronger in care for older people than in childcare, and a few show the reverse pattern. Overall, those in the South and the East provide much less than their counterparts in the West and the North (see Mai-Klose and Moreno-Fuentes, 2013; Lehmann and Havlíková, 2015). A recent review of Stoy (2014) suggests clusters roughly in line with earlier typologies, distinguishing liberal, conservative, social democratic and 'rudimentary' models. It presents some striking results; for instance, France is considered a liberal model, side by side with the UK.

Less surprisingly, the rudimentary type embraces countries from the South and the East that exhibit limited public spending on welfare services and a comparatively small volume of public sector employment in social (and health) care. To some extent, the picture changes depending on which kind of services is taken into account. For example, comparative assessments of childcare systems (e.g. Kröger, 2011) suggest that France is close to a universalistic (Nordic) model. Likewise, recent work on services for older people indicates that conservative welfare states such as Germany and Belgium have developed in *different* directions (Bode et al., 2013). As for social work, interventions have long been based on 'one-stop' *public* agencies or local welfare departments even in liberal welfare states. While this public infrastructure has been downsized in many places (Lorenz, 2016), an increased share of social work is now provided by *non-statutory* organisations (Lawrence and Lyons, 2013).

In a longitudinal perspective, social services have become more comprehensive *whatever the family of welfare states* to which they belong – although more recent trends exhibit some contradictions. Between 1990 and 2010, against the background of policies meant to enable women to enter into gainful employment, the growth of 'formalised' services in the domain of care work has been impressive across many European countries, including some of those that were traditionally sticking to a breadwinner culture, e.g. Ireland or Germany (Ferragina and Seeleib-Kaiser, 2015). Concerning recent developments in Eastern Europe after the fall of communism, a similar trend is discernible at least in some countries (see Kampichler et al., 2015). Regarding support to older people, the numbers of both facilities and users served have increased as well. Efforts were concentrated on residential care during the post-war decades whereas domiciliary provision has become more dynamic after 1980 (Bahle, 2008; Da Roit and Sabatinelli, 2013; Giraud et al., 2014). Again, this pattern is prominent in Eastern Europe, too (Österle, 2011; CAP Kováčová et al., 2014; Juska and Ciciurkaite, 2015; Kubalčíková and Havlíková, 2016). Until the financial crisis, all latecomers were trying to catch up with the more mature welfare states (Guillén and Matsaganis, 2000; Da Roit and Sabatinelli, 2013; CAP Vaiou and Siatitsa, 2013; CAP Pace and Vella, 2014).

Accordingly, there is evidence for *employment* in the social service sector mushrooming almost everywhere, at least between the early 1990s and the end of the 2000s. This is highlighted by statistics that reveal changes in the composition of the European workforce. Oesch (2013), scrutinising this development across a couple of countries since 1990, finds 'welfare state jobs' (in public administration, health, education and social work) growing much stronger than any other occupation (until 2008). Huber et al. (2008), summarising studies on the EU-15 and EU-25, come up with a similar result, although they stress exceptions to this rule in Bulgaria, Estonia, Latvia, Poland and (surprisingly) Sweden. In general, the Nordic countries appear as those with the highest share of social service jobs in the economy.

A further expression of social services becoming more important internationally is growing *public expenditure* for them. A recent report on 'Social investment policies' submitted to the European commission (Bouget et al., 2015) shows that public spending on childcare has increased in most European countries even after 2008; some parts of Europe have seen cuts (the Netherlands, Southern Europe, some Eastern countries), but on average, the expansive tendency is clear (see also Mills et al., 2014). According to the same source, expenditure on services for older people has remained stable over that period, after two decades of strong growth (albeit, with increased demand, this means reduced *per capita* expenditures). Moreover, there is international evidence that programmes for labour market activation that contain a significant component of social work have been extended, especially after the economic recession – despite cuts for other welfare programmes (Van Kersbergen et al., 2014).

Finally, the last decades have seen the *professionalisation* of social service provision. Compared to the 1970s, there is much more specialised education for social support activities, and academic social work has a firm place within the institutional set-up of European welfare states (Lawrence and Lyons, 2013). This movement, very salient in Nordic and Western countries, has also occurred in the South. Spain is a good example: it was a latecomer concerning the 'normalisation' of social work professions but has seen ample debate on these professions becoming 'agents of the welfare state' (Sáez and Sánchez, 2006). Likewise, Eastern Europe exhibits a (sometimes slow) investment in Western-style social work professions (Zavirsek, 2014). True, there is a debate on a latent deprofessionalisation of these occupations in some countries (Duyvendak et al., 2006), yet everywhere, 'organised' social intervention continues to be acknowledged as being indispensable to contemporary European societies.


## 3.   LOOPHOLES AND TRAGIC MOMENTS

Notwithstanding the expansion of social service provision over the last decades, the afore-sketched institutionalisation was anything but perfect. Rather, our 'success story' is *incomplete* as the development of social service provision exhibits various loopholes in terms of 'who gets what'; furthermore, the recent history presents some tragic moments, that is, first, the paradox of publicly promoted, work-centred and gender-neutral life course models being paralleled by trends towards (re)privatisation, and secondly, a tendency towards a mode of governance that provokes what can be referred to as 'disorganised' service provision.

## Loopholes: Limitations and Inequalities in Service Provision

In many countries, there continue to be various loopholes in the social service sector, meaning that the aforementioned developments have taken place with important limitations as well as multifaceted patterns of inequality. This, first of all, concerns the *access to social services*. Thus, in Southern and Eastern Europe, large groups of citizens do not receive such services even though they exist on paper. This for instance affects some regions in Italy that had never witnessed serious efforts in building childcare facilities for the very young and are currently hampered by austerity measures in moving forward in that direction (CAP Martinelli and Sarlo, 2014). In the East, the 'normalisation' process mentioned in the preceding section comes against the background of a 'denormalisation' agenda taking shape when communist institutions collapsed during the early 1990s. Company-based, more universalistic childcare services were cut back during this period, without this loss in facilities being compensated by the (growing) non-statutory service sector. Only some countries have built up new capacity in this area (CAP Győry and Szikra, 2014; Kampichler et al., 2015). Concerning services for old age, this part of Europe traditionally relied on residential care (of very modest quality), but the latter was challenged strongly following the fall of the iron curtain (Österle, 2011). In Southern Europe, the establishment of formal services for older people was rather slow from the 1980s onwards and stopped quite abruptly with the advent of the financial crisis (Mai-Klose and Moreno-Fuentes, 2013; Deusdad et al., 2016). More generally, recent public policies increase efforts in some areas (workfare and early education) while cutting expenditure elsewhere. The social investment agenda of the EU is a supra-national expression of this selectivity and prone to create new loopholes within the social service sector (Bothfeld and Rouault, 2015).

Moreover, *regional* disparities have remained strong in many places, with Southern and Eastern Europe being a case in point (CAP Javornik, 2014; CAP Martinelli and Sarlo, 2014; Oliver and Mätzke, 2014; Deusdad et al., 2016). Even in the Nordic world, the nature and amount of service supply partially depends on municipal politics and local prosperity (see e.g. Jensen and Lolle, 2013). There are also specific *social* divisions concerning service delivery. Thus, the British welfare state leaves large parts of service provision unmonitored for those parts of the population that are not entitled to means-tested benefits. Relevant sections of the population have difficulties in accessing services without public support. This residual-ism has become stronger from the 1990s onwards – even though there has been some investment in facilities for children (Lewis, 2011) and a raise in the individual asset threshold below which adults in need of assistance are entitled to state benefits (Burchardt et al., 2016). More generally, private co-payment for social services is a reality in many European welfare states, which implies an unequal distribution of these services across populations in need (see the section dealing with care for elderly people below).

In addition, important *aspects* of social support are often not included in what users receive, with services being *deficient in terms of quality*. Thus, in continental Europe, the social service sector, while covering increasingly larger sections of the population, has tended to leave certain needs uncovered and to set limits to professionalisation – at least when compared to other areas of human service provision such as healthcare or education. For instance, in the German home care sector, effective social support presupposes the presence of private or family caregivers because entitlements are confined to short periods of professional intervention focusing on paramedical needs (Bode et al., 2013). Moreover, a growing proportion of less qualified staff has recently entered the workforce in this sector. France, while investing in a professionalised home care sector, lets the latter develop side by side with public subsidies for the employment of low-skilled domestic workers who are incapable of applying professional standards (Le Bihan, 2012). In Italy, cash transfers represent the bulk of public support to older people, thereby encouraging the hiring of low-skilled – generally immigrant – private caregivers (Da Roit and Sabatinelli, 2013). And while some European countries have seen considerable invest-ment in publicly regulated childcare for under three years (see Oliver and Mätzke, 2014), this happened at the expense of quality as there frequently are fewer educators per child under the current conditions.

**Tragic Moments: Paradoxical (Re-)privatisation and Disorganisation**

Moreover, there is change that makes the development of social services appear *tragic*. First, concerning what is often labelled the 'welfare mix', certain institutional and sociopolitical developments sit uneasily with each other. In recent times, social services have been understood as a vehicle to enhance (full-time) employment and education for both men and woman and to relieve them (partially) from what is commonly referred to as the 'care burden' (Piovani and Aydiner-Avsar, 2015). As a response to such expectations, there have been various policy announcements including at the level of EU institutions (see e.g. Mills et al., 2014). However, this dual earner model clashes with tendencies to *(re)privatise* part of the responsibility for providing social support. The term 'privatisation' here refers to the productive role of citizens in welfare provision and not to the type of involved service suppliers. While some countries are wavering 'between resilience and erosion' (Gautié, 2015, referring to France), declining collective responsibility is an issue in many places. Thus, Finnish municipalities have reorganised their home help provision and dropped housekeeping services from what is offered by domiciliary care workers (Anttonen and Häikiö, 2011). England, the Netherlands and Sweden have taken a similar route by awarding smaller volumes of publicly funded service hours (see Grootegeld and Van Dijk, 2012; Ulmanen and Szebehely, 2015; Burchardt et al., 2016). Germany continues to endorse private caregiving by cash-for-care benefits granted to family members.

While these are gradual changes, the promised creation of a modern social service sector was seriously disappointed in the South or in the East of Europe where the outbreak of the financial crisis brought a turning point to the aforementioned 'catching up' process. Countries such as Portugal and Greece (but also Ireland) have been urged to reduce markedly the volume of publicly funded services during recent years. While budget cuts abound in such countries, some retrenchment mechanisms work below the surface: in the Spanish system of care for older people, extended co-payments, a reduction of subsidies to informal caregivers, and the abolition of social security contributions to caregiving relatives overall imply a reduced public input into the system. The East did not fare better. Thus, in the Czech Republic, policies meant to dissolve residential care facilities did not entail sufficient funding for domiciliary services replacing them.

Interestingly, such developments go alongside a strong *policy discourse* in favour of both 'hollow state arrangements', promoting non-statutory service co-production (Milward and Provan, 2003), and what is widely referred to as 'participatory' (welfare) governance (Fung, 2015), that is, private involvement in the design of service provision. Citizens or local communities are enticed to take over activities relevant to the production process – often according to a 'help to self-help' model (Dahl et al., 2015) and on a volunteer basis. Where pressures on informal involvement are high, citizens are facing tough challenges when striking a balance between paid employment, voluntary work, child-rearing and taking care of older people (Duxbury and Dole, 2015; Maestripieri, 2015). This hints at a first tragic moment in the recent episode of our 'social service story': the demand for service provision is growing also because more traditional forms of private social support are running dry; yet paradoxically, prevailing policies put their faith into precisely this shrinking reservoir.

A second tragedy resides in the proliferation of new governance models, with a systematic *disorganisation* of social service provision as a result (see Bode, 2003; 2006; 2010). This term stands for various movements reshaping the infrastructure of the welfare state, materialising in modes of governance driven by what has been coined 'New public management' (NPM). Anchored in the wider transformation of Europe's political economy (Lash and Urry, 1987; BRS, 2013), disorganisation makes itself felt in the interplay among the many collective actors involved in the horizontal division of labour endemic in contemporary welfare states (see Martinelli, Chapter 1, in this volume). In the pre-NPM settlement, most European welfare states had orchestrated their welfare programmes either by entrusting public (in-house) undertakings with administering and providing services (and social benefits) or by long-term contractual relations with non-profit agencies. Nowadays, in-house provision has often been outsourced, and interorganisational relations have become volatile.

To be sure, service-based undertakings always need some 'non-organised' spaces for flexible problem-solving (Herath et al., 2016). Moreover, certain problematic elements of disorganisation (e.g. poor response to acute needs by welfare bureaucracies) had already been contained in traditional, public sector-led social service settings. In addition, disorganisation can also occur with a lack of *any* public management. A case in point are less developed welfare states in which public agencies informally allocate places to handpicked users in the event of demand exceeding supply (Kovács, 2015, with respect to the Romanian childcare system). Having said all that, the recent history has seen developments that entail *systemic* disorganisation, including with respect to the regulation of social service sectors.

One facet of this movement consists of devolving responsibilities to *for-profit service providers* that tend to create and restructure activities according to what turns out to be lucrative in a given market context. Polacek et al. (2011) report a growing reliance on these providers in numerous countries. This trend is prominent in childcare and child protection (see Lloyd and Penn, 2012; Jones, 2015; Meagher et al., 2015, for the case of Sweden and England) as well as for organised work integration and services to older people. In these areas, commercial enterprises have often replaced public service units, but also non-profit providers (Damm, 2014, dealing with England; Puthenparambil and Kröger, 2016, concerning Finland).

Yet even where for-profit provision has remained small-scale, *competition* has become a frequent feature of the coordination process between funders, suppliers and users (Hendriksen et al., 2012; Brennan et al., 2012; Bode et al., 2013; CAP Anttonen and Karsio, 2013). Competition is a key driver of disorganisation because it is always unclear who will be a winner or a loser in dynamic and often untransparent welfare markets. Volatility in both the range of providers and service arrangements is a likely outcome. A similar effect is generated by the increased use of service vouchers and cash benefits (Ungerson and Yeandle, 2007) together with 'personalisation' (Mladenov et al., 2015), i.e. programmes that make users 'buy independence' (Glendinning et al., 2000) by hiring private assistants or shopping around for professional help. The latter trend is corroborated by the service market liberalisation strategy of the EU (see Gómez-Barroso et al., in this volume; CAP Barillà et al., 2016).

Moreover, new governance models are based on what is widely referred to as public sector '*managerialism*', which is a third facet of disorganisation. These models comprise quasi-commercial 'public–private partnerships', 'performance-based contracting', and meticulous process control mechanisms (Clarke et al., 2000; Harlow et al., 2013; Lawrence and Lyons, 2013; Carter and Withworth, 2015). In this context, collaboration between non-statutory instances and the state has become instrumental and troublesome in many places (Bode and Brandsen, 2014). Providers have turned into 'hybrids' (Evers, 2005; Bode, 2014) or 'social enterprises' eager to meet financial targets and objectives as specified in business-like contracts.

That this multifold process of permanent disorganisation is an international phenomenon is shown by the example of long-term care for older people, which represents an ever more important part of the social service sector (Ranci and Pavolini, 2013; Lehmann and Havlíková, 2015; Gori et al., 2016). This process comes in various forms. Thus, local governments in Norway have established mild versions of managerialism and provider pluralism, together with promises to enhance choice options. Recent years have also seen a technical separation of funding, assessment, and service provision within the public realm, together with sophisticated interregional benchmarking; this is widely perceived as entailing a more fragmented service supply (Wollscheid et al., 2013). In Germany, the long-term care system is based on users purchasing services individually, with expenses being partially refunded by social insurance. As the market is highly competitive and providers run a permanent risk of economic loss, coordination with other tiers of the care system is poor (Bode et al., 2013). In the English domiciliary care sector, private firms compete for both 'free market' customers (those not covered by public programmes) and care contracts commissioned by specialised bodies (local mergers of units from the National health system and social service departments). Staff fluctuation is considerable even as shifts in contracts can be frequent; in addition, citizens eligible for public support have become entitled to 'personal budgets' to be spent individually (Burchardt et al. 2016, p. 188). In Italy too, both the national cash transfer system and some municipal support schemes can be used to purchase home help on the 'free labour market'. In places where formalised services are available, public tenders are used to contract service provision out to social cooperatives, with users receiving a voucher for paying providers (Bode et al., 2013). Likewise, new regulation in the Czech Republic implies that frail older people can receive a care allowance for the same purpose. This was meant to replace residential care provision by domiciliary services, yet plans to professionalise these services have hardly been realised, so that municipalities are tinkering with meeting uncovered needs. There is also evidence on 'quasi-social' non-registered services filling the gap between the 'frozen' residential care sector and the shortage of publicly funded domiciliary care services meant to substitute it (Kubalčíková and Havlíková, 2016). This goes alongside shifting or dispersed responsibilities; in some places, undertakings employing agents without special training or degrees use programmes such as work integration schemes or funds for regional economic development in order to offer care services.

Among other things, the aforementioned movements turn out to be tragic in that they have come with wrong promises. Meant to make social service provision more effective, they frequently have implications running against that purpose, as the above evidence on long-term care systems demonstrates. Both the political elite and influential groups in the wider public wanted to save money by making the respective infrastructure less monolithic and by resorting to instruments such as output-based evaluation, public tendering and fixed-term contracts. However, whether coinciding with welfare state retrenchment *or* with overall stability in social budgets, this movement stirs disorder in many instances. While a stable institutional embeddedness based on trust and long-term relationships appears critical for both bringing professional expertise to bear and making social support sustainable (see Hasenfeld, 2010, discussing this in theoretical terms), systemic disorganisation – materialising in repeated interruptions and rearrangements, continuous fluctuation in staff and resource streams, constant administrative adjustments, and shifting, or dispersed, responsibilities for service planning and delivery – does endanger such embeddedness. It is prone to undermine the 'prosocial spirit' of organisations and professions inhabiting the sector, even as growing competitive orientations tend to impede network forms of collaboration (Evers and Hafkesbrink, 2014).

## 4.   CONCLUSIONS

During the second half of the twentieth century, social services have become a cornerstone of European welfare states – notwithstanding that they still prove the 'poor cousin' of social security pillars in many places and that their institutionalisation lags behind other areas of human service provision (education; mainstream health care). For those in favour of a perpetuation of the 'success story', the bad news is that, besides the loopholes left in the recent development of the social service sector, there are tragic moments in this story even when considering the more affluent countries.

Thus, on the one hand, the obvious (if sometimes timid) trend to make social services an integral component of the modern welfare state has been reversed, at least in some parts of Europe. A couple of countries have recently seen a containment of entitlements to 'organised' social support while some only invest in selected areas of social service provision. On the other hand, partial (re)privatisation and what has been labelled 'disorganisation' in this chapter have set clear limits to the improvement of social service provision even in countries that have maintained relatively generous welfare programmes. Concerning privatisation, there is the paradox of many users becoming dependent on *ever less practicable* informal solutions that sit uneasily with the full-time dual-earner model so strongly promoted by governments internationally. Volunteer work and private co-provision are still viewed, and sometimes increasingly so, as an indispensable component of social support systems, rather than an 'extra' on top of professional, institutionalised intervention. Citizens who are lacking social networks or resources to purchase services privately are particularly hit by this situation, which becomes a new source of social inequalities adding to those highlighted above. As for the new governance approach proliferating in several families of welfare states, dynamics of disorganisation entail both *novel constraints* on professionalised service delivery and *impediments* concerning the widely shared objective of better coordinated service systems.

The preliminary end of our story is an overall *more precarious arrangement* of social support to citizens in need. This becomes particularly obvious when considering the development of working conditions in the sector under study. Low pay, extra hours and insecure employment increasingly bear witness to social services forming *a second-class zone* in contemporary labour markets. 'Working under pressure' – and sometimes even for nothing – becomes a day-to-day experience in many service-providing undertakings, with staff often being involved in a 'race to the bottom' (Balloch et al., 1999; Cunningham, 2008). This is a clear expression of the post-industrial character of the current social service sector and of its ever less collectivistic organisation.

Across Europe, there certainly are different versions of the story presented in this chapter, with each exhibiting a specific dramaturgy. However, the aforementioned limitations and paradoxes show up in all these versions. Perhaps the common culmination point in the 'tragedy' recounted here is that, under the conditions depicted above, institutions meant to promote the inclusion of human beings rather tend to amplify those social divisions endemic to post-industrial societies. The poorer sections of the population, and all those who lack the knowledge and skills required for coping with privatised and disorganised patterns of service provision, will have to bear the costs. Moreover, not only the lack of services, but also low quality as brought about by dynamics of disorganisation, can undermine social cohesion (Andrews and Jilke, 2016). Hence, while the success story is not history, its happy end is yet to come.

## REFERENCES

Aiken, M. and I. Bode (2009), 'Killing the golden goose? Third sector organisations and back -to-work programmes in Germany and the UK', *Social Policy & Administration*, **43** (3), 209–25.

Andrews, R. and S. Jilke (2016), 'Welfare states and social cohesion. Does social service quality matter?', *Journal of Social Policy*, **45** (1), 119–40.

Anttonen, A. and L. Häikiö (2011), 'Care "going market". Finnish elderly-care policies in transition', *Nordic Journal of Social Research*, **2** (1), 70–90.

Anttonen, A. and O. Karsio (2013), 'From welfare Stateism to welfare markets: eldercare service redesign in Finland', presentation at the COST Action IS1102 Workshop, University of Iceland, Reykjavik, 3–7 June.

Anttonen, A. and J. Sipilä (1996), 'European social care services: is it possible to identify models?', *European Journal of Social Policy*, **6** (2), 87–100.

Bahle, T. (2008), 'The state and social services in Britain, France in Germany since the 1980s. Reform and growth in a period of welfare state crisis', *European Societies*, **10** (1), 25–47.

Balloch, S., J. McLean and M. Fisher (eds) (1999), *Social Services: Working under Pressure*, Bristol: Policy Press.

Barbier, J.-C. (2015), 'Legal uncertainty in social services: a threat to national social protection schemes?', in J.C. Barbier, R. Rogowski and F. Colomb (eds), *The Sustainability of the European Social Model. EU Governance, Social Protection and Employment Policies in Europe*, Cheltenham, UK and Northampton, MA, USA: Edward Elgar Publishing, pp. 255–75.

Barillà, S., J.L. Gómez-Barroso and I. Harsløf (2016), 'A critical overview of the European Union policy framework for social services: agendas, regulation and discourses', *COST Action IS1102 Working Papers*, no. 14, accessed at http://www.cost-is1102-cohesion.unirc.it/docs/working-papers/wg3.eu-policy-framework-s.barilla-et-al.pdf.

Bode, I. (2003), 'The creeping disorganization of welfare capitalism or what is the future of Germany's social sector?', *Review of Social Economy*, **61** (3), 341–63.

Bode, I. (2006), 'Disorganised welfare mixes. Voluntary agencies and new governance regimes in Western Europe', *Journal of European Social Policy*, **19** (4), 346–59.

Bode, I. (2010), 'Towards disorganised governance in public service provision? The case of German sickness funds', *International Journal of Public Administration*, **33** (2), 172–81.

Bode, I. (2014), 'In futile search of excellence. The "muddling through agenda" of service-providing "social enterprises" in contemporary Europe', in S. Denny and F. Seddon (eds), *Social Enterprise: Accountability and Evaluation around the World*, London: Routledge, pp. 196–212.

Bode, I. and T. Brandsen (2014), 'State–third sector partnerships. A short overview of key issues in the debate', *Public Management Review*, **16** (8), 1055–66.

Bode, I., B. Champetier and S. Chartrand (2013), 'Embedded marketization as transnational path departure. Assessing recent change in home care systems comparatively', *Comparative Sociology*, **12** (6), 821–50.

Bonoli, G. (2007), 'Time matters: Postindustrialization, new social risks, and welfare state adaptation in advanced industrial democracies', *Comparative Political Studies*, **40** (5), 495–520.

Bothfeld, S. and S. Rouault (2015), 'Families facing the crisis: is social investment a sustainable social policy?', *Social Politics*, **22** (1), 60–85.

Bouget, D., H. Frazer, E. Marlier, S. Sabato and B. Vanhercke (2015), *Social Investment in Europe. A Study of National Policies*, Brussels: European Commission.

BRS – Book Review Symposium (2013), 'Book Review Symposium: Scott Lash and John Urry *The End of Organized Capitalism*' (with contributions from G. Burrell, M.M. Lucio, I. Greer, S. Lash and J. Urry), *Work, Employment & Society*, **27** (3), 537–46.

Breimo, J., O. Firbank, H. Turba, I. Bode and J.T. Sandvin (2016), 'Networking enforced – comparing social services' collaborative rationales across different welfare regimes', *Social Policy & Administration*, accessed at http://dx.doi.org/10.1111/spol.12235.

Brennan, D., B. Cass and M. Szebehely (2012), 'The marketisation of care: rationales and consequences in Nordic and Liberal care regimes', *Journal of European Social Policy*, **22** (4), 377–91.

Burchardt, T., P. Obolenskaya and P. Vizard (2016), 'Adult social care', in R. Lupton, T. Burchardt, J. Hills, K. Stewart and P. Vizard (eds), *Social Policy in a Cold Climate. Policies and their Consequences since the Crisis*, Bristol: Policy Press, pp. 187–214.

Carter, E. and A. Withworth (2015), 'Creaming and parking in quasi-marketised welfare-to-work schemes: designed out of or designed into the UK Work Programme?', *Journal of Social Policy*, **44** (2), 277–96.

Castles, F.G. and H. Obinger (2008), 'Worlds, families, regimes: country clusters in European and OECD area public policy', *West European Politics*, **31** (2), 321–44.

Clarke, J., S. Gewirtz and E. McLaughlin (eds) (2000), *New Managerialism, New Welfare?*, Buckingham: Open University Press.

Cunningham, I. (2008), 'A race to the bottom? Exploring variations in employment conditions in the voluntary sector', *Public Administration*, **86** (4), 1033–53.

Da Roit, B. and S. Sabatinelli (2013), 'Nothing on the move or just going private? Understanding the freeze on child- and eldercare policies and the development of care markets in Italy', *Social Politics*, **20** (3), 430–53.

Dahl, M.H., L. Eskelinen and E. Boll-Hansen (2015), 'Coexisting principles and logics of elder care: help to self-help and consumer-oriented service?', *International Journal of Social Welfare*, **24** (3), 287–95.

Damm, C. (2014), 'A midterm review of third sector involvement in the Work Programme', *Voluntary Sector Review*, **5** (1), 97–116.

Deusdad, B.A., D. Comas-d'Argemir and S.F. Dziegielewski (2016), 'Restructuring long-term care in Spain: the impact of the economic crisis on social policies and social work practice', *Journal of Social Service Research*, **42** (2), 246–62.

Duxbury, L. and G. Dole (2015), 'Squeezed in the middle. Balancing paid employment, childcare and eldercare', in J. Burke, K. Page and C.L. Cooper (eds), *Flourishing in Life, Work and Careers. Individual Wellbeing and Career Experiences*, Cheltenham, UK and Northampton, MA, USA: Edward Elgar Publishing, pp. 141–68.

Duyvendak, J.W., T. Knijn and M. Kramer (eds) (2006), *Policy, People and the New Professional: De-Professionalisation and Re-Professionalisation in Care and Welfare*, Amsterdam: Amsterdam University Press.

Esping-Andersen, G. (1999), *Social Foundations of Postindustrial Economies*, Oxford: Oxford University Press.

Evers, A. (2005), 'Mixed welfare systems and hybrid organisations. Changes in the governance and provision of social services', *International Journal of Public Administration*, **28** (9–10), 737–48.

Evers, J. and J. Hafkesbrink (2014), 'Trust and its impacts on organizational change and innovation in social services', in G. Becke (ed.), *Mindful Change in Times of Permanent Reorganization. Organizational, Institutional and Sustainability Perspectives*, Berlin: Springer, pp. 167–87.

Ferragina, E. and M. Seeleib-Kaiser (2015), 'Determinants of a silent (r)evolution: understanding the expansion of family policy in rich OECD countries', *Social Politics*, **22** (1), 1–37.

Fung, A. (2015), 'Putting the public back into governance: the challenges of citizens participation and its future', *Public Administration Review*, **75** (4), 513–22.

Gautié, J. (2015), 'France's social model: between resilience and erosion', in D. Vaughan-Whitehead (ed.), *The European Social Model in Crisis. Is Europe Losing its Soul?*, Cheltenham, UK and Northampton, MA, USA: Edward Elgar Publishing, pp. 121–74.

Giraud, O., B. Lucas, K. Falk, S. Kümpers and A. Lechavalier (2014), 'Innovations in local domiciliary long-term care: from libertarian criticism to normalisation', *Social Policy & Society*, **13** (3), 433–44.

Glendinning, C., S. Halliwell, S. Jacobs, K. Rummery and J. Tyrer (2000), *Buying Independence: Using Direct Payments to Integrate Health and Social Services*, Bristol: Policy Press.

Gori, C., J.-L. Fernandez and R. Wittenberg (eds) (2016), *Long-term Care Reforms in OECD Countries*, Bristol: Policy Press.

Greve, B. and T. Sirovátka (eds) (2014), *Innovation in Social Services. The Public–Private Mix in Service Provision, Fiscal Policy and Employment*, Farnham: Ashgate.

Grootegeld, E. and D. van Dijk (2012), 'The return of the family? Welfare state retrenchment and client autonomy in long-term care', *Journal of Social Policy*, **41** (4), 677–94.

Guillén, A.M. and M. Matsaganis (2000), 'Testing the "social dumping" hypothesis in southern Europe: welfare policies in Greece and Spain during the last 20 years', *Journal of European Social Policy*, **10** (2), 120–45.

Győry, A. and D. Szikra (2014), 'Family policies and female labour force participation in the Visegrád-countries. Has there been a move towards flexibility since 2000?', unpublished paper presented at the COST Action IS1102 Workshop, University of Tampere, Tampere, 2–6 June.

Harlow, E., E. Berg, J. Barry and J. Chandler (2013), 'Neoliberalism, managerialism

and the reconfiguration of social work in Sweden and the United Kingdom', *Organization*, **20** (4), 534–50.

Hasenfeld, Y. (2010), *Human Services as Complex Organizations*, 2nd edn, Newbury Park: Sage.

Hendricks, J. and J. Powell (eds) (2009), *The Welfare State in Post-Industrial Society: A Global Perspective*, Berlin, Germany and New York, USA: Springer.

Hendriksen, L.S., S.R. Smith and A. Zimmer (2012), 'At the eve of convergence? Transformations of social service provision in Denmark, Germany and the United States', *Voluntas*, **23** (2), 458–501.

Herath, D., D. Secchi and F. Homberg (2016), 'The effects of disorganization on goals and problem solving', in D. Secchi and M. Neumann (eds), *Agent-Based Simulation of Organizational Behavior. New Frontiers of Social Science Research*, Berlin: Springer, pp. 63–84.

Huber, M., M. Maucher and B. Sak (2008), *Study on Social and Health Services of General Interest in the European Union: Final Synthesis Report*, Vienna: European Centre for Social Welfare Policy and Research.

Javornik, J. (2014), 'Urban variation in childcare provision: the case of Slovenia', unpublished paper presented at the COST Action IS1102 Workshop, University of Tampere, Tampere, 2–6 June.

Jensen, P.H. and H. Lolle (2013), 'The fragmented welfare state: explaining local variations in services for older people', *Journal of Social Policy*, **42** (2), 349–70.

Jones, R. (2015), 'The end game: the marketisation and privatisation of children's social work and child protection', *Critical Social Policy*, **35** (4), 447–69.

Juska, A. and G. Ciciurkaite (2015), 'Older-age care politics, policy and institutional reforms in Lithuania', *Ageing and Society*, **25** (4), 725–49.

Kahn, A.J. (1973), *Social Policy and Social Services*, New York: Random House.

Kampichler, M., E. Kispéter and D. Kutsar (2015), 'Childcare systems in post state-socialist countries: comparative cases from Brno, Szekesfehervar and Tartu', in D. Kutsar and M. Kuronen (eds), *Local Welfare Policy Making in European Cities*, Berlin: Springer, pp. 135–48.

Kaufmann, F.X. (1980), 'Social policy and social services. Some problems of policy formation, program implementation, and impact evaluation', in D. Grunow and F. Hegner (eds), *Welfare or Bureaucracy? Problems of Matching Social Services to Clients' Needs*, Cambridge: Oelgeschlager, Gunn & Hain, pp. 29–43.

Kováčová, J., G. Szüdi and S. Konečný (2014), 'Transformation of social services for the elderly in the context of deinstitutionalization of social services in Slovakia', unpublished paper presented at the COST Action IS1102 Workshop, University of Tampere, Tampere, 2–6 June.

Kovács, B. (2015), 'Managing access to full-time public daycare and preschool services in Romania: planfulness, cream-skimming and 'interventions', *Journal of Eurasian Research*, **6** (1), 6–16.

Kröger, T. (2011), 'Defamilisation, dedomestication and care policy: comparing childcare service provisions of welfare states', *International Journal of Sociology and Social Policy*, **31** (7/8), 424–40.

Kubalčíková, K. and J. Havlíková (2016), 'Current developments in social care services for older adults in the Czech Republic: trends towards deinstitutionalization and marketization', *Journal of Social Service Research*, **42** (2), 180–98.

Lash, S. and J. Urry (1987), *The End of Organized Capitalism*, Cambridge: Polity Press.

Lawrence, S. and K. Lyons (2013), 'Social work and social services in Europe – a changing landscape', *Cuadernos de Trabajo Social*, **26** (2), 371–83.

Le Bihan, B. (2012), 'The redefinition of the familialist home care model in France: the complex formalization of care through cash payment', *Health and Social Care in the Community*, **20** (3), 238–46.

Lehmann, S. and J. Havlíková (2015), 'Predictors of the availability and variety of social care services for older adults: comparison of central European countries', *Journal of Social Service Research*, **41** (1), 113–32.

Lewis, J. (2011), 'From Sure Start to Children's Centres: an analysis of policy change in English early years programmes', *Journal of Social Policy*, **40** (1), 71–88.

Lloyd, E. and H. Penn (2012), *Childcare Markets. Can they Deliver an Equitable Service?*, Bristol: Policy Press.

Lorenz, P. (2016), 'Rediscovering the social question', *European Journal of Social Work*, **19** (1), 4–17.

Maestripieri, L. (2015), 'Gendering social vulnerability. The role of labour market de-standardisation and local welfare', in D. Kutsar and M. Kuronen (eds), *Local Welfare Policy Making in European Cities*, Berlin: Springer, pp. 51–67.

Mahoney, J. (2007), 'Qualitative methodology and comparative politics', *Comparative Political Studies*, **40** (2), 122–44.

Mai-Klose, P. and F.J. Moreno-Fuentes (2013), 'The southern European welfare model in the post-industrial order. Still a distinctive cluster?', *European Societies*, **15** (4), 475–92.

Mangen, S. (2013), 'Cross-national qualitative research methods: innovations in the new millennium', in P. Kennett (ed.), *A Handbook of Comparative Social Policy*, 2nd edn, Cheltenham, UK and Northampton, MA, USA: Edward Elgar Publishing, pp. 243–62.

Marlier, E., A.B. Atkinson, B. Cantillean and B. Nolan (2007), *The EU and Social Inclusion: Facing the Challenge*, Bristol: Policy Press.

Martinelli, F. and A. Sarlo (2014), 'Early childhood services and territorial cohesion. A comparative analysis of supply trajectories in the Emilia Romagna and Calabria regions of Italy', COST Action IS1102 Working Papers, no. 6, accessed at http://www.cost-is1102-cohesion.unirc.it/docs/working-papers/wg2.italy-childcare-martinelli-and-sarlo.pdf?v=3.

Meagher, G., T. Lundström, M. Sallnäs and S. Wiklund (2015), 'Big business in a thin market: understanding the privatization of residential care for children and youth in Sweden', *Social Policy & Administration*, accessed at http://onlinelibrary.wiley.com/doi/10.1111/spol.12172/epdf.

Mills, M., F. Tsang, P. Präg, K. Ruggeri, C. Miani and S. Hoorens (2014), *Gender Equality in the Workforce: Reconciling Work, Private and Family Life in Europe*, report prepared for the European Commission Directorate General for Justice and Fundamental Rights, Brussels: RAND Europe, accessed at http://ec.europa.eu/justice/gender-equality/files/documents/140502_gender_equality_workforce_ssr_en.pdf.

Milward, H.B. and K.G. Provan (2003), 'Managing the hollow state', *Public Management Review*, **5** (1), 1–18.

Mladenov, T., J. Owens and A. Cribb (2015), 'Personalisation in disability services and healthcare: a critical comparative analysis', *Critical Social Policy*, **35** (3), 307–26.

Oesch, D. (2013), *Occupational Change in Europe. How Technology & Education Transform the Job Structure*, Oxford: Oxford University Press.

Oliver, R. and M. Mätzke (2014), 'Childcare expansion in conservative welfare states: policy legacies and the politics of decentralised implementation in Germany and Italy', *Social Politics*, **21** (2), 167–93.

Österle, A. (ed.) (2011), *Long-term Care in Central and South Eastern Europe*, Frankfurt am Main: Peter Lang.

Pace, C. and S. Vella (2014), 'Impacts on Malta's welfare: causes, experiences and expectations', unpublished paper presented at the COST Action IS1102 Workshop, University of Tampere, Tampere, 2–6 June.

Piovani, C. and N. Aydiner-Avsar (2015), 'The gender impact of social protection policies. A critical review of the evidence', *Review of Political Economy*, **27** (3), 410–41.

Polacek, R., D. McDaid, J.-L. Fernandez, T. Matosevic, H. Penn, M. Korintus, M. Verheyde et al. (2011), *Study on Social Services of General Interest*, Final report, European Commission, Directorate General for Employment, Social Affairs and Inclusion, Brussels: Belgium, accessed at: http://eprints.lse.ac.uk/43342/.

Puthenparambil, J.M. and T. Kröger (2016), 'Using private social care services in Finland: free or forced choices for older people?', *Journal of Social Service Research*, **42** (2), 167–79.

Ranci, C. and E. Pavolini (eds) (2013), *Reforms in Long-Term Care Policies in Europe. Investigating Institutional Change and Social Impacts*, New York: Springer.

Sáez, J. and M. Sánchez (2006), 'Trust and professionalism in social professions. The case of social education', *Current Sociology*, **54** (4), 595–606.

Stoy, V. (2014), 'Worlds of welfare services: from discovery to exploration', *Social Policy & Administration*, **48** (3), 343–60.

Ulmanen, P. and M. Szebehely (2015), 'From the state to the family or to the market? Consequences of reduced residential eldercare in Sweden', *International Journal of Social Welfare*, **24** (1), 81–92.

Ungerson, C. and S. Yeandle (eds) (2007), *Cash for Care in Developed Welfare States*, Basingstoke: Palgrave Macmillan.

Vaiou, D. and D. Siatitsa (2013), 'Current organisational framework of elderly care services', COST Action IS1102 Working Papers, no. 2, accessed at http://www.cost-is1102-cohesion.unirc.it/docs/working-papers/wg1.greece-care-for-older-peo ple-d.vaiou-and-d.siatitsa.pdf.

Van Kersbergen, K., B. Vis and A. Hemerijck (2014), 'The Great Recession and welfare state reform: is retrenchment really the only game left in town?', *Social Policy & Administration*, **48** (7), 883–904.

Wollscheid, S., J. Eriksen and J. Hallvik (2013), 'Undermining the rules in home care services for the elderly in Norway: flexibility and cooperation', *Scandinavian Journal of Caring Sciences*, **27** (2), 414–21.

Zavirsek, D. (2014), 'Social work education in Eastern Europe. Can post-communism be followed by diversity?', in C. Noble, H. Strauss and B. Littlechild (eds), *Global Social Work. Crossing Borders, Blurring Boundaries*, Sydney: Sydney University Press, pp. 283–98.

# 5. The vertical division of responsibility for social services within and beyond the State: issues in empowerment, participation and territorial cohesion

## Stefania Sabatinelli and Michela Semprebon

## INTRODUCTION

It is well known that public responsibility for social policies in Europe has been extensively 're-scaled' in the course of the last decades: from the national state it has shifted upwards (towards the European Union) and downwards (towards the local levels, including municipalities, sometimes even neighbourhoods in big cities, and/or intermediate levels, such as regions, provinces or districts) (see among others Ferrera, 2005; Kazepov, 2010).

The changing articulation of what we call the vertical division of responsibility (Aguilar Hendrickson and Sabatinelli, 2014; see also Martinelli, Chapter 1, in this volume) is a complex process that affects systems that by definition have been constituted, consolidated and expanded as national entities. The literature highlights ambivalences in the re-scaling of social policies. With reference to upward re-scaling, the non-binding character of most guidelines provided by the European Union on social policies (see also Goméz-Barroso et al., in this volume) has hindered harmonisation among member countries. In turn, this has raised issues in terms of social rights boundaries (Ferrera, 2005). On the other hand, the prolonged economic recession has led European and international bodies to be much more effective in imposing austerity measures, entailing direct and indirect cuts to social expenditure, in some countries more than in others (Saraceno, 2013). In what concerns downward re-scaling, on the one hand, the decentralisation of social policies has sometimes allowed for the development of innovative, flexible, place-specific declinations of policies; on the other hand, it has often entailed reduced accountability, public de-responsibilisation and increased territorial differences (Keating, 1998; Bonoli, 2012; Rodríguez-Pose and Ezcurra, 2010).

Re-scaling processes take different forms in different national contexts. They also assume different meanings when countries of different size are considered, in terms of both population and territory. Even the features of the multi-level governance (MLG) system and the initial degree of centralisation are relevant. Therefore, the above-described risks do not have the same impact in all contexts. In fact, they are more evident – and stronger – in Southern European countries, where the allocation of responsibilities among different institutional levels has remained fuzzy and has allowed for both potential loopholes and the overlapping of roles and competences. Moreover, there is a concrete risk of the existing territorial differentiation typical of these countries (Pavolini, 2015) becoming even more evident in the presence of decentralising pressures. Nonetheless, it has been reported that local differentiation occurs and can threaten the principle of equality also in countries where such threat is considered marginal, or is maybe underestimated (Trydegård and Thorslund, 2001).

Concerns about the ambivalent implications of shifts in the vertical division of responsibility vary also in relation to social policy domains. Implications differ depending on whether these changes concern policies involving cash transfers as opposed to the provision of in-kind services, such as social assistance, activation policies, early child education and care, long-term care and housing. In fact, while regulation, financing and planning of social policy can take place at national or regional levels, the organisation and implementation of services are necessarily carried out at the very local level. Therefore, the provision of services may display the most diversified MLG arrangements, since services that obtain legitimation in their respective policy fields usually become the object of national legislation and financing. On the other hand, services that lack institutionalisation are (almost) entirely left to local responsibilities. Furthermore, re-scaling trends can follow specific paths and directions in each policy domain, giving origin to different MLG patterns within the same country.

Against this backdrop, the chapter deals with the ambivalent implications that varying patterns of change in the vertical division of responsibility have on the delivery of social services. In particular, we explore the room for manoeuvre available to local bodies for pursuing quality, efficiency and innovation; the forms of local governance; citizens' participation and empowerment. These are all aspects that ultimately affect the possible impacts on territorial and social cohesion and equal opportunities for accessing welfare resources in each country.

The analysis is based on nine case studies produced within the COST

Action IS1102 *SO.S. COHESION – Social services, welfare states and places*, situated in six European countries. These cases have no ambition to be representative of the complex re-scaling trends that are occurring in Europe and across policy fields. Rather, they should be considered as illustrations of the diverse patterns, risks and potentials that can be found in the evolving scenario of social services throughout Europe. The chosen case studies refer to three policy fields – early childhood education and care, long-term care, and the social inclusion of migrants and Roma – which, in our view, best enable the issues at stake to be observed and discussed. The focus is mainly on Southern and Central-Eastern European countries, in which the issues explored are more evident, with the addition of the UK.

The chapter is organised as follows: the next section briefly recalls the theoretical discussions on re-scaling processes and synthetically frames the trajectories observed in European welfare systems, particularly in the countries of the selected case studies; the subsequent section elaborates on the possible repercussions of changes in the vertical division of responsibility, taking into consideration the case studies; in the last section some conclusions are drawn highlighting a number of critical policy issues.

## 1.  THE VERTICAL DIVISION OF RESPONSIBILITY WITHIN THE STATE AND THE CHANGING ROLE OF THE LOCAL LEVEL: THE DEBATE AND OUR ANALYTICAL TOOLKIT

This section provides a brief and, of necessity, non-exhaustive overview of the debate that has developed around the vertical division of responsibility within the state, with reference to social policy and especially social services. It provides an analysis of the main analytical concepts and variables with the aim of critically addressing the cases that will be discussed in the following section. The analytical framework draws on different streams of literature: studies on welfare models and on government styles, as well as analyses of re-scaling processes, MLG patterns and local welfare systems. Discussions on the implications of these (changing) configurations are then mobilised, paying particular attention to two aspects: (a) users' empowerment and participation; (b) the complex relation between re-scaling processes and territorial cohesion, also with reference to issues of institutional accountability.

**Localised Social Policies: Discourses, Strategies and Risks**

Re-scaling processes in welfare states are not a recent phenomenon. Indeed, the initial development of welfare states was a long-term re-scaling process. Specifically, it was a process of upward re-scaling from local charity-based assistance initiatives towards an increasing assumption of responsibilities and competences by the nation state in the field of social protection (Kazepov, 2010). For a few decades, the nation state represented the 'natural' space of welfare policies. Social policies, especially those at the core of the welfare systems (old-age pensions, unemployment benefits, education, health in many countries) were largely defined at the national level. The aim was to grant throughout the national territory an even distribution of access points to welfare benefits (that is local offices of national ministries) and services (schools, hospitals, nursing homes, day-care centres). This was consistent with the goal of pursuing universalism as a principle of entitlement to welfare and redistribution of resources.

With the crisis of Fordism in the mid-1970s, and the decline of Keynesian policies and 'spatial Keynesianism' (Brenner, 2004) after almost a century during which the nation state had played a predominant role, growing pressures emerged towards the decentralisation and/or devolution of responsibilities in social policies. A wave of 'implicit' downward re-scaling was observed – that is in the absence of formal regulative reforms – when local bodies acquired greater importance in the management of social protection, due to the interaction between changing economic patterns and the features of existing measures (Kazepov, 2008). For instance, with the increase of long-term unemployment, applications for social assistance schemes similarly increased and were mainly managed by local bodies, often municipalities. Later on – with different timing and speeds – most European countries started experiencing an 'explicit' wave of downward re-scaling, with reforms shifting responsibilities down to local bodies for the delivery, organisation, and increasingly also the financing and regulation of social policies and services (Kazepov, 2008). On the one hand, the claim for devolution originated from below, as local bodies sought more autonomy in managing the greater burden they were confronted with or greater 'institution building' opportunities. This was especially true in some contexts, in connection with the development of localist political parties. On the other hand, the nation state itself implemented decentralisation reforms as a response to its loss of legitimacy due to the fiscal crisis and a perceived lack of efficacy of the traditional, nation-based welfare programmes in the face of 'new social risks' brought about by post-Fordism (Bagnasco and Le Galès, 2000; O'Connor, 1971; Ranci et al., 2014; Taylor-Gooby, 2004).

The core answers to social needs in the Fordist decades were represented by monetary transfers (with the exception of education and health services); the new social risks (especially those related to care and employability) called for more in-kind services. But while cash transfer programmes can be designed and managed centrally by the nation state, services actually consist of personal interactions that cannot but take place (literally and physically) at the local level (Ranci et al., 2014), although they might be – and often are – regulated and/or financed nationally. Despite the fact that the implementation of services has traditionally been a local competence, since local bodies have been in many contexts the first movers in introducing social services, the increasing relevance of local governments is associated with the growth in size, expenditure and social and political importance of demands for and provisions of personal services.

The complex character of re-scaling processes stands in the articulation of responsibilities among government levels with reference to the key functions involved in delivering social services: regulation, funding, planning and production (see Martinelli, Chapter 1, in this volume). When examining the implications of re-scaling, impacts strongly depend on which institutional level does what.

**The Main Implications of Re-scaling**

As discourses portraying the national welfare state as outdated, inefficient and 'passive'[1] gained momentum, it was increasingly 'considered to be more effective, more participative and democratic and more sustainable' to 'localise' social policies, bringing decision-making closer to the local level (Andreotti et al., 2012, p. 1926). This rhetoric tended to develop independently from empirical evidence, even more so in systems that used to be strongly centralised and/or where monetary transfers played a comparatively dominant role vis-à-vis service provision, like Mediterranean countries. In this context, the three main dimensions to analyse are effectiveness, participation and sustainability.

As regards the first dimension, localised social policies are widely considered to be more effective. In fact, it is believed that, at the local level, it is possible to define solutions better consistent with the specific local features (labour market, housing market, family structures, migration flows). It is also deemed that these solutions allow to better build on the specific resources of the local context (such as the traits of the local economy, the variety and density of local actors, or the morphology of the area). If local welfare systems are understood as 'specific configurations of population needs and welfare providers and resources [. . .] deeply embedded in the specific feature of each local context' (Andreotti et al., 2012, p. 1927), it is then from this interplay – between specific demands and assets of the locality – that local welfare systems should draw.

As regards the second dimension, localised policies are believed to offer more scope for participation and innovation, on the basis of the argument that the 'localisation of policies will facilitate the activation and empowerment of citizens and [. . .] of non-governmental actors in decision making, therefore opening the arena to civil society organisations and strengthening democracy' (Andreotti et al., 2012, p. 1927). The re-scaling of welfare competences has been accompanied by a parallel gradual delegation of responsibilities to non-public actors, in the frame of a strong rhetoric on 'subsidiarity'. Non-public actors were the first initiators of service provision in many countries and were subsequently overshadowed by the predominant role of the central state during the golden age of the welfare state. Especially starting in the 1990s, the role of for profit and non-profit actors in the service sector increased. This was particularly the case of outsourced public services, as needs for personal services increased in quantity and diversity, although with a different timing across European countries. These actors' more flexible organisation – as opposed to big, hierarchical, public institutions – appeared to be better suited to grasp the changing nature of social needs and to experiment with innovative policy answers. At the same time, the local level was deemed the elective scale at which bottom-up and grassroots initiatives could develop to innovate contents, approaches and/or processes of social intervention.

As regards the third dimension – financial sustainability – the debate on federalism and/or decentralisation revolved for a long time around the supposed enhanced capacity of local governments to contain public spending. This was based on the argument that it is easier for citizens and voters to control expenditures since they are carried out at the scale of the locality where they live, and to verify how resources are used in practice. However, as stressed by Bonoli (2012), the most effective mechanism of spending control has often been sheer 'blame avoidance'. In many cases the transfer of responsibilities from the central state to sub-national institutional levels has masked attempts to elude commitments towards social demands that could not be addressed in the conditions of 'permanent austerity' which characterised post-Fordist Western societies (Pierson, 2001). This was especially the case when the transfer of responsibilities was not accompanied by the transfer of adequate resources – a mechanism labelled 'decentralisation of penury' (Meny and Wright, 1985, cited in Keating, 1998) – leaving local bodies either to raise more resources autonomously (often involving higher local taxes, if they had such power) and/or to manage citizens' discontent.[2]

In addition to the above, a key aspect that must be considered when discussing the implications of re-scaling processes – particularly downward ones – is the impact on territorial cohesion, that is, whether and under which conditions greater local responsibility affects the distribution of welfare resources and the access to welfare benefits. Local variations might concern the quantity of services and how widespread they are throughout the territory. However, they also concern their quality, the specific content nuances that similar services might take in different localities, or the degree of innovation in the programmes developed. The nation state is the only institutional level capable of guaranteeing rights, including social rights (Saraceno, 2005, p. 5). In contexts where the nation state's capacity to frame and control local differences is lower and where subjective entitlements are weaker and non-enforceable, the risk for citizenship rights to vary according to the place where people (happen to) live is higher (Kazepov, 2010). In the attempt to control such drifts, changes have been introduced in several countries. Said changes include soft governance tools, such as steering mechanisms, unification and reduction in the number of municipalities (for example in Finland), abolition, reduction of competences or transformation of intermediate levels into merely administrative bodies without elected councils (for example the reform of provinces in Italy), and/or re-centralising reforms. Similar to the case for decentralisation pressures, re-centralisation trends have also been observed, guided by the same concerns for curbing public expenditure, especially after the recent global recession.

Whether the re-scaling process occurs upward or downward, or even in both directions at the same time, an added concern is that it can lead to a less transparent system of responsibilities, with an overall reduction of accountability. This happens when the MLG system stemming from the implementation of re-scaling reforms does not define a clear vertical division of responsibility among institutional levels, especially in the attribution of competences and responsibilities with regard to regulation, funding, planning and production. A similar concern also regards horizontal subsidiarity among different public and non-public actors partaking in the provision of services. In an opaque system, blame-avoidance becomes easier, while it is more difficult for citizens to claim their rights.

**Diverse Trajectories**

The complex re-scaling processes briefly described above have involved most European Union member states, starting in the last quarter of the twentieth century. Yet, at a closer look, differences and specificities emerge in the paths followed by each country. This is partly dependent on the specific government style – 'Scandinavian', 'Napoleonic' or 'Anglo-Saxon'

(Bennett, 1993) – and on the inter-scalar configuration of power during the origin and consolidation phases of the welfare state. But it also depends on the morphology and population size of each country, as well as on the dimension that similar administrative bodies have in different contexts (for example small vs. large municipalities). These institutional features are then intertwined with the specific characteristics of the national welfare models (Esping-Andersen, 1990; Ferrera, 1996) and the broad paths and timing of the reforms that followed in the shift to post-Fordism (Esping-Andersen et al., 2002; Bonoli and Natali, 2012; see also Martinelli, Chapter 1, in this volume).

The MLG features of the countries generally included in the Nordic welfare model have been defined as a 'centrally framed local autonomy' (Kazepov, 2010, pp. 53–6). In this context, a long-lasting tradition of local autonomy – built also on a 'Scandinavian' system of local government (Bennett, 1993) – has allowed social citizenship rights to be warranted throughout the country, also owing to the recognition of several social entitlements, such as subjective rights, the definition of minimum standards of provision, and the use of soft governance tools.

In England – traditionally a 'centrally framed' context (Kazepov, 2010) – decentralisation trends have been more recent. Moreover, they are interacting in complex ways with the re-centralisation implications of austerity measures and the centrally-imposed limits on public expenditure of recent years (Lowndes and Pratchett, 2012).

Both continental German-speaking and Southern European countries share a 'regionally framed' MLG system in the domain of social policies (Kazepov, 2010) and a 'Napoleonic' style of local government (Bennett, 1993). Nevertheless, the national contexts of the local cases analysed here are profoundly different. In fact, Germany and Austria display forms of 'institutional isomorphism' (Di Maggio and Powell, 1983) that attempt to keep somehow under control territorial differences which – within a federalist organisation of the State – can be significant, especially in some policy fields.[3] By contrast, in Italy (similarly to what happens in other Southern European countries), a less inclusive social protection system (with the lack of subjective rights even in terms of minimum income support) goes hand in hand with the lack of centrally engineered steering mechanisms. Minimum standards – to be respected throughout the country – have been defined for health services, but not for social services. Besides, institutional bodies that should enhance coordination among institutional levels are largely ineffective. In such a context, the regionalisation of social policies – ratified in the Constitutional reform of 2001 – has increased the pre-existing very severe territorial divides, especially between North and South, but also within regions, in a sort of 'anarchic municipalism' (Saraceno, 2005).

Finally, 'transition' countries are much more dissimilar than generally assumed. During the Soviet period the prevalence of a monolithic nation state structure was a common denominator implemented in quite diverse pre-existent institutional systems. In Hungary, an intermediate institutional level (the counties) used to play a relevant role before the establishment of the Soviet system. The 1989–90 transition provided more autonomy for the local level, namely municipalities, whose number was doubled to promote local democracy (Fleischer et al., 2002).

## 2.　SOME IMPLICATIONS OF RE-SCALING: ILLUSTRATIONS FROM CASE STUDIES

This section builds on case studies presented in the course of the COST Action IS1102 *SO.S. COHESION*. In particular, it draws on nine cases which, among other aspects, dealt with the vertical division of responsibility within the state. The said cases are not necessarily representative of general national trends, but they shed light on re-scaling dynamics across various European countries and, at the same time, across different policy fields, including services for older people, childcare and the social inclusion of migrants and Roma. They all fall within the context of the general trends and national institutional frameworks described in the previous section. However, the cases examined are rather heterogeneous in terms of territorial scale: some address specific local initiatives, others the municipal or regional governance system, others yet national trajectories. Some of these cases stem from bottom-up initiatives. As such, although they are not the result of decentralisation processes, they still show an increase in the relevance of the local institutional level. In fact, they are at the forefront of pressing social problems, against the absence or inadequacy of intervention from other scales. Table 5.1 illustrates the case studies considered in this chapter, summarising some of their basic features.

As stressed earlier, the aim of this section is not to generalise or provide an exhaustive assessment of the trends at play. The cases examined here are used to exemplify different patterns of re-scaling and related implications. The review is focused on two such implications, in line with the literature: (a) changes in citizens' empowerment and participation; (b) impacts on social and territorial cohesion. Some attention is also paid to whether re-scaling has affected the degree of transparency of the overall governance system and its level of accountability. Overall, our analysis aims to highlight the ambivalent character of changes in the vertical division of responsibility.

*Table 5.1    The COST case studies examined*

| Place | Country | Users of social services | Authors |
| --- | --- | --- | --- |
| Leeds | UK | Older people | Yeandle, 2014 |
| Germany | DE | Older people | Bode, 2013 |
| Six Danish Municipalities | DK | Older people | Jensen and Fersch, 2013 |
| Reggio Calabria | IT | Older people | Martinelli, 2012 |
| | | | Bagnato et al., 2014 |
| Vienna | AT | Roma | Novy et al., 2015 (see also Weinzierl et al., in this volume) |
| Hungary | HU | Roma | Novy et al., 2015 (see also Weinzierl et al., in this volume) |
| Badolato and Riace | IT | Immigrants | Sarlo and Martinelli, 2016 |
| Austria | AT | Early childhood | Leibetseder, 2016 |
| Reggio Calabria | IT | Early childhood | Martinelli et al., 2012 |
| | | | Martinelli and Sarlo, 2014 |
| | | | Martinelli et al., 2014 |

*Source:*    Authors' own compilation.

## Empowerment and Participation

A number of our cases studies exhibit interesting features of the relationships that can develop between varying configurations of the vertical division of responsibility and bottom-up participatory initiatives (see also García et al., 2008; Moulaert et al., 2014; Brandsen et al., 2016). As argued above, a possible outcome of decentralisation can be improved forms of citizens' participation and/or empowerment, in line with Andreotti et al. (2012). Examples of such virtuous participatory practices are provided by the Austrian and Hungarian cases (CAP Novy et al., 2015; Weinzierl et al., in this volume).

In Austria, the Thara project addressed the participation of Roma in the labour market, an issue largely overlooked by national employment policies. Efforts were made to build an open and representative working consortium at the local level. Closer contacts with the communities were vital in raising awareness and in stimulating active engagement. The existing scepticism to collaborate with public institutions (and vice versa) was partly overcome, although social inclusion strategies normally involve long-term processes, particularly when facing a long history of exclusion, as in the case of Roma. The project also contributed to the empowerment of both individuals and the wider community: Romani women employed by Thara brought new competence to the wider field of employment services, which used to be characterised by homogeneous social profiles. They also filled a gap in Roma (political) representation (CAP Novy et al., 2015; Weinzierl et al., in this volume).

In Hungary, the movement for the Tanoda study halls provides another illustration of empowerment. Owing to the opening of study halls, Roma children could enjoy access to quality training and services they were unlikely to receive in the public school system. The movement implemented a positive discrimination strategy broadening the approach of the Hungarian educational system. Yet, despite the positive impact of the project, some potentially negative implications in terms of accessibility must be highlighted. First of all, although study halls are open to all students, they are specifically targeted to Roma. Therefore, they tend to exclude non-Roma students. Secondly, study halls are located in cities, where innovative capital and support are more easily available. It is thus legitimate to wonder whether the initiative would be capable of reaching more deprived territories. Thirdly, the project – as in the case of Thara – thrives on continuing (largely European) funding, which raises questions of sustainability over time (CAP Novy et al., 2015; Weinzierl et al., in this volume).

Despite their critical aspects, the above cases clearly show how civil society organisations can contribute to stimulate service quality and innovation through localised initiatives. This is evident also in the case of the 'Dorsal of hospitality' in Southern Italy (CAP Sarlo and Martinelli, 2016). The Dorsal includes a series of innovative projects for the reception of asylum seekers, in some municipalities of the Locri Plain in Calabria, a context long characterised by economic marginality and weak social capital. In the vacuum left by an inactive public sector, several local actors from the municipal administrations and the civil society developed a 'solidarity network'. Public funding was then put together to further support the project. In the most recent years, however, it has been hard for local actors to strike a balance between innovation and institutionalisation of the initiative. A first issue concerns financial sustainability. Although a regional law has institutionalised the Dorsal's approach, limited financial provisions were allocated for its implementation. Furthermore, although the municipalities have recently joined the SPRAR reception system,[4] the latter is not providing funding as it primarily targets large cities with higher reception capacity. A second issue concerns bureaucratic constraints to creativity and innovation. Being part of the SPRAR involves the fulfilment of bureaucratic requirements which often hinder experimentation and frustrate creative drives.

The case of Leeds in the UK well exemplifies the mixed implications of participatory processes with reference to the reorganisation of services for older people (CAP Yeandle, 2014). Alongside horizontal and vertical subsidiarisation processes, the City Council has developed bottom-up consultation mechanisms to ensure that citizens engage in service planning and feed into decisions about the shape of services. This has increased their awareness of needs and policy issues and has possibly helped to define more consistent welfare configurations. At first glance, thus, this case could be read in a positive light for its constructive implications in terms of participation and empowerment, but the picture is more complex. In its attempt to deal with inequalities and to achieve cost-efficiency objectives, the Council has supported the development of local partnerships by drawing on initiatives that mobilise local communities and volunteers to help the older population. This has led to service diversification and to the emergence of new forms of solidarity towards older people (and their caregivers). On the other hand, as a result of this reorganisation, part of the older community no longer has access to services, as publicly funded support is now limited to the poorest. The care system for older people has thus been substantially disrupted and citizens' participation has been somehow 'brought in' to respond to, and legitimise, this move.

## Social and Territorial Cohesion

In some European countries, strong territorial inequalities exist in the distribution of welfare resources. Re-scaling processes can further amplify this problem. Municipalities can gain considerable room for manoeuvre in social services programming and implementation and this can fuel innovative interventions to fill the gaps associated with underdeveloped or ineffective policies defined by other higher-level institutional actors. At the same time, however, with an increasing territorial diversification of welfare services, inequalities can emerge or grow stronger, thus impacting on social cohesion.

Childcare in Austria provides an example of how government efforts aimed at reducing territorial disparities in welfare service provision can be fraught with the threat of inequality (CAP Leibetseder, 2016). Up to 2008, only provinces and local communities had the responsibility to provide and pay for childcare services, whose coverage was comparatively low, with strong territorial differences. The Austrian Federal Government now provides financial support to provincial authorities and requires them to grant minimum access to care and the fulfilment of qualitative benchmarks. This was aimed at harmonising the provision and quality of services. An agreement between the Federal Government and the Provinces defines the minimum provision. Provinces are free to decide on the remaining aspects of the arrangements, while municipalities define the amount of fees and lunch provision (according to the standards set by the provincial legislation) and deliver the service. However, in some provinces care services are also provided by private firms and non-profit organisations. Following the reform, a minimum provision (for younger children) is also available in rural areas, but territorial differences still exist as regards distribution, and considerable discretion is left to provinces and municipalities for implementation. The evident risk is a limited capacity of welfare policies to ensure equal access in all territories.

Re-scaling processes have taken place also in Denmark, where territorial variations emerge rather strongly in the care for older people (CAP Jensen and Fersch, 2013). Through the Social Services Act, municipalities have been appointed with the main responsibility of care, and in particular with the task to run residential and nursing homes and provide home care (Jensen and Fersch, 2016). Since 1999, local authorities have been required to define quality standards for the care of older people and to plan and implement control mechanisms to ensure their fulfilment. However, they suffer from increasingly limited financial resources. Their budget is negotiated every year on the basis of an agreement between the Ministry of Finance and the Local Government Denmark (the institution representing Danish municipalities). Moreover, they end up competing among each other to attract citizens and related taxes, and they are pressured to cut back on care provisions. Both issues have translated into significant territorial disparities in the distribution of services. Combined with a wide availability of information on quality standards, this seems to have triggered a phenomenon of change of residency in order to enjoy access to what citizens perceive as better services (Jensen and Lolle, 2013).

Some observations on the uneven territorial distribution of services can be made also for long-term care in Germany (CAP Bode, 2013). Here, care provision presents variations in what concerns public funding available for suppliers, support given to traditional non-profit providers and the role of the for-profit sector. Some (richer) municipalities run more generous programmes, while others are less prodigal even in the delivery of basic 'care support' set out by national law. However, differences remain limited, considering that Länder do not invest consistently in the sector. In the 1980s and 1990s care work in the family was institutionally recognised in Germany and, within the framework of long-term care insurance, the option of 'cash-for-care' was introduced. This gave beneficiaries the possibility to choose among in-kind services (offered by non-profit and/or for-profit providers), cash-for-care payments or a combination of both. Yet access to care and the possibility to choose among services are far from universal, as the in-kind provision does not cover all needs and the long-term care schemes offer only 'partial insurance coverage', the rest having to be covered by families. As a result, access to care has grown unequal across regions and social classes. The poorest care-dependent citizens are now less likely to be granted access to adequate assistance, particularly in the poorest regions – as the subsidies available to municipalities are capped. While territorial differences in provision – although (to date) minor – are emerging across Germany, they are less a consequence of the vertical division of responsibility and more a result of changes in the horizontal welfare mix (CAP Bode, 2013; see also chapter by Leibetseder et al., in this volume), with the opening of provision to the market. This testifies how rising inequalities in accessing service provision can be a combination of both processes.

Variation in access can also be associated with ineffective MLG patterns that hinder policy implementation. This can take place when a national regulation is weak and grants significant freedom to the lower levels of authority, as in the case of Italy (Costa, 2009). In fact, following the 2001 devolution reform, regional governments have been in charge of social services, which has highlighted differences across regions depending on administrative traditions (CAP Martinelli et al., 2012). The case of the Region of Calabria is emblematic, both as regards childcare and the care of older people (CAP Martinelli and Sarlo, 2014; CAP Martinelli et al., 2014; CAP Bagnato et al., 2014). In contrast with other regions, the Regional Government of Calabria has not yet implemented the 'integrated system of social services' postulated by the National Law 328/2000 and the subsequent Regional Law 23/2003. Moreover, in spite of a significant growth in the demand for services, both childcare services and the care of older people remain inadequate and residual, at a level among the lowest in Italy. Such a deficit is explained by two factors: on the one hand, the regional model of governance and programming has discouraged local authorities from developing a public service provision; on the other, the public provision of such services has been given low political priority, endorsing social norms considering the family as the key care provider. As regards the former, even when some dedicated national resources were available, the regional authority did not manage to assess needs, define priorities and set up a consistent allocation of resources. The limited resources available have been centralised at the regional level despite the formal mandate to municipalities. Moreover, they have been spent on the basis of ad hoc and erratic regional decrees, through a series of public calls with changing beneficiaries and criteria – managed directly by the regional government itself – in a rather hierarchical, opaque and discretionary fashion. This resource allocation system has contributed to determine a scenario of uncertainty in relation to the transfer of funding to local administrations and a general disempowerment of local actors. Furthermore, municipalities have been 'forced' to compete among each other for regional resources, regardless of their actual service endowment and needs, and despite being often understaffed and lacking specific fundraising competences. The result has been a highly differentiated provision of services within the territory of Calabria itself, depending on each local authority's ability to obtain resources. In the case of childcare, an unregulated private supply has been attempting to meet the growing demand, with problems of accountability and quality, which only recently has been regularised. In the case of care of older people, since the municipal provision of in-kind services is residual, the national cash-for-care system has remained the main public funding source, supporting either family care or privately hired caregivers. The implications are evident: in Calabria, access to services is only for individuals and households that can afford to pay for services in the private market.

Finally, it is important to highlight that re-scaling processes can feature a situation in which the transfer of responsibilities is not coupled by a transfer of resources for implementation. Local authorities can thus be stranded, with no other choice but to raise resources autonomously, through higher local taxes, increased user fees or reduction in provision. The steady decrease in regional care service provision and severe hurdles in the municipal management of services in weak regions like Calabria illustrate the implications of national funds that, on top of being insufficient to start with, have also undergone frequent cuts (CAP Bagnato et al., 2014). The same seems to be occurring following the introduction of austerity measures in the UK, where the central government has reduced transfers and local authorities had to cut back on care provision to older people. In Leeds, this has resulted in reduced access to services, since publicly-funded support remains now available only to the poorest (CAP Yeandle, 2014).

## 3.   CONCLUDING REMARKS

In the current restructuring processes, changes in the vertical division of responsibility for social services within the state are a very relevant issue, which can have substantial impacts in terms of empowerment and participation, as well as social and territorial cohesion. Drawing from the case studies presented in this chapter, the following critical issues must be pointed out.

First, re-scaling reforms have not always brought about a clear and balanced attribution of competences and responsibilities among the various institutional levels in the four main functions involved in social service delivery – regulation, financing, planning and provision. Moreover, their re-allocation has not always involved an adequate parallel attribution of resources. As a consequence, lower-scale institutions might have been given greater space for discretionary action, but often with limited accountability and resources. In such opaque governance systems, blame-avoidance becomes easier, while it is more difficult for citizens to claim their rights.

Secondly, although empowerment – particularly that of the most vulnerable social groups – can be a positive stake and/or outcome of downward re-scaling processes, all efforts and initiatives towards empowerment and democratic participation must be balanced against the severe financial cuts that continue to affect the funding of social services and put the needs of the most vulnerable segments of the population increasingly at risk of remaining unaddressed.

Thirdly, re-scaling can create the conditions for developing localised innovative initiatives, focusing on unaddressed needs or targets, or developing more effective and/or efficient solutions. Yet the very localised character of policy innovations entails some critical aspects:

- In contexts where the vertical division of responsibility lacks a clear attribution of responsibilities, local bodies cannot really pursue innovative and localised interventions as they need to try and compensate for inadequate policies developed by other institutional levels (Aguilar Hendrickson and Sabatinelli, 2014).
- In the absence of the definition of enforceable social rights and/or of minimum standards of intervention, local policy innovation may further increase inequalities among citizens, depending on where they live, in a sort of 'territorial Matthew Effect'. This means that better-off areas can rely on innovative capacities, creative coalitions of actors and abilities to attract funds to finance experimentation more than deprived areas, which are those that would most benefit from innovative projects (Sabatinelli, 2015).
- Paradoxically, innovative drives can be hard to sustain when projects are up-scaled, mainstreamed and institutionalised into (more) permanent structures, which often introduce rigid management and accountability requirements.
- Local authorities can become trapped in a system in which they must compete among each other for resources distributed by higher levels. This causes a detrimental effect on local bodies that are often understaffed and lack specific competences to bid for co-funding.

Last but not least, most of the above issues contribute to increasing the risk of territorial differences in provision, access, quality and cost of social services, which is a threat to social and territorial cohesion. 'Local citizenships' can entail a positive meaning, being 'situated interactions between citizens sharing a territory and defining together public goods' (Saraceno, 2005, p. 5, our translation). Yet, at least four elements appear fundamental for pursuing a balance between local responsibility and the safeguard of universalism: (1) a well-defined distribution and balancing of responsibilities among all institutional levels, with a view towards greater accountability; (2) the definition of minimum enforceable rights, standards of service contents and costs; (3) territorial (re)distribution mechanisms; and (4) legitimate and effective structures for the mediation of possible institutional conflicts. In the absence of these elements, 'local citizenships' can also turn into 'local non-citizenships' (Saraceno, 2005, p. 5, our translation).

## NOTES

1. As opposed to what gradually came to be considered the 'new', 'empowering' types of intervention at the basis of the 'Enabling State' (Serrano-Pascual, 2007, p. 12).
2. It should not be forgotten that the objective to try and reduce public expenditures was also a powerful driver for horizontal subsidiarity (see Anttonen et al., in this volume).
3. In Germany, in particular, territorial differentiation has notably increased after the re-unification of Western and Eastern Länder in 1990 (Oliver and Mätzke, 2014; Ziblatt, 2002).
4. SPRAR stands for *Sistema Centrale di Protezione per Richiedenti Asilo e Rifugiati* (Central System for the Protection of Asylum Seekers and Refugees), a national network involving public actors and third sector organisations that manage integrated reception projects with the financial support of the National Fund for Asylum Policies.

## REFERENCES

Aguilar Hendrickson, M. and S. Sabatinelli (2014), 'Changing labour markets and the place of local policies', in C. Ranci, T. Brandsen and S. Sabatinelli (eds), *Social Vulnerability in European Cities. The Role of Local Welfare in Times of Crisis*, Basingstoke: Palgrave Macmillan, pp. 67–102.

Andreotti, A., E. Mingione and E. Polizzi (2012), 'Local welfare systems: a challenge for social cohesion', *Urban Studies*, **49** (9), 1925–40.

Bagnasco, A. and P. Le Galès (2000), 'European societies and collective actors?', in A. Bagnasco and P. Le Galès (eds), *Cities in Contemporary Europe*, Cambridge: Cambridge University Press, pp. 1–31.

Bagnato, A., S. Barillà and F. Martinelli (2014), 'The public supply of care for older people in Reggio Calabria. The impact of the crisis on a long-standing deficit', presentation at the COST Action IS1102 Workshop, Ekonomickà Univerzita, Bratislava, 3–7 November.

Bennett, R.J. (1993), 'European local government systems', in R.J. Bennett (ed.),

*Local Government in the New Europe*, London, UK and New York, USA: Belhaven Press, pp. 28–47.

Bode, I. (2013), 'The changing governance of domiciliary elderly care in Germany', unpublished paper presented at the COST Action IS1102 Workshop, Dunarea de Jos University, Galati, 5–8 November.

Bonoli, G. (2012), 'Blame avoidance and credit claiming revisited', in G. Bonoli and D. Natali (eds), *The Politics of the New Welfare State*, Oxford: Oxford University Press, pp. 93–110.

Bonoli, G. and D. Natali (2012), *The Politics of the New Welfare State*, Oxford: Oxford University Press.

Brandsen, T., S. Cattacin, A. Evers and A. Zimmer (2016), 'Social innovation: a sympathetic and critical interpretation', in T. Brandsen, S. Cattacin, A. Evers and A. Zimmer (eds), *Social Innovations in the Urban Context*, New York, USA and Heidelberg, Germany: Springer, pp. 3–18.

Brenner, N. (2004), 'Urban governance and the production of new state spaces in Western Europe, 1960–2000', *Review of International Political Economy*, **11** (3), 447–88.

Costa, G. (ed.) (2009), *La solidarietà frammentata*, Milan: Bruno Mondadori.

Di Maggio, P.J. and W. Powell (1983), 'The iron cage revisited: institutional isomorphism and collective rationality in organizational fields', *American Sociological Review*, **48**, 147–60.

Esping-Andersen, G. (1990), *The Three Worlds of Welfare Capitalism*, Princeton: Princeton University Press.

Esping-Andersen, G., D. Gallie, A. Hemerijck and J. Myles (eds) (2002), *Why We Need a New Welfare State*, Oxford: Oxford University Press.

Ferrera, M. (1996), 'The Southern model of welfare in social Europe', *Journal of European Social Policy*, **6** (1), 17–37.

Ferrera, M. (2005), *The Boundaries of Welfare. European Integration and the New Spatial Politics of Social Protection*, Oxford: Oxford University Press.

Fleischer, T., P. Futó, G. Horváth, I. Pálné Kovács (2002), *Multi-level Governance and the Impact of EU Integration in Hungarian Regional and Environmental Policies*, Report of the EU supported Research Project 'EU Enlargement and Multi-Level Governance in European Regional and Environment Policies', accessed at https://core.ac.uk/download/pdf/11856181.pdf.

García, M., M. Pradel and S.A. Eizaguirre (2008), 'Governance integration exercise', *KATARSIS Working papers*, Diss3, accessed at http://katarsis.ncl.ac.uk/.

Jensen, P.H. and B. Fersch (2013), 'Local variations and preferences in the organization of elder care: the Danish case', unpublished paper presented at the COST Action IS1102 Workshop, University of Iceland, Reykjavik, 3–7 June.

Jensen, P.H and B. Fersch (2016), 'Institutional entrepreneurs and social innovation in Danish senior care', in *Administration & Society*, published online 20 January.

Jensen, P.H. and H. Lolle (2013), 'The fragmented welfare state: variations in services for older people', Journal of Social Policy, **2** (42), 349–70.

Kazepov, Y. (2008), 'The subsidiarization of social policies: actors, processes and impacts. Some reflections on the Italian case from a European perspective', European Societies, **10** (2), 247–73.

Kazepov, Y. (ed.) (2010), *Rescaling Social Policies towards Multilevel Governance in Europe*, Avebury: Ashgate.

Keating, M. (1998), *The New Regionalism in Western Europe: Territorial*

*Restructuring and Political Change*, Cheltenham, UK and Lyme, NH, USA: Edward Elgar Publishing.

Leibetseder, B. (2016), 'The regulatory trajectory and organisational framework of childcare services in Austria', *COST Action IS1102 Working Papers*, no. 9, accessed at http://www.cost-is1102-cohesion.unirc.it/docs/working-papers/wg1. austria-childcare-services-b.leibetseder.pdf.

Lowndes, V. and L. Pratchett (2012), 'Local governance under the Coalition government: austerity, localism and the Big Society', in *Local Government Studies*, **38** (1), 21–40.

Martinelli, F. (2012), 'Current organisational framework of care services for older people – Italy', unpublished paper presented at the COST Action IS1102 Workshop, Rovira i Virgili University, Tarragona, 17–19 October.

Martinelli, F. and A. Sarlo (2014), 'Early childhood services and territorial cohesion. A comparative analysis of supply trajectories in the Emilia Romagna and Calabria regions of Italy', *COST Action IS1102 Working Papers*, no. 6, accessed at http://www.cost-is1102-cohesion.unirc.it/docs/working-papers/wg2. italy-childcare-martinelli-and-sarlo.pdf.

Martinelli, F., S. Barillà and A. Sarlo (2014), 'Daycare services in the municipality of Reggio Calabria. The impact of the crisis on a long-standing deficit', *COST Action IS1102 Working Papers*, no. 7, accessed at http://www.cost-is1102-cohe sion.unirc.it/docs/working-papers/wg2.italy-rc-childcare-martinelli-barilla-and-sarlo.pdf.

Martinelli, F., A. Sarlo, S. Sabatinelli and M. Semprebon (2012), 'Current organisational framework of childcare services – Italy, Calabria, Emilia Romagna and Lombardy', unpublished paper presented at the COST Action IS1102 Workshop, Rovira i Virgili University, Tarragona, 17–19 October.

Meny, Y. and V. Wright (1985), 'Introduction', in Y. Meny and V. Wright (eds), *Centre–Periphery Relations in Western Europe*, London: George Allen & Unwin, pp. 1–9.

Moulaert, F., D. MacCallum, A. Mehmood and A. Hamdouch (eds) (2014), *The International Handbook on Social Innovation. Collective Action, Social Learning and Transdisciplinary Research*, Cheltenham, UK and Northampton, MA, USA: Edward Elgar Publishing.

Novy, A., F. Wukovitsch, C. Weinzierl, A. Bernát and Z. Vercseg (2015), 'Social cohesion and the governance of social innovation. A comparative analysis of initiatives for the inclusion of Roma in Hungary and Austria', unpublished paper presented at the COST Action IS1102 Workshop, University of Lund, 8–12 June.

O'Connor, J. (1971), *The Fiscal Crisis of the State*, New York: St Martin's Press.

Oliver, R. and M. Mätzke (2014), 'Childcare expansion in conservative welfare states: policy legacies and decentralized implementation in Germany and Italy', *Social Politics*, **21** (2), 167–93.

Pavolini, E. (2015), 'How many Italian welfare systems are there?', in U. Ascoli and E. Pavolini (eds), *The Italian Welfare State in a European Perspective*, Bristol: Policy Press, pp. 283–301.

Pierson, P. (ed.) (2001), *The New Politics of the Welfare State*, Oxford: Oxford University Press.

Ranci, C., T. Brandsen and S. Sabatinelli (2014), 'Local welfare systems in Europe in the age of austerity', in C. Ranci, T. Brandsen and S. Sabatinelli (eds), *Social Vulnerability in European Cities. The Role of Local Welfare in Times of Crisis*, Basingstoke: Palgrave Macmillan, pp. 273–98.

Rodríguez-Pose, A. and R. Ezcurra (2010), 'Does decentralization matter for regional disparities? A cross-country analysis', *Journal of Economic Geography*, **10** (5), 619–44.

Sabatinelli, S. (2015), 'Aspetti critici dell'innovazione sociale nel contesto italiano', *Prospettive Sociali e Sanitarie*, **XLV** (4.1), 9–12.

Saraceno, C. (2005), *I livelli essenziali di assistenza nell'assetto federale italiano*, Milan: Associazione Reforme.

Saraceno, C. (2013), 'Three concurrent crises in welfare states in an increasingly asymmetrical European Union', *Stato e Mercato*, no. 3, pp. 339–58.

Sarlo, A. and F. Martinelli (2016), 'Housing and the social inclusion of immigrants in Calabria. The case of Riace and the "dorsal of hospitality"', *COST Action IS1102 Working Papers*, no. 13, accessed at http://www.cost-is1102-cohesion. unirc.it/docs/working-papers/wg2.italy-calabria-housing-and-social-inclusion-im migrants-sarlo-and-martinelli.pdf.

Serrano-Pascual, A. (2007), 'Reshaping welfare states: activation regimes in Europe', in A. Serrano-Pascual and L. Magnusson (eds), *Reshaping Welfare States and Activation Regimes in Europe, Work and Society*, Brussels: P.I.E. Peter Lang, pp. 11–35.

Taylor-Gooby, P. (ed.) (2004), *New Risks, New Welfare. The Transformation of the European Welfare State*, Oxford: Oxford University Press.

Trydegård, G.B. and M. Thorslund (2001), 'Inequality in the welfare state? Local variation in care of the elderly – the case of Sweden', *International Journal of Social Welfare*, **10** (3), 174–84.

Yeandle, S. (2014), 'Reconfiguring services for older people living at home in Leeds, UK: how have services changed?', unpublished paper presented at the COST Action IS1102 Workshop, University of Tampere, Tampere, 2–6 June; now published as S. Yeandle (2016) 'From provider to enabler of care? Reconfiguring local authority support for older people and carers in Leeds, 2008 to 2013', *Journal of Social Service Research*, **42** (2), 218–32.

Ziblatt, D.F. (2002), 'Recasting German federalism? The politics of fiscal decentralization in post-unification Germany', *Politische Vierteljahresschrift*, **43** (4), 624–52.

# 6.  The horizontal 're-mix' in social care: trends and implications for service provision

## Bettina Leibetseder, Anneli Anttonen, Einar Øverbye, Charles Pace and Signy Irene Vabo

## INTRODUCTION

This chapter re-conceptualises the notion of 'welfare mixes' in social care and addresses the main changes taking place in European countries. First, we provide a typology of care provision modes that refines the so-called 'welfare diamond' (Jenson, 2013) and we discuss the theoretical implications of welfare mixes, which originally set out to promote equality and partnership among different providers, striving for user-centred and universal social services. However, reviewing the changes that have been introduced over the past few decades, we detect a tendency whereby re-mixes accentuate social inequalities between lower and higher income groups due to increased fragmentation and marketisation, which threatens equality among service providers and universal provision.

We take a look at the main trajectories that frame and shape welfare mixes in social care. The latter are described in terms of the relative share of public, for-profit, non-for-profit or family-based providers. Our aim is to construct a conceptual map of the way responsibilities are shifting among care providers and producing re-mixes. First, we outline a framework for conceptualising welfare mixes. We then contrast this with changes that lead to re-mixes, and we develop a new typology of care provision modes. Next, we present a few illustrative examples drawn from the empirical material shared within the COST Action IS1102 *SO.S. COHESION – Social services, welfare states and places* to highlight such shifts in re-mixes. Finally, we attempt to discern the main social impacts that may result from different types of shifts, paying particular attention to the consequences for equality among users and partnership among providers.

# 1.   THE WELFARE RE-MIX IN SOCIAL CARE PROVISION

The 'welfare diamond' – with the state, family, community and market featuring at each of its four corners – has aroused much interest in social policy research and furthered our understanding of the complexity of care production (Evers et al., 1994; Jenson, 2013). Mixes are shaped and framed by many changes. The recent restructuring of social services in the wake of the financial crisis has, in many countries, taken the form of a retreat by the state from its role in welfare policies. The state's role has been, to a greater or lesser extent, (re)taken over by the market, the community and the family. Permanent austerity has also forced the state to seek ways to raise the productivity of services and care work. The result is a complex, differentiated – and at times contradictory – set of social care services that spans across countries and regions, across fields of social care.

The concept of 're-mix' relates to Martinelli's notion of 'horizontal' division of responsibility (Chapter 1, in this volume) and is used here to describe and analyse *shifts* in the providers' mix, i.e. among the four main actors involved in social care: the state, the family, the for-profit sector, and the non-profit or community sector.

Since the late 1980s, 'welfare pluralism' (Johnson, 1987), also known as the 'mixed economy of welfare' (Abrahamson, 1995), was seen as an emerging principle that re-shuffled the rights and responsibilities among the market, welfare organisations and households and redefined the role of the state (Evers, 1990). It provided an alternative model for social policy at a time when the privatisation of welfare was becoming a very powerful doctrine and policy trend. 'Welfare mix' theory was based on the idea that parallel providers, as well as close collaboration among them, were needed in social service provision in order to secure the best possible outcomes in terms of the satisfaction of needs, the participation of users, and the prevention of any kind of monopoly. It was assumed that multiple providers can offer a better variety of services, generate more diversity, and constitute equal players in the field. An important aim was to make the voluntary and for-profit sectors visible in welfare production (Evers, 1995). The 're-mix' idea also connects to current discussions which stress 'horizontal subsidiarity' (Kazepov, 2010), 'new welfare governance' (Bode, 2006) and 'hybridisation' of providers (Evers, 2005). The concept of horizontal 're-mix' is used to further develop approaches and concepts pertaining to the empirical dimensions of welfare mixes. Besides changing the nature of collaboration, re-mixes involve tasks being re-shuffled among actors involved in care in complex and contradictory ways. This can challenge parity among providers.

In this chapter, we focus on social care services. All people need social care, most particularly at the beginning and end of their life course. Social care (Anttonen and Zechner, 2011) covers a wide range of activities that help people to cope with their daily life. Compared to health and education, though, social care is a less specialised and professionalised service, as there is a less clear demarcation between informal and formal care, unpaid and paid care (see Kröger and Bagnato, in this volume). Therefore, it serves as a suitable illustration of re-mix trends in the European context.

Our empirical material consists of case studies presented in the context of our COST Action. As these cases do not systematically represent all social care services or all European countries, we also integrated findings from other sources. However, although these cases serve to illustrate our conceptual taxonomy and re-mix shifts, they do not enable us to generalise about countries or welfare regime trajectories. To foster accuracy, we also circulated the chapter among the authors of the COST Action case studies addressed here.

## 2.  FROM WELFARE MIX TO RE-MIX IN SOCIAL CARE

Before we outline the current trajectories leading to welfare re-mixes, we must first establish what welfare mixes mean for social care. The concept of 'mix' distinguishes analytically between four main actors that provide social services (Evers and Svetlik, 1993). The four providers are not perceived as mutually exclusive but as complementing each other (despite some rivalry and competition) in covering informal and formal provision, private and public sources of care, and voluntary and professional engagement (Evers and Olk, 1996; Evers and Guillemard, 2013).

The notion of 'mix' underscores the connectedness of informal and formal as well as public and private care provision. Table 6.1 summarises modes of provision, relating them to the four suppliers featuring in the diamond, and further refining the taxonomy.

First, we find the *family* or immediate community, which constitutes the main provider of care nearly everywhere, with different degrees of involvement depending on the user group, be it small children, frail older people or newly arrived immigrants. Altruism and/or reciprocity characterise the exchange, and users are mostly relatives or close community members. Consequently, the family or immediate community forms an exclusionary system of support and cannot guarantee equality in access to care. It may lead to neglect when moral obligations cannot be fulfilled, for instance due to lack of resources or mutual respect (Evers and Olk, 1996).

*Table 6.1    Care provision modes*

| Modes of provision | Provider | Resources mobilised | User | Care worker |
|---|---|---|---|---|
| Informal care | Family; immediate community | Reciprocity; love, responsibility | Member of family or community | Unpaid (female) family member; friend |
| Voluntary and charity work | Non-profit (I): community; charity and voluntary associations | Fundraising; voluntary work; public subsidies | Targeted user | Unpaid volunteer |
| Non-profit care service organisations | Non-profit (II): welfare organisations | Fundraising; membership or user fees; public subsidies | Member; targeted user, customer | Paid or semi-paid worker; unpaid volunteer |
| For-profit commercial providers | For-profit (I): companies; for-profit service organisations | Service charges; (public subsidies); social insurance | Customer | Paid (professionalised) worker |
| Privately hired caregivers | For-profit (II): self-employed caregiver | Service charges; (public subsidies); social insurance | Employer; customer | Paid (professionalised or informal) worker |
| Public providers | Central/ regional/ local authorities; subcontractors | Taxation; service fees; social insurance | Citizen; resident; user (more or less targeted) | Paid professionalised worker; sometimes volunteers |

*Source:*    Authors' compilation (based on Anttonen and Sipilä, 2005; Powell, 2007).

In the non-profit sphere, *community*, *voluntary* and other *civil society-based providers* are private actors that deliver services to approved categories of users needing help, sometimes members of the associations in question. They are divided into two main subcategories, the first based on voluntary, unpaid work, and the second based on more or less professionalised paid work. Users are cared for according to the organisation's targets and their own needs – an aspect that may hinder the equal distribution of services, while the voluntary nature of some of this work might hinder professionalisation. Although these private, non-profit organisations generally endorse solidarity and aim to ensure users' political and social participation and empowerment, over the past 20 years many had to transform into market actors due to increased participation in competitive tendering.

In the market sphere, we also find two main categories. On the one hand, there are *for-profit commercial enterprises*, which sell services directly to customers – who pay for them and enjoy the freedom to choose – or receive payments from public authorities, in the case of outsourcing. It is widely believed that private for-profit providers enhance competition, innovation and choice. On the other hand, we find *self-employed caregivers* who are privately hired by users or their families. Their work is more or less formalised and regulated, depending on the country.

Finally, there is the *public* sector, which carries out multiple tasks and plays different roles in social services and social care: it may regulate, finance and/or provide services depending on the welfare state context. The state may regulate the provision of care work, by setting for example minimum standards for public and private providers. The state can also directly provide services, which implies that the facilities are owned and financed by either the national, the regional or the local government; that those who work in those facilities are public employees; and that entitled users are citizens or residents. The state may also finance social services indirectly, via tax breaks or benefits for users, or via subcontracting or outsourcing services to private providers. In general, the state is regarded as an actor that aims to achieve social equality and the universal provision of services, but it may also inhibit private initiatives, neglect the needs of minorities, and act in a rather hierarchical and overly bureaucratic manner.

The welfare mix approach – in its optimistic version – is based on the idea that these diverse actors tend to complement each other. The various care providers do not typically possess the same strengths, and by combining efforts in different ways they can also cover care needs in different ways. This diversity can, in fact, offer a menu of choices for users and caregivers alike (Anttonen and Sipilä, 2005; Evers and Guillemard, 2013; Powell, 2007). On the other hand, boundaries between providers have also become blurred and a new hybridity has evolved which might endanger equality, universality and political accountability (Evers, 2005). Bode (2006) also underlines that all providers, with the exception of households, have experienced intensified competition and state regulation, abandoning their initial values as a result of the marketisation drive.

Seen from that perspective, the previous debate on how best to offer social provision in welfare mixes (Powell, 2007) might get lost in the re-mix process. Early welfare mix theorists criticised both the dominance of the public sector and marketisation, seeking instead a truly pluralist model that recognised the third sector as an important actor (Evers and Svetlik,

1993; Evers and Laville, 2004). How do recent trends fit into the theory and practice of welfare mixes? Are re-mixes leading towards increased marketisation of care production?

## 3. SHIFTS AND TRENDS: WELFARE RE-MIXES IN THE MAKING

Besides political-normative perspectives on how the distribution of social services and care *ought* to be organised, an analytical framework is needed in order to describe the rationalities and roles of different actors and the shifts occurring among them. We will therefore now propose some fine-grained distinctions within the most common trends in the reorganisation of tasks among the actors involved in welfare re-mixes, as defined above.

A lot of attention has been paid to the *shift away from public sector delivery* of welfare and social services in current market economies (Meagher and Szebehely, 2013). This pertains to at least three processes: (a) *marketisation*; (b) *familialisation*; (c) *communitarisation*.

*Marketisation* is a major component of the current transformation of care services. It refers to a growing role of the market provider. It is, however, a multi-faceted concept and phenomenon. Here we specifically address the process whereby an increasing share of formerly public services are contracted out to for-profit providers, usually through competitive tenders or customer choice models. In this way, market actors assume a central position not only in countries that previously featured substantial public provision, but also in contexts where this was not the case.

Marketisation can take place without public sector retrenchment. Care services can be generated by motivating market providers to produce services and consumers to purchase them with the help of public money, such as vouchers, or other financial incentives such as tax rebates. It can also occur by outsourcing the provision to for-profit providers: the national, regional or local governments issue a call for tenders and diverse providers compete for a government contract to provide the service. Very often, thus, marketisation implies that for-profit providers deliver care services which are still fully or partly funded through public sources – be these taxes or mandatory contributions.

It is important to note that while marketisation can be a state-led, active policy measure, it can also just occur through inaction or drift. *Active* marketisation takes place through tenders and the issuing of vouchers, leading towards a 'managed' social care market. *Passive* marketisation occurs instead when public funding and provisions do not keep pace with increased demands and for-profit providers develop to answer needs.

*Familialisation* implies an increase in the role of the family. The concept of 'de-familialisation' was extensively used to indicate social developments whereby functions previously handled by family members were removed from the domestic sphere and transferred to the state, market providers, or the voluntary and community sector. 'Re-familialisation' correspondingly refers to transitions whereby functions that were once removed from the family's sphere of responsibility are returned to the family (Leitner, 2003). Both forms of change can entail active or passive processes. *Passive* (or de facto) re-familialisation is a result of public withdrawal, market withdrawal (for example due to decreased ability to pay formal or informal market providers), or community withdrawal (if non-governmental or community organisations reduce their services). Conversely, *active* re-familialisation occurs when government authorities encourage the family to take on more care obligations, through, for example, the granting of allowances to parents caring for children or family members looking after frail relatives at home (Saraceno and Keck, 2011).

Whether family-based social care provision is actively supported by the state or taken for granted as a family's obligation, the provision of family care can, to some extent, be regulated by law. Regulated family care occurs, for example, when the state intervenes, through legal measures or economic and moral incentives, in how much and what kind of social care the family provides.

*Communitarisation.* Non-governmental organisations (NGOs) and community-based organisations (CBOs) are sometimes labelled 'community' organisations, or 'third sector' organisations. We suggest the concept of 'communitarisation' to describe increases in the role of the non-profit sector that have occurred as a consequence of shifts within the horizontal division of labour. 'De-communitarisation' implies a declining role for NGOs and CBOs as service providers, because more care is provided either by the state, the market or family. Conversely, 're-communitarisation' can take place when the state or other actors withdraw, or do not expand fast enough to meet increased demands and the community – whether in the form of voluntary associations or non-profit organisations – takes over again.

Because communitarisation may apply to diverse organisations, we distinguish between *formal* communitarisation, which involves large NGOs, and *informal* communitarisation, which involves less formalised CBOs, based on voluntary initiatives. Recently, however, the role of third sector organisations has changed, due to the overall marketisation of care production: third sector actors are increasingly expected to compete with for-profit providers and ask for user fees. There still are, however, genuine non-profits (charities, voluntary organisations) that provide 'services' and help free of charge.

\*\*\*

In conclusion, marketisation, familialisation and communitarisation are processes that alter the welfare mix in horizontal terms: there are different providers in each society, and their role and status vary, as do the relations among them, also in function of governments' policies. Since the 1990s, a major market 'turn' has taken place in a number of European countries. Marketisation, in particular, is often accompanied by a reduction of government expenditure on care and, in this respect, can be distinguished from outsourcing, in which private organisations deliver social services while public authorities bear the costs.

On the other hand, the public financing of social services can also expand, as has happened in both childcare and care for older people throughout Europe in the 1990s and early 2000s (Bouget et al., 2015). New social security schemes can be established, or access to free, tax-financed social services can be introduced. It may also provide larger direct and indirect subsidies to users or private providers, for example through tax deductions for users of private services or insurance or direct subsidies for private investments in services (e.g. for the construction of private kindergartens or nursing homes).

To sum up, the overall system of service provision in contemporary Europe is based on a variety of rationalities in care production, a complex set of relations among different providers, diversity in funding and steering mechanisms, and diversification in user behaviours.

## 4. WELFARE RE-MIXES IN THE CONTEXT OF EUROPEAN SOCIAL CARE

Our empirical evidence includes examples drawn from our COST Action, which focus on specific social services in a number of European countries, regions and municipalities. We especially looked at those that addressed re-mixes and changes in terms of marketisation, familialisation or communitarisation in provision, funding and regulation.

Based on our previous theoretical discussion, we have identified and grouped the observed shifts according to the taxonomy presented in Table 6.2. The table was devised as a *tool* to facilitate the *description* of how these changes played out in various cases, taking into account possible differences within countries in diverse service fields, and to help discern the *social impacts* of these changes.

*Table 6.2    Key shifts in welfare re-mixes*

| Directions of change | Forms of change | Mechanisms (examples) |
| --- | --- | --- |
| Marketisation | Active marketisation<br>Passive marketisation<br>Informal marketisation<br>De-marketisation | Choice/tender models/<br>  cash-for-care<br>Austerity/cuts<br>Immigrant care work<br>Insourcing |
| Familialisation | Active re-familialisation<br>Passive re-familialisation<br>De-familialisation | Cash for care/moral incentives<br>State withdrawal<br>Expansion in service provision |
| Communitarisation | Active communitarisation<br>Passive communitarisation<br>Formal communitarisation<br>Informal<br>  communitarisation<br>De-communitarisation | Partnership/network models<br>Increased competition, austerity<br>Bottom-up initiatives |

*Source:*   Authors' compilation.

Our focus is thus on re-mix trends as they have manifested themselves through the mechanisms of marketisation, familialisation and communitarisation. The deep and extensive changes in state and local government administration and management are touched upon only in relation to these processes. This means that the focus is not on changes within the public sector – or vertical governance changes (see Sabatinelli and Semprebon, in this volume) – but on transfers of responsibility for services away from governments and towards diversified social care mixes. Since shifts between providers (state, family, market, community) are more nuanced than is generally acknowledged in the debate, marketisation, familialisation and communitarisation have been further specified, for instance through the distinction between active and passive marketisation, as proposed in Table 6.2. In what follows, we will illustrate these more specific trends.

**Active and Passive Marketisation**

Marketisation is a widespread ideology, doctrine and policy strategy in most European countries (Bode et al., 2011; Brennan et al., 2012; Salamon, 1993; Yeandle et al., 2012). It is, however, important to underline differences among prevailing forms of marketisation. Active marketisation is used here to refer to the active or proactive role of the state in ensuring the shift to the market. Passive marketisation denotes a growing role for market provision as a consequence of weak or retrenching state intervention in social care, often amid growing demand.

In care for older people in Denmark, for example, services have undergone a significant marketisation shift, with users regarded as customers who make informed choices, a shift justified by population ageing, fiscal stress and neo-liberal principles. The emphasis on users as customers was ushered in by national legislative reforms enacted by a centre-right government in the early 2000s, which reduced municipal autonomy. Until 2002, in fact, municipalities could choose whether they preferred direct provision or outsourcing to private providers, but in 2003, national legislation granted users the right to choose between municipal and private services. In practice, this has introduced 'tender-marketisation', where private providers have to meet specified quality standards in order to be authorised by municipalities. Private and public providers then receive the same fixed payment (CAP Jensen and Fersch, 2013).

The system is supposed to encourage competition among providers, but has led to new issues in service provision. Jensen and Fersch (CAP 2013) talk about a 'tyranny of the clock', where strict schedules prevent home help providers from responding to unexpected urgent needs. The case of Danish care for older people well illustrates how governments can be active in their marketisation efforts, particularly in promoting different choice models and outsourcing public services through tenders to for-profit providers.

In Finland, marketisation has taken place primarily through outsourcing via competitive tendering, which is now in use in most municipalities. The share of for-profit service provision in Finland has risen sharply since the early 1990s, most notably in child welfare services and intensive 24-hour care for older and disabled persons. For-profit provision in 2013 accounted for roughly half of all publicly funded services (CAP Leinonen et al., 2012; CAP Anttonen and Karsio, 2013; see also Anttonen and Karsio, in this volume) compared to the early 1990s, when the share of for-profits was close to zero.

In Austria and Germany, social service provision has always been strongly tied to public as well as non-profit providers (besides the family) (Evers and Laville, 2004). This is the case both in care for older people and childcare. In terms of care for older people, however, a shift has been observed from non-profit towards for-profit providers, as well as towards informal care-giving, albeit with some regulation (CAP Bode, 2013; CAP Leibetseder, 2016a). Austria and Germany have also introduced cash allowances to motivate citizens to purchase private services. The introduction of a universal care allowance in Austria and of a social care insurance option in Germany represent a further expansion of the public financing of private suppliers (see Bode, in this volume; CAP Leibetseder, 2016b). Thus, marketisation does not necessarily mean the withdrawal of state funding. Both countries have also stepped up the financing and provision of childcare services, as has also occurred in many other European countries (Ferragina and Seeleib-Kaiser, 2015).

Both the Czech Republic and Slovakia, which have a strong tradition of state provision of residential care for older people, have embraced a marketisation approach when they joined the EU. The Czech Republic has moved away from exclusive provision by government agencies towards the participation by non-profit and for-profit providers in long-term residential care for older people. There has also been an increase in state support for informal care-giving. In Slovakia, care service provision for older people is still mainly a government responsibility, but this is changing in the direction of a plurality of providers (Kubalčíková et al., in this volume).

The United Kingdom has undergone a number of changes in its service design. Among others, it has introduced a new type of economic support for family carers. It is unlikely, though, that these indirect subsidies to private providers (including family providers) will be sufficient to reverse the overall downward trend in public funding in the UK. Although new legislation in the UK, including the Localism Act of 2011 and the Welfare Reform Act of 2012, has given local authorities new autonomy, it has become rather difficult to exercise it within the financial restraints emanating from years of centrally imposed budget cuts, as shown in the case of the municipality of Leeds (CAP Yeandle, 2014). Moreover, local citizens are now asked to approve any increase in council taxes above national guideline levels.

Southern European countries historically had a comparatively small public service sector in social and health care (Stoy, 2014; Martinelli, Chapter 1, in this volume). Only in the 1980s, increased state provision began supplementing existing residual (mostly church-related) non-profit service organisations. However, rising demands have also led to an expansion of market- and community-based care. With the 2008 financial crisis, the development both of public support and private provision has ground to a halt.

In the municipality of Reggio Calabria, in Southern Italy, the very limited development of both direct public provision and outsourced public childcare services, in parallel to a significant growth in demand, has triggered a clear process of passive marketisation or marketisation by default, with the development of an unregulated system of private for-profit or non-profit childcare providers (CAP Martinelli et al., 2014).

In Malta, a significant shift has taken place from public provision and church-related NGOs in the field of care services for older people towards market-based services. The government has not outsourced any pre-existing public services to private organisations, although new residential homes have been created as public–private partnerships, and the government purchases places within private residences. Meanwhile NGO provision of meals-on-wheels was transferred to for-profit providers in 2015. And yet, public or NGO-based provision of social care in Malta has not kept pace with the increased demand, and non-subsidised market-based services nowadays fill the void (Pace et al., 2016).

In many of the Action's other case studies concerning Southern Europe, 'passive' marketisation is at work, as direct and indirect public support of care services is not keeping up with demand. This kind of passive marketisation leads many users who cannot afford for-profit services to exit the formal social service systems, resorting instead to the re-familialisation of care and/or to situations where care needs are not properly met.

**The Informal Marketisation of Care**

In elderly care, some cases bear witness to the detrimental effect of the provision of cash benefits, low public provision of services and rather mediocre regulation and enforcement. These factors tend to lead to the creation of *informal markets*, where mostly informal private caregivers (usually immigrants) deliver service provision.

Public support of care services for older people in Mediterranean countries such as Spain or Italy began to develop in the 1980s, spurred by increased demand (CAP Deusdad, 2013; CAP Martinelli, 2012). The financial crisis of 2008, however, interrupted this 'catch-up' process and provoked a sharp retrenchment of public funding. Therefore, direct and indirect public funding of care services for older people, as well as for people with disabilities and children, has remained residual. Doñate et al. (CAP 2013) show in their case from Spain that the very advanced legislation on 'personal autonomy' from 2007 upgraded the country from a residual (family- or charity-centred) system to a quite encompassing caring state. In 2013, however, benefits for residential care, as well as care allowances for family carers, were simply discontinued. In Italy, which also followed a 'latecomer' trajectory (Da Roit and Sabatinelli, 2013; CAP Martinelli, 2012; CAP Bagnato et al., 2014), dramatic cuts in public support since 2010 have resulted in the disappearance, or at least severe reduction, of many services, especially in Southern regions and municipalities, forcing many users to fall back on the family or turn to the informal market (private hiring of immigrant caregivers). In Malta, unregulated informal marketisation of care for older people has also increased.

Families who can afford it often do not provide care services themselves, preferring to employ informal home care workers (mostly Filipinas). This solution, however, is unaffordable for those who only receive old age pensions (Pace et al., 2016). Ultimately, even the informal market option has become more limited in these countries, for instance in Greece, due to huge unemployment and loss of income among all social groups (CAP Konstantatos, 2013).

The use of cash benefits for the care of older people has stimulated informal market provision also in Germany, Austria and the Czech Republic. For example, the introduction of 'care allowance' has supported informal care given either by family members or informally hired, sometimes undocumented, migrant caregivers in the Czech Republic (CAP Kubalčíková and Havlíková, 2013). In Austria, recent legislation has introduced a special status for 'informal' care workers with very low wages and less protected working conditions compared to 'native' employees, in an attempt to introduce some degree of formal regulation (CAP Leibetseder, 2016b). In Germany, the growth of informal care work has not led to any legislative changes, but non-profit care providers have been demanding reforms for years (Neuhaus et al., 2009; Lutz, 2015).

**Active and Passive Re-familialisation of Care**

Historically, a significant share of care work has been progressively removed from the realm of the private household and entrusted to formal services, whether public or private. However, the nature of this change differs across social services and countries. Care model researchers have shown that, even today, some countries lean much more on families for care provision than others (León, 2015). The term 're-familialisation' describes a situation where households and families have to take up again a share of care responsibilities. Here too there can be passive and active re-familialisation.

An important difference between childcare and care for older people must be stressed here. Childcare service provision has grown steadily in most European countries, most particularly pre-school services, whereas there is much more variation in the scale, scope and targeting of care services for older people and other dependent adults. Re-familialisation thus takes very different forms depending on which services and countries or regions within countries are studied.

A clear trend of passive re-familialisation is evident, for instance, in Malta with regard to care for older people. Here, low-income people have had to turn to family members for care, while better-off people can purchase (informal immigrant) services with their own money (Pace et al.,

2016). In the municipality of Reggio Calabria (CAP Martinelli et al., 2014; CAP Bagnato et al., 2014), the limited provision of public services and, recently, the further reduction of public support for both childcare and care for older people have prompted many families who cannot afford private care to resume care responsibilities. Deusdad and Zafra (CAP, 2013) show how the heavy cuts in public funding of both care services and housing services for older people in Tarragona (Catalonia) have reversed previous service gains and have triggered passive re-familialisation, whereby deprivation and inequality between classes and genders have resumed.

Passive re-familialisation can also be observed in the field of care for older people in the Nordic countries (Rostgaard and Szebehely, 2012). Local case studies in Finland indicate that stricter targeting of residential and home care services has accompanied reduced government expenses. Families have had to take on more responsibility for care tasks than before and this has also become an official objective that is enshrined in many government documents (CAP Anttonen and Karsio, 2013). The newly revised Social Services Act of 2016 supports this development, turning passive re-familialisation into an active endeavour. The new law underlines the participation not only of users but also of their family members, and makes the role of family members much more explicit than before. Conversely, in the Danish case, according to the law it is not families who must take over care responsibilities but the clients themselves, who are 'activated' (enablement policy). This also strengthens the clients' decision-making discretion, fostering individualisation (CAP Jensen and Fersch, 2013).

A relevant exception is childcare services in the Nordic countries, the Netherlands, France, Austria and Germany. In this field, continued *de-familialisation* is observed, in the form of increased subsidised or publicly financed and sometimes even publicly provided kindergartens (Ferragina and Seeleib-Kaiser, 2015), which continued after the 2008 crisis. Some countries have also extended mandatory parental leave schemes. A move towards increased kindergarten coverage and longer periods of paid parental leave can be detected in other European countries as well, although not as strongly (Ferragina and Seeleib-Kaiser, 2015). Indeed, childcare and care for older people have historically had different statuses, the former traditionally enjoying stronger political and legal support. Nevertheless, there is some evidence that, to save money, Finnish municipalities prefer to grant cash benefits to parents of small children than to provide publicly funded childcare services, a policy that has widened the gap between higher- and lower-educated mothers, the latter preferring cash benefits (Mahon et al., 2012). Such a development would indicate a process of stratified, active re-familialisation.

**The Communitarisation of Care**

'Communitarisation' implies that the role of third sector organisations – whether large Non-governmental organisations (NGOs) or smaller Community-based organisations (CBOs), whether based on voluntary work or paid professional work – is increasing in the overall production of care services. If the state withdraws public funds for social services, these organisations may move in 'by default' and fill the gap. After the 2008 economic crisis, in many places the third sector has become more active in the provision of social services. Compared to previous phases, this features a form of passive re-communitarisation.

Small, ad hoc neighbourhood-based, but often networked, CBOs are filling the gap left by the dramatic reduction of the public care sector in many contexts as a result of austerity measures. In Greece, for example, there has been an increase in local self-organising, bottom-up networking initiatives, addressing health, housing and neighbourhood support (CAP Adam and Papatheodorou, 2014; Häikiö et al., in this volume). Semprebon and Vicari (CAP 2014) examine an initiative to empower immigrants to build their own houses. Vaiou and Siatitsa (CAP 2013) reported on community-based organisations in Athens that provide services such as soup kitchens, food banks, communal cooking, medical wards, as well as counselling and support centres. In Catalonia, Escobedo and Escapa (CAP, 2014) describe the role played by parents' organisations in the management of out-of-school care in times of crisis, albeit supported by government resources.

These community initiatives sometimes take the form of political mobilisation (CAP Vaiou and Siatitsa, 2013). Persons risking eviction or court proceedings are helped by community initiatives offering legal support, as well as initiatives to organise public demonstrations and civil disobedience. García and De Weerdt (CAP 2013) analyse how such a community initiative in Spain mobilised against paying mortgages in a context of rising unemployment and the burst real estate bubble. Jolanki (CAP 2014; Jolanki and Vilkko, 2015) describe a commune of older adults that was established in order to respond to the problems of access to public care services and to help develop their own design for life within a shared residence in Finland.

There are also instances of 'active' communitarisation, when local governments actively engage with third sector organisations, albeit often with insufficient funding. In the UK, for example, the financial crisis has generated severe cuts in national funding, putting further pressure on local government budgets. As illustrated in the case of services for older people in Leeds (Yeandle, 2014), local governments are therefore increasingly involving community-based – often voluntary – organisations in the delivery of social services, sometimes by awarding them contracts for publicly funded services, sometimes by encouraging grassroots and voluntary organisations to develop additional support, following the ideal of a conservative Big Society that functions without state resources. A similar active communitarisation trend is observed by Fraisse (CAP 2014) in his analysis of childcare services in the French cities of Lille and Nantes. There, left-wing local governments have implemented a centrally-directed expansion of childcare by involving mainly third sector and user associations rather than for-profit providers. The increased role of local organisations is thus 'publicly-led', with local authorities supporting the development of new services, with strong support from the central state as well. In contrast to the UK, however, the French welfare re-mix remains embedded in a national regulatory and funding framework.

## 5.    THE SOCIAL IMPACTS OF HORIZONTAL RE-MIXES

The concept of 'horizontal re-mix' has been used in this chapter to describe changes that are re-shuffling welfare mixes in multiple and contradictory ways. Our main conclusion is that impacts of the current horizontal re-mix diverge substantially from those postulated by the welfare mix theory of the 1980s and 1990s. The idea of partnership and close collaboration among the sectors has become eroded as a result of increasing market dominance in many countries. If one actor gains a (near) monopoly in the mixed economy of care and influences all other actors' performance, one would hardly expect to find equal partnerships and mutual ties among service providers. Even increased competition among service providers might hinder such fruitful partnerships.

It appears that market-, third sector- and family-based care provision modes have attained a stronger position than earlier; most particularly, countries that used to rely significantly on the direct public provision of services have taken steps to introduce welfare mixes. Following the early assumptions of welfare mix theory, diverse providers were thought to lead to greater variety in welfare provision and, through collaboration between equal players, tailored services were supposed to cater for individualised needs. In contrast, the more recent re-mixes feature multiple trends that do not support these claims. These trends, as shown in our taxonomy and examples, suggest problematic and sometimes even negative re-mix effects.

First, care inequality is increasing. On the one hand, higher income groups can access better and more individualised service provision, as they can afford to pay out of their own pockets or combine individual payments with cash benefits in order to secure higher quality services. On the other hand, stricter targeting and means testing exacerbates social exclusion and stratification, as publicly supported services just provide a bare minimum for the poor, and low-income populations above the minimum income threshold may be too poor to pay for care services. The latter groups must increasingly rely on family networks (passive familialisation) or local CBOs (passive communitarisation). Thus, while the richer users have been transformed into consumers enjoying ample choices, in the case of the poorer users, services are provided unevenly, across social groups, service fields and places, creating new inequalities that threaten universalism and social citizenship. In other words, welfare re-mixes tend to benefit better-off citizens, which was not what welfare mix supporters aimed at, when the argument was first brought into welfare theory.

Secondly, government involvement in the governance of social services is diminishing in many contexts, although with different intensities across places and services. The retraction of public funding largely results in a greater role for profit providers and self-employed care workers. But governmental withdrawal also opens up ungoverned spaces that lower the potential for productive collaboration between diverse providers or the active state-led coordination of these. This leads us to ask: should the role of the state be stronger than is suggested in the welfare mix literature, which placed so much faith in equal partnership? Less state involvement easily leads to the dominance of market providers.

Finally, the growing complexity of care services is becoming a major problem. Not only does it result in splits among diverse providers in the same area; sometimes clients have to engage with multiple providers to cover one specific care need. Furthermore, the fragmentation and disruption of services challenge accountability and assessment, as matters of responsibility and factual service provision are rather arduous to address.

Our main conclusion is, thus, that the concept of 'horizontal welfare re-mix' is needed to assess the overall transition from state care service provision towards a mixed provision of such services, as well as towards a more market-based provision of care. The retreat of state provision and public funding in social care tends to result in a lower integration of, and greater fragmentation among, service providers. The original idea of welfare mixes – idealised as bringing together the best of the service sector actors, including families and households, while lowering expenditure – has certainly not been fulfilled. Instead, a social care landscape has emerged that operates less harmoniously than before.

# REFERENCES

Abrahamson, P. (1995), 'Welfare pluralism: towards a new consensus for a European social policy?', *Current Politics and Economics of Europe*, **5** (1), 29–42.

Adam, S. and C. Papatheodorou (2014), 'Social medical centers of solidarity in turbulent times', unpublished paper presented at the COST Action IS1102 Workshop, University of Tampere, Tampere, 2–6 June.

Anttonen, A. and O. Karsio (2013), 'From welfare stateism to welfare markets: eldercare service redesign in Finland', presentation at the COST Action IS1102 Workshop, University of Iceland, Reykjavik, 3–7 June. Now published as Anttonen and Karsio (2016), 'Elder care service redesign in Finland: deinstitutionalization of long-term care?', *Journal of Social Service Research*, **42** (2), 151–66.

Anttonen, A. and J. Sipilä (2005), 'Comparative approaches to social care: diversity in care production modes', in B. Pfau-Effinger and B. Geissler (eds), *Care and Social Integration in European Societies*, Bristol: Policy Press, pp. 115–34.

Anttonen, A. and M. Zechner (2011), 'Theorizing care and care work', in B. Pfau-Effinger and T. Rostgaard (eds), *Care between Work and Welfare in European Societies*, Basingstoke: Palgrave Macmillan, pp. 15–34.

Bagnato, A., S. Barillà and F. Martinelli (2014), 'The public supply of care for older people in Reggio Calabria. The impact of the crisis on a long-standing deficit', presentation at the COST Action IS1102 Workshop, Ekonomickà Univerzita, Bratislava, 3–7 November.

Bode, I. (2006), 'Disorganized welfare mixes: voluntary agencies and new governance regimes in Western Europe', *Journal of European Social Policy*, **16** (4), 346–59.

Bode, I. (2013), 'The changing governance of domiciliary elderly care in Germany', unpublished paper presented at the COST Action IS1102 Workshop, Dunarea de Jos University, Galati, 5–8 November.

Bode, I., L. Gardin and M. Nyssens (2011), 'Quasi-marketisation in domiciliary care: varied patterns, similar problems?', *International Journal of Sociology and Social Policy*, **31** (3/4), 222–35.

Bouget, D., H. Frazer, E. Marlier, S. Sabato and B. Vanhercke (2015), *Social Investment in Europe. A Study of National Policies*, Brussels: European Commission.

Brennan, D., B. Cass, S. Himmelweit and M. Szebehely (2012), 'The marketisation of care: rationales and consequences in Nordic and liberal care regimes', *Journal of European Social Policy*, **22** (4), 377– 91.

Da Roit, B. and S. Sabatinelli (2013), 'Nothing on the move or just going private? Understanding the freeze on child- and eldercare policies and the development of care markets in Italy', *Social Politics: International Studies in Gender, State and Society*, **20** (3), 430–53.

Deusdad, B. (2013) 'Regulatory trajectory and current organisational framework of social services and social care', *COST Action IS1102 Working Papers*, no. 1, accessed at www.cost-is1102-cohesion.unirc.it/docs/working-papers/wg1.spain-catalonia-social-services-b.deusdad.pdf.

Deusdad, B. and E. Zafra (2013), 'Older adults, housing accessibility and consequences of the economic crisis', unpublished paper presented at the COST Action IS1102 Workshop, Dunarea de Jos University, Galati, 5–8 November.

Doñate, A., C. García and I. Monsonís (2013), 'Regulatory trajectories and organisational frameworks of social services in the Valencian region of Spain', *COST Action IS1102 Working Papers*, no. 3, accessed at www.cost-is1102-cohesion. unirc.it/docs/working-papers/wg1.spain-and-valencian-region-social-services-a. donate-et-al.v2.pdf.

Escobedo, A. and S. Escapa (2014), 'Participation of parents in the management of out-of- school care services as a source of solidarity at the local level', unpublished paper presented at the COST Action IS1102 Workshop, Faculty of Economics and Business, Barcelona, 3–6 March.

Evers, A. (1990), 'Shifts in the welfare mix: introducing a new approach for the study of transformations in welfare and social policy', in A. Evers and H. Wintersberger (eds), *Shifts in the Welfare Mix. Their Impact on Work, Social Services and Welfare Policies*, Frankfurt am Mein, Germany and New York, USA: Campus Verlag, pp. 7–30.

Evers, A. (1995), 'Part of the welfare mix: the third sector as an intermediate area', *Voluntas: International Journal of Voluntary and Nonprofit Organizations*, 6 (2), 159–82.

Evers, A. (2005), 'Mixed welfare systems and hybrid organizations: changes in the governance and provision of social services', *International Journal of Public Administration*, 28 (9–10), 737–48.

Evers, A. and A.-M. Guillemard (eds) (2013), *Social Policy and Citizenship: the Changing Landscape*, Oxford: Oxford University Press.

Evers, A. and J.L. Laville (eds) (2004), *The Third Sector in Europe*, Cheltenham, UK and Northampton, MA, USA: Edward Elgar Publishing.

Evers, A. and T. Olk (1996), 'Wohlfahrtspluralismus: analytische und normativ-politische Dimensionen eines Leitbegriffes', in A. Evers and T. Olk (eds), *Wohlfahrtspluralismus: vom Wohlfahrtsstaat zur Wohlfahrtsgesellschaft*, Opladen: Westdeutscher Verlag, pp. 9–61.

Evers, A. and I. Svetlik (eds) (1993), *Balancing Pluralism: New Welfare Mixes in Care for the Elderly*, Aldershot: Avebury.

Evers, A., M. Pijl and C. Ungerson (eds) (1994), *Payments for Care: A Comparative Overview*, Aldershot: Avebury.

Ferragina, E. and M. Seeleib-Kaiser (2015), 'Determinants of a silent (r)evolution: understanding the expansion of family policy in rich OECD countries', *Social Politics: International Studies in Gender, State and Society*, 22 (1), 1–37.

Fraisse, L. (2014), 'Ambivalences of social innovations discourses and strategies in local childcare governance in the time of crisis', unpublished paper presented at the COST Action IS1102 Workshop, University of Tampere, Tampere, 2–6 June.

García, M. and J. de Weerdt (2013), 'Housing crisis and the "Plataforma Afectados por la Hipoteca" organization', unpublished paper presented at the COST Action IS1102 Workshop, University of Iceland, Reykjavik, 3–7 June.

Jensen, P.H. and B. Fersch (2013), 'Ideas about good care at the municipal level', presentation at the COST Action IS1102 Workshop, Dunarea de Jos University, Galati, 5–8 November.

Jenson, J. (2013), *Social Innovation: Redesigning the Welfare Diamond*, accessed at http://www.transitsocialinnovation.eu/content/original/Book%20covers/Local%20 PDFs/100%20SF%20Jenson%20Social%20innovation%20redesigning%20the%20 wlfare%20diamond%202013.pdf.

Johnson, N. (1987), *The Welfare State in Transition*, Brighton: Wheatsheaf.

Jolanki, O. (2014), 'Senior cohousing community as a way to organize help and support for older people', unpublished paper presented at the COST Action IS1102 Workshop, University of Tampere, Tampere, 2–6 June.

Jolanki, O. and A. Vilkko (2015), 'The meaning of a "sense of community" in a Finnish senior cohousing community', *Journal of Housing for the Elderly. Special Issue: Nordic Housing Research*, **29** (1–2), 111–25.

Kazepov, Y. (2010), 'Rescaling social policies towards multilevel governance in Europe: some reflection on processes at stake and actors involved', in Y. Kazepov (ed.), *Rescaling Social Policies. Towards Multilevel Governance in Europe*, Farnham, UK and Burlington, USA: Ashgate, pp. 35–72.

Konstantatos, H. (2013), 'Regulatory trajectories and organisational frameworks of social services – Greece', unpublished paper presented at the COST Action IS1102 Workshop, Catholic University of Portugal, Porto, 18–21 February.

Kubalčíková, K. and J. Havlíková (2013), 'The current development of social services in the care of older people: deinstitutionalization and/or marketization?', unpublished paper presented at the COST Action IS1102 Workshop, Dunarea de Jos University, Galati, 5–8 November.

Leibetseder, B. (2016a), 'The regulatory trajectory and organisational framework of childcare services in Austria', *COST Action IS1102 Working Papers*, no. 9, accessed at http://www.cost-is1102-cohesion.unirc.it/docs/working-papers/wg1.austria-childcare-services-b.leibetseder.pdf.

Leibetseder, B. (2016b), 'The regulatory trajectory and organisational framework of social services in Austria', *COST Action IS1102 Working Papers*, no. 10, accessed at http://www.cost-is1102-cohesion.unirc.it/docs/working-papers/wg1.austria-social-services-b.leibetseder.pdf.

Leinonen, E., T. Sihto and T. Kröger (2012), 'Current organisational framework of care services for older people – Finland', unpublished paper presented at the COST Action IS1102 Workshop, Rovira i Virgili University, Tarragona, 17–19 October.

Leitner, S. (2003), 'Varieties of familialism: the caring function of the family in comparative perspective', *European Societies*, **5** (4), 353–75.

León, M. (ed.) (2015), *The Transformation of Care in European Societies*, London: Palgrave Macmillan.

Lutz, H. (2015), 'Ausländische Pflegekräfte in deutschen Privathaushalten. Interview mit Redaktion focus Migration', *Kurzdossiers: Zuwanderung, Flucht und Asyl: Aktuelle Themen*, accessed at http://www.bpb.de/gesellschaft/migration/kurzdossiers/211011/interview-mit-helma-lutz?p=0.

Mahon, R., A. Anttonen, C. Bergqvist, D. Brennan and B. Hobson (2012), 'Convergent care regimes? Childcare arrangements in Australia, Canada, Finland and Sweden', *Journal of European Social Policy*, **22** (4), 419–31.

Martinelli, F. (2012), 'Current organisational framework of care services for older people – Italy', unpublished paper presented at the COST Action IS1102 Workshop, Rovira i Virgili University, Tarragona, 17–19 October.

Martinelli, F., S. Barillà and A. Sarlo (2014), 'Daycare services in the municipality of Reggio Calabria. The impact of the crisis on a long-standing deficit', *COST Action IS1102 Working Papers*, no. 7, accessed at http://www.cost-is1102-cohesion.unirc.it/docs/working-papers/wg2.italy-rc-childcare-martinelli-barilla-and-sarlo.pdf.

Meagher, G. and M. Szebehely (eds) (2013), *Marketisation in Nordic Eldercare: A Research Report on Legislation, Oversight, Extent and Consequences*, Stockholm: Stockholm Studies in Social Work.

Neuhaus, A., M. Isfort and F. Weidner (2009), *Situation und Bedarfe von Familien mit Mittel- und Osteuropäischen Haushaltshilfen*, Cologne: Deutsches Institut für angewandte Pflegeforschung, accessed at http://www.dip.de/fileadmin/data/pdf/material/bericht_haushaltshilfen.pdf.

Pace, C., S. Vella and S.F. Dziegielewski (2016), 'Long-term care of older adults in Malta: influencing factors and their social impacts amid the international financial crisis', *Journal of Social Services Research*, **42** (2), 263–79.

Powell, M. (ed.) (2007), *Understanding the Mixed Economy of Welfare*, Bristol: Policy Press.

Rostgaard, T. and M. Szebehely (2012), 'Changing policies, changing patterns of care: Danish and Swedish home care at the crossroads', *European Journal of Ageing*, **9** (2), 101–109.

Salamon, L.M. (1993), 'The marketization of welfare: changing nonprofit and for-profit roles in the American welfare state', *Social Services Review*, **67** (1), 16–39.

Saraceno, C. and W. Keck (2011), 'Towards an integrated approach for the analysis of gender equity in policies supporting paid work and care responsibilities', *Demographic Research*, **25** (11), 371–406.

Semprebon, M. and S. Vicari (2014), 'Innovative housing practices involving immigrant communities: the case of self-building in Italy', paper presented at the COST Action IS1102 Workshop, Faculty of Economics and Business, Barcelona, 3–6 March, now published (2015) in *Journal of Housing and the Built Environment*, Special Issue: Housing and community needs and social innovation responses in times of crisis, **30** (3), 439–55.

Stoy, V. (2014), 'Worlds of welfare services: from discovery to exploration', *Social Policy & Administration*, **48** (3), 343–60.

Vaiou, D. and D. Siatitsa (2013), 'Current organisational framework of elderly care services', *COST Action IS1102 Working Papers*, no. 2, accessed at http://www.cost-is1102-cohesion.unirc.it/docs/working-papers/wg1.greece-care-for-older-people-d.vaiou-and-d.siatitsa.pdf.

Yeandle, S. (2014), 'Reconfiguring services for older people living at home in Leeds, UK: how have services changed?', paper presented at the COST Action IS1102 Workshop, University of Tampere, Tampere, 2–6 June; now published as Yeandle (2016), 'From provider to enabler of care? Reconfiguring local authority support for older people and carers in Leeds, 2008–2013', *Journal of Social Service Research*, **42** (2), 218–32.

Yeandle, S., T. Kröger and B. Cass (2012), 'Voice and choice for users and carers? Developments in patterns of care for older people in Australia, England and Finland', *Journal of European Social Policy*, **22** (4), 432–45.

# 7. The 'activation turn' and the new horizontal division of labour at the local level: the case of social assistance services in Austria, Belgium, Norway and Switzerland

**Peter Raeymaeckers, Bettina Leibetseder, Robert Fluder, Erika Gubrium and Danielle Dierckx**

## INTRODUCTION

In this chapter we focus on social assistance *services*, such as housing, childcare, counselling, food and other types of benefits, that are provided to people receiving a guaranteed subsistence income from the state, defined here as social assistance beneficiaries. These services are delivered by social workers in public agencies, often collaborating with other public and non-profit service providers at the local level. We will specifically address how the 'horizontal division of labour' (Martinelli, Chapter 1, in this volume) among government actors and a variety of social service providers (public, non-profit and for-profit) has been affected by the so-called 'activation turn' (Kazepov, 2010; Raeymaeckers and Dierckx, 2013) in social assistance.

In recent decades, most European countries have made a transition to an 'active' welfare state, whereby social policies are aimed at facilitating the transition of people in poverty to the labour market. This shift is defined as the 'activation turn'. In most European welfare states, this turn has reallocated the tasks of social workers and caseworkers at the local level from supporting the vulnerable target group of social assistance beneficiaries by providing services in different life domains towards supporting labour market activation (Raeymaeckers and Dierckx, 2013). In some countries, such as Switzerland, a trend towards vertical subsidiarity is observed, whereby responsibilities concerning services for and the activation of social assistance beneficiaries are shifted from the state to the local level. Other countries, such as Finland and Norway, show a trend towards an upward re-scaling, whereby specific regulations and responsibilities of local governments and municipalities are taken over by the central state. In all countries, however, even when an upward re-scaling is observed, local actors still exhibit a high level of discretion regarding how and what types of services are delivered (Kazepov, 2010; Sabatinelli and Semprebon, in this volume; Andreotti et al., 2012). In this chapter we analyse the extent to which the freedom local actors experience when providing these services goes hand in hand with horizontal subsidiarisation (Kazepov, 2010; see also Leibetseder et al., in this volume). More specifically, we examine four case studies developed in the context of the COST Action IS1102 *SO.S. COHESION – Social services, welfare states and places*, to document the horizontal division of labour between local government actors and a variety of service organisations (public, non-profit and private) to provide services and activation trajectories in four European cities: Graz in Austria, Antwerp in Belgium, Berne in Switzerland and Oslo in Norway. Our analysis shows that in all cases a horizontal division of labour has emerged between actors involved with the activation of social assistance clients, on the one hand, and a variety of service organisations providing different types of services, on the other hand (housing, food, material aid, counselling, etc.). We hypothesise that this accrued horizontal division of labour results in a selection mechanism we define as 'creaming the crop'. This mechanism appears when local actors favour the 'best' clients, i.e. those who are able to make the transition towards the labour market, over the 'worst' clients, those who are not capable to find a job.

## 1.   SUBSIDIARISATION AND ACTIVATION POLICIES

According to Lorenz (2001), the growing emphasis on activation has had important consequences for social policy and the provision of services in European countries. Some authors even propose that a new welfare state has emerged grounded in the new activation paradigm (Cantillon and Vandenbroucke, 2014). Because of this change, local service providers are increasingly challenged when confronted with the need to activate people falling through the cracks of the labour market.

Two different activation policy approaches can be found in the literature: a narrow, 'disciplining' perspective and a broad, 'emancipatory' perspective (Raeymaeckers and Dierckx, 2013; Mätzke et al., in this volume). When adopting a disciplining approach, access to services is made contingent upon the client's individual motivation and efforts to find a job. Additionally, social assistance beneficiaries are seen as unwilling and/or incapable of work and, as a consequence, their behaviour must be changed through conditionality and stimulus (Wright, 2012). This disciplining perspective stems from the idea that social assistance beneficiaries are themselves responsible for their (un)employment (Dalrymple, 2001). Accordingly, social policies must focus on disciplining beneficiaries instead of supporting them. The right to cash benefits and in-kind services is thus contingent upon the efforts beneficiaries deploy in job seeking.

Other scholars, however, stress the detrimental effects of disciplining strategies (Standing, 1999). A primary argument is that disciplining policies do not take into account the specific needs and contexts of vulnerable groups such as social assistance beneficiaries (Quaid, 2002), who are confronted with significant problems across different life domains, such as lack of access to basic services. Consequently, these beneficiaries need support to meet these different needs *before* they can be activated and do not benefit from disciplining strategies. Scholars critical of disciplining strategies defend a broad and emancipatory conceptualisation of activation. According to this perspective, the transition towards the labour market is not the sole goal: integration into the broader social community is central, ultimately leading to reduced social isolation (Lødemel and Moreira, 2014).

Throughout Europe, local governments have attempted to reconcile these different perspectives and aims through new organisational arrangements, which have changed the horizontal division of labour among different local actors. According to Kazepov (2010), the horizontal dimension of subsidiarisation refers to the multiplication of actors involved in the production and delivery of social services (see also Leibetseder et al., in this volume). This entails the formation of local welfare systems consisting of a mix of formal and informal actors (Andreotti et al., 2012). The new horizontal division of labour involves a mix of local actors that may include state (public institutions), market (for-profit) or non-profit organisations, all of which are involved in the provision of welfare services.

## 2. SOCIAL SERVICES FOR SOCIAL ASSISTANCE BENEFICIARIES AT THE LOCAL LEVEL

The case studies addressed in this chapter – Graz (Austria), Antwerp (Belgium), Berne (Switzerland) and Oslo (Norway) – were assessed on the basis of national policy documents and earlier empirical investigations conducted by the authors in their respective cases (Altreiter and

Leibetseder, 2015; CAP Gubrium, 2013; CAP Gubrium and Øverbye, 2012; Raeymaeckers and Dierckx, 2013; CAP Raeymaeckers and Dierckx, 2012; CAP Leibetseder, 2016; CAP Hauri et al., 2012).

In a comparative perspective, our four case studies are relatively homogeneous (Yin, 2013). In all four countries, social policy was significantly influenced by the activation paradigm. Furthermore, all four countries exhibit high levels of discretion at the local level in the way service delivery and activation trajectories are implemented. We therefore argue that these cases are relevant to understanding the extent to which a specific horizontal division of labour influences the activation trajectories and provision of services to social assistance beneficiaries. In Table 7.1, basic information on the cases is provided.

In the remainder of this section, we first elaborate on how activation policies and the provision of services to social assistance beneficiaries are regulated at the national level, and the extent to which local actors are entrusted with the responsibility of implementing the national regulatory framework. Subsequently, we focus on how service delivery and activation are implemented in the four cities.

### Austria

#### The Austrian regulatory framework
In Austria, the new Needs-Oriented Minimum Income Framework (*Vereinbarung zwischen dem Bund und den Ländern gemäß Art. 15a B-VG über eine bundesweite Bedarfsorientierte Mindestsicherung*) was approved and accepted by all provinces in 2010. This regulatory framework, which was to be adopted and implemented at the provincial level, determined activation trajectories and the provision of social services for social assistance beneficiaries. Within this new framework, the task of the provinces was to ensure that social assistance beneficiaries obtained counselling and support, 'to avoid and overcome situations of social needs'.

An important aspect of the reform is that the local Public Job Centres (*Arbeitsmarktservice*), which are financed by unemployment insurance and the national state and are centrally organised, must focus on the activation trajectories of social assistance beneficiaries and unemployment benefit beneficiaries. They offer job search advice and provide job offers and other job-related programmes and courses (Vereinbarung zur Mindestsicherung, 2010, Article 7). The national government supports the Job Centres with funds to establish specific programmes for the long-term unemployed. Nevertheless, the regulation leaves the implementation of these programmes to provincial agreements between Job Centres and provincial governments. More specifically, the provinces and their respec-

Table 7.1  *The four case studies*

| Case studies | Inhabitants (2014) | Social assistance beneficiaries (2014) | % of social assistance beneficiaries (2014) | Regulatory framework | Local government level | Local actors involved |
|---|---|---|---|---|---|---|
| Graz (Austria) | 269 997 | 8 961 | 3.31 | Needs-Oriented minimum income framework (2010) | Municipality | Municipality, Public Job Centres, non-profit service providers |
| Antwerp (Belgium) | 514 532 | 10 526 | 2.06 | Law on Public Centres for Social Welfare (1976); Law on the right for societal integration | Municipality | Public Centres of Social Welfare |
| Berne (Switzerland) | 1 009 418 | 42 760 | 4.23 | No Federal Law. Only guidelines and criteria for the determination of poor law support | Canton | Cantons and municipalities, non-profit service providers |
| Oslo (Norway) | 647 676 | 19 797 | 3.05 | Act in Social Assistance Services in NAV (2009) | Municipality | Municipal or district 'One-stop shops' |

*Source:*  Authors' compilation.

tive municipalities can decide which services are offered to social assistance beneficiaries (Vereinbarung zur Mindestsicherung, 2010, Article 17). In addition to the Job Centres that provide activation trajectories, the provinces may organise 'low-threshold' services (*niederschwellige*), such as, for example, employment in sheltered work for social assistance beneficiaries (Vereinbarung zur Mindestsicherung, 2010, Article 16). Those services are mostly organised by non-profit organisations and provide an activation trajectory for vulnerable people unable to enter the regular labour market. The Job Centres provide services for target groups who are considered (almost) ready for the regular labour market.

The reform has thus introduced a new vertical and horizontal division of labour in activation. First, the services for beneficiaries are now co-financed by the Job Centres, the province and the municipality. Second, the reform enables a harmonisation of the services provided to social assistance beneficiaries within the province, whereas in the previous regime these varied from one municipality to another. More specifically, the province and the Job Centres have now implemented a province-wide delivery of outsourced activation services. Third, some municipalities have handed over the main responsibility for activation to the local Job Centre. On the other hand, social services for adults with multiple problems still vary within the province and rely on the administrative and financial resources of municipalities.

### Activation and services in Graz

In Graz, the municipality grasped the opportunity offered by the new legislation and transformed its administrative procedures. Now, a service centre provides an initial access point established on the ground floor. New beneficiaries pick a number and receive an invitation to have an initial discussion within half a day. The caseworkers, as trained administrators, are experienced in the financial and legal aspects of the minimum income protection. When caseworkers identify further social problems, they refer the beneficiaries to other services, such as child welfare service or crisis counselling. Their role is limited to screening beneficiaries, assessing eligibility and demanding employable recipients to register at the Job Centre (Altreiter and Leibetseder, 2015).

In the new scheme, the ongoing check of eligibility only requires beneficiaries to attend short meetings every three months. Nevertheless, strict compliance for those classified as employable with the requirements of the Job Centre is enforced. Every morning, the municipal caseworkers monitor their beneficiaries online. They check whether Job Centres have reported any sanctions due to missed appointments or courses or failed attempts to contact potential employers (CAP Leibetseder, 2016).

In Graz, the Job Centre offers activation trajectories, but only for social assistance beneficiaries who are classified as employable. The Job Centre controls the applications and job interviews of beneficiaries and, depending on individual characteristics, offers training and courses or further education. In specific circumstances, beneficiaries who are considered as hardly employable obtain a case manager who places them in step-wise programmes, which are outsourced. These services are mostly delivered by non-profit organisations, which take over the beneficiary when they are referred from the local Job Centre. Services of these non-profit organisations concern social employment or intensive training and job search support to find employment in the regular labour market.

The new framework and the provincial regulation also allow support in different life domains through case management. For the beneficiaries considered as non-employable, however, the municipality of Graz has limited its services to the provision of financial means and some minor services from other departments and non-profit organisations. In contrast, for beneficiaries who are able to enter the labour market, services have been improved and are provided by the Job Centre. We conclude that the discretionary clauses in the new framework and in the provincial legislation have generated a gap between beneficiaries who are not employable and those who are at least classified as somehow employable. The former receive a low level of services while the latter receive a more intensive level of support.

## Belgium

### The national regulatory framework in Belgium

For the Belgian context, we focus on the role and responsibility of the *Openbare Centra voor Maatschappelijk Welzijn* or Public Centres of Social Welfare (PCSWs). The policy context of these centres is shaped by two federal laws, both defining their main tasks: *de Wet op de Openbare Centra voor Maatschappelijk Welzijn* or Law on Public Centres of Social Welfare (1976) and *het Recht op Maatschappelijke Integratie* (Wet van 26 mei 2002) or Law on the Right for Societal Integration (2002).

According to the Law of 1976, the Public Centres of Social Welfare (PCSWs) are responsible for the welfare of their beneficiaries in different life domains, such as housing, financial means, education, childcare, etc. The Law gives PCSWs the responsibility to provide a wide variety of services, including financial aid (social assistance), but also social housing, home care, activation trajectories, support for financial debt, psychosocial support, judicial guidance, and support for participating in cultural activities. The Law of 2002 confirms that PCSWs maintain their responsibility to provide a *Leefloon*, i.e., a guaranteed subsistence income, based on relatively well-defined conditions, such as nationality, age, family situation, residence, willingness to work, and need; however, the PCSWs are also required to 'activate' their beneficiaries towards the labour market.

The centres thus have two main goals. The first goal is to support the well-being of their beneficiaries by providing different types of services in a variety of life domains. The second goal concerns the insertion of beneficiaries into the labour market. In what follows, we elaborate on how the PCSW of Antwerp combines these two tasks in everyday practice, stressing the high level of discretion in the way these tasks are implemented at the local level.

**The case of Antwerp**
In the case of Antwerp, we draw a distinction between the Local Centres (*Sociale Centra*), which operate at the neighbourhood level, and the Activation Department (*Departement Activering*), which operates at the city level, although both are part of the Public Centre of Social Welfare (PCSW) of Antwerp.

In Antwerp, the PCSW consists of 25 Local Centres, each taking care of the residents of their respective neighbourhood. In these centres, the beneficiaries are prepared for an activation trajectory. The municipal Activation Department specialises in activating social assistance beneficiaries and takes over beneficiaries from all Local Centres when they are ready for activation. Below, we provide a more specific outline of the division of labour between the Local Centres and the Activation Department in Antwerp, relying on a study written for the Federal Public Service for Social Integration (Raeymaeckers et al., 2009) and other research we conducted for the PCSW of Antwerp (Raeymaeckers and Vranken, 2009; Raeymaeckers and Dierckx, 2013; CAP Raeymaeckers and Dierckx, 2012).

We will stress that the PCSW of Antwerp organises a trajectory that can best be described as a succession of steps. In this 'staircase' model, the activation process starts with a broad perspective on the general welfare of the beneficiary. Only when 'all problems are solved' is the beneficiary considered ready to start the activation trajectory.

The first step is defined as 'working on preconditions', i.e., eliminating obstacles that prevent the client from entering the actual activation trajectory (as yet). One of the most common obstacles is housing (Raeymaeckers and Dierckx, 2013). Other problems such as childcare, educational needs, problems related to addiction, insufficient knowledge of the Dutch language and physical or psychological problems also appear. In Antwerp, this stage is the main responsibility of the Local Centres at the neighbourhood level. The social workers in these centres provide the necessary services or refer beneficiaries to other specialised providers of services, such as childcare, in-kind material aid (food, clothing), housing services or other service agencies in different life domains. These agencies are both public and non-profit service providers.

The second step concerns the start of the actual activation route, after the main obstacles have been removed. The screening phase is still carried out at the Local Centre. When collecting information on the beneficiary, attention is given to his or her labour market history and to the problems he or she experiences when looking for a job. In some cases, beneficiaries are sent to training courses to learn how to do job interviews and write a résumé. The tasks of the counsellor at this stage are very diverse. They must have knowledge of screening, guidance on and away from the shop floor, they must network with external organisations and they must keep up to date on activation measures. After this stage, the counsellor of the Local Centre can start the beneficiary on a social activation trajectory or a professional trajectory. Both of these further stages are organised by the Activation Department of the PCSW in Antwerp.

Step three can be defined as a social activation process and is organised for beneficiaries who experience difficulties finding a job on the regular labour market. Social activation can be either a step towards full employment or an end point. This means that beneficiaries in this group are engaged in a useful activity, in an easily accessible and protected work environment (employment care). They are not pressured to find employment in the social or regular circuit.

Step four, the professional trajectory, is a step closer to employment in the regular labour market. The PCSW provides time-limited (one year) work experience by allowing social assistance beneficiaries to work in employment settings where there is still some guidance. Three months before the end of this form of employment the counsellors of the Activation Department organise job interview training to prepare their beneficiaries for employment in the regular labour market. At the end of the professional trajectory, beneficiaries are sent to the local Job Centres or *Vlaamse Dienst voor Arbeidsbemiddeling*. These Job Centres are publicly funded agencies, regulated at the level of the Flemish Government, that guide the beneficiaries in finding a job on the regular job market.

According to the Belgian regulatory framework, thus, the goals of the PCSWs are twofold: on the one hand, they seek to enhance the well-being of vulnerable target groups; on the other, they seek to enhance their position in the regular labour market. However, our analysis shows that in Antwerp the goal of activation has become prominent. To enhance the welfare of vulnerable target groups is considered important, but only in order to complete the activation of social assistance clients. Clients make progress on the staircase model when they are capable of finding and maintaining a job on the regular labour market. To meet this goal, the collaboration between the different non-profit and public actors is crucial. As the target group of the PCSWs is affected by needs that decrease their chances of finding a job in the regular labour market, social workers find it important to collaborate with a variety of non-profit service agencies that are able to face the many problems of their clients. Moreover, our analysis shows that collaboration with the specialised job centres is key to completing the activation trajectory.

## Norway

### The Norwegian regulatory framework
In Norway, municipalities have been responsible for social assistance and attached services since before the 1845 Poor Law (Vabo and Øverbye, 2009). The 1992 *Kommuneloven* or Local Government Act provided local governments with the power to decide how services should be provided, i.e., whether publicly or through outsourcing to for-profit or non-profit organisations.

In a trend toward re-centralisation, however, in 2006 the management of social assistance was merged with the national unemployment (*Aetat*) and social insurance (*Trygdeetaten*) agencies (the so-called 'NAV Reform'), creating a new agency – the *Ny arbeids- og velferdsforvaltning* (NAV) or New Labour and Welfare Administration – with NAV One-Stop Offices located in municipalities for service provision. Local governments were required to make formal cooperation agreements concerning the division of labour for the provision of municipal social assistance and social services. At a minimum, the administration of NAV benefits and services were to be physically located in the same building(s) as the local administration of social assistance cash benefits. With this co-location, the administration of social assistance was, in effect, increasingly centralised, in contrast to prior arrangements. The unification of service provision into a one-stop shop opened the possibility for broader programmatic offerings to eligible social assistance clients. There was less emphasis on traditional social work and more emphasis on the sorts of employment services formerly provided only at the national level (by *Aetat*). State-level workers and leaders formerly housed within the national unemployment agency were merged into offices with local social assistance providers, and the strategies implemented were heavily influenced by a state-level ethos focused on the needs and labour market realities of the 'regular' unemployed. The move created new arenas for the sanctioning of those social assistance clients unwilling or unable to partake in such work-oriented activities (Gubrium and Lødemel, 2014).

The late 2000s saw further re-centralisation. Building on the foundation laid by the NAV reform and with a heightened state employment agency ethos (Gubrium et al., 2014), the 2007 revision of the 1991 Law on social services – the *Sosialtjenesteloven* or Social Services Act – introduced a semi-compulsory work-directed programme, the *Kvalifiseringsprogrammet* or Qualification Programme. The target group was individuals of working age with reduced working capacity. Emphasis was on preparation for the labour market and participants were to receive a nationally set cash benefit, which was higher than the average social assistance. The programme was nationally managed, with local social service agencies responsible for the provision of services. While the state was initially to provide extra financial support to cover such additional expenditures at the local level, no earmarked grants are available for the Qualification Programmes and local authorities were forced to finance social assistance from their own tax revenues, block grants or other general transfers from the national government (Gubrium et al., 2014).

The 2009 Act on Social Assistance Services in NAV (*Lov om sosiale tjenester i arbeids- og velferdsforvaltningen*: LOV-2009-12-18 No. 131, 2009) further centralised services. Cash benefits and the work-oriented Qualification Programme were administratively separated from social care services (e.g., help in case of crises, family counselling, drug abuse, centres for battered women, re-establishment centres, temporary/emergency housing), which had a strong local service tradition. This new arrangement reflected the strong work-oriented ethos driving the new NAV administration. The Act also introduced the possibility for the county governor to review the social assistance services and new requirements for municipalities to carry out internal controls on service provision.

Yet the story is mixed: while there has been increased state intervention in social assistance through the administrative presence of NAV, the moves can also be interpreted as vertical subsidiarisation, in the sense that labour activation strategies that were formerly the exclusive responsibility of the state have been moved into local social assistance service agencies. This shift is in line with broader changes in the Norwegian organisation of social services and in the direction of administrative devolution, such as in the domain of health and care services (the 2011 'Coordination Reform').

To summarise, while in Norway responsibility for social assistance (or poor relief) services had traditionally been the responsibility of municipalities, recent changes highlight increased state governance and a heightened state employment ethos. On the other hand, within social services at large, shifts have occurred away from the county level, primarily to the municipal level, with the introduction of new tasks such as labour activation programming (in the case of the Qualification Programme), formerly the domain of national agencies. The incentive strategy providing the premise for the Qualification Programme was based on the idea that it would serve as a motivation to move users into work. Yet the strategy did not fit the realities of much of the social assistance target group. Changes to the financing structure have placed further pressure on programme providers to produce 'good outcomes' in the form of moving clients into the labour market. This has resulted in stricter eligibility requirements for the programme across Norway, indicating that the incentive 'to cream' has increased (Herud and Ohrem Naper, 2012; Gubrium et al., 2014).

### Activation at the local level in Oslo

As stressed above, Norwegian social assistance cash benefits and services have long been the responsibility of local governments. In urban areas such as Oslo, the 'local' is below the municipal, i.e. at the level of the 15 Oslo districts. Each is considered an administrative unit, with its own elected district council and responsibility for service provision to residents (Oslo Municipality, 2016). In an international comparison, Norway is near the top of the list in terms of economic equality and near the bottom in terms of poverty level. However, within Norway itself, the Oslo region has the highest level of poverty (15.5 per cent, according to the 60 per cent threshold conventionally used as the indicator of those at risk of poverty in the EU) and the highest level of wage inequality. Oslo comprises district areas with relatively high levels of child poverty and large immigrant populations facing chronic unemployment (Langeland et al., 2016). Across Norway, however, a wide discretionary berth is reflected in significant geographical differences in the level of cash benefits and services allocated to beneficiaries of social assistance. This is also the case across the various Oslo districts.

Oslo's socioeconomic realities are not necessarily matched by more generous social assistance allocations. Districts are free to determine the benefit amount as well as the provision of other forms of support, including housing or electricity. Payments depend upon the generosity, priorities and financial resources of the particular local authority (Terum and With, 2007). The national government issues recommended but non-binding 'guidelines' for the award of cash support, including suggested expenditures based on current, daily costs (NMHSA, 2001). Local authorities may decide to adopt an internal organisation of social assistance provision and related services provided within the local NAV One-Stop Offices, to provide a specialised social assistance office, or to provide social assistance in tandem with other forms of cash transfers and services.

Moreover, the local 'street level bureaucrat' (employed by the municipality), the person usually sitting face to face with the claimant, is the actual deliverer of social assistance. The law specifies that he/she should use his/her 'professional best judgement' both to decide if a claimant should receive a benefit, and how much the claimant should receive, subject to a household means test. However, there are no specified national protocols for conducting the test. The local authorities may or may not issue local guidelines for the caseworker to follow. It is thus up to the professional discretion of the caseworker.

Thus, although the merger of local and state services in a One-Stop Office may represent a form of centralised authority, the decision of whether an individual is eligible for entry to the programme and the types of activation measures and services offered are left to the local level, thereby allowing for great variations according to local (often office level) resources and priorities (Andreassen and Fossestøl, 2011; Ot. prp. nr 70, 2006–2007; Schafft and Spjelkavik, 2011).

The degree of horizontal subsidiarity, i.e., the 'mix' of service providers, has also become more territorially diverse (CAP Gubrium and Øverbye 2012). Since 1992, local governments have had the freedom to choose organisational solutions for their various activities, and recent years have seen a rise in the external provision of activation services. Within the context of the Qualification Programme, the use of private providers has been a strategy employed by many of Oslo's larger NAV offices, as they must manage the expanded set of duties accompanying the programme's new provisions (NAV Directorate, 2011; Norwegian Board of Health Supervision, 2011). There has also been a push toward increased horizontal diversity with a 2004 amendment to the Social Services Act and the more recent Social Assistance Act within NAV (Ot. prp. nr 103, 2008–2009). These acts specify that the social policy department in the municipality should cooperate with other relevant agencies (voluntary organisations, health service providers, the local branch of the national employment directorate, etc.) when setting up and executing individual plans, introducing elements of 'network-management' (by national dictate) at the local level. Again, however, the level of cooperation established with relevant agencies is left to the professional discretion of caseworkers.

In conclusion, despite a re-centralisation trend, especially with regard to activation, there is still a significant degree of discretion in programme eligibility and services at the local level, and a heightened work-orientation further enhances the tendency towards a discretion that values work ability over need.

## Switzerland

### The national regulatory framework in Switzerland

In Switzerland, regional authorities have great freedom of action and financial autonomy in the implementation of social assistance schemes (Fluder and Stremlow, 1999). For social security, i.e., the compulsory insurance system related to employment, the legislation and the supervision lie at the federal state level, but for social assistance, i.e., supporting vulnerable people in different life domains, the power of legislation is in the hands of the regional governments (i.e., the 26 Swiss cantons). There is no federal law for social assistance. To fill this regulation gap, the *Schweizerische Konferenz für Sozialhilfe* or Swiss Conference on Social Welfare (SCSW) drew up Guidelines and Rates for the Determination of Poor Law Support (*Richtlinien für die Ausgestaltung und Bemessung der Sozialhilfe*), which are recommendations to the cantons and municipalities. Today all cantons refer to these guidelines when determining public welfare measures (Hänzi, 2011).

With the economic and social changes beginning in the 1990s, unemployment in Switzerland has increased rapidly, new social risks have emerged and, consequently, the number of beneficiaries of unemployment and invalidity benefits, as well as social assistance benefits, has increased significantly. In this context, the concept that financial support for these beneficiaries needed to become conditional, meaning that the beneficiary had to do something in return – the so-called 'activation turn' – became the dominant guiding idea of the relationship between beneficiaries and the state (CAP Hauri and Fluder, 2012). This concept was introduced as early as the new Guidelines of 1998, and with the revision of the Guidelines in 2005, the promotion of social integration and vocational training was embedded in a system of bonuses and penalties (Knöpfel, 2006). If beneficiaries refused to cooperate, to participate in these integration programmes or to accept the offer of a suitable job, the social worker could reduce or even cancel the benefits. At the same time, the amount of the basic cash benefit was reduced and a supplement for working beneficiaries (*Einkommensfreibetrag/Integrationszulage* or allowance for working) was introduced to eliminate negative incentives for finding employment and to reward efforts at integration.

While the Regional Service Centres (*Regionale Arbeitsvermittlungszentren*) managed unemployment benefits and services, cantons and municipalities had to activate social assistance and provide services to people who were not or no longer eligible for unemployment benefits. These services include employment offers and offers for professional reintegration, as well as support for social integration, e.g., for stabilising the life situation or overcoming isolation.

**The case of Berne**

In Berne, the canton is responsible for the provision of social integration services and programmes (*Sozialhilfegesetz des Kantons Bern vom 11. Juni 2001* or Welfare Act of the Canton of Berne 2001). With the changing priority towards an activation policy, a shift in responsibility from the municipal to the cantonal level was observed. The canton has taken over the steering of the social integration services by building a cantonal network of employment providers and social integration schemes (*Beschäftigungs- und Integrationsangebote der Sozialhilfe* or BIAS) (Office des affaires sociales, 2015). To this purpose, the canton was divided into ten zones. A strategic partner is responsible for each zone (four of these are public agencies, i.e., in bigger municipalities, and six are private organisations). With each of these partners, the canton has service agreements that regulate the planned provision, the quantity and the financing. The supply is organised by a public or private funding body. The strategic partners are responsible for the cooperation of all concerned parties (municipalities, social service agencies, providers of integration programmes, job networks, enterprises). Five types of measures are relevant: job programmes, qualification programmes, specific offers for young adults, job networks, and long-term training programmes (Neuenschwander and Winkelmann, 2011).

In addition to the services of the BIAS Network, the Regional Employment Centres and the Offer for School Leavers (*Motivationssemester, Brückenangebote und Berufsberatung*) are the most important services in the Berne Canton (Hauri and Zürcher, 2015, p. 18). There are also services in the area of health, professional and financial counselling. In recent years, the supply of services has significantly increased. Only a small part of the BIAS provisions is oriented towards direct job achievement, as reintegration in the labour market is often not a realistic objective and beneficiaries must first regain their employability. For most beneficiaries, the priority is the stabilisation of their life situation and social integration. The low proportion of employable beneficiaries is caused, among other reasons, by the relatively long duration of the unemployment insurance scheme, which covers approximately two years.

In what concerns activation policy, the cantons set up a multitude of specialised offers that support work integration. Only a relatively small number of beneficiaries have access to these services, however, and most of them focus more on the broader perspective of social integration rather than professional integration. The failed chance for reintegration in the labour market, the lack of suitable offers and the high cost are the main factors for the restricted entitlement for integration measurements. Because the beneficiaries in social assistance are often outside the labour market for a long time, the number of employable beneficiaries is relatively low. For employable beneficiaries there exists a great deal of pressure to re-enter the labour market, i.e., to search for a job and participate in work integration programmes. If they do not cooperate they can be sanctioned, but this enforcement is often dependent on the discretion of social workers. For this target group, social assistance cooperates with the Regional Employment Centres (RAV) of the unemployment administration, and some of these beneficiaries are also entitled to attend the programmes of the RAV. For all others, there are low threshold services (*niederschwellige Angebote*; e.g., employment in sheltered work places), but only a few of them participate in such support programmes (Salzgeber, 2012).

## 3.   CONCLUSIONS

In this chapter we examined the horizontal division of labour that has emerged among a variety of local actors (public, non-profit and for-profit) under the influence of the 'activation turn' in social policy in four European countries and cities: Austria (Graz), Belgium (Antwerp), Switzerland (Berne) and Norway (Oslo). In all four cases, local governments at the level of the municipality (or the canton) have a significant degree of freedom or discretionary power as to how they combine their activation tasks with the provision of both cash transfers and services to social assistance beneficiaries. With the rise of the active welfare state and the introduction of activation policies at the national level, local governments in Graz, Antwerp, Oslo and Berne are confronted with the tension between the task of labour activation and the task of providing social services to social assistance beneficiaries to address their myriad problems in different life domains. In the context of our theoretical framework, we argue that local actors are struggling with the tension between the narrow – 'disciplining' – perspective on activation, in which reinsertion into the regular labour market is central, and the broader – 'emancipatory' – perspective, in which supporting social assistance beneficiaries via the provision of services that address their needs within different life domains is considered crucial.

To understand how local governments address this tension, assessing the horizontal division of labour and the collaboration among local providers becomes important. In all four cases, the horizontal division of labour between a variety of local service agencies proves crucial in ensuring the delivery of services to support social assistance beneficiaries and to organise activation trajectories. In all four cases, local actors experience some level of discretionary power to develop collaborative structures among a variety of job centres and service delivery agencies in the four cities. In Austria, there is collaboration between the Job Centres and the municipalities organising counselling and referral to specialised service agencies. While Job Centres have the main responsibility for supporting activation trajectories for social assistance beneficiaries, provinces and municipalities provide case management for beneficiaries who are not yet employable. In Belgium, the Public Centres of Social Welfare provide support to beneficiaries and organise activation trajectories. When beneficiaries are considered 'ready for labour', they are sent to the Job Centres, which take care of the transition into the labour market. For the beneficiaries requiring additional support for specific needs, social workers collaborate with other specialised service agencies. In Norway, One-Stop Offices are the key actors. Although intensive activation strategies have been introduced at the national level, state and local services have been co-located with these locally managed offices. Social service provision to social assistance beneficiaries thus remains a matter of municipal/district discretion and the scope and aim of activation measures varies widely between local offices. A trend towards networking is observed, but it is dependent on social workers' discretion. In Switzerland, most cantons such as Berne have developed a network of service providers, most of them giving support for integration, and partly also providing counselling in cases of debt and/or in the area of health.

An important question concerns the consequences of this horizontal division of labour at the beneficiary level. The hypothesis we put forward here is that the division of tasks in the field of activation policies results in a stratification of the target group – social assistance beneficiaries – according to their capabilities to enter the labour market. Local actors are de facto involved in a process we define as 'creaming the crop', whereby a distinction is made between three types of beneficiaries: the *deserving and strong* beneficiaries who are able to find a job on the labour market, the *vulnerable* beneficiaries, and the *non-deserving* beneficiaries (those valued within the more traditional social service domain).

The deserving and strong beneficiaries have the skills and the right attitude to enter the labour market, and they therefore gain easier access to activation trajectories. Efforts are made to provide the appropriate route and services to move these beneficiaries into the labour market as soon as possible. In most of our cases, these beneficiaries are sent to specialised Job Centres that guide them to the regular labour market.

The more vulnerable beneficiaries, who seem to suffer from different problems in a variety of life domains, are considered unable to hold a job on the regular labour market. These beneficiaries gain access to a range of different services. Our case studies show that for these people, the collaboration among different specialised service agencies becomes important. In Austria, the Job Centres collaborate with a number of not-for profit providers that provide different forms of more or less intensive support for beneficiaries. In Belgium, the PCSWs collaborate with various service agencies. In Norway, networks are established at the level of the NAV One-Stop Offices. In Switzerland, networks are established at the cantonal level.

The undeserving beneficiaries, those unwilling or unable to conduct any effort to find a job, are refused access to new services and support. For these beneficiaries, an administrative structure is being put in place to control and sanction them. In Belgium, the PCSWs are responsible for this task. In Austria, this controlling task is a collaborative action between Job Centres and Provinces. In Norway, the NAV One-Stop Offices are responsible, and in Switzerland, the social service agencies fulfil this role.

In conclusion, our analysis suggests that the turn to activation has heightened tensions at the local level. While the traditional provision of services to beneficiaries of social assistance focused on specific local and individual needs, nationally introduced (and EU prescribed) activation measures have been accompanied by rearranged governance structures, as local authorities feel the pressure of the mandate to move beneficiaries into work. This has resulted in additional tasks for local actors, putting pressure on individualised, tailor-made solutions. These findings would then support the claim put forward by Lødemel and Gubrium (2014) that activation trajectories across Europe have moved in the direction of a disciplining perspective on activation.

We nevertheless acknowledge that our exploratory analysis must be supported by further research. First, the horizontal division of labour in activation trajectories and service delivery should be investigated in other types of welfare states, such as those in Southern and Eastern European countries. Next, we believe that further work should also pay attention to the role and training of individual social workers and the way they use their discretionary power to establish collaboration among service agencies in the field. Finally, further research should be devoted to assessing how stronger central regulation – and financial redistributive support – might ensure a more homogeneous supply of social assistance services.

## REFERENCES

Altreiter, C. and B. Leibetseder (2015), 'Constructing inequality: deserving and undeserving clients in Austrian Social assistance offices', *Journal of Social Policy*, **44** (1), 127–45.

Andreassen, T.A. and K. Fossestøl (2011), *NAV ved et Veiskille* [*NAV at a Crossroads*], Oslo: Gyldendal.

Andreotti, A., E. Mingione and E. Polizzi (2012), 'Local welfare systems: a challenge for social cohesion', *Urban Studies*, **49** (9), 1925–40.

Cantillon, B. and F. Vandenbroucke (2014), *Reconciling Work and Poverty Reduction: How Successful are European Welfare States?*, Oxford: Oxford University Press.

Dalrymple, T. (2001), *Life at the Bottom: The Worldview That Makes the Underclass*, Chicago: Ivan R. Dee.

Fluder, R. and J. Stremlow (1999), *Armut und Bedürftigkeit. Herausforderungen für das Kommunale Sozialwesen* [*Poverty and Vulnerability. Challenges for the Municipal Social Services*], Bern: Haupt.

Gubrium, E. (2013), 'Activation policies in Norway: personal impact of vertical re-organization on social assistance users', unpublished paper presented at the COST Action IS1102 Workshop, Catholic University of Portugal, Porto, 18–21 February.

Gubrium, E. and E. Øverbye (2012), 'Current organisational framework of economic social assistance services – Norway', unpublished paper presented at the COST Action IS1102 Workshop, Rovira i Virgili University, Tarragona, 17–19 October.

Gubrium, E., I. Harsløf and I. Lødemel (2014), 'Norwegian activation reform on a wave of wider welfare state change: a critical assessment', in I. Lødemel and A. Moreira (eds), *Activation or Workfare? Governance and the Neo-Liberal Convergence*, New York: Oxford University Press, pp. 19–46.

Gubrium, E.K. and I. Lødemel (2014), '"Not good enough": social assistance and shaming in Norway', in E. Gubrium, S. Pellissery and I. Lødemel (eds), *The Shame of it: Global Perspectives on Anti-poverty Policies*, Bristol: Policy Press, pp. 85–111.

Hänzi, C. (2011), *Die Richtlinien der Schweizerischen Konferenz für Sozialhilfe. Entwicklung, Bedeutung und Umsetzung der Richtlinien in den deutschsprachigen Kantonen der Schweiz* [*The Guidelines of the Swiss Conference for Social Welfare. Development, Importance and Implementation of the Guidelines in the German-speaking Cantons of Switzerland*], Basel: Helbing Lichtenhahn.

Hauri, R. and P. Zürcher (2015), *Kooperationsformen im Bereich der Sozialen Grundversorgung. Schlussbericht* [*Forms of Cooperation in the Field of Social Basic Services. Final Report*], Bern: BFH.

Hauri, R., R. Fluder and R. Ruder (2012), 'Current organisational framework of social assistance services – Switzerland, Canton of Bern', unpublished paper presented at the COST Action IS1102 Workshop, Rovira i Virgili University, Tarragona, 17–19 October.

Herud, E. and S. Ohrem Naper (2012), 'Fattigdom og levekår i Norge: Status 2012 (Report 1)' ['Poverty and living conditions in Norway: status of 2012 (Report 1)'], Oslo: NAV Directorate.

Kazepov, Y. (2010), 'Rescaling social policies towards multilevel governance in Europe: some reflections on processes at stake and actors involved', in Y. Kazepov (ed.), *Rescaling Social Policies: Towards Multilevel Governance in Europe*, London: Ashgate, pp. 35–72.

Knöpfel, C. (2006), 'Sozialhilfe – grundsicherung – grundeinkommen in der Schweiz. Neue richtlinien – und ein systemwechsel' ['Social assistance – basic security – basic income in Switzerland. New guidelines – and a change in the system'], in E. Carigiet, U. Mäder, M. Opielka and F. Schultz-Nieswandt (eds), *Wohlstand durch Gerechtigkeit: Deutschland und die Schweiz im sozialpolitischen vergleich* [*Prosperity Through Righteousness: A Comparison Between Germany and Switzerland*], Zurich: Rotpunktverlag, pp. 159–69.

Langeland, S., T. Dokken and A. Barstad (2016), *Fattigdom og Levekår i Norge* [*Poverty and Living Conditions in Norway*], NAV report 2016: 1, Oslo: Arbeids- og velferdsdirektoratet.

Leibetseder, B (2016), 'The restructuring of social assistance services in Austria. A case study in 35 municipalities of Styria and Upper Austria', COST Action IS1102 Working Papers, no. 11, accessed at http://www.cost-is1102-cohesion.unirc.it/docs/ working-papers/wg2.austria-styria-and-upper-social-assistance-b.leibetseder.pdf.

Lødemel, I. and E. Gubrium (2014), 'Trajectories of change: activation reforms from inception to times of austerity', in I. Lødemel and A. Moreira (eds), *Activation or Workfare? Governance and the Neo-Liberal Convergence*, New York: Oxford University Press, pp. 327–48.

Lødemel, I and A. Moreira (2014), *Activation or Workfare? Governance and the Neo-Liberal Convergence*, New York: Oxford University Press.

Lorenz, W. (2001), 'Social work responses to "new labour" in Continental European countries', *British Journal of Social Work*, 31 (4), 595–609.

LOV-2009-12-18 no. 131 (2009), *Lov om sosiale tjenester i arbeids- og velferdsforvaltningen, Kapittel 4, Individuelle tjenester* [*Social Services Law in the Labour and Welfare Management Agency (NAV), Chapter 4 Individual Services*], Oslo: Arbeids- og sosialdepartementet.

NAV Directorate (2011), *Sluttrapport: Implementering av kvalifiseringsprogrammet 2007–2010* [*Final Report: Implementation of the Qualification Programme*], 11 February, Oslo: Arbeids- og velferdsdiektoratet.

Neuenschwander, P. and A. Winkelmann (2011), *Arbeitsintegration in der Sozialhilfe. Bestandesaufnahme von Angeboten der beruflichen und sozialen Integration* [*Labor Integration of Social Assistance. Inventory of Offers of Professional and Social Integration*], Bern: BFH.

NMHSA – Norwegian Ministry of Health and Social Affairs (2001), *Statlige Veiledende Retningslinjer for Utmåling av Stønad til Livsopphold etter Sosialtjenestelovens § 5-1* [*Guidelines from the State regarding Level of Financial Assistance Norwegian Ministry of Health and Social Affairs*] Circular (I-13/2001), Oslo: Arbeids- og sosialdepartementet.

Norwegian Board of Health Supervision (2011), *Kommuner bryter loven ved henvendelser om økonomisk stønad* [*Municipalities Break the Law Concerning Social Support Inquiries*] (Report 4/2011), Oslo.

Office des affaires sociales (2015), *Auswertungen und Ergebnisse des Reportings 2014* [*Employment and Integration Programmes of Social Assistance. Evaluations and Results of the Reporting 2014*], Bern: Gesundheits und Fürsorgedirektion des Kantons Bern.

Oslo Municipality (2016), *Geographical Sections*, accessed at https://www.oslo. kommune.no/politikk-og-administrasjon/statistikk/geografiske-inndelinger/.

Ot. prp. nr 70 (2006–2007), *Om lov om endringer i sosialtjenesteloven og i enkelte andre lover* [*Concerning the Act on Changes to the Social Welfare Services Law and Individual Other Acts*], Oslo: Norwegian Ministry of Labour and Inclusion.

Ot. prp. nr 103 (2008–2009), *Om lov om sosiale tjenester i arbeids- og velferdsforvaltningen* [*Concerning the Act on Changes to the Social Welfare Services Law and Individual Other Acts*], Oslo: Norwegian Ministry of Labour and Inclusion.

Quaid, M. (2002), *Workfare: Why Good Social Policy Ideas go Bad*, Toronto: University of Toronto Press.

Raeymaeckers, P. and D. Dierckx (2012), 'Current organisational framework of social services to social assistance clients – Belgium, Flanders', unpublished paper presented at the COST Action IS1102 Workshop, Rovira i Virgili University, Tarragona, 17–19 October.

Raeymaeckers, P. and D. Dierckx (2013), 'To work or not to work? The role of the organisational context for social workers' perceptions on activation', *British Journal of Social Work*, **43** (6), 1170–89.

Raeymaeckers, P. and J. Vranken (2009), *Hulpverleners over 'A'ctivering: de rol van organisatie en buurt bij de hulpverlening in het Antwerpse OCMW* [*Social Workers about Activation: the Role of Organisation and Neighbourhood for Service Delivery in the Antwerp PCSW*], Leuven: Acco.

Raeymaeckers, P., L. Nisen, D. Dierckx, J. Vranken and M.-T. Casman (2009), *Activering binnen de Belgische OCMW's: op Zoek naar Duurzame Trajecten en Goede Praktijken* [*Activation in the Belgian PCSW's: In Search of Durable Trajectories and Good Practices*], Brussels: POD Maatschappelijke Integratie.

Salzgeber, R. (2012), *Kennzahlen zur Sozialhilfe in Schweizer Städten, Berichtsjahr 2012, 13 Städte im Vergleich* [*Indicators on Social Services in Suisse States: Year 2012*], Bern: BFH.

Schafft, A. and Ø. Spjelkavik (2011), *Evaluering av Kvalifiseringsprogrammet: Sluttrapport* [*Evaluation of Qualification Programme: Final Report*], WRI Report Series: 4, Oslo: Work Research Institute.

Standing, G. (1999), *Global Labour Flexibility: Seeking Distributive Justice*, London: Palgrave Macmillan.

Terum, L. and M.-L. With (2007), *Klager på Økonomisk Stønad* [*Complaints about Financial Support*], Report for the Norwegian Health Authority, 6/2007, Oslo: Norwegian Health Authority.

Vabo, S.I. and E. Øverbye (2009), *Decentralisation and Privatisation in the Norwegian Welfare State since 1980. HIO-Report, No. 3*, Oslo: Oslo University College.

Vereinbarung zur Mindestsicherung (2010), 'Vereinbarung zwischen dem Bund und den Ländern gemäß Art. 15a B-VG über eine bundesweite Bedarfsorientierte Mindestsicherung' ['Agreement between the federal and state governments in accordance with Art. 15a of a nationwide social minimum'], accessed 12 September 2016 at https://www.ris.bka.gv.at/GeltendeFassung.wxe?Abfrage=Bundesnormen&Gesetzesnummer=20006994.

Wet van 26 mei 2002 (2002), 'Wet betreffende het recht op maatschappelijke integratie' ['Law of 26th May 2002 concerning the right on societal integration'], accessed 12 September 2016 at http://www.ejustice.just.fgov.be/cgi_loi/change_lg.pl?language=nl&la=N&cn=2002052647&table_name=wet.

Wright, S. (2012), 'Welfare-to-work, agency and personal responsibility', *Journal of Social Policy*, **41** (2), 309–28.

Yin, R. (2013), *Case Study Research: Design and Methods*, London: Sage Publications.

# 8. Care in the wake of the financial crisis: gender implications in Spain and the United Kingdom

**Blanca Deusdad, Jana Javornik, Rosa Mas Giralt and Raquel Marbán-Flores**

## INTRODUCTION

Focusing on national provisions on care in Spain and the UK, this chapter explores government intervention and trajectories of policy change between 2008 and 2015, based on case studies developed in the course of the COST Action IS1102 *SO.S. COHESION – Social services, welfare states and places.* We examine whether and how care infrastructures support female employment and males' involvement in caregiving, considering the intersections of familistic dynamics in economically adverse circumstances from a gender perspective.

The selection of countries allows us to examine a combination of commonalities and differences. The two have very different welfare systems and trajectories, providing distinctive scenarios in which to study those issues. On the one hand, different histories and economies aside, both countries were significantly affected by the global financial crisis in 2008, during which they introduced austerity programmes and deficit management plans. The effects have been deeper in Spain, which continues to experience high rates of unemployment and slow economic recovery (Lin et al., 2013). By contrast, the UK returned to its pre-crisis economic levels by the second quarter of 2014 (O'Connor, 2015). On the other hand, the combination of changes introduced in parental leave and care systems provides a trajectory of significant interest for gender equality. While both countries show significant policy transformation in parental leave schemes to challenge gendered parenting, they vary in the amount of policy change introduced to provisions of care for children and older people. In Spain the long-term care system saw a significant overhaul, whereas in the UK gradual changes in this area have been taking place since the 1990s due to the political weight and lobbying influence of carers' organisations (e.g. Yeandle et al., 2012).

In both countries government interventions show a trajectory towards more state support for care policies. However, austerity measures in response to the financial crisis have led to budget cuts, which negatively affect financing of policies and potentially widen inequalities in access. Such mixed dynamics in the care sector disrupt progress towards gender equality in practice, which negatively affects women's opportunity to continuously engage in the labour market and compete with men for the best paying jobs, and men's to actively engage in family care. With policies on care being central to the current reforms and transformation of the welfare states, policy programming around parental leave (used hereafter as an umbrella term for different types of child-related rights), childcare and care for older people is emblematic of interventions that cut across domains such as employment, children and care, gender and income.

Against this background, this chapter analyses policy change and the multilevel dynamics that shape policy provisions in these two European countries, to examine whether and how public support differently shapes women's and men's opportunities after they become parents. We argue that public policy provisions have gendered opportunity ramifications. Whilst care is a universal human need, it is embedded in the culture of social obligation that women are the primary carers (e.g. Anttonen and Zechner, 2011).

Comparative welfare state research highlights that welfare states differ in the extent to which they consider women's uneven capability to invest in paid employment and the family (e.g. Korpi, 2000; Leitner, 2003). Governments choose combinations of policy instruments, that is the services, the money to purchase services and/or familial care (Korpi, 2000), and these vary across countries. These choices represent the framework within which people and companies operate, making it easier/harder to be a carer in some countries than others. Public services are a necessary precondition for freeing women's time to participate in the labour market; if women remain locked into familial care obligations, they forgo an important source of (independent) income and self-realisation (Esping-Andersen, 2009, p. 80). When both services and cash benefits are low, women's opportunities depend on their households' resources, namely access to the market, which exacerbates socioeconomic inequalities with gendered consequences. This opens up both the conceptual and analytical space for comparative analysis of recent policy developments. Using Javornik's (2014) analytical approach to comparative policy analysis we conceptualise these as publicly provided opportunity structures for carers, creating and constraining their possibilities to work and care. We focus on parental leave, childcare and care for older people as specific public policy instruments whose designs express multiple interpretations of gendered opportunities.

The chapter starts with a theoretical discussion to set the conceptual framework of the analysis. To identify and understand connections between current politics and policy developments, the next two sections flesh out 'the environment at the [austerity] time' (Page, 2006, p. 92) in Spain and the UK. They present accounts of policy dynamics related to the economic difficulties between 2008 and 2015 through national policy trajectories. We conclude with a discussion of the insights learnt from these cases in relation to gender equality.

## 1.  THEORETICAL PERSPECTIVES

Care has long been a 'woman-specific concept' (Daly and Lewis, 2000, p. 283). It has been firmly established in welfare state research that normative assumptions about gender roles underpin policies on care (Thane, 1991, p. 93); these may reinforce or challenge the conventional gender roles, both in terms of women's employment opportunities and men's involvement in care (e.g. Gornick and Meyers, 2003). As Wilson (1977, p. 9) reiterates, the welfare state is 'not just a set of services; it is also a set of ideas about society, about the family and – not least importantly, about women who have a centrally important role within the family, as its linchpin'.

Access to paid employment has conspicuous economic, political, cultural and social implications, for both personal autonomy and gender equality. However, women's access to independent income remains largely structured by widespread gendered division of caring, whereby women still bear the brunt of responsibility for care (Kröger and Yeandle, 2013). A growing body of comparative research on female employment has found that female employment rates generally drop subsequent to childbirth and that, in general, women who provide care are economically disadvantaged across countries (e.g. Gupta and Smith, 2001). The proportion of women withdrawing from paid employment and the size of their disadvantage over the life course, however, vary significantly across welfare states.

Public policies may either bolster or undermine women's early and continuous attachment to waged labour and men's active care, thus shaping carers' prospects for (adequate) income during their working lives and into retirement (Thane, 1991). Orloff (1993, pp. 303–4) argues that 'the character of public social provision affects women's material situations, shapes gender relationships, structures political conflict and participation, and contributes to the formation and mobilisation of specific identities and interests.'

Nevertheless, welfare states differ in the extent to which they acknowledge the uneven capacity of primary carers (i.e. women) to invest in paid employment: whilst most assume that men and women equally need to earn for their own security, they do not necessarily assume equal care responsibilities (Pascall and Lewis, 2004, p. 391). States can provide a mix of policies coming from various public policy institutions, including time off from work (leave), the money for familial care, the services, and the money to purchase services (Korpi, 2000). Each represents different policy combinations, which differently constrain carers' choices, exacerbating socioeconomic and gender inequalities (e.g. Javornik, 2014).

To illustrate, parental leave may come with penalties, including discriminatory treatment in pay and promotion. Thus, for some, taking leave could be an option to fall back on instead of a first choice, especially when childcare services are limited (Javornik, 2014). Alternatively, welfare states may use leave policies to challenge the normative parenthood ideals (e.g. Leitner, 2003). Likewise, in the area of care for older people, cash transfers and allowances for family care may reinforce gendered roles. Women may prefer staying at home and this becomes the best option due to a lack of public funding for fostering entrance into the labour market. This suggests that government initiatives may transform gendered roles, which Javornik (2014) calls 'policy transformative potential', referring to the extent to which the state supports female employment over the life course and male involvement in care.

Using the gendered-magnifying glass, comparative welfare state research has developed conceptual and analytical tools to investigate how welfare states vary in the extent to which they reinforce or challenge gendered care (e.g. Leitner, 2003). They show that policies that regulate family responsibilities in care influence the choices and possibilities of women between work and care, and may have familistic or de-familistic effects (e.g. Leitner, 2003; Saraceno and Keck, 2011). Familistic welfare states promote and rely on family care, either explicitly (by financially investing in family care) or implicitly (by withdrawing any support to carers). By contrast, de-familistic policies facilitate carers' labour force participation and challenge gender-specific care, via public services, either the state or the market.

Leitner (2003) and Javornik (2014) show how each welfare state combines elements of both familialism and de-familialism, whereby familistic policies too could challenge gender roles when providing 'incentives to ensure that care provision is shared on equal terms among male and female family members' (Leitner, 2003, p. 367). Alternatively, whilst policies may enhance carers' employment, they could also 'threaten to recreate earlier forms of gender inequality in a new form' (Mandel and Semyonov, 2005, p. 951). What matters, then, is the overall policy constellation, which signals whether or not the state supports gender equality. From the gender equality perspective, what is particularly relevant is the extent to which policy acknowledges familial care, supports women's continuous employment and men's involvement in care, recognises and rewards care responsibilities and the changes therein. We argue that national statutory entitlements present material opportunities (resources) that shape the boundaries of what is possible and pave the way towards policy uptake. But multiple pressures and hurdles dictate carers' real possibilities to claim their statutory entitlements.

Against this background, we adapt Saraceno and Keck's (2011) and Javornik's (2014) analytical frameworks of de-familialism to evaluate changes in parental leave and services for children and older people in Spain and the UK. These policy areas were chosen because parental leave and childcare services form a 'package' available to parents following childbirth (Javornik, 2010; 2014). As families and populations age, care provisions for older people become relevant; together, then, 'care policies' determine women's and men's opportunities over their lives (Anttonen and Sipilä, 1996).

## 2.  CARE POLICIES, AUSTERITY AND GENDER EQUITY IN SPAIN AND THE UNITED KINGDOM

This section turns to trends in parental leave and care for children and older people in Spain and the UK. As we will show, the two have very different welfare systems and trajectories, demonstrating significant policy transformation in parental leave schemes, but vary significantly in policy provision for children and older people.

### Spain

Spain has been a latecomer to welfare state development and gender equality. Democracy brought about significant changes in women's rights and a new conception of the family and its values, which differed from those during Franco's regime (1939–75). When the social democratic party (PSOE) came to power in 1982, significant progress was achieved with the development and institutionalisation of social services. An important feature of the Spanish structure of social services is its de-centralisation in Autonomous Communities (*Comunidades Autónomas*), which translates into diversity across different parts of the country. There is only one national state law on social and care services, namely the 2006 long-term care law for the promotion of personal autonomy and care for older and disabled people (*Ley 39/2006 de Promoción de la Autonomía Personal y Atención a las personas en situación de dependencia*, hereafter LAPAD).

In terms of gender equality, the most remarkable social policy transformations were introduced during President Zapatero's first term in office (2004–08), a period which saw the increasing influence of Spanish feminist lobbies (Comas d'Argemir, 2015). However, as will be explored below, the progressive policy trajectory initiated in this period was interrupted by the onset of the economic crisis and subsequent austerity measures and changes of government.

Women's caregiving position is closely related to the challenges that Spanish women face in the job market. In 2014, 73.28 per cent of part-time workers were women (UGT, 2015) and 62.5 per cent of women working part-time would have liked to work full-time (INE, 2014). In most cases, it seems, a part-time job is not a choice and women may be 'forced' to provide family care, given the high rates of unemployment and/or a lack of skills to enter/re-enter the job market. In addition, the gender pay gap increased with the recession, moving from 19.3 per cent in 2002 to 20.2 in 2014 (UGT, 2015). These circumstances, along with other impacts of the 2008 economic crisis, have strengthened intergenerational solidarity, including an 'exploitation' of family resources, whereby families increasingly rely on grandparents' pensions (or adult children being forced to move back home) as the only source of income for the whole family (Moreno, 2009; Deusdad et al., 2016).

The following sections will focus on those social policies that have improved gender equality conditions in relation to care in general, paying attention to representative policies in the area of parental leave, childcare and care for older people.

**Parental leave and childcare**
In Spain, it was not until 1986 with the consolidation of democracy that maternity leave was extended up to 16 weeks and paternity leave was recognised. Initially, fathers only had two days of leave after the birth of a child. The Gender Equality Act (*Ley de Igualdad* 35/2007), introduced to address gender discrimination, increased this allowance to fifteen days. In the proposal, paternity leave was to be offered for four weeks, but because of austerity measures this has been postponed until January 2017 (Escobedo et al., 2016). As of 16 December 2016, the government has proposed the reintroduction of the four-week optional paternity leave with a budgeted cost of EUR 400 million for 2017 (*El Economista*, 2016). Furthermore, although there is parental leave, only a few fathers use it (1.7 per cent in 2014; Escobedo et al., 2016). Although they recognise fathers' rights to

care, these provisions do not go far enough in transforming traditional gendered parenting.

Another important achievement promoted by the Gender Equality Act was the 'birth benefit', known as 'baby cheque' (*cheque bebé*), providing an amount of EUR 2500 for every newborn child (initially introduced in 2007). To be eligible, one had to have Spanish nationality or have resided in Spain without interruption during the two previous years. In the case of single mothers, large families (three or more children) or children with disabilities, the cash transfer was EUR 3500. Nevertheless, this benefit was subject to criticism and was considered to be a populist measure. Furthermore, this lump-sum payment did not assist with long-term childcare needs nor could it be guaranteed that it was spent on the children. Eventually, it was abolished (in 2011) as the consequence of austerity cuts.

Parental leave and childcare are national policies, although regional differences exist also in parental leave in terms of benefits (Table 8.1). GDP expenditure for childcare is about 0.6 per cent, with an enrolment rate of 39.3 per cent for children under 3 years of age (above the averages of 29 per cent for the EU-27 and 32.6 per cent for the OECD), whilst the enrolment rate of 3–5-year-olds is 99.3 per cent (OECD, 2016). Such universal coverage has positively affected women's opportunity to participate in paid employment, but the effect was more positive for mothers with higher levels of education (Nollenberger and Rodríguez-Planas, 2011).

Childcare (0–3) is the responsibility of regional departments of education and thus the supply can vary between regions. For example, in the Basque Country, the enrolment rate was 51.3 per cent, in Extremadura 16.8 per cent and in The Canary Islands only 7.9 per cent (Síndic de Greuges, 2015). The average for the whole of Spain was 33.7 per cent, of which 17.2 per cent was public and 16.3 private (Síndic de Greuges, 2015). This proportion differs significantly between regions and municipalities and even between neighbourhoods, which affects inequalities in access. Private provision is higher in regions with more services, except for Murcia, where almost half of the services are private (7.9 per cent) with low enrolment rates (17.2 per cent) (Síndic de Greuges, 2015).

Private services are on average more expensive, which negatively affects service affordability and thus service accessibility. Access to state funding is means-tested and requires co-payments for the services provided, depending on the family's resources. This reinforces family care, largely by grandmothers, who often find themselves sandwiched between caring for grandchildren and their own parents or partners. Insufficient childcare provisions weaken women's position in the labour market, thus widening the gender opportunity gap (World Bank, 2014).

*Table 8.1   Changes in parental leave, Spain*

| Type of leave | 2008–10 | 2011–17 |
|---|---|---|
| Statutory maternity leave | 16 weeks (6 weeks compulsory, following birth). 100% of earnings (with a ceiling). A flat-rate benefit (EUR 532.51 per month or EUR 17.75 per day, for 42 days) to non-eligible employed mothers. | Remains in place. Total earnings to a ceiling of EUR 3606.00 a month in 2015 and EUR 3642.00 in 2016. |
| Statutory paternity leave (father of the child, spouse, partner or civil partner) | 13 days of paternity leave + 2 days of birth leave. 100% of earnings (with a ceiling). Some regions have improved entitlements for public sector employees. | Extension of paternity leave up to four weeks in 2011. Due to austerity measures it was postponed until January 2017. |
| Parental leave | Individual right to 12 weeks but the outstanding four weeks have to be taken by mothers. Each parent is entitled to take leave until three years after childbirth. During the first year, return to the same job position is protected. Seven regional governments have introduced flat-rate benefits: Navarre (2000); Castile and León (2001); Basque Country and Castile-La Mancha (2002); La Rioja (2003); Balearic Islands and Murcia (2008). | Remains in place. Regions in which flat rate payments were abolished: Murcia (2011); Castile and León and Castilla-La Mancha (2012); Navarre (2013). Regions in which flat rate payments remain in place: Basque Country (EUR 271.25 per month in 2016); La Rioja (EUR 250 per month in 2016 to families with an annual income below EUR 40 000). Optional 4 weeks as of 1 January 2017. |

*Source:*   Authors' compilation based on Escobedo et al. (2016).

**Care for older people**

The Spanish long-term care law 39/2006 LAPAD is a key piece of legislation regulating care for older people, but also covering people with disabilities of all ages. It represents a significant improvement in the recognition of care needs and is an important achievement for gender equality (Deusdad, Lev et al., in this volume; Rodríguez-Cabrero and Marban-Gallego, 2013). As families (particularly women) are the main care providers, LAPAD helped to reduce the care burden of women, or, at least, to recognise and make their unpaid care work visible.

LAPAD was supposed to introduce new services (telecare, day centres, residential care and home care), as well as family care allowance (*Prestación económica para cuidados en el entorno familiar*). People applying for this allowance must first have their autonomy assessed. The assessment is first undertaken by a regional agency and then forwarded down to the social workers at the municipal level; these are in charge of implementing an individual care programme (*Pla Individual de Atenció*) for end-users. The way in which LAPAD has been implemented since 2007 has given priority to this allowance for family carers, even though it was initially considered as 'an exceptional measure' (Deusdad et al., 2016).

Social workers prioritise the allowance over other types of support because it is less costly for the administration and more easily accepted by the users. Furthermore, most carers are women in their fifties or sixties, and this allowance has been a source of income and social security contribution, which, in turn, provides the possibility of receiving a pension once they reach retirement age. This allowance has been key to recognising care as paid work, giving an economic value to activities traditionally carried out by women within the family. However, it has also reinforced women's role as family caregivers (Comas d'Argemir, 2015; CAP Deusdad, 2013). Overall, it improved somewhat the situation of women but has not radically transformed it.

The austerity cuts introduced by the Conservative Government since 2011 have further deteriorated gender equality. First, implementation of the allowance for people with the lowest level of autonomy was postponed until 2015; thus, people who were in need of care were left unattended, leaving care to the family, particularly women. Secondly, the maximum amount of monthly allowance for family caregivers has been reduced (from EUR 442.59 to EUR 387.64 after 2012). Thirdly, women who receive care allowance are no longer included in the social security system. Fourthly, the assessment criteria for determining one's level of autonomy have become stricter, as has the means-testing, which in some regions includes end users' property as well as income. Furthermore, the scarcity of resources and low to non-existent income have forced some men to become caregivers. That is, men have been forced by their personal family situation and financial needs to become caregivers and, in turn, to apply for the LAPAD allowance.

Overall, the effects of the austerity measures and policy changes introduced in response to the crisis have brought about important cutbacks in service delivery; this has had a detrimental effect on the rights previously acquired by family caregivers. The implementation of LAPAD brought about a hope of building a more universal welfare system by providing benefits that would meet citizens' care needs. However, in practice there remains a significant gap and unmet care needs of older adults in most of the regions; thus, care remains prevailingly a family responsibility, which most critically affects women.

**The United Kingdom**

This section presents an overview of policy processes between 2008 and 2015, focusing on UK-wide national provisions in parental leave, childcare and care for older people. This period covers two key changes of policy-making context: in 2010, a Conservative-led Coalition Government replaced the Labour Government; and in 2015, a Conservative Government took office. It also marks the launch of an austerity programme, a deficit reduction plan and a process of decentralisation to 'make public services more competitive', with significant local budgets cuts and welfare reforms (Ward, 2013). Our analysis also makes reference to key turning points in the past when a clear path dependency emerges.

In the UK's liberal welfare state, many aspects of work–care organisation are determined by employers. Legislation provides only minimum statutory entitlements, leaving any enhanced occupational packages to employers (for example, top-up payments over and above the statutory entitlements). This means that, in practice, the conditions under which women can access and engage with the labour market, but also men's access to caring over the family's lifecycle, differ between companies and sectors and can either exacerbate or reduce gender inequalities (e.g. Gornick and Meyers, 2003).

Childcare and parental leave are both national policies and apply across the UK as a whole. However, policy implementation has been a largely devolved responsibility since 1998 (Lloyd, 2015), with a more mixed policy landscape starting to develop under the 2010 (Conservative-led) Coalition and the 2015 Conservative Government, alongside ongoing fiscal constraints. The Coalition Government articulated a vision for challenging gendered care and boosting female employment by first extending paternity leave in 2011, followed by a policy redesign in 2014, when Shared parental leave was introduced. Plans to double free childcare for 'working families' were announced by the 2015 Conservative Government. This occurred in the context of increasing female employment and upward demand for childcare, but was accompanied with decentralisation, bringing along significant local budget cuts (Hastings et al., 2015). The Comprehensive Spending Review of 2010 set out an austerity programme and a 4-year deficit reduction plan, which significantly affected English local authorities (Ward, 2013). Significant income cuts created challenges in maintaining and extending care services for older people and children, leading to large-scale service re-planning. This is reflected in increasing user fees, co-payments for care services and in one of the most expensive childcare services in the OECD, with significant regional disparities (Javornik and Ingold, 2015). These developments occurred alongside an evolving national policy on ageing, an approach that predated both the financial crisis and the Coalition Government (Yeandle, 2016, p. 221). Overall, central funding of public services in England has been fundamentally restructured since 2010, with a differential impact in different parts of the country (Kispéter and Yeandle, 2015; Javornik and Ingold, 2015). Next we present these developments by policy areas.

**Parental leave and childcare**
The 2010 general election represents a critical juncture for distributing parenting responsibilities between parents. The Coalition Government first extended paternity leave and pay replacement, to allow fathers to take up to six months' leave during the child's first year, if the mother returned to work before the end of her maternity leave (Table 8.2). But soon, there appeared a stark contrast in the uptake of the short but paid paternity leave (91 per cent of fathers; Chanfreu et al., 2011) and the additional unpaid paternity leave. Failing to provide financial security, paternity leave was criticised for not challenging gender norms. To further address a relatively stubborn pattern of gendered parenting, and to advance women's employment, the same government introduced Shared parental leave (SPL) in 2014 (entered in force in April 2015). By taking a symbolic step towards explicitly promoting men's role in caring, this represents a milestone: by treating men as likely carers, it was introduced as a major advance for gender equality, enabling couples to distribute care more fairly (Table 8.2). The policy was initially put forward by the Liberal Democrats as a pre-2010 election pledge; but the final legislation significantly differs from the proposed, more flexible scheme, reflecting the response to the views expressed by the Conservatives (coalition partner), business, parents and child welfare organisations.

SPL creates a total of 52 shareable weeks available to eligible parents, 39 weeks of which are paid at the statutory rate (Table 8.2). Couples may switch from maternity leave to SPL after two weeks, which softens the distinction between maternity (pregnancy and childbirth) and parenthood (Javornik and Oliver, 2015). Both leave and pay are contingent upon

*Table 8.2    Changes in parental leave, United Kingdom*

| Type of leave | Before 2015 | 2015–16 |
| --- | --- | --- |
| Statutory maternity leave/pay | 52 weeks: 26 of ordinary + 26 of additional leave + compulsory 2 weeks following the birth, with 39 weeks of statutory pay at 90 per cent of woman's average earnings for 6 weeks with no ceiling + a flat-rate payment of either GBP 139.58 or 90 per cent of average gross weekly earnings (whichever is lower) for 33 weeks. The remaining 13 weeks are unpaid. | Remains in place. |
| Statutory paternity leave/pay (father of the child, spouse, partner or civil partner) | Up to 2 weeks of statutory paid leave. Flat-rate payment of GBP 139.58 a week, or 90 per cent of average weekly earnings, if less. | Remains in place. |
| Additional paternity leave | In 2011–15, possibility for mothers to transfer part of maternity leave (up to 26 weeks) to the person taking paternity leave 20 weeks after the birth of the child. Unpaid. | Abolished. |
| Parental leave/pay | 18 weeks' unpaid leave per parent, per child (born or adopted). Employees can take it at any time up to the child's 18th birthday. To be taken in blocks of a week or multiples of a week, unless the employer agrees otherwise or the child is disabled. Max. 4 weeks per year. An employee remains employed, with some terms of the contract (contractual notice and redundancy terms) apply. | Remains in place (unpaid). |

*Table 8.2*   (continued)

| Type of leave | Before 2015 | 2015–16 |
|---|---|---|
| Shared parental leave/pay | | Established on 5 April 2015. Qualifying mothers can end maternity after 2 compulsory weeks and switch over to SPL; 50 weeks can be shared between the mother & father/other parent. The father/other parent's right to paternity leave remains in place but is lost once s/he takes SPL. |
| | | *Pay* is available for eligible employees meeting prescribed qualifying requirements, paid at the lesser between 90 per cent of earnings and the flat rate of GBP 139.58. The remaining 13 weeks of the first year are unpaid. |
| | | To qualify, an individual must meet a length of service qualifying criterion, a partner must meet an economic activity test (worked for 26 weeks out of the 66 weeks before the expected week of childbirth and have earned at least GBP 30 per week for 13 weeks – min. GBP 390 in total) plus the continuous employment test; these replicate those for paternity leave/maternity allowance. |

*Source:*   Authors' compilation based on the Children and Families Act 2014, accessed December 2016 at http://www.legislation.gov.uk/ukpga/2014/6/pdfs/ukpga_20140006_en.pdf and ACAS, accessed December 2016 at http://www.acas.org.uk/.

maternity leave, and any time/pay taken as maternity leave gets subtracted from the total.

From the gender equality perspective, this policy is flawed for different reasons. First, it is grafted onto the existing framework of maternity leave. Because the Government failed to create a stand-alone right, it merely allows parents to split the existing maternity leave. Secondly, the state failed to introduce a forceful structure that provides sustainable statutory replacement pay levels. Instead, it provides modest statutory pay and leaves the decision about any enhanced packages to employers. Not mandating equivalent schemes for mothers and fathers is problematic because fathers' use of parental leave is significantly influenced by the benefit level. A clear line between the civil service and commercial employers has emerged over the past year, with the former more often offering enhanced options. No official data on uptake will be available before 2018, when the policy will be evaluated, but thus far, many employers have seen no business reasons to offer anything beyond statutory obligations; as a consequence, and in contrast to the policy aim, couples who choose to share leave are few. Overall, this new scheme has so far failed to enshrine gender equality as a societal ideal (Javornik and Oliver, 2015).

By contrast, two distinct factors define the childcare policy area: (1) a disconnect between childcare and other social welfare policy approaches; and (2) the strong impact of a political focus on market operations as the delivery model for childcare services. There is a continuing split concerning responsibilities for childcare at the level of central government; service provision has been a largely devolved responsibility since 1998 (Lloyd, 2015). This results in an array of actors operating across sectors; a complex and expensive funding mechanism with fees set by providers to maximise profitability lead to prohibitively high parental fee costs and chronic shortage of public childcare services. Namely, childcare is offered by a mix of private for-profit and not-for-profit childcare businesses, operating within a mixed market economy.

The UK appears a generous spender on childcare and early education (1.1 per cent of GDP in 2011; OECD, 2016). This is largely due to the demand-priming approach, where parents are reimbursed through the tax and benefit systems for services purchased in the open market (provided by private, voluntary and not-for-profit organisations and local council services), although such support is limited. Such a model challenges service affordability, and thus hardly enables mothers as primary carers to work (Brewer et al., 2014).

This has been a growing concern ever since the Labour Government introduced the universal 'early years' provision in 1998, equating it to 15 hours of care per week for 3- and 4-year-olds for 38 weeks a year (Javornik and Ingold, 2015). However, such limited free childcare conflicts with the reality of parents' working lives and with the tax/benefits system, which only recognises employment of 16 hours or more. The increase in casualised work means that it has become even more difficult for families to organise care arrangements, with time required to travel between childcare and places of work often being a hidden factor.

Despite efforts to remedy the childcare crisis over successive governments there is significant unmet need among parents, especially among the poorest and most disadvantaged, and parents with disabled children and those living in rural/remote areas. With recently reduced Working Tax Credit from 80 to 70 per cent, alongside decentralisation and local budget cuts, such disparity is likely to become more pronounced. Namely, facing increased childcare demand and not coping with the scale of cuts, many local authorities imposed additional charges; for instance, fees increased by 33 per cent for a child under 2 (Family and Childcare Trust, 2015). As childcare costs operate in the same way as a reduction in female wages, this may exacerbate gender inequality (Javornik, 2010).

The Coalition Government announced new plans in 2013 for a tax-free replacement for the existing employer-provided voucher system starting in 2015 (HM Treasury, 2014). Families would receive 20 per cent of yearly childcare costs, up to GBP 10000 per child; to be eligible both parents need to be in work, each earning less than GBP 150000 per year and not receiving support for childcare costs from tax credits or Universal Credit. From 2016 the childcare costs covered under Universal Credit were planned to increase to cover 85 per cent of eligible childcare. However, subject to the cap on social spending, this has now been rescheduled for autumn 2017 and it is unclear how it would be financed over time (Javornik and Ingold, 2015). The Coalition and Conservative Governments have done this at the expense of childcare provision for the most disadvantaged children: in 2010, they discontinued central funding for 'Sure Start' children's centres, which resulted in many centres closing down, cutting provision or raising fees (Kispéter and Yeandle, 2015, p. 109). This runs counter to the social mobility policy ideas reflected in the expansion of childcare and the social justice rationale underpinning investment in services and infrastructure (Lloyd, 2015).

Alongside these developments, the Conservative Government forged ahead with its pre-election pledge to double the current 15 hours per week of free childcare to 30 hours, to get more women into work. However, there are concerns over the sector's capacity to expand and the quality of such scaled-up provision (McLean, 2015). Moreover, state-funded support is tied to being in work. This suggests that the government sees childcare largely as a support strategy for *employed parents*. But for parents, particularly mothers in education, training, seeking a job or starting a business, having quality childcare in place is essential before they can undertake these activities (Ingold and Javornik, 2015). Families with young children seem to have borne the brunt of the welfare policy changes under the Coalition (Stewart and Obolenskaya, 2015). But if the government is assuming equal economic participation of men and women, then limiting access to affordable childcare will further intensify segregation between parents.

**Care for older people**
The provision of public services for older people is the statutory obligation of local authorities, and the system varies significantly across the country. Despite fundamentally restructuring central government funding of English local authorities in 2010, these duties have not been reduced (Kispéter and Yeandle, 2015, p. 107). Moreover, demand for local services has grown through a combination of demographic changes, higher unemployment and cuts in social insurance benefits, all resulting in a differential impact on the ability of local authorities to provide public services.

In England, the role of unpaid carers has been recognised in the system, largely due to the voluntary sector carer organisations (Yeandle, 2016, p. 226). Actually, the UK was one of the first countries to address the needs of carers of older people (Yeandle and Cass, 2013). The process began in the 1960s, and the Coalition Government included priorities to support carers in the 2010 National Carers' Strategy. This led to three main types of public support for carers:

1.  The Carer's Allowance, which is a national cash welfare benefit administered outside local authority systems, available to people with low income who care for at least 35 hours per week for a person receiving certain disability benefits. These are intended to help towards higher costs incurred by carers of people with disability. Carers are entitled to claim Carer's Allowance when earning up to GBP 110 per week, so some carers are able to retain a part-time job. But as many cannot manage the burden of full-time care and part-time work, they are dependent on Carer's Allowance (Citizens' Advice, 2015, p. 3).
2.  Local services designed to support carers comprise in-kind services provided by some local authorities, often following a Carer's Assessment, and include information, advice, training and respite care (at home or in a care home).
3.  Legislated employment rights to flexible working and unpaid leave (Kröger and Yeandle, 2013); and, from 2010, the protection from being discriminated against in the workplace because of the care they

provide to a disabled person (Yeandle and Joynes, 2012, p. 825). The right to request flexible working represents the key policy change affecting carers of older people, in addition to emergency time off (unpaid leave) to address caring emergencies.

Since 2010, public resources have increasingly focused on those with greatest needs: public spending on home care for older people has reduced by a fifth between 2010/11 and 2013/14, with 15 per cent fewer older people getting support (Mortimer and Green, 2015, p. 5). Spending on meals on wheels has halved in the last three years and approaching two-thirds fewer older people now receive them. A similar pattern can be seen regarding daycare (including day centres).

Studies show that a rebalancing is needed between the core, public and private economy in care provision (e.g. Mortimer and Green, 2015). Because of a mixture of spending cuts and rising demands, service provision is considered inadequate. In the coming years, the ability of the public economy to provide adequate support for those who cannot afford to pay for care may have to be compromised in terms of quantity and quality (Penny, 2012). As with childcare, those most adversely affected will be those without access to private care.

To address this issue, the Care Act was introduced in 2014. While this represents a significant change in social care law, it applies only to England (National Audit Office, 2014). In a nutshell, the act aims to explicitly shift responsibility to the local authorities (through a duty to ensure people's well-being), introduce the right to request a personal budget, and provide preventative services that could reduce or delay one's need for care. The law entered into force in April 2015, but there will be a lengthy settling-down period, with the final arrangements for the funding of care (including the cap on one's care costs) to be in place only in 2020 (originally announced for 2016). As only some of its aspects have come into force, it is premature to draw any conclusions about its effects. However, with its introduction, local councils were expected to undertake about half a million extra assessments; the new rights for carers are also very likely to put more pressure on public resources, which, as considered above, have been considerably reduced since 2010.

Overall, provision across the different policy areas under New Labour, the Coalition and the Conservatives has been piecemeal; the complexity of subsidies, combined with inadequate quality monitoring, has resulted in patchwork arrangements, largely not suited to families' needs and with worse consequences for those in disadvantaged economic situations. Cuts to social benefits and public services will disproportionately affect women as unpaid but also as paid carers themselves. They are also likely to disrupt the support offered by extended families and friends, and thus affect women indirectly. Namely, this involves more women helping adult children/grandchildren, and women are more likely to increase unpaid help, to make up for the deficit from the public purse.

## 3.  DISCUSSION

Focusing only on care in Spain and the UK, this chapter explored government interventions and trajectories of policy change from 2008 and until 2015. It investigated the dynamics in this sector from a gender perspective in economically adverse circumstances.

We found an increased policy interest in this area, with both countries explicitly seeking ways to address gendered care provision. This was to a large extent the function of national governments seeking to improve female employment, which represents a significant shift away from the male-breadwinner family model in both countries. To do so, and despite their different welfare systems and histories, they both introduced new leave legislation (still awaiting full implementation in the case of Spain), which could significantly reform gendered care by supporting more active fatherhood. By contrast, changes to childcare and care for older people have been mixed. Here too several acts/laws have recently come into force, but evidence was provided that budget cuts and marketisation risks are deepening in care both for children and older people. Interventions in both countries, especially after 2010, seem to lack a strategic and sustainable approach to support gender equality in care, and have instead exacerbated socioeconomic and gender inequalities.

Ongoing fiscal constraints post-2008 seem to have halted the initial vision in both countries, disrupting the 'policy transformative potential' and reinforcing instead gendered care with familistic dynamics. These similar dynamics are remarkable given the different histories and welfare traditions of the two countries, and thus it is worth considering how different welfare contexts, diverging paths post-financial crisis and disparate political agendas have resulted in similar gendered dynamics. Each country started from different positions in terms of the provisions for carers and a gender division of care pre-crisis, and despite new policies, they continue to offer contrasting levels of public support (for example, parental leave being more developed in the UK). The governments that initially opted for gender equality principles in care policies in both countries were of left ideologies (i.e. the 2000s' Socialist government in Spain and 1990s' Labour in the UK). Subsequent moves to the centre and right of the political spectrum, intersecting with the effects of the economic crisis, led to a near complete halt of the gender equality push in Spain while, in the UK, it led to a dilution of more ambitious ideas. This dynamic of 'disrupted equality policy trajectories' coincides with Conservative cabinet ministers' commitment to austerity in both countries, using the crisis discourse to justify cutbacks. In Spain, however, the persisting effects of the economic crisis in terms of high unemployment rates may have reinforced the return to family (gendered) care dynamics as families navigate a precarious financial climate. In the UK, despite a recovered economy, the austerity ideology has continued to be used to justify cuts in the public sector, with detrimental impacts on local authorities' ability to provide care services for older people and childcare.

Overall a lack of sufficient benefits and cash transfers for care at national levels maintains the brunt of care tasks in the family and, as a result, adds further responsibility on to women. This has significant consequences for gender equality, as women's opportunities to access independent income are skewed. Both cases exemplify how the 'policy transformative potential' cannot be realised without adequate resourcing and complementing policies. It has been established that service unavailability and unaffordability alongside unsustainable benefits or pay replacements undermine gender equality, both in terms of women's employment opportunities and men's involvement in care. The situation of scarcity has re-established family intergenerational solidarity, particularly in the case of Spain. However, research covering a longer time period is required to show exactly how recent interventions will play out for different populations.

## REFERENCES

Anttonen, A. and J. Sipilä (1996), 'European social care services: is it possible to identify models?', *Journal of European Social Policy*, **6** (2), 87–100.

Anttonen, A. and M. Zechner (2011), 'Theorizing care and care work', in B. Pfau-Effinger and T. Rostgaard (eds), *Care Between Work and Welfare in European Societies*, London: Palgrave Macmillan, pp. 15–34.

Brewer, M., S. Cattan, C. Crawford and B. Rabe (2014), 'The impact of free, universal pre-school education on maternal labour supply', Colchester: Institute for Social and Economic Research.

Chanfreu, J., S. Gowland, Z. Lancaster, E. Poole, S. Tipping and M. Toomse-Smith (2011), 'Maternity and paternity rights and Women Returners Survey 2009/10', Research Report No. 777, Sheffield: Department for Work and Pensions Research Report, accessed 16 January 2016 at http://goo.gl/OqGGHK.

Citizens Advice (2015), 'The role of carer's allowance in supporting unpaid care', London: Citizens Advice, accessed 12 August 2016 at www.citizensadvice.org.uk.

Comas d'Argemir, D. (2015), 'Los cuidados de larga duración y el cuarto pilar del sistema de bienestar', *Revista de Antropología Social*, **24**, 375–404.

Daly, M. and J. Lewis (2000), 'The concept of social care and the analysis of contemporary welfare states', *British Journal of Sociology*, **51** (2), 281–98.

Deusdad, B. (2013), 'Regulatory trajectory and current organisational framework of social services and social care', *COST Action IS1102 Working paper*, no. 1, accessed 10 January at http://www.cost-is1102-cohesion.unirc.it/docs/working-papers/wg1.spain-catalonia-social-services-b.deusdad.pdf.

Deusdad, B., D. Comas d'Argemir and S. Dziegielewski (2016), 'Restructuring long-term care in Spain: the impact of the economic crisis on social policies and social work practice', *Journal of Social Service Research*, **42** (2), 246–62.

El Economista (2016), 'El permiso de paternidad en España pasará de dos a cuatro semanas en 2017', accessed 16 December 2016 at http://www.eleconomista.es/economia/noticias/8030711/12/16/El-permiso-de-paternidad-se-ampliara-a-un-mes-a-partir-de-enero.html.

Escobedo, A., G. Meil and I. Lapuerta (2016), 'Spain country note', in A. Koslowski, S. Blum and P. Moss (eds), *International Review of Leave Policies and Research 2016*, accessed 8 January 2016 at: http://www.leavenetwork.org/lp_and_r_reports/.

Esping-Andersen, G. (2009), *The Incomplete Revolution. Adapting to Women's New Roles*, Cambridge: Polity Press.

Family and Childcare Trust (2015), 'Childcare costs survey 2014', accessed 20 April 2016 at http://www.familyandchildcaretrust.org/childcare-cost-survey-2015.

Gornick, C.J. and K.M. Meyers (2003), *Families that Work. Policies for Reconciling Parenthood and Employment*, New York: Russell Sage Foundation.

Gupta, N.D. and N. Smith (2001), *Children and Career Interruptions: The Family Gap in Denmark*, Bonn: Institute for the Study of Labor (IZA).

Hastings, A., N. Bailey, G. Bramley, M. Gannon and D. Watkins (2015), *The Cost of the Cuts: The Impact on Local Government and Poorer Communities*, York: Joseph Rowntree Foundation.

HM Treasury (2014), *Budget 2014 (HC1104)*, London: House of Commons.

INE (National Institute of Statistics) (2014), 'Participación de los trabajadores a tiempo parcial y con contrato temporal', accessed 5 January 2016 at http://www.ine.es/dynt3/inebase/index.htm?padre=2128&capsel=2415.

Ingold, J. and J. Javornik (2015), 'Focusing free childcare on "working parents" is short-sighted', *The Conversation*, 22 July, accessed 15 January 2016 at https://theconversation.com/focusing-free-childcare-on-working-parents-is-short-sighted-44623.

Javornik, J. (2010), *Exploring Maternal Employment in Post-Socialist Countries: Understanding the Implications of Childcare Policies*, PhD Thesis, Southampton: University of Southampton.

Javornik, J. (2014), 'Measuring state de-familialism: contesting post-socialist exceptionalism', *Journal of European Social Policy*, **24** (3), 240–57.

Javornik, J. and J. Ingold (2015), 'A childcare system fit for the future?', in L. Foster, A. Brunton, C. Deeming and T. Haux (eds), *In Defence of Welfare 2*, Bristol: Policy Press, pp. 75–8.

Javornik, J. and L. Oliver (2015), 'Legal battles loom on shared parental leave from fathers not getting equal benefits', *The Conversation*, 14 December, accessed 8 January 2016 at https://goo.gl/BYunIE.

Kispéter, E. and S. Yeandle (2015), 'Local welfare policies in a centralized governance system: childcare and eldercare in a period of rapid change in Leeds', in D. Kutsar and M. Kuronen (eds), *Local Welfare Policymaking in European Cities*, Cham: Springer International Publishing, pp. 101–16.

Korpi, W. (2000), 'Faces of inequality: gender, class, and patterns of inequalities in different types of welfare states', *Social Politics*, 7 (2), 127–91.
Kröger, T. and S. Yeandle (2013), *Combining Paid Work and Family Care*, Bristol: Policy Press.
Leitner, S. (2003), 'Varieties of familialism. The caring function of the family in comparative perspective', *European Societies*, 5 (4), 353–75.
Lin, C.Y.-Y., L. Edvinsson, J. Chen and T. Beding (2013), 'Impact of the 2008 global financial crisis', in C.Y.-Y. Lin, L. Edvinsson, J. Chen and T. Beding (eds), *National Intellectual Capital and the Financial Crisis in Greece, Italy, Portugal, and Spain*, New York: Springer, pp. 5–15.
Lloyd, E. (2015), 'Early childhood education and care policy in England under the Coalition Government', *London Review of Education*, 13 (2), 144–56.
Mandel, H. and M. Semyonov (2005), 'Family policies, wage structures, and gender gaps: sources of earnings inequality in 20 countries', *American Sociological Review*, 70 (6), 949–67.
McLean, A. (2015), 'Promising more free nursery care is one thing, delivering it is quite another', *The Conversation*, 1 May, accessed 15 January 2016 at https://theconversation.com/promising-more-free-nursery-care-is-one-thing-delivering-it-is-quite-another-41105.
Moreno, L. (2009), *Reformas de las Políticas del Bienestar en España*, Madrid: Siglo XXI.
Mortimer, J. and M. Green (2015), *Briefing: The Health and Care of Older People in England 2015*, London: Age UK.
National Audit Office (2014), *Adult Social Care in England: Overview*, London: National Audit Office.
Nollenberger, N. and N. Rodríguez-Planas (2011), 'Child care, maternal employment and persistence: a natural experiment from Spain', Discussion paper no. 5888, Bonn: Institute for the Study of Labor (IZA).
O'Connor, S. (2015), 'UK economy returns to pre-crisis level', *Financial Times*, accessed 8 January 2016 at http://www.ft.com/cms/s/0/bad33d56-13d5-11e4-8485-00144feabdc0.html#axzz3vjNPR0k2.
OECD (2016), *OECD Family Database*, accessed 8 August 2016 at www.oecd.org/social/family/database.htm.
Orloff, A.S. (1993), 'Gender and the social rights of citizenship: the comparative analysis of gender relations and welfare states', *American Sociological Review*, 58 (3), 303–28.
Page, S.E. (2006), 'Path dependence', *Quarterly Journal of Political Science*, 1 (1), 87–115.
Pascall, G. and J. Lewis (2004), 'Emerging gender regimes and policies for gender equality in a wider Europe', *Journal of Social Policy*, 33 (3), 373–94.
Penny, J. (2012), 'Coproduction and the core economy: a solution to care in crisis', *The Nef Blog*, accessed 8 January 2016 at http://www.neweconomics.org/blog/entry/coproduction-and-the-core-economy-a-solution-to-care-in-crisis.
Rodríguez-Cabrero, G. and V. Marban-Gallego (2013), 'La atención a la dependencia en una perspectiva europea de la asistencialización a la quasi-universalización', in E. del Pino and M.A. Rubio (eds), *Los Estados del Bienestar en la Encrucijada: Políticas Sociales en Perspectiva Comparada*, Madrid: Tecnos, pp. 337–61.
Saraceno, S. and W. Keck (2011), 'Towards an integrated approach for the analysis of gender equity in policies supporting paid work and care responsibilities', *Demographic Research*, 25 (11), 371–406.

Síndic de Greuges de Catalunya (2015), *Informe sobre la Igualdad de Oportunidades en la Educación Infantil (0–3 años)*, Barcelona: Síndic de Greuges, accessed 8 August 2016 at http://www.sindic.cat/site/unitFiles/3904/Informe%20escolaritza cio%200_3%20anys_cast_ok.pdf.

Stewart, K. and P. Obolenskaya (2015), 'The coalition's record on the under fives: policy, spending and outcomes 2010–2015', Working Paper No. 12, London: STIRCED & LSE, accessed 10 August 2016 at: http://sticerd.lse.ac.uk/dps/case/spcc/wp12.pdf.

Thane, P. (1991), 'Visions of gender in the making of the British welfare state: the case of women in the British Labour party and social policy, 1906–1945', in G. Bock and P. Thane (eds), *Maternity and Gender Policies*, New York: Routledge, pp. 93–118.

UGT (2015), 'Trabaja igual, cobra igual y concilia igual', Madrid: UGT, accessed 5 January 2016 at: http://www.ugt.es/Publicaciones/Informe_8_%20de_ Marzo_2015_UGT_Mujer_Trabajadora.pdf.

Ward, M. (2013), *Public Services North: Time for a New Deal?*, London: The Smith Institute.

Wilson, E. (1977), *Women and the Welfare State*, London: Tavistock.

World Bank (2014), 'Gender at work. A companion to the *World Development Report on Jobs*', accessed 16 January 2017 at http://documents.worldbank.org/curated/ en/884131468332686103/pdf/892730WP0Box3800report0Feb-02002014.pdf.

Yeandle, S. (2016), 'From provider to enabler of care? Reconfiguring local authority support for older people and carers in Leeds, 2008–2013', *Journal of Social Service Research*, **42** (2), 218–32.

Yeandle, S. and B. Cass (2013), 'Working carers of older people: steps towards securing adequate support in Australia and England?', in T. Kröger and S. Yeandle (eds), *Combining Paid Work and Family Care. Policies and Experiences in International Perspective*, Bristol: Policy Press.

Yeandle, S. and V. Joynes (2012), 'Challenges in combining work and care: evidence from investigating women's work in Leeds', *Local Economy*, **27** (8), 816–30.

Yeandle, S., T. Kröger and B. Cass (2012), 'Voice and choice for users and carers? Developments in patterns of care for older people in Australia, England and Finland', *Journal of European Social Policy*, **22** (4), 432–45.

PART III

Recent Trajectories in Care for Older People

# 9. Care for older people in early twenty-first-century Europe: dimensions and directions of change

**Teppo Kröger and Angela Bagnato***

## INTRODUCTION

Provisions and patterns of care for older people have recently undergone significant change all over Europe (Ranci and Pavolini, 2013). Many European nations have been reaching out for innovations in care as their populations continue to age at an increasing speed and new models are clearly necessary in order to deal with growing needs (Leichsenring et al., 2013; Gori et al., 2016). On the one hand, countries like Spain (Deusdad et al., 2016a) and Ireland (Timonen et al., 2012), which earlier had not been particularly active in developing long-term care, have launched new policies and, on the other hand, countries that had introduced care policies earlier, like Britain and the Nordic countries, have been reforming their provisions (Anttonen and Karsio, in this volume; Yeandle, 2016). At the same time, countries in Central Eastern Europe have been trying to depart from an overly institution-based provision, that is, from the legacy of the socialist period (Kubalčíková et al., in this volume). One issue that has been prominent in reform efforts is the redefinition of the 'vertical division of authority' or 're-scaling of responsibility' between local and central government (see Martinelli, Chapter 1, as well as Sabatinelli and Semprebon, in this volume; Kazepov, 2010). The European Union has also been searching for a role in long-term care policy, attempting to influence policy-making in member states at least indirectly (see Gómez-Barroso et al., in this volume). In addition, the development of care systems has been affected by the progress of neo-liberal thinking and NPM-inspired governance models (see Martinelli, Chapter 1, in this volume).

However, the conditions of policy-making were changed radically when the financial crisis spread to Europe in 2008. Many national economies were hit hard, especially in Southern Europe. Progressive policy reforms were halted in a number of policy fields, also in care for older people, and austerity measures came into focus instead. However, a general European-wide view on the implications of the economic crisis for care policy developments has been missing. This chapter makes a contribution to filling this knowledge gap by mapping the main directions of change in long-term care in different parts of Europe during the early twenty-first century.

The analysis presented here is based on information reported in working papers produced by national teams in the course of the COST Action IS1102 *SO.S. COHESION – Social services, welfare states and places*. All working papers that describe developments in the care for older people were selected to be reviewed in this chapter. These COST Action papers or presentations (CAPs hereafter) cover 11 European countries in total, representing the Nordic countries (with Denmark, Finland, Iceland), Central/Central Eastern Europe (with the Czech Republic, Germany, Slovakia) and the Mediterranean region (Greece, Italy, Malta, Spain), plus the United Kingdom.[1]

Being based on the information that these reports offer, this chapter is thus the result of a collective effort and it aims to summarise the similarities and differences of recent changes in care provisions for older people in these 11 countries. Summing up these reports has not been uncomplicated, due to the richness of their details and because some of them are local case studies in character while others describe developments at the national level. Their contents and, sometimes, terminology differ. Moreover, there are many local and regional variations within countries, Italy being a prime example with its substantial differences between the North and the South of the country. Furthermore, these 11 countries do not represent the whole of Europe. As a result, the picture drawn here of changes in European care provisions remains unavoidably incomplete and fractional.

Nevertheless, these reports are a valuable source of information on recent policy developments in different parts of Europe, written by social policy and long-term care researchers. We made a thematic analysis of these reports, aiming to interpret and summarise their key findings. According to Braun and Clarke (2006, p.79), thematic analysis is a method for 'identifying, analysing and reporting patterns (themes) within data. It minimally organises and describes your data set in (rich) detail. However, frequently it goes further than this, and interprets various aspects of the research topic'. This description fits the way this chapter was written.

Based on a careful reading of extended abstracts of the reports, common themes were identified that appeared in a number of the reports. Five such themes became especially visible. Next, all the full reports were read carefully and summarised using a framework that consisted of these five key themes. Most key discussions of the reports centred around these five themes and each of them was featured in several reports. Each theme appeared as a specific dimension of policy development and design, consisting of a dichotomous double concept and of the distance in between. These *five dimensions* were: (1) decentralised care–centralised care; (2) social care–health care; (3) outsourcing–in-house provision of care; (4) home-based care–institutional care; and (5) formal care–informal care. These five policy dimensions are thus based on the themes we identified in our reading and analysis of the reports, representing an interpretation of key issues of recent change in long-term care.

The chapter is structured according to the framework that emerged from our thematic analysis of the reports and presents their observations one key dimension after another. The contents of this chapter overlap partly with previous chapters of this collection as they are based on the same COST Action local and national studies. However, earlier chapters focus on a particular theme or group of countries, whereas this chapter aims to synthesise the general observations on recent developments of care from all the participating countries that addressed care for older people.

## 1.   DECENTRALISED CARE–CENTRALISED CARE

How have European care systems changed recently, seen through the lens of decentralisation? Unlike most social security benefits, care services are only rarely delivered to citizens through national welfare agencies. Instead, they are part of the local welfare state, organised and produced usually by local and regional authorities. Nevertheless, this is done in an administrative framework created by the central state through legislation, central regulation and central grant systems (Burau and Kröger, 2004; Kazepov, 2010; Kröger, 2011). Care is thus an issue of multilevel governance where the vertical division of labour between the national and sub-national levels of government – and increasingly supra-national levels like the EU – plays a major role (Kutsar and Kuronen, 2015; Martinelli, Chapter 1, in this volume). Local and regional levels always have at least some discretion in the implementation of care policies but the national government may aim to either limit or broaden the scope of this discretion.

The COST Action working papers show that in the twenty-first century, local/regional governments have been given additional responsibilities for care for older people in several European countries. In *Italy*, for example, after 2001, regional governments were given authority over all social services. However, a corresponding transfer of resources did not accompany this change. As a result, regional governments, especially in the poorer regions of Italy, have not been able to deliver adequate care services. National government has avoided responsibility also by not defining national quality benchmarks. In the absence of centrally defined criteria for a minimum level of services, local and regional variations in coverage and quality of services have further increased in Italy (CAP Bagnato et al., 2014).

The developments in the *Slovak* and *Czech Republics* are similar to the situation in Italy: in both countries long-term care has experienced a process of legislative and financial decentralisation. Local authorities have been delegated the responsibility for care but, like in Italy, without guaranteeing the necessary financial resources and thus, without guaranteeing that local authorities are really able to deliver adequate services (Kubalčíková et al., in this volume; Szüdi et al., 2016).

In the *UK*, the central government has imposed new constraints on the spending of local authorities. These spending caps represent a kind of re-centralisation in financing, limiting the action of local authorities. At the same time, local authorities have nevertheless been granted greater autonomy and responsibility in implementation (Kispéter and Yeandle, 2015; CAP Yeandle, 2014; Yeandle, 2016). Also in *Denmark*, local authorities are under increasing pressure and economic control as the central state is aiming to cut local spending (CAP Jensen and Fersch, 2013).

Danish municipalities and Southern Italian regions are certainly in a different situation: the former provide universal free-of-charge care services to a large proportion of their population aged 65 and over, while the latter can offer only limited care provisions to their inhabitants. Nevertheless, both – as well as local authorities in a number of other European countries – face rather similar tendencies: national governments have been eager to delegate the responsibility for care for older people to subnational units, that is, to regional and local authorities (Ranci and Pavolini, 2013). However, this decentralisation of responsibility has not been accompanied by a corresponding transfer of economic resources to the local and regional levels. On the contrary, despite continuously increasing care needs, several central governments have cut their funding to long-term care and capped local spending, thus reducing in practice the opportunities of local and regional governments to meet the needs of their older citizens (see also Sabatinelli and Semprebon, in this volume).

## 2.   SOCIAL CARE–HEALTH CARE

Needs for social care in old age are associated with difficulties with health, which makes social and health care fundamentally interrelated. In most countries, both social welfare agencies and health care providers are involved in the provision of care services, helping people in old age to manage their daily activities. The exact boundary between the two sectors is nevertheless up to national and local definitions. In many European countries, the health sector and the social sector have major difficulties in their collaboration, do not manage to provide integrated services and continue to work separately from each other (Leichsenring, 2004; Colombo et al., 2011; Rodrigues et al., 2012; Ranci and Pavolini, 2013).

Very often social services are provided by local governments, while health services are the responsibility of regions or sometimes the central state. Such an administrative separation has brought additional complications for the co-operation of the two sectors and made their full integration impossible. Recently, some efforts have been made to overcome this institutional dualism. For example, the *Slovak Republic* attempted in 2005 to integrate health care services, financed by health insurance payments, and social care services, which are provided by the social welfare system and funded through regional and local taxation and co-payments of care users. However, this integration effort failed and, in the end, the proposed law was not enacted (CAP Kováčová et al., 2014; Szüdi et al., 2016). *Italy* has launched a new service concept of 'integrated socio-health domiciliary care' (*assistenza domiciliare integrata*), but in regions like Calabria this new service is still organised by regional health districts alone, seldom in collaboration with municipal welfare agencies (CAP Bagnato et al., 2014).

In *Iceland*, in the early 2000s the largest municipalities assumed responsibility for all social and health care, while previously the responsibilities had been divided between the state, the municipality and the providers. A similar integration of management of the two sectors is planned to take place at the national level in the near future. However, in this case, it is necessary to remember that the whole nation has only about 329 000 citizens, which explains why the central state has until now taken an exceptionally large role in care provision (CAP Sigurðardóttir, 2014).

In some countries, particularly in Southern Europe, the slow development of social care and the resulting lack of access to its services have produced the phenomenon of 'social hospitalisation' (Colombo and Mercier, 2012). In *Spain*, for example, social care has remained unavailable to many, and using health care services, in particular hospitals, has been the usual way to try to obtain assistance for the activities of daily life, causing an overuse of health care and long waiting lists (Garcés et al., 2013; CAP Ródenas et al., 2013). However, due to austerity measures brought by the recent economic crisis, the Spanish public health care system has lately lost many of its universalistic features: access depends now on membership with the social security system, the unemployed being excluded. Co-payments for medications have also been introduced. These and other recent changes have made public health care inaccessible or unaffordable to many older people and have thus ended a large part of the earlier 'social hospitalisation' (CAP Deusdad and Zafra, 2013; Deusdad et al., 2016b).

On the other hand, in several parts of Europe the crisis seems to have affected the social care component of services at least as much as the health care component. Home-based social care has been cut in several countries. For example, local authorities in *Denmark* and *Finland* have made their spending cuts in home care primarily in services for household tasks and social support, not in health-related services for personal care (Kröger and Leinonen, 2012; CAP Jensen and Fersch, 2013; CAP Kröger et al.. 2013).

The duality of social care and health care has not disappeared during the new century. Some countries have recently aimed to integrate these two domains, particularly within home-based care for older people. These efforts have not always been successful but many integration efforts and experiments are going on (e.g. Leichsenring and Alaszewski, 2004; Hixon, 2016). Austerity measures have in many places heightened the earlier tensions between social and health care as both domains are trying to manage under cuts and are retargeting their activities. So far, the question of how to bring social and health care into close co-operation and integrate their services in a way that covers both the health needs and social needs of the older population remains mostly unanswered.

## 3.   OUTSOURCING–IN-HOUSE PROVISION OF CARE

For-profit long-term care provision has traditionally been untypical in Europe, which has instead been characterised by public provision (especially in Northern and Eastern Europe), provision by non-profit organisations (in Central European countries) or a delegation of care tasks to the family (in Southern Europe and parts of Eastern Europe) (EC, 1999). However, several European countries have recently started to outsource publicly funded care services to for-profit or non-profit providers through competitive tenders, leading to a decrease of the share of direct 'in-house' provision by local authorities (e.g. Meagher and Szebehely, 2013).

In the late 1980s and early 1990s, *Britain* was the first country in Europe to start a determined policy push towards broadening the role of the 'independent' sector in care (Means et al., 2002). Many local authorities in Britain are still continuing to contract out their care provisions to for-profit (and non-profit) organisations under 'public–private partnerships'. Central government guidance has urged local authorities to keep stimulating local care markets and to develop new models of 'co-production'. For example, in Leeds in 2006 the City Council provided 79 per cent of home care hours itself while the for-profit and non-profit sectors provided 21 per cent. By 2011 this situation had effectively reversed, with the private sector providing 75 per cent and the local authority only 25 per cent (Yeandle, 2016, p. 223).

In 2000, *Italy* enacted national legislation that encouraged outsourcing. In regions like Calabria where public care services were very limited, the new legislation actually led to an enlargement of publicly funded services: the law was used to initiate new services, the provision of which was delegated to non-profit organisations. However, this way to extend services came to an end with the economic recession, as a result of budget cuts. Austerity has recently placed many Italian non-profit organisations and their employees in a vulnerable position as competitive bidding procedures have led to a worsening of contractual relations and, as a result, to decreasing salary levels, longer shifts and a move from permanent to temporary work contracts. Moreover, the payments from local authorities to non-profit organisations have often been delayed or fully suspended, which has brought many organisations to the verge of bankruptcy (CAP Martinelli, 2012; Gambardella et al., 2013; CAP Bagnato et al., 2015).

Non-profit organisations have faced difficulties in other countries, as well. For example, in *Germany*, since the 1995 introduction of the long-term care insurance scheme, commercial providers have been admitted to the field of care services for older people, hitherto dominated by the non-profit sector. The traditional large German non-profit players have not disappeared, but have adapted their management policies to market-inspired models (CAP Mätzke, 2012; CAP Bode, 2013).

Outsourcing of publicly funded care services has become a powerful trend in long-term care for older people in Europe. Local and regional authorities in different parts of Europe increasingly use competitive tendering of care provisions, and this tendency has given for-profit organisations a stronger position. As a result of outsourcing, for-profit services are growing rapidly in several countries in Europe. The new situation has also challenged non-profit organisations. Their non-profit provisions have traditionally supplemented public provisions in a number of countries – or even formed the bulk of services in some countries – but now they have to compete against for-profit providers, which has led to a reduction in differences between the for-profit and non-profit sectors.

## 4.   HOME-BASED CARE–INSTITUTIONAL CARE

In the last decades, care policy for older people has emphasised de-institutionalisation all over Europe. Institutional care has come to be seen as paternalistic, unable to promote quality of life, self-determination or quality of care. Furthermore, higher budgetary constraints have strengthened the push to find less expensive alternatives to institutional provisions. 'Ageing in place' has instead become the slogan of new policies (Colombo et al., 2011; Deusdad et al., 2016a). As a result, many governments in Europe have issued policy documents and programmes that promote de-institutionalisation, such as the 'National action plan for the transition from institutional to community-based care 2012–15' (*Národný akčný plán prechodu z inštitucionálnej na komunitnú starostlivosť v systéme sociálnych služieb na roky 2012–2015*) in *Slovakia*.

Following the 'ageing in place' principle, institutional provisions are being cut in different parts of Europe. The *Czech Republic*, representing a country where institutional care used to dominate the care service scene, has made drastic cuts in the number of places in long-term care institutions, albeit waiting lists remain long (CAP Kubalčíková and Havlíková, 2013; Kubalčíková and Havlíková, 2016). In *Iceland*, the number of nursing home beds decreased somewhat from 2006 to 2011, while needs have considerably increased, and access has become more strictly controlled than earlier (CAP Sigurðardóttir, 2014). In *Finland*, too, the number of nursing homes has gone down, leading to an increasing number of older people with high levels of needs living at home and in intensive service housing units (CAP Kröger et al., 2013; CAP Anttonen and Häikiö, 2014; Anttonen and Karsio, 2016). In several Southern European countries there never was a large coverage of institutional services, and the de-institutionalisation policy, together with the economic crisis, have prevented them from growing.

Growing waiting lists are the unintended result of shrinking institutional provisions. Needs for institutional care have not vanished but instead there seems to be a widening gap between needs and actual provisions. In *Malta*, which has fewer than 450 000 inhabitants, the government has calculated that 300 new residential beds would be needed every year over the next ten years in order to keep pace with the ageing of the population – but such an increase in beds is not taking place (CAP Pace and Vella, 2014; Pace et al., 2016). In *Catalonia*, the regional government ended its financial support for residential care in 2013, which led to further lengthening of waiting lists that were already long (CAP Deusdad and Zafra, 2013; Deusdad et al., 2016b). The recession brought the upgrading and expansion of *Icelandic* nursing homes to a standstill, as well, which resulted in longer waiting lists and in poorer health of those on the waiting lists (Sigurðardóttir et al., 2016). In some parts of *Italy* the undersupply of institutional care is a critical issue: for example, in the city of Reggio Calabria, with 185 000 people, there are only two publicly supported residential units for older people, with a total of 42 beds (Bagnato et al., 2015). In the *Czech Republic*, people do not trust home care services to provide adequate support in case of high care needs, which has resulted in long waiting lists for institutional care and in the emergence of private residential quasi-services of questionable quality. (CAP Kubalčíková and Havlíková, 2013; Kubalčíková et al., in this volume).

Waiting lists for institutional care show that home-based services have fallen short of the expectation that they could support 'ageing in place' on a grand scale. Institutional care seems to continue to be required in the case of high care needs. This 'failure' of home-based care is to a large extent explained by the fact that, usually, the resources of home care have not been increased to meet the growing needs caused by population ageing and de-institutionalisation. In some places these resources have even been cut down during the economic crisis. In the city of Reggio Calabria in *Italy*, for example, the number of users of publicly supported home-based social care decreased by more than a half from 2009 to 2014 and the remaining beneficiaries of home care services, all with extensive care needs, receive only three hours of services per week on average (Bagnato et al., 2015).

Some countries, particularly in the Nordic region, that earlier used to provide home care support for both personal care and household tasks, have recently prioritised one area above the other. In a local *Danish* case study it was found that cuts have been made in practical home help but not in personal care (CAP Jensen and Fersch, 2013). Similarly in *Finland*, municipal home care services have minimised providing help in several household tasks such as cleaning and shopping and have focused their resources on personal care (CAP Anttonen and Häikiö, 2014; CAP Kröger et al., 2013). In *Iceland*, on the other hand, assistance at home has been available mainly for domestic tasks, such as cleaning, cooking, shopping and laundry, and less for personal care, getting out of bed, toilet visits, clothing and feeding (CAP Sigurðardóttir, 2014).

The emphasis on 'ageing in place' and de-institutionalisation, accepted widely as a policy principle all over Europe (e.g., Means, 2007; Troisi and von Kondratowitz, 2013), has created a general understanding that institutional care is outdated and no longer necessary. However, the actual situation in different parts of Europe shows growing waiting lists for institutional care as families do not find that their older members receive adequate services at home. Expectations of the capability of home care to support people with high needs seem to have been exaggerated. The inability of European countries to increase resources for home-based service provisions in step with growing needs has clearly contributed to this 'failure of home care'. Instead of the necessary investments, the development of home care services has been characterised by cuts and implementation of stricter access criteria. Situations vary in individual countries, but overall both institutional provisions and home-based care services have ended up as targets of austerity measures throughout Europe.

## 5.  FORMAL CARE–INFORMAL CARE

The term 'formal care' refers usually to care services provided by public, for-profit or non-profit organisations, while 'informal care' may refer either to care from the family and social networks or to grey market care, performed outside the formal economy (Colombo et al., 2011). Concerning the first component of 'informal care', research has shown that in all countries, Nordic countries included, care is provided overwhelmingly by the family and that formal care provisions represent only a minor share of the total volume of support for older people. When informal family care has been recognised as the real mainstream of care, the interplay between formal and informal care has become a key issue in long-term care policy (Kröger, 2001; Bettio and Verashchagina, 2012). The second component, grey market care, has always occurred in some form but recently it has become more important as families in many European countries have started to employ migrant women to provide care for older people. The phenomenon has been particularly present in Southern Europe in countries like Italy and Greece but it occurs to some extent in many other European countries (Pfau-Effinger et al., 2009; Bettio and Verashchagina, 2012; Ranci and Pavolini, 2013).

Cuts in the provision of institutional and home-based public care do not leave families unaffected. As *Icelandic* home care services are primarily focused on household tasks, a large proportion of care is expected to come from the family (CAP Sigurðardóttir, 2014; Sigurðardóttir and Kåreholt, 2014). In a local case study from the *Czech Republic* the situation was found to be the same: there too home care services focus on providing assistance with housekeeping and shopping, while assistance with personal care remains very limited (CAP Kubalčíková and Havlíková, 2013). On the other hand, in *Denmark* household tasks are currently left to the families of older people to take on (CAP Jensen and Fersch, 2013). Such policy decisions on the limitation of available support are made with little concern for whether older people really have families that can take on these responsibilities.

In some countries, informal family carers have received new rights and forms of support, such as for example in Britain, in Finland and in Germany. In the *UK*, family carers have since the turn of the century had some, albeit limited, employment rights through new legislation and they have also gained the right to have their own needs assessed by local authorities. According to the national census 2011 data, there are nevertheless considerable unmet needs for support among carers (Yeandle et al., 2013; CAP Yeandle, 2014; Yeandle, 2016). In *Finland*, the 2005 revision of the Informal Care Act (*Laki omaishoidon tuesta*) extended carers' rights for respite and made regulation of their financial support and additional services clearer, though these did not end local variations. In 2011, care responsibilities for older family members were modestly recognised in *Finland*'s labour legislation, when employees were offered the right to unpaid care leave, which, however, requires the agreement of the employer (Kröger and Yeandle, 2013; CAP Kröger et al., 2013).

*Germany* reformed its long-term care insurance scheme in 2008 in order to improve the situation of frail older people and to support their carers. This reform introduced new forms of unpaid leave for people who take care of a family member, thereby preserving a key role for family members in providing care and helping them to combine their jobs with their care tasks (CAP Bode, 2013). *Malta* has also launched a pilot project to offer a subsidy for qualified domiciliary carers who look after people put on a waiting list for a residential home, but other measures supporting people who care for an older family member have not yet been forthcoming (CAP Pace and Vella, 2014; Pace et al., 2016).

*Spain* is an example of a country that launched progressive policy reforms in the early 2000s, in particular with the 2006 Law of promotion of personal autonomy and care for older and disabled people (*Ley de Promoción de la Autonomía Personal y Atención a personas en situación de dependencia*), but was later hit by the economic crisis. As a result of the 2006 legislation, some informal family carers, mostly wives or daughters, started to receive care allowances and were for the first time included in pension schemes. However, these rights were short-lived as, due to the cutbacks of social spending, from 2012 caring relatives were excluded from the social security system (CAP Deusdad, 2013; CAP Deusdad and Zafra, 2013; Deusdad et al., 2016b).

The economic crisis has also brought some unforeseen changes in the behaviour of families. Though long waiting lists for institutional care are reported in Southern Europe, it has been noticed that in both *Spain* and *Italy* cash-for-care benefits to older people (In Italy, *Indennità di accompagnamento*), as well as pensions of older family members, are now used to help children and grandchildren economically, that is, to even out the gaps in family economies caused by the crisis. As a result, willingness to use institutional care or other formal care services in these countries has decreased (CAP Deusdad and Zafra, 2013; Bagnato et al., 2015; Deusdad et al., 2016b).

In *Greece* and *Italy*, other changes have also been observed. Until 2008, the number of grey market migrant care workers had increased rapidly, the use of such workers becoming an important strategy for families to organise care for their older members in these countries (Bettio and Verashchagina, 2012; Ranci and Pavolini, 2013). This development had raised great concern about migrant workers' lacking job protection and social security. But now this trend has suddenly changed. In *Greece*, severe cuts in pensions and salaries have decreased family incomes significantly, especially in low-income households. As a result, employing a migrant care worker (or using formal care services) is no longer a viable option for the majority of families. Consequently, the responsibility for care of older people has reverted to the family, in practice, to female family members (CAP Vaiou and Siatitsa, 2013, p. 12). Also in Southern *Italy*, many families have been hit so hard by the economic crisis that they can no longer afford to employ a migrant care worker (called '*badante*'). As a result, the employment opportunities of migrant women have been reduced considerably since 2008 (Bagnato et al., 2015).

The above described developments have deeply affected the relationship between formal and informal care in many European countries. Cuts in home-based and institutional care provisions have pushed responsibilities back to the family in different parts of Europe. The most radical setbacks have taken place in Southern Europe, where formal care provisions were developing when the economic crisis hit. Moreover, it was not just the development of formal care that was disrupted there – the expansion of grey market care work has also been affected, due to the economic problems of families. But also in other parts of Europe, cuts in institutional and home care provisions have pushed responsibility for care of older people back to families.

## 6.    CONCLUSION: DIRECTIONS OF POLICY CHANGE

This chapter is based on the reports and working papers written by 11 national teams of the COST Action. The picture they paint is surprisingly consistent: recent developments are rather parallel in different parts of Europe, despite substantial differences in the starting point of the long-term care policy of individual nations before the economic recession. The overall conclusion is that European countries seem to be moving mostly in the same direction, though from different positions.

Using the framework of five key dimensions of change, as outlined in this chapter, the directions of recent long-term care policy change can be summarised as follows. On the first dimension, there has been a movement towards decentralisation in the implementation of care policy: more responsibility has been given to local and regional authorities. The central state has reduced its commitments in several European countries, also in financial terms, which means that the increase in the tasks transferred to local and regional governments has not been compensated by a growth in central funding. From countries like Denmark and the UK, there are also examples of the central state's growing control on the spending of local authorities. Overall, central governments seem to be trying to reduce their responsibility for long-term care – and to 'avoid blame' for its shortcomings (Sabatinelli and Semprebon, in this volume).

Concerning the complicated relation between social care and health care, that is, the second dimension, the direction is unclear. There have been some efforts, for example in the Slovak Republic and in some regions of Italy, to bring about more co-ordination or integration between these two sectors but these efforts have been mostly unsuccessful. The economic crisis has further complicated the collaboration: cuts have targeted the funding of health care as well as social care so both have been curtailing their provisions. This has changed some earlier practices: for example, the tendency in Southern Europe to compensate for the non-existence of social care by an overuse of health care has now decreased. However, the original problem, the lack of social care services, has not been resolved, nor have the difficulties in co-operation between social and health care.

Looking through the lens of the third dimension, new outsourcing practices adopted by public authorities have led to a distinctive decrease of 'in-house' direct public provisions and to a corresponding growth of for-profit and non-profit provisions. Contracting out through competitive tenders seems to have strengthened the position of for-profit providers. Although many non-profit organisations are also providing these services, they have had to adapt to a new competitive context and adopt new market-based practices. In Southern Europe, where public budgets have been hit most severely by the economic crisis, non-profit organisations have seen a worsening of their contractual conditions with local and regional authorities, which reverberates also in the quality of their services and employment conditions.

Fourth, the widely adopted 'ageing in place' principle has not delivered on its promises in Europe. Based on this principle, institutional provisions have been cut in different parts of the continent but, as this has not been accompanied by major investments in home care provisions, long-term care has failed to meet people's needs. Access to home care has instead become stricter in several countries and the range of home care services has been narrowed. Long waiting lists for institutional care all around

Europe are a result of this development, together with the emergence of residential quasi-services of questionable quality in some countries.

Finally, regarding the fifth dimension, the direction has clearly been away from formal care and towards informal care. As a consequence of cuts in institutional and home care services, families have been required to take increasing responsibility for the care of their older relatives. In this respect, the development seems to be parallel throughout Europe, from North to South and from West to East. A large proportion of needs are left to the family to deal with. The share of this family responsibility depends on the starting point at which national and local care systems entered the economic crisis: in the Nordic countries, publicly funded provisions still cover a sizeable proportion of needs, while in many in Southern and Eastern European countries the responsibility of families is currently very high.

Where does all this leave us? What is the state of long-term care in Europe after several years of deep economic recession? Based on the findings of the COST papers, the key directions of recent change are: from the central state to the local level, from public provision to for-profit (and non-profit) services, from institutional care to (insufficient) home care, and from formal care (and informal migrant care) to informal family care. Put together, these changes mean that governments in Europe are trying to reduce their responsibilities for care for their older populations, hoping that someone else will do the work and pay the bill.

## NOTES

\* The writing of this chapter has been partly supported by a project grant from the Academy of Finland (LinkAGE, No. 299053).
1. Newer revised versions of some of these COST Action papers and presentations have been published in 2016 in a special issue of the *Journal of Social Service Research*. In these cases, references are given to both the earlier versions and the newer published versions.

## REFERENCES

Anttonen, A. and L. Häikiö (2014), 'Eldercare service redesign in six Finnish municipalities: welfare market in the making', unpublished paper presented at the COST Action IS1102 Workshop, Faculty of Economics and Business, Barcelona, 3–6 March.
Anttonen, A. and O. Karsio (2016), 'Eldercare service redesign in Finland: deinstitutionalization of long-term care', *Journal of Social Service Research*, **42** (2), 151–66.
Bagnato, A., S. Barillà and F. Martinelli (2014), 'The public supply of care for older

people in Reggio Calabria. The impact of the crisis on a long-standing deficit', presentation at the COST Action IS1102 Workshop, Ekonomickà Univerzita, Bratislava, 3–7 November.

Bagnato, A., S. Barillà and F. Martinelli (2015), 'L'offerta pubblica di servizi di cura per gli anziani a Reggio Calabria. L'impatto della crisi su un deficit strutturale', paper presented at the ESPAnet Italy eighth conference, University of Salerno, Salerno, 17–19 September.

Bettio, F. and A. Verashchagina (2012), *Long-Term Care for the Elderly: Provisions and Providers in 33 European Countries*, Luxembourg: Publications Office of the European Union.

Bode, I. (2013), 'The changing governance of domiciliary elderly care in Germany', unpublished paper presented at the COST Action IS1102 Workshop, Dunarea de Jos University, Galati, 5–8 November.

Braun, V. and V. Clarke (2006), 'Using thematic analysis in psychology', *Qualitative Research in Psychology*, **3** (2), 77–101.

Burau, V. and T. Kröger (2004), 'The local and the national in community care: exploring policy and politics in Finland and Britain', *Social Policy & Administration*, **38** (7), 793–810.

Colombo, F. and J. Mercier (2012), 'Help wanted? Fair and sustainable financing of long-term care services', *Applied Economic Perspectives and Policy*, **34** (2), 316–32.

Colombo, F., A. Llena-Nozal, J. Mercier and F. Tjadens (2011), *Help Wanted? Providing and Paying for Long-Term Care*, Paris: OECD Health Policy studies, OECD Publishing.

Deusdad, B. (2013), 'Regulatory trajectory and current organisational framework of social services and social care', *COST Action IS1102 Working Papers*, no. 1, accessed at http://www.cost-is1102-cohesion.unirc.it/docs/working-papers/wg1. spain-catalonia-social-services-b.deusdad.pdf.

Deusdad, B. and E. Zafra (2013), 'Older adults, housing accessibility and consequences of the economic crisis', unpublished paper presented at the COST Action IS1102 Workshop, Dunarea de Jos University, Galati, 5–8 November.

Deusdad, B., D. Comas-d'Argemir and S.F. Dziegielewski (2016b), 'Restructuring long-term care in Spain: the impact of the economic crisis on social policies and social work practice', *Journal of Social Service Research*, **42** (2), 246–62.

Deusdad, B., C. Pace and A. Anttonen (2016a), 'Facing the challenges in the development of long-term care for older people in Europe in the context of an economic crisis', *Journal of Social Service Research*, **42** (2), 144–50.

EC (1999), *Social Protection for Dependency in Old Age in the 15 EU Member States and Norway*, Luxembourg: Office for Official Publications of the European Communities.

Gambardella, D., E. Morlicchio and M. Accorinti (2013), 'L'illusione riformista delle politiche di assistenza in Italia', in Y. Kazepov and E. Barberis (eds), *Il welfare frammentato. Le articolazioni regionali delle politiche sociali italiane*, Roma: Carocci, pp. 25–44.

Garcés, J., F. Ródenas and T. Hammar (2013), 'Converging methods to link social and health care systems and informal care – confronting Nordic and Mediterranean approaches', in K. Liechsenring, J. Billing and N. Henk (eds), *Long-Term Care in Europe*: *Improving Policy and Practice*, London: Palgrave Macmillan, pp. 100–17.

Gori, C., J.L. Fernández and R. Wittenberg (eds) (2016), *Long-Term Care Reforms in OECD Countries: Successes and Failures*, Bristol: Policy Press.

Hixon, L.L. (2016), 'The relationship between social and health services in care for older people', in C. Gori, J.L. Fernández and R. Wittenberg (eds), *Long-Term Care Reforms in OECD Countries: Successes and Failures*, Bristol: Policy Press, pp. 247–70.

Jensen, P.H. and B. Fersch (2013), 'Local variations and preferences in the organization of elder care: the Danish case', unpublished paper presented at the COST Action IS1102 Workshop, University of Iceland, Reykjavik, 3–7 June.

Kazepov, Y. (ed.) (2010), *Rescaling Social Policies towards Multilevel Governance in Europe: Social Assistance, Activation and Care for Older People*, Farnham: Ashgate Publishing.

Kispéter, E. and S. Yeandle (2015), 'Local welfare policy in a centralized governance system: childcare and eldercare services in a period of rapid change in Leeds', in D. Kutsar and M. Kuronen (eds), *Local Welfare Policy Making in European Cities*, Cham: Springer International Publishing, pp. 101–16.

Ková čová, J., G. Szüdi and S. Konečný (2014), 'Transformation of social services for the elderly in the context of deinstitutionalization of social services in Slovakia', unpublished paper presented at the COST Action IS1102 Workshop, University of Tampere, Tampere, 2–6 June.

Kröger, T. (2001), *Comparative Research on Social Care: The State of the Art*, Luxembourg: European Communities.

Kröger, T. (2011), 'Retuning the Nordic welfare municipality: central regulation of social care under change in Finland', *International Journal of Sociology and Social Policy*, **31** (3/4), 148–59.

Kröger, T. and A. Leinonen (2012), 'Transformation by stealth: the retargeting of home care services in Finland', *Health and Social Care in the Community*, **20** (3), 319–27.

Kröger, T. and S. Yeandle (eds) (2013), *Combining Paid Work and Family Care: Policies and Experiences in International Perspective*, Bristol: Policy Press.

Kröger, T., E. Leinonen and M. Kuronen (2013), 'Restructuring of care for older people in Jyväskylä', unpublished paper presented at the COST Action IS1102 Workshop, University of Iceland, Reykjavik, 3–7 June.

Kubalčíková, K. and J. Havlíková (2013), 'The current development of social services in the care of the older people: deinstitutionalization and/or marketization?', unpublished paper presented at the COST Action IS1102 Workshop, Dunarea de Jos University, Galati, 5–8 November.

Kubalčíková, K. and J. Havlíková (2016), 'Current developments in social care services for older adults in the Czech Republic: trends towards deinstitutionalization and marketization', *Journal of Social Service Research*, **42** (2), 180–98.

Kutsar, D. and M. Kuronen (eds) (2015), *Local Welfare Policy Making in European Cities*, Cham: Springer International Publishing.

Leichsenring, K. (2004), 'Developing integrated health and social care services for older persons in Europe', *International Journal of Integrated Care*, **4** (3), 1–15.

Leichsenring, K. and A. Alaszewski (eds) (2004), *Providing Integrated Health and Social Care for Older Persons: A European Overview of Issues at Stake*, Aldershot: Ashgate.

Leichsenring K., J. Billing and N. Henk (eds) (2013), *Long-Term Care in Europe: Improving Policy and Practice*, London: Palgrave Macmillan.

Martinelli, F. (2012), 'Current organisational framework of care services for older people – Italy', unpublished paper presented at the COST Action IS1102 Workshop, Rovira i Virgili University, Tarragona, 17–19 October.

Mätzke, M. (2012), 'Regulatory trajectories and organisational frameworks of social services. Country profile – Germany', unpublished paper presented at the COST Action IS1102 Workshop, Oslo and Akershus University College, Oslo, 18 June.

Meagher, G. and M. Szebehely (eds) (2013), *Marketisation in Nordic Eldercare: A Research Report on Legislation, Oversight, Extent and Consequences*, Stockholm: Stockholm University (Stockholm Studies in Social Work 30).

Means, R. (2007), 'Safe as houses? Ageing in place and vulnerable older people in the UK', *Social Policy & Administration*, **41** (1), 65–85.

Means, R., H. Morbey and R. Smith (2002), *From Community Care to Market Care? The Development of Welfare Services for Older People*, Bristol: Policy Press.

Pace, C. and S. Vella (2014), 'Impacts on Malta's welfare: causes, experiences and expectations', unpublished paper presented at the COST Action IS1102 Workshop, University of Tampere, Tampere, 2–6 June.

Pace, C., S. Vella and S.F. Dziegielewski (2016), 'Long-term care of older adults in Malta: influencing factors and their social impacts amid the international financial crisis', *Journal of Social Service Research*, **42** (2), 263–79.

Pfau-Effinger, B., L. Flaquer and P.H. Jensen (eds) (2009), *Formal and Informal Work: The Hidden Work Regime in Europe*, New York, USA and London, UK: Routledge.

Ranci, C. and E. Pavolini (eds) (2013), *Reforms in Long-Term Care Policies in Europe*, New York: Springer.

Ródenas, F., J. Garcés, I. Monsonís, C. García and A. Doñate-Martínez (2013), 'Case-management: social and health care for older people', unpublished paper presented at the COST Action IS1102 Workshop, Dunarea de Jos University, Galati, 5–8 November.

Rodrigues, R., M. Huber and G. Lamura (eds) (2012), *Facts and Figures on Healthy Ageing and Long-term Care: Europe and North America*, Vienna: European Centre for Social Welfare Policy and Research.

Sigurðardóttir, S.H. (2014), 'Older people with limitations – aging at home in Iceland', unpublished paper presented at the COST Action IS1102 Workshop, University of Tampere, Tampere, 2–6 June.

Sigurðardóttir, S.H. and I. Kåreholt (2014), 'Informal and formal care of older people in Iceland', *Scandinavian Journal of Caring Sciences*, **28** (4), 802–11.

Sigurðardóttir, S.H., O.H. Kristmundsson and S. Hrafnsdóttir (2016), 'Care of older adults in Iceland: policy objectives and reality', *Journal of Social Service Research*, **42** (2), 233–45.

Szüdi, G., J. Kováčová and S. Konečný (2016), 'Transformation of social care services for the elderly in Slovakia', *Journal of Social Service Research*, **42** (2), 199–217.

Timonen, V., M. Doyle and C. O'Dwyer (2012), 'Expanded, but not regulated: ambiguity in home-care policy in Ireland', *Health and Social Care in the Community*, **20** (3), 310–18.

Troisi, J. and H.J. von Kondratowitz (eds) (2013), *Ageing in the Mediterranean*, Bristol: Policy Press.

Vaiou, D. and D. Siatitsa (2013), 'Current organisational framework of elderly care services', *COST Action IS1102 Working Papers*, no. 2, accessed at http://www.cost-is1102-cohesion.unirc.it/docs/working-papers/wg1.greece-care-for-older-peo ple-d.vaiou-and-d.siatitsa.pdf.

Yeandle, S. (2014), 'Reconfiguring services for older people living at home in Leeds, UK: how have services changed?', unpublished paper presented at the COST Action IS1102 Workshop, University of Tampere, Tampere, 2–6 June.

Yeandle, S. (2016), 'From provider to enabler of care? Reconfiguring local authority support for older people and carers in Leeds, 2008 to 2013', *Journal of Social Service Research*, **42** (2), 218–32.

Yeandle, S., T. Kröger, B. Cass, Y.-C. Chou, M. Shimmei and M. Szebehely, (2013), 'The emergence of policy supporting working carers: developments in six countries', in T. Kröger and S. Yeandle (eds), *Combining Paid Work and Family Care: Policies and Experiences in International Perspective*, Bristol: Policy Press, pp. 23–50.

# 10. How marketisation is changing the Nordic model of care for older people

**Anneli Anttonen and Olli Karsio**

## INTRODUCTION

The last thirty years have witnessed significant changes in the ethos and organisation of public services. There has been a profound market shift not only in the liberal welfare states but recently also in the Northern European countries representing the social democratic model. The Nordic countries were well known for their extensive care service delivery for both children and older people. Services were financed by general tax revenues, produced by municipalities, and provided to all the people who needed these services. The Nordic model of care reflected the capability of social democratic states to extend social rights to cover the care needs of adults and to recognise women's right to employment and independence by providing high-quality care services. This model, among other things, contributed to move unpaid female care work from the sphere of the private household economy to the publicly funded care labour market with high professional opportunities.

This is a major reason to look more closely at the avenues and mechanisms through which an increasing proportion of publicly funded care services for older people are recently being removed from the entirely public sphere of state and municipal provision towards a greater involvement of the private household, the formal economy of the market, and the voluntary or third sectors. The Nordic care model thus reflects current welfare re-mixes as discussed in this book (see Martinelli, Chapter 1, in this volume; Leibetseder et al., in this volume). Clear signs of intensified marketisation are emerging most particularly in Finland and Sweden (Karsio and Anttonen, 2013; Meagher and Szebehely, 2013). Here, care services for older people are, among publicly funded services, the most extensively outsourced to private for-profit providers; and, among these services, residential care is proving to be a lucrative opportunity for large international companies.

By marketisation we refer to the growing presence of private for-profit providers and the increasing influence of market ideas, logics and mechanisms within public service delivery (Anttonen and Meagher, 2013). From the point of view of the Nordic model, marketisation is now the major rationality shaping and framing public sector service provision. As with many other concepts in social theory, marketisation is of course a complex and context-bound term taking different meanings in different times, places and academic disciplines. In this chapter, our aim is to map out what marketisation is about in the Nordic countries and in the context of care for older people. We also ask how marketisation fits into the Nordic model of care. Most importantly, does it alter the principle of universalism that in social services refers to *equal access* to services and to the *inclusiveness* of the care service system, meaning that all people, in principle, *use the same services and are treated in the same way in similar care situations*? Universalism also implies that citizens might have a legal right to services and that *service fees – if any – are low and affordable* to users (Anttonen, 2002; Vabø and Szebehely, 2012). The two countries looked at more closely are Finland and Sweden, where marketisation has been a stronger force than in Denmark and Norway.

## 1.   MARKETISATION: A POWERFUL TRANSFORMATIVE IDEA AND IDEOLOGY

Marketisation reflects the overall economisation and commercialisation of social policies and the production of public goods (Brown, 2015; Crouch, 2004; Newman, 2013; Streeck and Thelen, 2005). It was pushed forward by the administrative reform movements pursuing economic efficiency and effectiveness (Hood, 1998), such as New public management (NPM). Reformers in different countries have favoured techniques taken from the private business sector as a solution to a wide range of perceived problems of public sector service provision. For instance, according to early-stage NPM architects, instead of hierarchical and large organisations, preference would be given to lean and small organisational forms. Similarly, an array of market-type instruments, including outsourcing, competitive tendering and performance-related pay, were recommended and widely introduced in the public sectors of many countries (Pollitt and Bouckaert, 2011).

The marketisation of public services has been further advanced by the austerity measures many governments have adopted since the 1990s to cope with the long-lasting crisis in the public financing of social transfers and services. The recent financial crisis has also played a part, leading policy-makers to seek ways of cutting costs, often through greater targeting of services, cuts in social welfare programs, as well as the outsourcing of services (Gingrich, 2011; Meagher and Szebehely, 2013).

The market shift is deeply rooted in neo-liberalism. Economic reasoning has changed so that economic organisations are increasingly seen as appropriately organising every domain of life (Brown, 2015). Public sector and public service provision are not left untouched. This is, as Brown argues, very different from the doctrine of unregulated laissez-faire capitalism. It is now widely thought that markets are also the best way to organise public goods such as education and social care, and that this development has to be supported through laws and governmental interventions. Marketisation has turned into such a powerful idea and logic that it has become difficult to oppose it. Markets are a beautiful idea, as Clarke (2010) has noted. This might be one reason why the political Left has supported market reforms in many countries (Erlandsson et al., 2013; Gingrich, 2011). Changes in citizens' values and expectations have also had a role to play, as users' choice is a widely supported idea. The disability movement, for instance, has strongly supported policies that favour freedom of choice and the use of vouchers and personal budgets (Yeandle, 2016; Kremer, 2006).

In Europe, the United Kingdom was among the first countries to reform thoroughly its public service model back in the late 1980s. These reforms have 'led the way in making welfare more conditional, more targeted and more oriented to market logics' (Clarke, 2010, p. 384). Other countries have followed the British route, at least to some extent. International organisations such as the OECD and the EU also have paved the way for the 'new politics of social care' with recommendations and regulation structured along market logics (Jenson, 2009). All this has changed the ethos of social service delivery and the governance of these services. The active creation of 'managed markets' has obtained a strong foothold in different public policy fields, such as health and social care, housing and education, leaning on a wide range of mechanisms (Gingrich, 2011; Brennan et al., 2012): purchaser/provider split, competitive tendering, vouchers and personal budgets (Clarke, 2006; Newman and Tonkens, 2011; Vabø, 2006). The benefits of coordination through competition – or 'market discipline' – have been advocated, whether driven by the re-organisation on the supply side or by consumer choice on the demand side (Martinelli, Chapter 1, in this volume; Gingrich, 2011).

New public management and other market-centred doctrines have also emphasised the notion of service *users*, reframing them as 'consumers' or even 'customers', who are entitled to more choice and voice (Clarke, 2006; Glendinning, 2008; Clarke et al., 2007; Rostgaard, 2006). The reframing of the service user as a consumer is linked not only to marketisation, but also to the personalisation and individualisation of the service provision. These processes invoke tailor-made solutions that are very different from the so-called 'one-size-fits-all' conception of services and they also refer to a shift in responsibilities. People themselves and their families are expected to take over greater responsibility over meeting care needs than earlier (CAP Anttonen and Häikiö, 2014; Yeandle, 2016). Along marketisation there are of course other ideas and logics that are contributing to changing the provision of public services, such as 'network governance', public–private 'partnerships' and 'mixed economies of welfare' (Anttonen and Häikiö, 2011; Leibetseder et al., in this volume), but they are not addressed in this chapter.

Marketisation and consumerism are deeply rooted in theories advocating 'freedom of choice', 'rational choice' and 'public choice' in public service delivery (Pollitt and Bouckaert, 2011). These theories have influenced public policies and political decision-making and finally actual service delivery all over the world, although the pace and timing of implementing market-intensive reforms vary (e.g. Bouckaert et al., 2010; Gingrich, 2011). One interesting finding is that public sector change has been deep in countries, such as for instance Finland, Sweden and the UK, where service provision was previously built upon hierarchically and professionally organised systems, rule of the law, and incremental budgeting (Pollitt and Bouckaert, 2011). Marketisation has thus got a fairly strong foothold in countries where the grand idea of universalism was first launched after the second world war (Sipilä and Anttonen, 2012) and, most importantly, extended to cover numerous social services. This brings us to argue that marketisation in the Nordic countries means that governments are marketising their welfare state and its institutions in the first instance 'from within'. In fact, most of the mechanisms of marketisation adopted are leaving the *funding* of services to the public sector and are marketising only the *production* side of these social goods. This is a clear difference with countries where marketisation has taken place more or less outside the public sector because there was no notable public service provision to start with, or because the public sector is not growing sufficiently to meet rising needs.

## 2.   MARKETISATION *FROM WITHIN*: THE NORDIC WELFARE MARKET MODEL IN THE MAKING

Marketisation takes different forms and is accelerated and implemented through diverse strategies and mechanisms in different countries. Marketisation *from within* is advanced mainly through the *outsourcing* of public services to for-profit providers and through implementing *customer choice models.* These two strategies represent the two main marketisation avenues in the Nordic countries.

## The Legislative Milestones

The beginning of marketisation is fairly similar in the Nordic countries. Up until the early 1990s virtually all care services were provided by the public sector. A series of legislative changes made it easier for the state and municipalities to start outsourcing services to private providers in the course of the 1990s.

In Sweden, the Social Democratic government introduced a new Local Government Act in 1992 (*Kommunallag 1991:900*), which 'codified norms and rules that had, in practice, already been in use in some municipalities' (Erlandsson et al., 2013, p. 26). The subsequent Conservative-led government made further amendments to the law, strengthening the role of private for-profit producers. Changes were made also to many other laws so that, in practice, only services that included the direct exercise of public authority were not outsourced. Since in Sweden public authority includes also the assessment of needs in care services for older people, the 1992 law meant that the assessment of needs and the provision of services became separated. Also in 1992, the Act on Public Procurement (*Lag om offentlig upphandling 1992:1528*, hereafter LOU) came into force, regulating the outsourcing of public services to private producers and introducing the obligation of competitive tendering.

In Finland, the revised Social Welfare Act came into force in 1984 (*Sosiaalihuoltolaki 710/1982*), ruling that local authorities are obliged to organise social services, to provide social assistance, and to pay allowances for their residents. State subsidies can be used for purchasing social services provided not only by the municipal authorities but also by not-for-profit and for-profit providers, as well as for making payments for informal care. The act represents a framework legislation that gives a 'right' to services or assistance only if needs cannot be met in any other way. The legislation does not include detailed regulations or subjective rights but guarantees access to needs assessment, which must be done by professional service workers. As in Sweden also in Finland decisions are mainly left to public authorities, most particularly with functions such as decisions over involuntary placements in child protection and mental health care (Huhtanen, 2012).

In Norway, the Procurement Act of 1992 (*Lov om offentlige anskaffelser, hereafter LOA*) gave more autonomy to the local authorities to choose whether to produce public services in-house or outsource them to private producers (CAP Øverbye et al., 2012). The act was amended in 1999,

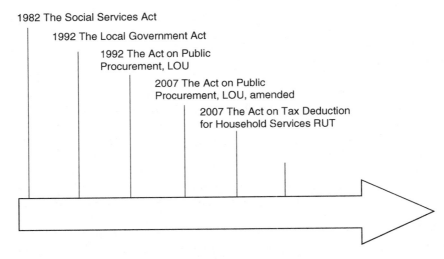

*Source:*   Authors' compilation, based on Erlandsson et al. (2013).

*Figure 10.1    The marketisation timeline in Sweden*

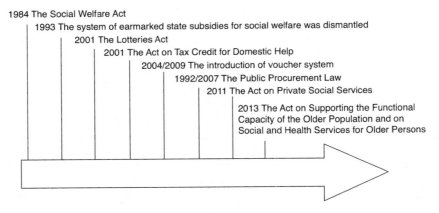

*Source:*   Karsio and Anttonen (2013, p. 97).

*Figure 10.2    The marketisation timeline in Finland*

stating that public procurements should be based on competition as far as possible. It resulted in increasing outsourcing in some municipalities, but not to the extent it reached in Sweden and Finland. Furthermore, Norway protected the participation of the non-profit sector in the production of social and health services. In 2006, an amendment was introduced in the public procurement legislation, whereby public authorities could outsource services to non-profit organisations without using a competitive bidding procedure. In other words, the Norwegian public sector can award non-profit organisations contracts to produce services without putting them on the same line with for-profit producers, unlike its Swedish and Finnish counterparts (Vabø et al., 2013, p. 176).

Thus, through changes in political preferences and several legislative reforms, more space for market provision within social services has been opened up in all three Nordic countries. It is important to stress, though, that local authorities are not *obliged* to outsource any of their social and health services in Finland, Sweden or Norway. Outsourcing is always a *voluntary* option in public service provision. In Finland, municipalities can outsource services and use vouchers if they prefer, but they can also provide services themselves or in collaboration with other local authorities. Thus, outsourcing in itself does not automatically lead to an increase of market provision. In fact, Finnish municipalities have a long tradition of outsourcing to purchase care services from non-profit providers, which has not been the case in Sweden.

The first wave of marketisation was thus mostly about *outsourcing* former publicly produced services. In Sweden services were outsourced through competitive tenders to for-profit providers from the very beginning, while in Finland the early years of outsourcing favoured non-profit providers. This was due to the special status of Finland's Slot Machine Association (in Finnish RAY), which had (and still has) a monopoly over slot machines in the nation and was, and is, obliged to use its profits for the public good. With financial aid from RAY, about 50 old age homes were built as early as the 1960s; whereas about 14 000 'service' housing flats were constructed between the mid-1980s and the mid-1990s, for older people who needed some help in their daily affairs but not 24-hour attendance (Pasanen, 2010, p. 22). RAY subsidies were thus crucial for the expansion of care services for older people. Moreover, since 'service' housing, funded by RAY, could not be provided by local authorities or for-profit providers, it gave a very strong position to third sector organisations.

The close partnership between municipalities and third sector associations, however, ended in 2001 with the Lotteries Act (*Arpajaislaki 1047/2001*), which marked a clear turn towards a policy of competitive neutrality. This principle was written in the legislation of public procurements and was a key factor behind the rapid growth of for-profit providers and the *incorporation* of welfare associations that took place after 2001. In Finland, non-profit organisations and associations provided welfare service as registered associations (registration was and is required for these organisations to sign contracts with local authorities to provide services). In recent years, many of these registered non-profit organisations have separated the service provision part of their operations from other activities, and changed the registered organisation into a for-profit provider by establishing a new company, which is, however, owned by the registered organisation or association (Kananoja et al., 2008). There are also other reasons for the incorporation of non-profit providers, for instance changes in national taxation practices (Kettunen, 2010). Similar process concerning competitive neutrality took place in Sweden in 2007, when the LOU was amended and market friendlier rules were introduced.

Further steps toward the creation of a welfare market in social care were taken when legislation establishing *tax credits for domestic help* came into force in 2001 in Finland (*Tuloverolaki 995/2000*) and in 2007 in Sweden (*Lag om skattereduktion för hushållsarbete 2007:346,* hereafter RUT). The main political forces behind tax credit reforms were right-wing parties and employers' associations that had been most outspoken in their demands for *free choice* policies and tax rebates to enable people to *purchase* services with their own money and/or to employ domestic or care workers in private households. In Finland, this measure provided a tax rebate on the purchase of domestic or care services or on employing a private caregiver to assist old persons in their homes (Karsio and Anttonen, 2013). The tax rebate clearly represented a market-friendly policy alternative to publicly funded service provisions and further accelerated the market turn.

**Customers' Choice**

After the above-described first wave of marketisation, Nordic countries increasingly embraced *free choice models* as a way to organise both social and health care. The customer choice model in the Nordic countries refers to a system where users of services can choose an authorised provider following needs assessment made by the public authorities (Erlandsson et al., 2013). In Sweden, the Act on System of Choice in the Public Sector (*Lag om valfrihetssystem* 2008:962, hereafter LOV) came into force in 2009 and marked a very clear shift from the outsourcing model to a customer choice model. 'The Act regulates what conditions apply when a procuring authority allows individuals to choose the provider of service from a list of approved providers in a system of choice' (Erlandsson et al., 2013, p. 30).

The customer choice model was adopted in Denmark in a slightly different form than in Sweden (CAP Jensen and Fersch, 2013). According to Bertelsen and Rostgaard (2013), Denmark, unlike other Nordic countries, has no specific legislation promoting or restricting outsourcing of social and care services. However, although the marketisation process in

Denmark had been more cautious than in the eastern Nordic countries, free choice legislation was implemented in the case of home care and residential care for older people. In 2002 legislation concerning free choice was enacted for home care services with the Law on Free Choice of Provider of Practical Assistance and Personal Care (*Lov nr. 399 af 6. juni 2002 Frit valg af leverandør af personlig og praktisk hjælp*) and in 2007 it was extended to residential care and nursing homes with the Act of Social Services & Law on Independent Nursing Homes (*Lov om friplejeboliger 2007*). Despite the fact that Danish municipalities are forced to offer free choice to customers and there has been some increase in private producers providing care for older people (CAP Jensen and Fersch, 2013), on the whole this has not resulted in a wide use of private producers (Bertelsen and Rostgaard, 2013).

In Finland, individual choice has been promoted through a voucher system first piloted in the 1990s (Heikkilä et al., 1997; Vaarama et al., 1999). Vouchers were then integrated into social legislation in 2004 (CAP Leinonen et al., 2012). In 2009, a specific law, the Act on Health and Social Service Vouchers (*Laki sosiaali- ja terveydenhuollon palvelusetelistä 569/2009*) was passed. This act made it possible for the municipalities to organise all social and health services through a voucher model, excluding emergency and involuntary services (such as involuntary placements in child protection and mental health care). It was justified with arguments that it would enhance customer choice and improve the effectiveness of services through competition. The main difference between outsourcing and the service voucher system is that in the former case it is the local authority that arranges the competition among different providers, whereas in the latter case it is the service user who makes the decision among different service providers. Although, on the whole, the voucher system in Finland has remained fairly marginal, a new reform under preparation is likely to change the entire system of health and social service provision in Finland by introducing a full choice model, first in primary health care in 2017–19 and later in almost all health and social services, if the government proposal is approved in parliament. This reform will also move the responsibility of arranging services from more than 300 municipalities to 18 counties (https://www.alueuudistus.fi).

In a country where municipal services constituted the core of the welfare state (CAP Kröger and Leinonen, 2012), the Finnish social and health care reform represents a comprehensive change and has spurred a strong discussion. Among the main advocates of the reform are big national and international for-profit companies operating in social and health care, since the free choice model, the centralised system and the 18 new counties (embedding a promise of larger market areas) paint a lucrative and successful future. The critics of the reform see black clouds above it. In contrast to the huge saving potential hoped for by the government, a rise in the costs of the system seems to be inevitable unless the service quality or level is lowered, or the client fees are raised. In addition, private producers might well start choosing their customers due to cream-skimming, in contrast to the original idea of free choice. Moreover, free choice is questionable in the context of care for older people, because of the limited ability of frail older people to make informed choices in the emerging care market.

## 3.   WHAT HAS CHANGED IN THE NORDIC MODEL? AND WHAT ARE THE IMPLICATIONS?

### Increase in For-profit Service Production and the Role of the Non-profits

A major result of marketisation is changes in the *providers* of care services. The share of the private for-profit sector within all publicly funded services has risen steadily in the last 20 years, especially in Sweden and Finland (Erlandsson et al., 2013; Karsio and Anttonen, 2013; CAP Kröger et al., 2013; CAP Knutagård, 2012). It appears that Norway and Denmark have been more resistant to market forces in the field of care for older people (CAP Vabo and Øverbye, 2012; Meagher and Szebehely, 2013), but in Sweden and Finland the presence of private providers is now significant.

In Sweden, the share of privately produced care services for older people, measured as the proportion of employees working in the private sector, was 3 per cent at the beginning of the 1990s (Erlandsson et al., 2013, pp. 23, 47). After over 20 years, the corresponding figures were 24 per cent in home care (measured in hours) and roughly 20 per cent in residential care (measured in beds) (Socialstyrelsen, 2016). Moreover, the presence of private for-profit companies in the Swedish care service sector for older people has increased from almost nothing to one fifth of all services.

Finland has experienced a similar change. Here, the share of social service personnel working in public social services fell from 88 to 66.5 per cent between 1990 and 2013 (Ailasmaa, 2015; Karsio and Anttonen, 2013). In care services for older people the proportion of personnel working in private for-profit companies rose from 6.7 to 21 per cent between 2000 and 2013, while that of the public sector fell from 74 to 64 per cent (Ailasmaa, 2015). The increase of for-profit private producers has been intense especially in 'service' housing and other 24-hour residential care. In 2000, the share of for-profit providers within publicly funded services in residential care was 16.4 and in 2013 it had reached 35.6 per cent (Ailasmaa, 2015). On the whole, these figures strongly support the thesis that there is a strong movement towards intensified marketisation and there really are profound changes in the ways services are produced in Finland.

Another important consequence of marketisation in Finland is that non-profit service providers have to resemble their for-profit counterparts to be successful in competitive bids. They have to compete in terms of service prices to win the bid because the system of direct award is not common in Finland. Thus, there is no longer room for developing innovative but costly services typically piloted and run by non-profits (Lith, 2013). The same is true with the special arrangement within the non-profit service provision that was earlier justified on communitarian principles. These principles have been replaced by the logic of market competition, meaning that traditional non-profit service provision and competitive neutrality do not necessarily fit together.

Competitive neutrality, placing both non-profits and for-profits on the same level in the bidding for public contracts, is applied differently within the Nordic countries. Norway has chosen to exercise positive discrimination in favour of the non-profits by means of legislation (Bertelsen et al., 2013). In contrast, in Finland the national procurement legislation is very strict on the competitive neutrality between the for-profit and the non-profit providers (Karsio and Anttonen, 2013). It is also worth remembering that the values of public goods and the non-profit service ideology might be endangered if welfare associations are forced to give up the communitarian and piloting rationality that their earlier performance was based on. Non-profit welfare associations have been very active in creating personalised services for older people with disabilities or drinking problems. The for-profit sector has so far paid much less or nearly no attention to these groups and their needs.

**The Changing Role of the State**

Nordic countries have been exceptional in their reliance on the state, public provision of in-kind service and universalism being their leading trademark (Sipilä and Anttonen, 2012; Kallio, 2010; Vaarama et al., 2014). Citizens and decision-makers in the Nordic countries viewed the state and the public sector as the best guarantor of citizens' social rights and of the common good. Accordingly, the welfare state was supposed to correct the failures of the market rather than work for the market (Esping-Andersen, 1985). When welfare is delivered through the market, then the question arises: how are social rights and the common good to be secured?

With reference to the main functions identified by Martinelli (Chapter 1, in this volume), we argue that in the new model the state continues to perform the *regulation*, *financing* and *planning* functions: through its legislative power it sets the legal frame and defines the rules for service provision; it collects resources (mainly through taxation) and finances the provision of social and other services; it also coordinates the regional and local service provision through old and new functions, such as procurement and tender legislation. But it plays a diminishing role in the actual *production* of services. We can thus expect a growing partnership between the public sector and private service providers, including for-profit companies, non-profit organisations and household provision of care and services. It can also be argued that the state and the public sector are not actually withdrawing from service provision, but are turning into enabler, financer and purchaser of services. Consequently, the role of the state is changing, but so also is the role of citizens and service workers or managers.

Market actors are much more central partners than earlier. This development might lead to a 'differentiated polity', which would encompass diverse features and processes, such as fragmentation, networks, hollowing-out and new governance modes (Rhodes, 1988). A differentiated polity is about mixed markets, hierarchies, and networks (or governance structures) in contemporary states. If universalisation referred to institutional generalisation, uniformity and predictability in processes and outcomes, differentiation refers to the processes of functional and institutional specialisation, fragmentation of policies and politics, increase in complexity and loss of central steering capacity. As Newman (2013) notes, 'divesting' is one of the processes occurring in complex environments, which involves a stripping away of government functions.

The phrase 'hollowing-out of the state' is used to summarise some of the changes taking place in the Nordic countries, such as the decreasing scope of public intervention. It also refers to the loss of functions upwards to the European Union and outward to new service actors. Yet the role of the state in Finland and Sweden has been, and is even today, fairly strong in regulating these new managed markets and, most importantly, in the funding of services. Funding principles have not changed very much: even in the late 2010s the state, regional and municipal governments still finance care and other services for older people on the basis of general taxation. Moreover, there are no notable changes in legislation when it comes to the right to the assessment of care service needs. These parts of the Nordic care model have remained more or less untouched and the huge increase in the for-profit provision of care services has not yet changed all pillars of the model.

On the other hand, the changes that have already taken place might lead into a further radical reorganisation of the public sector and a much more extensive use of for-profit services. The marketisation shift in Nordic countries has already proved to be a lucrative opportunity for large international care companies. This is by no means a small aspect in the discussion about the impact of marketisation on the Nordic care model and welfare state. The concentration of the care markets in a few large, private, for-profit companies in Finland and Sweden has been highlighted in several studies (Karsio and Anttonen, 2013; Erlandsson et al., 2013) and has many implications. First, international companies become powerful political actors, capable of influencing the development and planning of care systems (Brennan et al., 2012). Their lobbying power is on a very different level compared to small and often local companies or associations providing services, i.e. those lean and small units praised by the early stage NPM architects. Secondly, international companies are quite efficient in tax avoidance. OECD (2015) and national non-governmental organisations have assessed the amount of tax revenues lost due to aggressive tax planning by multinational companies. Finnwatch estimated that in Finland alone the state loses between 430 and 1400 million in tax revenues annually (Ylönen and Purje, 2013; Finér and Telkki, 2016). The share of this annual loss due to care companies is not known but is significant. Thirdly, as private companies provide more and more publicly funded services, a larger share of people work now in the private sector.

Finally, we need to pay attention to the new identity of 'customers' involved in the market shift, meaning that the user of services as a buyer now has the right to complain. Fountain (2001, p. 63) noted that in earlier times 'legislators may never have intended to promise service excellence when passing legislation to mandate certain services'. The same applied to public servants: they had the obligation to provide services equitably. Service universalism is at least partly about meeting needs of large numbers of people in a decent but not luxury way. Freedom of choice might instead lead into a situation where the 'customer' has the right to set the standard and pay extra for better or more luxury services compared to an average situation. This might in the longer run change the Nordic care model. There are also other differences emerging between the system of public service provision and the system of customer choice models: customers possess no particular loyalty to their for-profit service providers. They are motivated by risk avoidance and price. The more services are outsourced and commercialised, the less there is motivation to maintain 'the public interest' or the 'community feeling'. This again might change the relation between the citizen and the state and citizens' willingness to pay taxes. Another development might be, as the father of the voucher system Milton Friedman (1955) stated in a later article: 'Vouchers are not an end in themselves, they are a means to make transition from a government to a market' (Friedman, 1997, p. 343). Thus, Nordic countries might just be at the beginning of the marketisation development.

## 4.   CONCLUDING REMARKS

Our main finding is that marketisation is a process that is intensively and comprehensively re-organising and re-shaping the public provision of care for older people and other social services in the Nordic countries (Meagher and Szebehely, 2013). Thus, if marketisation first involved liberal welfare states, such as the UK (Newman, 2001), it has now reached the Nordic countries, where the state earlier assumed a wide responsibility for both financing and producing care services for its residents.

It is important to stress that the emerging welfare market model, which includes publicly governed and subsidised social and health care markets, is not just an evolution. It has to be created, and once the welfare market model is created it has to be maintained and reproduced. Both its establishment and maintenance require considerable use of public interventions, public money and public regulation. We have highlighted the main avenues and mechanisms behind creating and maintaining managed care markets in the Nordic countries. We also provided a more concrete definition of marketisation, which refers to the growing presence and influence of market ideas, logics and mechanisms in public and publicly funded service provision, which we also define as marketisation 'from within'. In the Nordic countries, there has been very little increase in free market care service provision, irrespective of the introduction of tax rebate schemes.

When we speak about Nordic countries it is important to underline that care is still regarded as a social right: it is not considered a private responsibility of individuals and families but a public good among other tax-financed services. All people, irrespective of their economic and social status, have a right to claim for care and other services, and public authorities are obliged to assess their needs and ensure they are met. Actual access to these services is based on a professional, individual assessment of the person who claims services. This is the case even today and marketisation has not changed this principle. Nevertheless, marketisation is introducing many other changes that, in the end, might also undermine this well-established principle.

As we have shown, marketisation is triggered by both bottom-up and top-down pressures. We have referred to these mechanisms as marketisation from within and from without. The Nordic countries are a grand example of marketisation taking place mostly from within. Marketisation has advanced mainly through local choices and decisions made by municipalities. The national legislations enable municipalities to marketise their service and governance systems, but do not force them to do so, with the exception of Denmark, where – surprisingly – marketisation has not proceeded as rapidly as in Finland and Sweden. It is difficult to evaluate the power of marketisation pressures from without. The EU, OECD and other powerful international actors have clearly favoured market mechanisms in their policy guidelines and directives (Jenson, 2009), but, as the examples from Finnish and Swedish legislation show, these countries have implemented more market-friendly laws than EU directives call for. Why then Finland and Sweden have been more anxious to marketise from within than Norway and Denmark, is an important question and should be studied further. Although marketisation from within seems to be a stronger mechanism than marketisation from without, we are not underestimating the power of travelling ideas and discourses mobilised by the EU and other international advocates of marketisation. We have, however, shown that the actual marketisation processes are context-dependent and reforms take place in processes driven by both bottom-up and top-down forces (see also Martinelli, Chapter 1, in this volume).

Marketisation from within has advanced mainly through two avenues, outsourcing of services and free choice models. Although the Nordic principle of care as a social right remains more or less untouched, the increasing involvement of for-profit companies in service provision and the expanding free choice model are changing the welfare state ethos. The principles of universalism, inclusiveness and equality are threatened by the logics of profit making and free choice. First, the more the access to public care services is dependent on individual choices and resources, whether money or the ability to make rational informed choices, the further the principles of inclusiveness and equality are undermined. Secondly, as private for-profit companies strive for profit in the area of social and health services, the integrity of the welfare state system is compromised. Advocates of marketisation argue that profit making and its implications can be regulated by state, but as research shows, this is not always the case, and regulation has many unintended consequences (e.g. Gingrich, 2011; Armstrong, 2013; Banerjee, 2013). Even though market forces can be controlled – at least for the time being – by the public authority, the more radical advocates of marketisation have no intention to stop here (Friedman, 1997).

Finally, marketisation is changing the identity – status and rights – of service users. In the context of the welfare state, an individual is understood as a citizen with social rights. In marketised welfare states individuals are seen as rational consumers and decision-makers who, by making active choices, shape the welfare markets and systems and make them more effective. According to the market ethos, the social right to welfare and care is not a priority, but a right to make free choices as a consumer in the market. Thus, it is possible that rights will be weakened. We must then ask ourselves for how long the citizen-consumer will support and legitimise the welfare state. Since consumers do not need to turn to bureaucrats but only to market actors to fulfil their needs, the loyalty toward state and municipal (or regional) public agencies might vaporise. Due to outsourcing and the increasing share of for-profits in the provision of care services, this change of the user identity from citizen to consumer might already be a reality. We should also stress that, while the shift from citizen to consumer is already a focus of research (Clarke, 2006; Clarke et al., 2007), we know very little of what happens to the identity of care workers.

To conclude, marketisation in the context of care and its implications do challenge the core principles of Nordic welfare states. Our evidence from the COST Action IS1102 *SO.S. COHESION – Social services, welfare states and places* and from other critical research does support the argument that the ethos of the welfare state is changing – and rapidly so – as a consequence of the growing role of markets within public service provision. Marketisation from within and from without, the increasing share of private for-profit producers, the changing roles and identities of service users and employees are all factors that might question the very roots of the Nordic welfare state and universalism. On the other hand, despite the directions of change discussed in this chapter and the increasing pace of marketisation, some basic features of the Nordic model are standing their ground. Universalism is still a fundamental idea and principle, at least if we refer to inclusiveness and the extensiveness of public funding of care services.

# REFERENCES

Ailasmaa, R. (2015), *Sosiaali- ja Terveyspalvelujen Henkilöstö 2013*, THL Statistical Report 26/2015, Helsinki: THL.

Anttonen, A. (2002), 'Universalism and social policy: a Nordic-feminist revaluation', *NORA – Nordic Journal of Feminist and Gender Research*, **10** (2), 71–80.

Anttonen, A. and L. Häikiö (2011), 'Care "going market": Finnish elderly-care policies in transition', *Nordic Journal of Social Research*, **2**, 70–90.

Anttonen, A. and L. Häikiö (2014), 'Eldercare service redesign in six Finnish municipalities: Welfare market in the making', unpublished paper presented at the COST Action IS1102 Workshop, Faculty of Economics and Business, Barcelona, 3–6 March.

Anttonen, A. and G. Meagher (2013), 'Introduction', in G. Meagher and M. Szebehely (eds), *Marketization in Nordic Eldercare: A Research Report on Legislation, Oversight, Extent and Consequences*, Stockholm: Stockholm University, pp. 13–22.

Armstrong, P. (2013), 'Regulating care: lessons from Canada', in G. Meagher and M. Szebehely (eds), *Marketization in Nordic Eldercare: A Research Report on Legislation, Oversight, Extent and Consequences*, Stockholm Studies in Social Work 30, Stockholm: Stockholm University, pp. 217–28.

Banerjee, A. (2013), 'The regulatory trap: reflections on the vicious cycle of regulation in Canadian residential care', in G. Meagher and M. Szebehely (eds), *Marketization in Nordic Eldercare: A Research Report on Legislation, Oversight, Extent and Consequences*, Stockholm Studies in Social Work 30, Stockholm: Stockholm University, pp. 203–16.

Bertelsen, T.M. and T. Rostgaard (2013), 'Marketisation in eldercare in Denmark: free choice and the quest for quality and efficiency', in G. Meagher and M. Szebehely (eds), *Marketization in Nordic Eldercare: A Research Report on Legislation, Oversight, Extent and Consequences*, Stockholm Studies in Social Work 30, Stockholm: Stockholm University, pp. 127–62.

Bouckaert, G., G. Peters and K. Verhoest (2010), *The Coordination of Public Sector Organizations. Shifting Patterns of Public Management*, New York: Palgrave.

Brennan, D., B. Cass, S. Himmelweit and M. Szebehely (2012), 'The marketization of care: rationales and consequences in Nordic and liberal care regimes', *Journal of European Social Policy*, **22** (4), 377–91.

Brown, W. (2015), *Undoing the Demos. Neoliberalism's Stealth Revolution*, Cambridge: MIT Press.

Clarke, J. (2006), 'Consumers, clients or citizens? Politics, policy and practice in the reform of social care', *European Societies*, **8** (3), 423–42.

Clarke, J. (2010), 'After neo-liberalism? Markets, states and the reinvention of public welfare', *Cultural Studies*, **24** (3), 375–94.

Clarke, J., J. Newman, N. Smith, E. Vidler and L. Westmarland (2007), *Creating Citizen-Consumers: Changing Publics & Changing Public Services*, London, UK and Thousand Oaks, USA: SAGE.

Crouch, C. (2004), *Post-Democracy*, Cambridge: Polity Press.

Erlandsson, S., P. Storm, A. Stranz, M. Szebehely and G. Trydegård (2013), 'Marketising trends in Swedish eldercare: competition, choice and calls for stricter regulation', in G. Meagher and M. Szebehely (eds), *Marketization in Nordic Eldercare: A Research Report on Legislation, Oversight, Extent and Consequences*, Stockholm Studies in Social Work 30, Stockholm: Stockholm University, pp. 23–84.

Esping-Andersen, E. (1985), *Politics Against Markets: The Social Democratic Road to Power*, Princeton: Princeton University Press.

Finér, L. and H. Telkki (2016), 'Jäävuorta mittaamassa. Arvioita monikansallisten yritysten aggressiivisen verosuunnittelun laajuudesta Suomessa', Finnwatch: Helsinki, accessed 21 December 2016 at http://finnwatch.org/images/pdf/jaavu ori.pdf.

Fountain, J.E. (2001), 'Paradoxes of public sector customer service', *Governance: An International Journal of Policy and Administration*, **14** (1), 55–73.

Friedman, M. (1955), 'The role of government in education', in R.A. Solo (ed.), *Economics and the Public Interest*, New Brunswick: Rutgers University Press.

Friedman, M. (1997), 'Public schools: make them private', *Education Economics*, **5** (3), 341–44.

Gingrich, J. (2011), *Making Markets in the Welfare State. The Politics of Varying Market Reforms*, Cambridge, UK and New York, USA: Cambridge University Press.

Glendinning, C. (2008), 'Increasing choice and control for older and disabled people: a critical review of new developments in England', *Social Policy & Administration*, **42** (5), 451–69.

Heikkilä, M., S. Törmä and K. Mattila (1997), *Palveluseteli lasten Päivähoidossa: Raportti Valtakunnallisesta Kokeilusta*, Raportteja 216, Helsinki: Stakes.

Hood, C. (1998), *The Art of the State: Culture, Rhetoric, and Public Management*, Oxford: Oxford University Press.

Huhtanen, R. (2012), 'Kunnan sosiaali- ja terveyspalvelujen yksityistäminen: oikeudellinen näkökulma', in A. Anttonen, A. Haveri, J. Lehto and H. Palukka (eds), *Julkisen ja Yksityisen Rajalla. Julkisen Palvelurakenteen Muutos*, Tampere: Tampere University Press, pp. 81–110.

Jensen, P.H. and B. Fersch (2013), 'Local variations and preferences in the organization of elder care: the Danish case', unpublished paper presented at the COST Action IS1102 Workshop, University of Iceland, Reykjavik, 3–7 June.

Jenson, J. (2009), 'Redesigning citizenship regimes after neoliberalism. Moving towards social investment', in N. Morel, J. Palme and B. Palier (eds), *What Future for Social Investment?*, Research Report 2/2009, Stockholm: Institute for Future Studies.

Kallio, J. (2010), *Hyvinvointipalvelujärjestelmän Muutos ja Suomalaisten Mielipiteet 1996–2006*, Sosiaali- ja terveysturvan tutkimuksia 108, Helsinki: Kelan tutkimusosasto.

Kananoja, A., V. Niiranen and H. Jokiranta (2008), *Kunnallinen Sosiaalipolitiikka: Osallisuutta ja Yhteistä Vastuuta*, Jyväskylä: PS-kustannus.

Karsio, O. and A. Anttonen (2013), 'Marketisation of eldercare in Finland: legal frames, outsourcing practices and the rapid growth of for-profit services', in G. Meagher and M. Szebehely (eds), *Marketization in Nordic Eldercare: A Research Report on Legislation, Oversight, Extent and Consequences*, Stockholm Studies in Social Work 30, Stockholm: Stockholm University, pp. 85–126.

Kettunen, R. (2010), *Sosiaalipalvelut*, Toimialaraportti 11/2010, Helsinki: Ministry of Employment and the Economy, accessed at http://www.temtoimialapalvelu.fi/files/1199/Sosiaalipalvelut_2010web.pdf.

Knutagård, M. (2012), 'Regulatory trajectories and organisational frameworks of social services. Country and regional profile – Sweden', unpublished paper presented at the COST Action IS1102 Workshop, Oslo and Akershus University College, Oslo, 18 June.

Kremer, M. (2006), 'Consumers in charge of care: the Dutch personal budget and its impact on the market, professionals and the family', *European Societies*, **8** (3), 361–83.

Kröger, T. and E. Leinonen (2012), 'Regulatory trajectories and organisational frameworks of social services. Country and regional profiles – Finland', unpublished paper presented at the COST Action IS1102 Workshop, Oslo and Akershus University College, Oslo, 18 June.

Kröger, T., E. Leinonen and M. Kuronen (2013), 'Restructuring of care for older people in Jyväskylä', unpublished paper presented at the COST Action IS1102 Workshop, University of Iceland, Reykjavik, 3–7 June.

Leinonen, E., T. Sihto and T. Kröger (2012), 'Current organisational framework of care services for older people – Finland', unpublished paper presented at the COST Action IS1102 Workshop, Rovira i Virgili University, Tarragona, 17–19 October.

Lith, P. (2013), *Vanhusten ja Erityisryhmien Yksityisen Palveluasumisen Kilpailutilanne*, TEM raportteja 9/2013, Helsinki: Ministry of Economic Affairs and Employment, accessed 21 December 2016 at https://tem.fi/documents/14108 77/2872337/Vanhusten+ja+erityisryhmien+yksityisen+palveluasumisen+kilpail utilanne+08022013.pdf.

Meagher, G. and M. Szebehely (eds) (2013), *Marketization in Nordic Eldercare: A*

*Research Report on Legislation, Oversight, Extent and Consequences*, Stockholm: Stockholm University.

Newman, J. (2001), *Modernising Governance: New Labour, Policy and Society*, London: Sage.

Newman, J. (2013), 'Performing new worlds? Policy, politics and creative labour in hard times', *Policy and Politics*, **41** (4), 515–32.

Newman, J. and E. Tonkens (eds) (2011), *Participation, Responsibility and Choice: Summoning the Active Citizen in Western European Welfare States*, Amsterdam: Amsterdam University Press.

OECD (2015), *Measuring and Monitoring BEPS, Action 11 – 2015 Final Report*, Paris: OECD Publishing, accessed 21 December 2016 at http://www.keepeek.com/Digital-Asset-Management/oecd/taxation/measuring-and-monitoring-beps-action-11-2015-final-report_9789264241343-en#.WC6_kk27rnM.

Øverbye, E., E. Gubrium and I. Harsløf (2012), 'Regulatory trajectories and organisational frameworks of social, education and health services – Norway', unpublished paper presented at the COST Action IS1102 Workshop, Oslo and Akershus University College, Oslo, 18 June.

Pasanen, S. (2010), *Vanhusten Palveluasumisen Vaiheet Tampereella. Asiantuntijoiden Kokemuksia ja Näkemyksiä*, Tampereen kaupunki, Tiedontuotannnon ja laadunarvioinnin julkaisusarja C1/2010, Tampere: City of Tampere.

Pollitt, C. and G. Bouckaert (2011), *Public Management Reform: A Comparative Analysis – New Public Management, Governance, and the Neo-Weberian State*, Oxford: Oxford University Press.

Rhodes, M. (1988), 'Globalization, labour markets and welfare states: a future of "competitive corporatism"?', in M. Rhodes and Y. Meny (eds), *The Future of European Welfare: A New Social Contract?*, London: Macmillan.

Rostgaard, T. (2006), 'Constructing the care consumer: free choice of home care for the elderly in Denmark', *European Societies*, **8** (3), 443–63.

Sipilä, J. and A. Anttonen (2012), 'Universalism in British and Scandinavian social policy debates', in A. Anttonen, L. Häikiö and K. Stefansson (eds), *Welfare State, Universalism and Diversity*, Cheltenham, UK and Northampton, MA, USA: Edward Elgar Publishing, pp. 16–41.

Socialstyrelsen (2016), *Vård och Omsorg om Äldre – Lägesrapport 2016*, Stockholm: Socialstyrelsen, accessed 21 December 2016 at http://socialstyrelsen.sosdmz.se/publikationer2016/2016-3-9.

Streeck, W. and K. Thelen (2005), *Beyond Continuity. Institutional Change in Advanced Political Economies*, Oxford: Oxford University Press.

Vaarama, M., S. Törmä, S. Laaksonen and P. Voutilainen (1999), *Omaishoidon Tuen Tarve ja Palvelusetelillä Järjestetty Tilapäishoito. Omaishoidon Palvelusetelikokeilun Loppuraportti*, Selvityksiä 1999:10, Helsinki: Ministry of Social Affairs and Health and Stakes.

Vaarama, M., S. Karvonen, L. Kestilä, P. Moisio and A. Muuri (eds) (2014), *Suomalaisten Hyvinvointi 2014*, Helsinki: THL.

Vabø, M. (2006), 'Caring for people or caring for proxy consumers?', *European Societies*, **8** (3), 403–22.

Vabø, M. and M. Szebehely (2012), 'A caring state for all older people?', in A. Anttonen, L. Häikiö and K. Stefánsson (eds), *Welfare State, Universalism and Diversity*, Cheltenham, UK and Northampton, MA, USA: Edward Elgar Publishing, pp. 121–43.

Vabø, M., K. Christensen, F.F. Jacobsen and H.D. Trætteberg (2013), 'Marketisation in Norwegian eldercare: preconditions, trends and resistance', in G. Meagher and M. Szebehely (eds), *Marketization in Nordic Eldercare: A Research Report on Legislation, Oversight, Extent and Consequences*, Stockholm Studies in Social Work 30, Stockholm: Stockholm University, pp. 163–202.

Vabo, S.I. and E. Øverbye (2012), 'Decentralisation and privatisation in the Norwegian welfare state since 1980', unpublished paper presented at the COST Action IS1102 Workshop, Oslo and Akershus University College, Oslo, 18 June.

Yeandle, S. (2016), 'From provider to enabler of care? Reconfiguring local authority support for older people and carers in Leeds, 2008 to 2013', *Journal of Social Service Research*, **42** (2), 218–32.

Ylönen, M. and H. Purje (2013), *Ei Tietoja, ei Tuloja? Outotec, Attendo ja Vastuullinen Veronmaksu*, Finnwatch 3/2013 Finnwatch: Helsinki, accessed 21 December 2016 at http://www.finnwatch.org/images/ei_tietoja_finnwatch.pdf.

# 11. The de-institutionalisation of care for older people in the Czech Republic and Slovakia: national strategies and local outcomes

**Kateřina Kubalčíková, Gábor Szüdi, Jaroslava Szüdi and Jana Havlíková**

## INTRODUCTION

In this chapter we address changes occurring in the public provision of long-term care (henceforth LTC) for older people in the Czech Republic and Slovakia, with particular attention to the process of 'de-institutionalisation', on the basis of two case studies developed in the course of the COST Action IS1102 *SO.S. COHESION – Social services, welfare states and places*. These two countries shared a common trajectory – under the Soviet rule – up to 1989, which may explain a number of similar problems they are facing in the domain of social services. This is especially true in the case of care for older people, a service historically organised in residential structures, the financial viability of which has come under severe strain because of demographic changes and austerity measures.

In the Czech case, changes in the provision of such services started in 2006 when the notion of de-institutionalisation entered Czech social policy at the national level and the first – and still only valid – Social services act was approved. In Slovakia, the first act on social services was adopted in 2008, introducing decentralisation, de-institutionalisation and diversification of services.

In what follows, we address the following questions:

1. How has the concept of de-institutionalisation influenced the Czech and Slovak national strategies, legislation and organisation of social services for older people?
2. What has been the actual 'response' of the regional and local authorities, as well as the providers of care services for older people, to the new national policy strategies and regulation in this area?

To answer these questions, we first review the national policy strategies that followed the new Social service acts in both countries and the interplay between national strategies and regulation, on the one hand, and the regional and municipal provision of care services for older people, on the other. Subsequently we critically assess two case studies: (1) the organisation of domiciliary services for older people in the municipality of Blansko in the South Moravian region of the Czech Republic; (2) the innovative solutions implemented for the delivery of domiciliary care services to older people in the municipality of Kalná nad Hronom in the Nitra region of Slovakia. We focus on domiciliary care as a way to assess the current de-institutionalisation process, also because this form of care takes a central role as a 'substitute' for outdated or too expensive residential care. Through these two case studies we seek to highlight the ambivalent nature of the de-institutionalisation agenda: the Blansko case is somewhat representative of an ambiguous de-institutionalisation process trapped between policy discourse and socioeconomic reality, while the Kalná nad Hronom case is rather an outlier and represents a more optimistic example of how de-institutionalisation can be creatively implemented. The above case studies may also be seen as different outcomes of the implementation of national strategies: in the Czech Republic the stronger role of the established system of social services plays a regulative role, whereas in Slovakia there is room for innovative projects of de-institutionalisation.

The chapter is structured in five parts. In the next section the conceptual framework guiding the analysis of the case studies is briefly presented. Subsequently, the changes in national social policy of the last ten years are described in the two countries, with a focus on de-institutionalisation discourses and strategies. In the third and fourth sections the two municipal case studies are detailed. Finally, some concluding remarks are drawn.

## 1.   THE ANALYTICAL APPROACH

In this section we briefly review the literature about welfare state models and 'transition' countries, de-institutionalisation strategies and the emerging vertical and horizontal division of responsibility in the provision of care services.

### 'Transition' Countries

Current differences in, and the potential future direction of, the organisation of social services may be explained by the welfare state type under which an individual state can be categorised (Rothgang and Engelke,

2009). However, in the case of Central European countries it is complicated to classify systems of social services in general, and for older people in particular. Early works by welfare model theorists (Esping-Andersen, 1990) did not include Central European countries among the liberal, conservative or social democratic models, which led to a subsequent discussion on whether post-Communist countries should be categorised into one of the established welfare models, constitute a separate welfare model – in the case of the Visegrad countries mainly resembling the conservative welfare state (Fenger, 2007) – or be regarded as a hybrid model – as argued by Hacker (2009). In what concerns LTC more specifically, based on the features of their demand for care and their provision of formal and informal care, researchers have classified these new EU members as a separate, hybrid model 'in transition' towards other established models (Lamura et al., 2007). Taking into account the fact that Rodrigues and Nies (2013) suggested that not only the Central European but all European LTC systems are currently in a transitional state, we regard LTC systems of the Czech Republic and Slovakia as 'transition' models and analyse their de-institutionalisation process within this analytical framework.

**De-institutionalisation and Care of Older People**

Institutional care came under attack following the mental illness reform movement of the 1960s and 1970s and the disability movement (for independent living) of the 1980s. The main argument was that the situation of residents living in institutions, including LTC institutions such as nursing homes or mental health hospitals was humiliating (Shen and Snowden, 2014). This line of reasoning was strengthened by the cost-saving agenda of neo-liberal, economically conservative politicians promoting individualised and often privatised care (Chesters, 2005).

Since the mid-1990s, several reforms have been undertaken in the field of care for older people in almost every welfare state, promoting community and domiciliary care services instead of institutional LTC (Pavolini and Ranci, 2008). These reforms have first and foremost been undertaken by governments seeking socially and economically sustainable solutions to create high-quality LTC for a higher number of older people without raising costs (OECD, 2013). This goal was reinforced by the outbreak of the financial crisis in 2008.

Whether for ethical, political or economic reasons, de-institutionalisation currently refers to a process through which institutional care is either reduced and replaced by community and home-based (or domiciliary) care arrangements or is radically reorganised. Thus, de-institutionalisation may not only refer to the notion that traditional institutions are closed down, but also to the concept that large institutions are replaced with smaller, home-like residences (Anttonen and Karsio, 2016).

Albeit a generalised strategy, de-institutionalisation is a highly context-bound phenomenon: the transition from institutional care to domiciliary or community care in Europe is implemented in rather different ways in different countries (Anttonen and Karsio, 2016). In the case of the Czech Republic and Slovakia, de-institutionalisation started later than in other European welfare states, as part of a radical transformation from one social services model to another. Although the end point of the transformation is still not visible, the beginning is clear: it was the denial of the old Soviet-style welfare model consisting of the state as a dominant service provider and an overall change from state monopolism to plurality, from direct control to market relations and from paternalism to self-governance (CAP Kubalčíková and Havlíková, 2013; CAP Kováčová et al., 2014). In this framework, policy-makers and experts now in both countries promote a shift to care in the community and at home.

### The 'Vertical' Division of Authority and the New 'Horizontal' Welfare Mix

As part of the Soviet bloc, Czechoslovakia adopted the Soviet-style, paternalistic model of social protection, with a centralised, state-run system that did not allow for private providers but tolerated (informal) residential care. After 1989, state paternalism was gradually replaced with more flexible and decentralised mechanisms, based on the following new principles: administrative decentralisation, new forms of social services provision and new ways of funding social services (Koldinská and Tomeš, 2004).

In 1990, social services were transferred from the central state to municipalities, also giving responsibilities to newly formed non-state actors, such as churches and NGOs (Mansfeldová et al., 2004). After the split of Czechoslovakia into two countries in 1993, social service providers and social workers – supported by the emerging non-profit, non-governmental sector striving to provide modern social services – started to discuss the parameters of a new conception of social services provision in both countries: in the Czech Republic the overall reform of the social services system culminated in the 2006 adoption of the Act on social services (*Zákon o sociálních službách*) (CAP Havlíková and Kubalčíková, 2014), while in Slovakia substantial changes in social service provision (including decentralisation of competences and funding in the care system for older people) were brought about by the 2008 Act on social services (*Zákon o sociálnych službách*) (CAP Kováčová et al., 2014).

If we apply the 'vertical division of authority' concept laid out by Martinelli (Chapter 1, in this volume), the general re-scaling of authority

Table 11.1   The 'vertical division of authority' in the field of care for older people in the Czech Republic and Slovakia

| Level and function | Central state | | Region | | Municipality | |
|---|---|---|---|---|---|---|
| | CZ | SK | CZ | SK | CZ | SK |
| Regulation | X | X | | | | |
| Funding | X | X | | X | X | X |
| Organisation/planning | | | X | X | X | X |
| Monitoring | | X | X | | | |
| Provision | | | | X | X | X |

*Source:* Authors' compilation.

that took place in the Czech Republic and Slovakia in the last twenty years looks as summarised in Table 11.1.

In both countries, a decentralisation of planning responsibilities occurred and regional and local actors became jointly responsible with the relevant ministries in the area of social services: in accordance with national social policy priorities, regions and municipalities must now elaborate plans for the development of social services and also take part in the funding of social services. But the most important change is that municipalities and regions must now provide social services by establishing suitable conditions for the development of such services and securing the resources necessary to satisfy people's needs, in addition to setting up organisations to provide social services (CAP Havlíková and Kubalčíková, 2014).

Parallel to the vertical 're-scaling' of authority, a new 'horizontal' mix of service providers (see Martinelli, Chapter 1, as well as Leibetseder et al., in this volume) is also being established in place of state monopolism. In the Czech Republic, regional governments and municipalities still provide the majority of social care services for older people (87 per cent), but non-governmental organisations and churches now account for around 10 per cent, while the share of the for-profit sector is around 3 per cent (Pfeiferová et al., 2013). In Slovakia, a slightly lower share of LTC services is provided by public bodies (75 per cent), while the share of private non-profit providers is higher (23 per cent) and for-profit providers remain at 2 per cent (CAP Kováčová et al., 2014).

In conclusion, the current state of care services for older people in the Czech Republic and Slovakia is a consequence of different restructuring processes, the roots of which are found in the early decentralisation process of the 1990s (Kazepov, 2010) and the changes in the division of responsibility among territorial levels. Subsequently, a new horizontal mix of service providers also developed through reforms advocating pluralism of supply and 'ageing in place', especially with the accession to the EU in 2004. As will be stressed in the next section, the current system of care for older people is thus characterised, in both countries, by a mix of continuity and new principles, such as decentralisation, pluralisation and privatisation, which is subject to growing financial pressures (Österle, 2011; Barvíková and Österle, 2013).

## 2. NATIONAL STRATEGIES FOR THE CARE OF OLDER PEOPLE IN THE CZECH AND SLOVAK REPUBLICS

The growing concerns over the ageing of the population, along with the increasing costs of providing social services, are reflected in a number of recent policy documents approved by both the Czech and the Slovak governments.

In the case of the Czech Republic, of particular importance are the 'National report on strategies for social protection and social inclusion 2008–10'(*Národní akční plan sociálního začleňování 2008–2010*) and the 'Quality of life in old age: National programme of preparation for ageing 2008–12' (*Kvalita života ve stáří: Národní program přípravy na stárnutí*), which focus on active ageing, integration and involvement of older people in daily activities within the community, promoting the idea that older persons with care needs should remain living in their own homes ('ageing in place'). Two other key documents, 'The concept of transition from residential service to different types of social service provided to users in their home environment and promoting social integration of the user into society' (*Koncepce podpory transformace pobytových služeb v jiné typy sociálních služeb, poskytovaných v přirozené komunitě uživatele a podporující sociální začlenění uživatele do společnosti*) of 2006 and the 'Priorities of the development of social services for the period 2009–12' (*Priority rozvoje sociálních služeb pro období let 2009–2012*), contain concrete suggestions and methods for achieving these goals. The recent 'National action plan to support positive ageing for the period 2013–17' (*Národní akční plán podporující pozitivní stárnutí pro období let 2013 až 2017*) confirms the strategies of the previous documents.

A key issue highlighted in these documents is the lack of an integrated conception of LTC. There is still poor or non-existing interdepartmental cooperation between the Ministry of labour and social affairs and the Ministry of health, and health care is provided separately from social care. The same separation applies to the financing of both types of care.

In the case of Slovakia, the orientation and organisation of social services began to change after the adoption of the Act on social services in 2008. Subsequently, two documents were approved in 2011: the 'Strategy of de-institutionalisation of social services and substitute care in the Slovak Republic' (*Stratégia deinštitucionalizácie systému sociálnych služieb a náhradnej starostlivosti v Slovenskej republike*) and the 'National action plan of transition from institutional to community-based care in the system of social services for the period 2012–15' (*Národný akčný plán prechodu z inštitucionálnej na komunitnú starostlivosť v systéme sociálnych služieb na roky 2012–2015*).

The reforms recommended in these documents aimed at improving the quality of care services, creating sustainable financing mechanisms, and increasing social inclusion. All social services were to be exclusively financed from regional and local budgets. In what concerned the division of responsibilities between the two sub-national tiers of government, municipalities were in charge of providing services for senior citizens and legally obliged to provide both domiciliary care and institutional care to those in need, whereas self-governing regions were obliged to provide institutional care. In both cases, however, community-based social services were to be preferred.

Thus, in both the Czech Republic and Slovakia, as in many other European countries, there is now a strong explicit policy preference for de-institutionalisation, i.e. for domiciliary care as opposed to institutional care. This national preference is supposed to be increasingly adopted at the local level (Carrera et al., 2013).

## 3. THE CASE OF BLANSKO IN THE SOUTH MORAVIAN REGION OF THE CZECH REPUBLIC

The South Moravian region, with its 1.17 million inhabitants, is the fourth largest of the 14 regions of the Czech Republic. The region has seven districts and 21 municipalities with extended competences. It is one of the three regions with the oldest population in the Czech Republic. In 2014, 231 228 people aged over 65 lived in this region and it is expected that at least 16 per cent of the region's population will be over 80 in 2060, which means that the proportion of persons aged 80+ will have almost quadrupled compared to 2010. This proportion is projected to be greater in the region than in the Czech Republic as a whole and the EU-28, which implies that the demand for care and social care services in the region will increase dramatically.

## De-institutionalisation in Regional and Local Care Strategies for Older People

The regional strategic documents on social services development approved by the South Moravia region for the periods 2006–09, 2010–13 and 2014–20[1] and their priorities concerning social care for older people are fully in line with national goals. They all state that the region should support non-residential (daycare centres, short-term care centres) and domiciliary services (i.e. provided at the person's place of residence). However, the strategic documents for the first two periods did not specify any indicators for measuring the fulfilment of these goals, nor the allocation of funding from the regional budget, thereby betraying that although de-institutionalisation was officially a priority, political support for its implementation was lacking. In fact, no substantive measures were established. In 2014, 13 100 people used domiciliary services in the region, compared to 5643 users in residential facilities for older people, but there were as many as 17 725 unmet applications for the latter service (MoLSA, 2014a).

The magnitude of the demand for places in residential care facilities was acknowledged in the last regional strategic document (although in many cases older people submit an application for residential services as a back-up plan in the event of future loss of self-sufficiency). The objective to further develop domiciliary care services and respite care was thus stressed again, but this time indicators were introduced to measure achievements.

### Care for Older People in the Municipality of Blansko

Against this background, a qualitative case study carried out in 2009–10 on a domiciliary care service agency established by the Municipality of Blansko[2] helps to shed light on the gap between policy strategies and actual implementation (Kubalčíková and Havlíková, 2015). Blansko is a medium-sized town in South Moravia with a population of 20 103. Here, the desirability of promoting ageing-in-place was as apparent at the municipal as at the regional level, but with a similarly limited impact in terms of the actual development of municipal care services. From 2008 to 2012, the main priorities of the Blansko municipality, as specified in its strategic plans[3] were: first, to preserve the 2008 level of domiciliary care delivery; second, to increase the number of beds in residential care (using funding from the regional and state budgets) given the great demand for this type of service; and, third, to sustain leisure and cultural activities for older people. The 'Third community plan' for social services of Blansko for the period 2013–16 seemed to underscore the change in attitude observed at the regional level. However, the municipal plan presumed that the proposed changes concerning domiciliary care service would not require additional funding, which gives rise to doubts about the possibility of successful implementation.

The findings from the case study of domiciliary care services in Blansko, complemented by updated administrative data, indicate that the present approach to these services in the Czech Republic is rather problematic for de-institutionalisation. There are two main reasons: first, the need for a greater involvement of social workers in the provision of domiciliary care has not been recognised yet; second, domiciliary services still largely consist of the provision of 'practical' assistance, especially meals-on-wheels.

At the time of the survey (2009), the number of users in Blansko was 475, cared for by 21 frontline workers (of whom 18 were care workers and only two were actual social workers). Although the ratio of social workers to users has slightly improved over time (to approximately 154 users per social worker in 2013), their very limited number does not allow either individualised social work or care management. The type of assistance provided by the domiciliary care agency predominantly involved the delivery of meals. This became even more pronounced over time, as this service came to represent 78 per cent of interactions with users in 2013, compared to 56 per cent in 2009, to the detriment of other kinds of assistance. Although this model of domiciliary care service runs counter to trends in other countries, which involves eliminating practical help in favour of providing more personal care (Yeandle et al., 2012), the head of the service in Blansko advocated that the delivery of meals was very popular among users.

In contrast, the domiciliary care service agency only rarely provided assistance in the form of long-term supervision or monitoring of the users' health condition and life situation. In 2009, this type of support represented only 5.5 per cent and in 2013 it had shrunk to 2.5 per cent of the total range of services, despite the fact that users perceived this kind of assistance as most important and stated that without it their only alternative would be residential care.

**A Preliminary Assessment**

Evidence from the qualitative case study points to four main explanations for the above trends in the implementation of domiciliary care services in Blansko.

First, only tasks falling under the categories of 'practical help' and 'personal care' were prescribed as compulsory by the national Act on social services, whereas medical care (nursing) is not part of social services provision. Therefore, domiciliary services cannot offer comprehensive care. Second, monitoring is voluntary and care management is not codified. Both are too expensive, as explicitly stated by the head of the service in Blansko; in the case of supervision, the worker's attention is devoted to a sole user for a significant period of time and the hourly fee provided by the user, as stipulated by the Social services act, does not cover the real cost of the service per hour. Third, although the provision of intensive domiciliary care is promoted in the strategic document, it has not become a real priority for the Blansko municipality. Since the municipality covers the majority of the domiciliary care budget, it also has a marked influence on the conception of domiciliary care itself. Moreover, budget constraints do not allow the domiciliary care agency to take on older people who need more intensive care. Fourth, and most importantly, the municipal implementation of the national priority of de-institutionalisation was not supported by appropriate financial transfers from the national or regional government. Although state contributions towards the funding of domiciliary care have risen over time, the direct allocation of these funds towards more intensive care is still missing.

In conclusion, domiciliary care service agencies have continued to focus on the provision of practical help with little or no care service. And yet, given their reduced self-sufficiency, older people expect more from social services than just ensuring basic practical help with household tasks, shopping or laundry. Moreover, since social care and health care are provided by different Czech agencies, these services can only be integrated within residential facilities, where the provision of complex social and health care is guaranteed by law. The current situation can, thus, be described as a major gap in care services, producing a significant degree of discomfort for older people and their families.[4]

### The Development of a 'Grey' Private Market

A major fallout of the above situation is the rise of a 'grey' market of institutional care. The narrow conception and limited availability of domiciliary care, coupled with the shortage of places in registered homes for older people, have created the conditions for the growth of non-registered private institutions that accept the vulnerable older people with the highest level of care allowance.

According to the experts' comments,[5] these 'quasi-services' for older people are primarily housing facilities, without legal registration for providing care service. Care for the residents is provided with the help of so-called 'care assistants', whom the recipients of care allowance may hire instead of relying on their own relatives. These assistants do not need to have any training in caring or nursing and they do not even have the status of employees (CAP Kubalčíková and Havlíková, 2013; MoLSA, 2014b).

As these quasi-service structures are not registered, there are no official statistics about the number of users they serve. The experts' guess was that in the South Moravian region alone tens of these facilities existed and in the Czech Republic as a whole these facilities may constitute at least 14 per cent of all homes for older people (MoLSA, 2014b). It can be assumed that this 'grey' marketisation is likely to have a greater negative impact on the quality of provided care in the Czech Republic than 'regulated' marketisation in Germany (Bode et al., 2011), Great Britain (Ferguson and Woodward, 2009) or the United States (Harrington, 2013). At the same time, even if such facilities were surveyed, there are no instruments for evaluating the quality of the care provided and the working conditions of care workers (MoLSA, 2014b).

## 4. THE CASE OF KALNÁ NAD HRONOM IN SLOVAKIA

The Slovak Republic had 5.4 million inhabitants in 2012, of which 13.1 per cent were aged 65+. The old age population is relatively smaller in Slovakia than in Western European countries, but forecasts put the number of people aged 65+ at around 33 per cent by 2060 (and people 80+ around 12 per cent), indicating that Slovakia will have one of the highest economic dependency ratios in the EU (CAP Kováčová et al., 2014). This implies a huge rise in the demand for care services and a projected increase of 237 per cent in public spending in LTC by 2060, just to keep up the present level of service (Österle, 2011).

This service level is already comparatively low, since roughly 4 per cent of older people (65+) receive social care services (Rodrigues and Nies, 2013). Residential care institutions include homes for older people and specialised homes providing care services according to type of disability. They typically accommodate large numbers and provide social services over the whole year. In 2012, Slovakia had 271 homes for older people, with a total capacity of 13 922 places (50 beds per facility on average), whereas about 34 000 people aged 65+ were cared for by family members eligible for care allowance (which is possible in the case of severe disabilities since 2009) and only 7085 caregivers were employed by municipalities for domiciliary care services as of 2010 (CAP Kováčová et al., 2014).

## The Health and Care Component of Domiciliary Services

In Slovakia, as in many other countries, domiciliary care services are subdivided into two main components: (1) health care services such as home nursing care; and (2) social care services. After a failed legislative attempt to integrate these two kinds of services, a strict division still exists in terms of financing: health care services are covered by health insurance, while social care services are financed through municipalities and self-governing regions (from general taxation) for roughly two-thirds and user co-payments for the remaining one third (Radvanský and Páleník, 2010).

Domiciliary or home nursing care is provided by 162 agencies (*Agentúra Domácej Ošetrovateľskej Starostlivosti,* hereafter ADOSs) that are free of charge after the insurance companies have assessed the individual level of disability and found the user eligible (Ležovič et al., 2007). ADOSs are part of the primary health care system and do not generally provide any home assistance in non-medical tasks, such as help with shopping, cooking or cleaning. In order to get the latter services, an older person has the choice of resorting to: (1) informal care provided by a relative; (2) paying for a private service provider (which is usually too expensive for an average retired person); or (3) applying for social care provision to the municipality responsible for providing social care (except for people with disabilities for whom the regional government is responsible).

Since it is financed at the regional and local level, the eligibility for social services provided in a home environment is assessed with a more complex procedure than health services: while disability or unfavourable health status is assessed by a medical examiner, the individual needs, family background and living conditions are assessed by a social worker employed by the municipality or regional government, based on national guidelines (Radvanský and Páleník, 2010).

Partly due to the division between medical and social care provision, the domiciliary care system in Slovakia faces several challenges. Among these are: (a) some eligible people do not receive adequate care since municipalities and other providers are not sanctioned for non-provision; (b) the assessment procedure for municipal domiciliary care may be ineffective due to regulatory overlaps and redundancy (Bode et al., 2011); (c) there are insufficient financial resources since they are mostly spent on residential care (Ležovič et al., 2007); (d) access to social services strongly varies according to local and regional policies (Genet et al., 2012); (e) funding regulations of private providers are so complicated that they can be viewed as an obstacle to competition between private and public service providers (Brichtová and Repková, 2009).

**An Innovative Solution for the Integration of Services: The Case of Kalná nad Hronom**

The local case study examined in Slovakia concerns the very innovative domiciliary service agency established in the Municipality of Kalná nad Hronom, a small town of 2082 inhabitants, located in the Nitra region.[6] Here, the municipality attempted to overcome the abovementioned national shortcomings through a new type of service provider, an NGO called Help Centre Kalná, established specially for this purpose in 2014. The aim of the NGO – financed at the local level – was to provide older people in need with integrated social and medical care, without going through the established multiple eligibility determination procedures.

The main support for this new kind of service provision came from the mayor, who wanted to ensure that older people could get comprehensive quality services at their homes. In addition to already existing social care services, since June 2014 Help Centre Kalná has started to offer an extended service, called 'family assistance'. This service can be provided to those older persons in the Kalná municipality who are not entitled to the official domiciliary care services but still need some assistance with routine household, personal and social activities. 'Family assistance' includes activities such as support in shopping, carrying out medical-related activities (visits to doctors or pharmacy), assistance in daily activities (farmyard, animal feeding or housekeeping), facilitating social contacts with peers, supervision in the absence of family members, assistance in contacts with authorities (social insurance, health insurance, post office), and visits to other older people in hospitals.

The pool of users is small in scale: there were 11 users at the beginning of the agency's activities (June 2014), which more than doubled (27) in 2015, showing a successful mutual trust-building process and underlined by the fact that one more family assistant was employed with the help of a grant from the European Social Fund. At least seven volunteers, including students and mothers on maternity leave, were continuously supporting the agency's work in service provision and monitoring. The funding has allowed the assistance to be provided in very favourable financial terms for users (in comparison to private providers): the single use of a service is charged at EUR 1 per hour, while the repeated use of a service is charged at EUR 0.50 per hour.

Another type of service offered by Help Centre Kalná since November 2014 is integrated nursing care, usually not provided at the local level, which is targeted at older people who fit the eligibility criteria determined by the current national legislation (which defines the minimum degree of dependence). It is not financed through public funds, social or health insurance, but paid by the user (or his/her relatives), with a contribution from the municipality. The current rate is EUR 0.29 per hour, in exchange for which older people receive some practical medical assistance (such as administering of medicines, blood pressure checks, insulin injections, etc.), but also standard care services (such as help with hygiene, clothing, eating and drinking) and support in household chores (cleaning, tidying, or fixing problems with running water or heating) and social activities (driving services or support in administrative matters).

Thus, the nursing services provided by the Help Centre Kalná try to bridge the need between the nursing care provided by the health insurance system after eligibility determination and the less formal social care services. The aim is to support relatives who cannot undertake the role of informal carers and/or have an older person in the family who might be in a situation requiring care, but who is not currently eligible for state provision. With this initiative, not only were the current institutional boundaries between health and social care provision made less sharp, but also formal care gained an officially recognised role of complement to informal social care provision. In order to provide monitoring, municipal employees and volunteers in Kalná visit the older persons in their households and check their condition, listen to their wishes and needs, and provide them with information about care possibilities that would fit their individual needs. The future plan of Help centre Kalná is to provide the whole portfolio of services from basic care to rehabilitation.

The initial infrastructural and human resources investments needed for the implementation of these services at the Help centre Kalná were partly financed by the Slovak government, through a project run by the SOCIA foundation, which allowed the purchase of vehicles and the re-training of social workers. As mentioned, the project extension was also financed through the European social fund.

**Replicability of the Kalná Experience**

A positive restructuring of the current institutional care model of Slovakia could be envisaged if domiciliary service provisions similar to our case study were implemented in more places across the country. The Kalná experience, however, has certain specificities that explain its success but also make it difficult to replicate.

First and foremost, the municipality has a proactive leadership strongly supporting the centre's management in fulfilling their innovative ideas, while building on existing legislative opportunities. As seen in Table 11.1, certain responsibilities are divided among local, regional and national levels, which can serve as both opportunity and hindrance in implementing new types of service provision for older people. In Kalná's case the local political, administrative and professional decision-makers could work in harmony to get the family assistance and nursing care service functioning.

Funding was also a crucial factor, because the new ideas would not become a reality without adequate financial resources. The Kalná municipality is in a better position than many of its counterparts (particularly in Eastern Slovakia) due to a steady flow of local taxes (partly stemming from the nearby nuclear plant contributing to the local budget through land leases and business taxes) but the success in finding, applying for, and effectively using 'out-of-the-box' funding opportunities such as EU or national funds is also a sign of an effective political and administrative management and an efficient interplay between them.

In sum, the replicability of such a novel de-institutionalised experience, through effective domiciliary care services for older people, is largely dependent upon the presence of proactive and motivated leaders in the municipality and a stable financing flow. However, this is not the case in the majority of Slovak municipalities. In order to make 'outliers' such as Kalná more replicable around the country, legislative changes would be needed to ensure a steady flow of financial resources to every municipality and balance out the territorial differences in tax bases. The strict division in financing of health and social care services should also be re-thought since a large part of LTC officially belongs to health care services which can only be financed at a central level. Some practical assistance to municipalities in finding the necessary funding resources (e.g. state or EU tenders) should also be considered.

## 5.   CONCLUDING REMARKS

During the first decade of the millennium the concept of de-institutionalisation significantly influenced legislation in both the Czech Republic and Slovakia. It was introduced in the context of an ongoing administrative restructuring process based on the principles of decentralisation, pluralisation and privatisation, whereby many competences in the domain of social care for older people were transferred to lower administrative levels and to non-governmental organisations. While implicit re-scaling was prevalent in the 1990s, when the adaptation of social assistance legislation resulted in changes of the relative weight of specific LTC policies, since the accession to the EU in 2004 all national-level strategies in this area have put 'ageing in place' at the forefront, leading to a more explicit form of vertical re-scaling and horizontal re-mixing through various de-institutionalisation reform packages.

However, despite discourses and legislation, there are still relevant organisational challenges in both countries, which prevent the actual implementation of de-institutionalisation. In the first place, there still is a strict division between health care and social care provision in both countries, resulting in the fact that nursing care is not part of social services provision (in the Czech Republic) or can only be provided after cumbersome administrative procedures for eligibility determination (in Slovakia). The social care services provided to older people are then generally limited to the most elementary (practical) assistance, a fact which is also a side-effect of the vertical reorganisation of competences. Secondly, there is significant fragmentation among the various levels of government regarding funding, leading to financial means that are often insufficient at the local level. Fragmentation and legal uncertainty also result in neglecting the proper monitoring of social services provided within the framework of the new systems. Therefore, the actual outcome of the re-organisation of care provisions based on the new regulations and strategies embracing de-institutionalisation might result in an inadequate level of service provision, consisting only of practical assistance in the best cases, which runs in parallel with the decreasing number of official opportunities for institutionalised care. Moreover, since social care services are now more dependent on local funding, the services provided to older people can vary significantly among different regions and communities within regions.

In terms of policy discourse, regions and municipalities do embrace de-institutionalisation (reflected in regional and municipal strategic documents), which often translates into restrictions to the development of residential services. But, in practice, regional and local policies do not support domiciliary social services, since the financial resources that are no longer allocated to residential services are not invested in the qualitative and quantitative development of domiciliary services. Thus, despite the fact that policy priorities similar to those existing in 'older' European countries were introduced at the national level in the Czech Republic and Slovakia, the transition to a 'new' conception of care for older people has been rather slow at the local and regional level, while the lack of political will to provide the necessary funding to expand service provision indicates a convergence with the Mediterranean welfare model, rather than the Continental or Nordic ones.

In conclusion, an official de-institutionalisation strategy was adopted in both countries – including the legislative and financial decentralisation of state responsibilities to regional and local governments – as a possible solution for a rapidly ageing population and as a modernisation strategy. However, this shift was implemented without guaranteeing adequate financial resources, while at the same time the demand for care in shrinking and understaffed residential facilities – as witnessed by the steady migration of nurses to the neighbouring Germany and Austria to provide care as personal assistants in private households – kept growing.

This has led to two 'spontaneous' but very distinct 'responses' that are well illustrated by our case studies: in one case (Blansko in the Moravia region of the Czech Republic) the development of a significant number of new private for-profit 'grey' residential structures, of questionable quality and with no legal accreditation, thereby with no guarantee of safeguarding the rights of older people; in the other case (Kalná in the Nitra region of Slovakia) a re-defined and innovative domiciliary care centre, in the form of an NGO supported by the municipality, which was able to overcome national legislative shortcomings.

However, while the Czech case exemplifies a rather widespread response, the Slovak one exhibits rather special features. Although the lack of funding at the local level made the emergence of market forces visible in both countries, it is still unclear whether innovative solutions such as the Help Centre of Kalná can diffuse to remedy the problems faced by other municipalities in the public provision of care for older people. Moreover, the fact that implementation of a national policy principle can lead to the exact opposite outcome than originally intended at the local level has significant policy implications. Sufficient funding and real support from policy-makers at all levels of government, as well as a prompt response to reduce the unintended impacts of the policy reforms seem thus to be vital for a successful implementation of the de-institutionalisation strategy in both countries.

## NOTES

1. 'South Moravian region development strategy 2006–2009'; 'South Moravian region development programme 2010–13'; and 'Strategy for the South Moravian region 2020'.
2. Evidence was gathered in 2009–10 through semi-structured interviews with representatives of the Blansko municipality, the agency's management staff, over half of its front-line workers (11) and 17 representatives of users. Furthermore, in 2013, a Panel of experts was organised in the context of the COST Action IS1102, to update information on the case study.
3. The 'First', 'Second' and 'Third community plans for social services of the Blansko Municipality' covering the periods of 2008–09, 2010–12, and 2013–16.
4. This has long been subject to debate by the Panel of experts established in 2013.
5. Panel of experts established in 2013; see note 4.
6. The functioning and relevance of this novel help centre was assessed in 2014–15 through semi-structured interviews with the local stakeholders (municipal leaders, social workers and users).

# REFERENCES

Anttonen, A. and O. Karsio (2016), 'Eldercare service redesign in Finland: deinstitutionalization of LTC', *Journal of Social Service Research*, **42** (2), 151–66.

Barvíková, J. and A. Österle (2013), 'LTC reform in Central-Eastern Europe. The case of the Czech Republic', in C. Ranci and E. Pavolini (eds), *Reforms in LTC Policies in Europe: Investigating Institutional Change and Social Impacts*, New York: Springer, pp. 243–65.

Bode, I., L. Gardin and M. Nyssens (2011), 'Quasi-marketisation in domiciliary care: varied patterns, similar problems', *International Journal of Sociology and Social Policy*, **31** (3/4), 222–35.

Brichtová, L. and K. Repková (2009), *Sociálna Ochrana Starších Osôb a Osôb so Zdravotným Postihnutím – Vybrané Aspekty* [*Selected Issues of Social Security for Older People and People with Health Disabilities*], Bratislava: EPOS.

Carrera, F., E. Pavolini, C. Ranci and A. Sabbatini (2013), 'LTC systems in comparative perspective: care needs, informal and formal coverage, and social impacts in European countries', in C. Ranci and E. Pavolini (eds), *Reforms in LTC Policies in Europe: Investigating Institutional Change and Social Impacts*, New York: Springer, pp. 23–52.

Chesters, J. (2005), 'Deinstitutionalisation: an unrealised desire', *Health Sociology Review*, **14** (3), 272–82.

Esping-Andersen, G. (1990), *The Three Worlds of Welfare Capitalism*, Princeton: Princeton University Press.

Fenger, H.J.M. (2007), 'Welfare regimes in Central and Eastern Europe: incorporating post-Communist countries in a welfare regime typology', *Contemporary Issues and Ideas in Social Sciences*, **3** (2), 1–30.

Ferguson, I. and R. Woodward (2009), *Radical Social Work in Practice: Making a Difference*, Bristol: Policy Press.

Genet, N., W. Boerma, M. Kroneman, A. Hutchinson and R.B. Saltman (2012), *Home Care across Europe – Current Structure and Future Challenges*, Copenhagen: World Health Organization, Regional Office for Europe, Observatory Studies Series.

Hacker, B. (2009), 'Hybridization instead of clustering. Transformation processes of welfare policies in Central and Eastern Europe', *Social Policy & Administration*, **43** (2), 152–69.

Harrington, C. (2013), 'Understanding the relationship of nursing home ownership and quality in the United States', in G. Meagher and M. Szebehely (eds), *Marketisation in Nordic Eldercare: A Research Report on Legislation, Oversight, Extent and Consequences*, Stockholm: Stockholm University, pp. 229–40.

Havlíková, J. and K. Kubalčíková (2014), 'The regulatory trajectory and current organisational framework of social services and social care in the Czech Republic', *COST Action IS1102 Working Papers*, no. 5, accessed 10 May 2016 at www.cost-is1102-cohesion.unirc.it/docs/working-papers/wg1.czechrepublic-social%20services-j-havlikova-k-kubalcikova.pdf.

Kazepov, Y. (2010), 'Rescaling social policies towards multilevel governance in Europe: some reflections on processes at stake and actors involved', in Y. Kazepov (ed.), *Rescaling Social Policies: Towards Multilevel Governance in Europe*, Farnham: Ashgate, pp. 35–73.

Koldinská, K. and I. Tomeš (2004), 'Social services in accession countries', *Social Work and Society, International Online Journal*, **2** (1), 110–17.

Kováčová, J., G. Szüdi and S. Konečný (2014), 'Transformation of social services for the elderly in the context of deinstitutionalization of social services in Slovakia', unpublished paper presented at the COST Action IS1102 Workshop, University of Tampere, Tampere, 2–6 June; now published as G. Szüdi, J. Kováčová and S. Konečný (2016), 'Transformation of social care services for the elderly in Slovakia', *Journal of Social Service Research*, **42** (2), 199–217.

Kubalčíková, K. and J. Havlíková (2013), 'The current development of social services in the care of the older people: deinstitutionalization and/or marketization?', unpublished paper presented at the COST Action IS1102 Workshop, Dunarea de Jos University, Galati, 5–8 November; now published as K. Kubalčíková and J. Havlíková (2016), 'Current developments in social care services for older adults in the Czech Republic: trends towards deinstitutionalization and marketization', *Journal of Social Service Research*, **42** (2), 180–98.

Kubalčíková, K. and J. Havlíková (2015), 'The potential of domiciliary care service in the Czech Republic to promote ageing in place', *European Journal of Social Work*, **18** (1), 65–80.

Lamura, G., E. Mnich, B. Bien, B. Krevers, K. McKee, E. Mestheneos and H. Döhner (2007), 'Dimensions of future social service provision in the ageing societies of Europe', *Advances in Gerontology*, **20** (3), 13–30.

Ležovič, M., M. Raučinová, A. Kováč, Š. Moricová and R. Kováč (2007), 'LTC in developed countries and recommendations for Slovak Republic', *Central European Journal of Public Health*, **16** (1), 21–5.

Mansfeldová, Z., S. Nalecz, E. Priller and A. Zimmer (2004), 'Civil society in transition. Civic engagement and nonprofit organizations in Central and Eastern Europe after 1989', in A. Zimmer and E. Priller (eds), *Future of Civil Society. Making Central European Nonprofit Organizations Work*, Wiesbaden: VS Verlag für Sozialwissenschaften, pp. 99–119.

MoLSA (Ministry of Labour and Social Affairs) (2014a), *Statistická Ročenka z Oblasti Práce a Sociálních Věcí 2009–2014* [*Statistical Yearbook of Labour and Social Statistics 2009–2014*], Prague: MoLSA.

MoLSA (Ministry of Labour and Social Affairs) (2014b), *Neregistrované Sociální Služby Porušují Zákon* [*Unregistered Social Services Break the Law*], Press release form 1 December 2014.

OECD (2013), *A Good Life in Old Age? Monitoring and Improving Quality in LTC*, OECD Health Policy Studies, Paris: OECD.

Österle, A. (2011), 'LTC in Central and South-Eastern Europe. Challenges and perspectives in addressing a "new" social risk', *Social Policy & Administration*, **44** (4), 461–80.

Pavolini, E. and C. Ranci (2008), 'Restructuring the welfare state: reforms in long term care in Western European countries', *Journal of European Social Policy*, **18** (3), 246–59.

Pfeiferová, Š., M. Lux, T. Dvořák, J. Havlíková, M. Mikeszová and P. Sunega (eds) (2013), *Housing and Social Care for the Elderly in Central Europe: WP 3 Main Findings Report*, Prague: Institute of Sociology, Academy of Science of the Czech Republic.

Radvanský, M. and V. Páleník (2010), 'The LTC System for the Elderly in Slovakia', *Economic Policy*, ENEPRI Research Reports.

Rodrigues, R. and H. Nies (2013), 'Making sense of differences – the mixed economy of funding and delivering LTC', in K. Leichsenring, J. Billings and

H. Nies (eds), *LTC in Europe. Improving Policy and Practice*, New York, USA and Basingstoke, UK: Palgrave Macmillan, pp. 191–213.

Rothgang, H. and K. Engelke (2009), 'LTC: how to organise affordable, sustainable LTC given the constraints of collective versus individual arrangements and responsibilities', discussion paper, Bremen: University of Bremen.

Shen, G.C. and L.R. Snowden (2014), 'Institutionalization of deinstitutionalization: a cross-national analysis of mental health system reform', *International Journal of Mental Health Systems*, **8** (47), 1–23.

Yeandle, S., T. Kröger and B. Cass (2012), 'Voice and choice for users and carers? Developments in patterns of care for older people in Australia, England and Finland', *Journal of European Social Policy*, **22** (4), 432–45.

# 12. Care for older people in three Mediterranean countries: discourses, policies and realities of de-institutionalisation

**Blanca Deusdad, Sagit Lev, Charles Pace and Sue Vella**

## INTRODUCTION

This chapter seeks to shed light on de-institutionalisation and the way people are 'ageing in place' in Mediterranean countries, based on case studies developed in the context of the COST Action IS1102 *SO.S. COHESION – Social services, welfare states and places*. Israel, Malta and Spain are chosen to represent diversity in size and demography, but also in culture, religion, history and sociopolitical context. De-institutionalisation can be defined as a policy emphasising care in or by the community rather than care within an institution, but it also refers to the prevention of institutional placements (Bachrach, 1976). Although the de-institutionalisation movement was mobilised by criticism addressed at mental health institutions, it expanded to also include the care of older people, children and persons with disabilities (Lerman, 1985; EEGTICC, 2012). The concomitant need for an expansion of appropriate community-based services makes de-institutionalisation an important object of study (Bachrach, 1976; Fakhoury and Priebe, 2007; EEGTICC, 2012).

De-institutionalisation of care for older people has been studied in the Nordic, Central and Eastern European countries (Deusdad et al., 2016a), while little is known about how this process has played out in Mediterranean countries (Deusdad et al., 2016b; Pace et al., 2016), in spite of the fact that de-institutionalisation is a subject of the Common European Guidelines (EEGTICC, 2012). Looking at the three Mediterranean countries one notices, first, that the share of older people in institutions has been low, particularly in Spain, compared to other European countries. Second, there are differences as to how far there has been a clear policy discourse fostering de-institutionalisation or ageing in place. Third, de-institutionalisation in the three countries has not been a homogeneous process. Its implementation has varied in extent and even, one can say, in its validity, where insufficient resources raise the question of whether it might have amounted to a *false de-institutionalisation* policy.

The first section of this chapter focuses on the relevant research and literature, the next three sections describe the situation in the three countries and section 5 reflects on similarities and differences among these countries with respect to the policies and discourses on de-institutionalisation and ageing in place.

## 1.  SHIFTS OF CARE AMONG INSTITUTIONS, FORMAL COMMUNITY SERVICES AND FAMILY

De-institutionalisation is a widely used concept and policy option. Preference for de-institutionalised care, even where care needs are extensive, is grounded in the belief that living in the community protects those fundamental human rights that institutional care might deny (Ilinca et al., 2015). This is reminiscent of the concept of the total institution, coined by Erving Goffman (1968) to refer to 'a place of residence and work where a large number of like-situated individuals, cut off from the wider society for an appreciable period of time, together lead an enclosed, formally administered round of life' (Goffman, 1968, p. xiii). Researchers have identified these features as applying to a considerable extent to typical institutions for older adults (Lang et al., 2007; Thomas, 2004), exerting pressure for conformity and obedience (Solomon, 2004) through a functional efficiency begetting rigid routines, low privacy and autonomy, and limited choice (Angelelli, 2006; Harnett, 2010).

In respect of the elderly, de-institutionalisation aims to promote ageing in place, defined as 'remaining living in the community, with some level of independence, rather than in residential care' (Davey et al., 2004, p. 133). Ageing in place requires services and facilities to be located close to the homes of older adults, affordable and known to potential users through clear information (WHO, 2007).

The philosophy of ageing in place is underpinned by the European Union's Charter of fundamental rights, which declares that 'The Union recognises and respects the rights of older adults to lead a life of dignity and independence and to participate in social and cultural life' (European Parliament, 2010). To simply reduce beds in institutional care is, by contrast, more about cost reduction than about the best interests of older adults (EC, 2008). Evaluation of ageing in place should look into the adequacy of services available in the local community (Bachrach, 1976; Fakhoury and Priebe, 2007). Adequate community-based services, including home-based care, all facilitate ageing in place through different means (Doyle and Timonen, 2007; Lehmann and Havlíková, 2014). Such services provide the support which older adults need and which enable them to participate in everyday life (EC, 2008).

Community care is taken, in the usual British sense, to refer to care given to people while they live 'in the community', normally at home (even when they go to outpatients' hospitals to receive care). Home care or domiciliary care refers to care received at home, for example 'meals-on-wheels' and home help. In many contexts, the concepts of community care and home care are not distinguished. Living in home-like and 'not-so-total' small shared residences is often not referred to as institutional care (Moise et al., 2004).

Preference for community-based over institutional care is supported by an increasing body of evidence to the effect that the former generally provides better results for users, families and staff, at comparable cost (EC, 2008). Furthermore, most Europeans perceived ageing in place as the best care for older adults (European Commission, 2007). Developing different forms of community to improve living conditions of older adults also involves reinforcing and enlarging social networks at the neighbourhood level.

Still, recent evaluations have questioned the universal appropriateness of ageing in place, the success of which is linked to the degree of disability and the type of available services (Grabowski, 2006; Mansell et al., 2007; Wysocki et al., 2015). Thus, where 24-hour care is needed, institutions may be preferred (Fakhoury and Priebe, 2007), but there is of course a need to create residences that are 'less institutional' by being small and more home-like. This need is reflected in the cultural shift from a medical and institutional model to a client-oriented model with home-based features (Kane and Kane, 2001; Koren, 2010; Thomas, 2004), and being part of the wider community rather than separated from it (Rabig et al., 2006; Thomas, 2004).

In this chapter de-institutionalisation is studied in a Mediterranean context. A number of welfare state researchers contend that Southern European or Mediterranean countries are a distinct welfare regime with unique characteristics (Damiani et al., 2011; Ferrera, 1996; Leibfried, 1992; Rhodes, 1996). Gal (2010) extended the Mediterranean regime to include the islands of Cyprus and Malta, as well as Turkey and Israel in the East (a cluster admittedly considered too broad by Guillén and León, 2011; see also Pace, 2009).

While acknowledging differences among Mediterranean countries' social policies, religion, cultural heritage, social conditions and standards of living, Gal (2009; 2010) claimed that they shared enough common features to distinguish them from other European regimes. Common shaping factors were a history of late industrialisation linked to lingering non-democratic or colonialist regimes as well as strong influence of religion, family and clientelistic networks. All this contributed to a common pattern of a relatively weak welfare and economic system (Gal, 2009; 2010) and a family that is strongly relied upon for care, often involving resource pooling and soft budgeting by the household or extended family (Moreno, 2000; Petmesidou, 1996).

Family care is thus prominent in Mediterranean countries, where women are expected to take responsibility for the care of older relatives. Israel, Malta and Spain, as other Mediterranean countries, also feature large numbers of home-based migrant women care workers, often hired by families from within the low-paid black economy, a common Mediterranean trend (Torrens-Bonet, 2012; Vara, 2014).

Like most of Europe, Mediterranean countries experience processes of restructuring, marketisation and promotion of choice (Deusdad et al, 2016a; Mathew-Puthenparambil and Kröger, 2016; Moreno-Fuentes and Mari Klose, 2015). These processes have deeply influenced the de-institutionalisation of care for older people aimed at ageing in place, as expressed in EU guidelines and social workers' discourse. The 2008 economic crisis, affecting Mediterranean countries in different ways, has in its turn widely provoked restructuring and, for instance, in the case of Spain has affected the implementation of long-term care (LTC) policy (Deusdad et al., 2016b).

This chapter focuses on Israel, Malta and Spain, with the aim that this study of similarities and differences may help shed light upon the de-institutionalisation of care in the Mediterranean welfare regime in a time of economic crisis. The selection of the three countries emerged from their geographical spread across the Mediterranean (Israel in the East, Spain in the West and Malta in the centre), their different population size and also their largely varied historical roots. Furthermore, while Portugal, Spain, Italy and Greece are most often studied, we felt it important to include Israel and Malta which, though seen by Gal as Mediterranean regime countries, are studied far less often. Meanwhile, statistics in Table 12.1 set the scene through some comparisons.

De-institutionalisation and ageing in place policies will be compared in the light of each country's legislation, formal and informal care systems, processes of marketisation or privatisation, family strategies and other changes in the face of the economic crisis. Through the three country case studies and the subsequent comparative discussion, we shall be addressing

*Table 12.1    Selected comparative data for Israel, Malta and Spain*

| Indicator | Israel | Malta | Spain |
|---|---|---|---|
| Percent of population aged ≥ 75 in 2015 | 4.89[1] | 7.41[2] | 9.23[2] |
| Old-age dependency ratios (persons aged ≥ 65/ persons aged 15–64) | 15.7[3] | 21.4[2] | 24.6[2] |
| Number of persons in the population aged ≥ 65, per available bed in nursing & residential facilities | 46.0[7] | 18.0[10] | 24.0[10] |
| Life expectancy for men aged 60 in 2013 | 23.3[5] | 22.5[4] | 23.1[4] |
| Life expectancy for women aged 60 in 2013 | 25.7[5] | 25.9[4] | 27.9[4] |
| % of GDP spent on welfare (2013) | 10.9%[8] | 18.5%[7] | 25.2%[7] |
| Long-term care expenditures as a % of GDP | 0.4[6] (2010) | 1.1[9] (2013) | 1.0[9] (2013) |

*Source:*   Authors' elaboration based on 1) Central Bureau of Statistics – Israel (2016a; 2016b; 2016c); 2) Eurostat (2016a); 3) Central Bureau of Statistics – Israel (2016a); 4) Eurostat (2016b); 5) OECD (2016a); 6) OECD (2016b); 7) Eurostat (2016c); 8) Central Bureau of Statistics – Israel (2016b; 2016c); 9) European Commission (2015); 10) Eurostat (2016d).

– with varied levels of intensity – the following three questions that articulate our underlying conceptual framework: (1) How far were the discourses of deinstitutionalisation and ageing in place embraced in actual policy strategies? (2) Which older adults are considered to require institutionalisation? (3) To what extent have policy discourses and strategies corresponded to reality?

## 2.    THE CASE OF ISRAEL

In Israel in 2014, persons over 65 accounted for 11 per cent of the general population. Most older adults in Israel lived in the community, while approximately 3 per cent lived in LTC institutions (Brodsky et al., 2015).

Institutional care of the older population in Israel is under government responsibility, while financing and regulation are shared between the Ministry of Welfare and Social Affairs, responsible for semi-independent and frail older adults, and the Ministry of Health, responsible for severely disabled older adults. These services are means-tested. The government is also responsible for home-based care, provided mainly by the Ministry of Social Affairs and Social Services (Azary-Viesel and Stier, 2014).

Another significant resource for older people in Israel is the National Insurance Institute (NII) (*Bituach Leumi*). According to the NII Law of

1995, two major allowances are available: the old age benefit, paid monthly on a universal basis to each insured person after retirement, and long-term care benefit, supporting services to older persons needing assistance and supervision in their daily functioning in the community (Azary-Viesel and Stier, 2014; Borowski, 2015). The cash benefits from the social security system pertaining to older adults in Israel comprise four layers. The two first layers are provided by National Insurance (NI) and include universal old age benefit (which was mentioned earlier) and selective financial support for older adults who need it. The third level includes work-related pensions. Finally, the fourth layer includes retirement saving (Gal and Pesach, 2002).

The most significant expression of de-institutionalisation of older people in Israel is the Long-term care insurance programme (LTCIP) (*Bituach Seeood*). We shall first briefly describe the background and the causes for the enactment of the LTCIP and the services that are included in it. Then we will focus on challenges facing the programme, since its enactment, relating to de-institutionalisation. LTCIP, administered since 1968 by National Insurance, promotes in-kind services for frail older people living at home (Iecovich, 2012), one of its goals being the reduction of demand for residential care (Borowski, 2015; Iecovich, 2012). Prior to the implementation of LTCIP, most services for older people were provided by the social assistance system. Limited in their scope, these were given mostly to poor older adults on a discretionary basis. Older adults who were ineligible for home-based services applied for publicly subsidised institutional care. Since the 1970s, the necessity arose for wider and more adequate resources, due to four main factors: (a) the enormous gap between the needs of the frail older population and the assistance available; (b) high cost of institutional care; (c) actual and predicted growth in the older population; and (d) a growing official recognition of the implications of the burden of care borne by family caregivers. In light of these needs, LTCIP was enacted in 1986, aiming to provide in-kind benefits for frail older adults through an array of personal care and homemaking services, and to enable 'ageing in place', alleviating the family caregivers' burden and reducing national expenditure on institutional care (Borowski, 2015; Borowski and Schmid, 2001; Iecovich, 2012; Schmid, 2009; Schmid and Borowski, 2004). Eligibility for LTCIP requires applicants to be Israeli citizens living in Israel and over the official age of retirement (age 64 for women and 67 for men). Applicants must be mentally and/or physically frail and in need of assistance or supervision with daily activities. They must live in their home in the community or in continuing care retirement communities and undergo an income test. The latter is quite generous and a vast majority meet these income criteria (Iecovich, 2012). Most prominent within LTCIP is home care, ranging from 9.75 to 18 hours per week (Borowski, 2015). Other services include daycare centres, alarm systems, laundry services and free incontinence pads (Iecovich, 2012).

A study that compared the patterns of institutionalisation prior to the implementation of LTCIP with those of several years later found a reduction of 25 per cent in the number of older adults in residential care. Additionally, the composition of the applicants for residential care changed. They were older, more disabled and more likely to have been widowed (Naon and Strosberg, 1996). However, the future of this de-institutionalisation in the context of LTCIP is less certain and further research is necessary to further explore this process (Asiskovitch, 2013; Borowski, 2015). Despite a significant increase in community-based assistance to older people, its coverage is still partial. The concept underlying this policy is providing a moderate degree of aid to a larger number of beneficiaries, rather than providing comprehensive assistance to a more limited number (Ben-Zvi, 1990). This policy also draws upon the values of Israeli and Jewish society, emphasising the involvement and the responsibility of family members in the care of older relatives (Iecovich, 2003). However, when there is need for institutional care, the government, through the Ministry of Health and the Ministry of Labour and Social Affairs, can provide full funding after an income test of the older adult and their children (Brodsky et al., 2003).

Thus, although the move of the older person to institutional care is often a result of decline in health or functional ability, in some cases the transition can occur due to a shortage in the economic or social resources of the older person and their family. This difficulty could worsen due to current processes of privatisation and liberalisation in Israel (Doron, 2007) alongside changes in family structure, mainly reflected in the growing participation of women in the labour market (Lavee and Katz, 2003; Toren, 2003). Thus women, who carry most of the informal caregiving responsibility, are left with less time and fewer resources to support older family members (Iecovich, 2003). Although amendments and adjustments in LTCIP have occurred over the years (Asiskovitch, 2013), these changes pose new challenges to LTCIP and to the continuation of the de-institutionalisation process in Israel.

## 3.  THE CASE OF MALTA

Malta's population of 420 000 is one of the fastest-ageing in the EU-28, flagging serious challenges for the future, even if the constant rise of GDP in recent years should enable the growth and not necessitate the reduction of services. By 2030, the over-65s and the over-80s will make up 25 per cent and 8 per cent respectively of the population.

Since the mid-1980s, discourse has been led by the terms 'community care', 'remaining in one's community' and, lately, 'ageing in place', though 'primary care' has also lingered longer than strictly appropriate as a competing term within health services vocabulary. Outside mental health, de-institutionalisation – taken to mean moving older people out of institutions – has not been a key goal in Maltese policy. The exception was the optimism that marked the newly-formed junior ministry for the elderly around 1987, which aspired to make such moves out of the state's 1000+ bed institution. This proved to be a short-lived dream amid the then undeveloped community services and residents' reluctance to relinquish their prized places in the institution.

Maltese expectations of care in old age by family or institutions exceed European averages: 53 per cent of Maltese (but 45 per cent in the EU) expect care at home by a relative. This is a tradition with a diminishing future, as Malta's female employment rate – while low – is the fastest-rising in Europe. Maltese are less than half as likely as other Europeans to expect to be cared for at home by a formal carer, while one in five Maltese (more than twice the EU average) expect to receive institutional care (European Commission, 2007).

The bulk of Malta's public expenditure on LTC goes into residential institutions. Specific cash benefits for LTC do not exist in Malta, and state home-based care costs amount to less than 0.1 per cent of GDP, as opposed to 0.53 for EU-27 in 2010 (European Commission, 2012). Meanwhile, government encouragement of 'ageing in place' has not been matched by a progressive growth of community services. There has been underinvestment in social work, disregarding its potential to improve support and survival in the community.

No law caters specifically for the care of older adults, although an Active Ageing Strategy has been in place since 2013. In Malta, welfare provision is within the capacity of only one tier of government, and its development is frequently driven by ministerial executive action, without the support of specific legislation beyond the Budget Act. Means-tested old age pensions were introduced in 1948, followed in 1956 by a contribution-based system. Since 1979, Malta has had a mandatory earnings-related contributory pension targeted to provide a pension equivalent to two-thirds of the average earnings of the insured person. However, due to a long frozen pensionable earnings cap, this objective has become a progressively rarer attainment in reality. Those who do not meet eligibility criteria for an NI pension can benefit from the non-contributory scheme as long as they satisfy conditions of residency and financial means (both income and capital assets of household members). While there is no LTC allowance as such, public residential care is usually paid by withholding about 70 per cent of one's state pension at source.

Residential care accommodation is now of four broad types: purely statutory; purely church; purely private; and public–private initiatives, including 'bed purchasing' by government. State hostels, started in the late 1980s for the able-bodied, have since become nursing homes. As far as community services are concerned, 1987 saw the growth almost from scratch of home care (meals-on-wheels, home helps, handyman, alarm-type Telecare) and, later, daycare. All this has increased in volume, only to reach a plateau in the last decade.

A significant move has been made to outsourcing. Public–private partnerships have been the declared path to increasing bed availability, through building and running new homes for older persons on the one hand, and publicly paid beds in private homes on the other. In 2015, the government transferred the provision of two key services (home nursing and meals-on-wheels) from NGOs to a for-profit provider (Pace et al., 2016). It is too early yet to assess the managerial, political and ideological significance of this little-discussed move. While no notable cuts have taken place, government provision has not kept pace with growing need. This has led to 'privatisation by default' or 'passive privatisation', through increasing recourse to private paid care (especially residential), to home-based care by immigrant care workers or, least likely, to community support.

Strikingly, populations in state-run residences have grown by 4 per cent a year since 2008, while use of the main home care services has barely grown at all. Similarly, the budget for residential care since 2006 has grown six times faster than that for community services. Clearly, community care growth has been deeply impeded by insufficient investment, although efforts are being made. A scheme to lighten residential waiting lists through subsidising home-based care workers was piloted in 2016, and has been extended into 2017. The budget for 2017 also includes a significant increase in the Carer's Pension and Carer's Allowance, payable to those caring for persons with high or medium dependencies in their own home.

A potentially positive move has been the transfer in 2013 of community care from the Health to the Social Solidarity ministry. The opportunity to correct the narrow view of the medical and institutional model at the expense of a social support model that could reduce recourse to residential care should not be lost. Yet, for a population of about 100 000 persons aged over 60, there are still only six social workers working in the community. These social workers play an important role in assessments, and as gatekeepers to home and residential services. The demands on their time result in an emphasis of quantity over quality while their potential to fine-tune care networks and prevent overuse of residential care is wasted.

The major challenges now, in order not to be overwhelmed by the fast-approaching demographic growth in dependency, are to study the lessons of international good practice, to robustly expand the needed resources for effective community care, to espouse its holistic and especially its social dimension, and to expand social work to develop the support capacities of local networks. Additional challenges are to develop a philosophy of community care overarching the care of older, disabled and mentally challenged persons and to introduce a flexible case management system (Pace, 2002) to achieve the necessary care programming and interagency coordination that makes best use of finite resources.

## 4. THE CASE OF SPAIN

In Spain, persons aged 65 and over represented 18.1 per cent of the total population in 2014 and this is increasing with the ageing of the baby-boomer generation. Those over-65 in care homes (*residencias asistidas*) account for 2.8 per cent (Imserso, 2014). The social services system in Spain has largely developed during the 1980s after the arrival of democracy. Pensions are the most important income for older adults, and in the Spanish case are particularly relevant because of their incidence in family solidarity strategies as we will explain later on. The Spanish pensions system is a mixed system, with contributions by workers and companies towards contributory pensions (*pensiones contributivas*). The state also provides non-contributory pensions (*pensiones no contributivas*). Older adults are eligible for a pension, although there are important gender differences, due to the fact that during Franco's dictatorship married women were forced to resign.

While pensions are low but assured, there is no specific Spanish social policy on the care of older people. Nevertheless, 1 January 2007 saw the promulgation of the Law 39/2006, for the promotion of personal autonomy and care for elderly people and disabled people (*Ley de Promoción de la Autonomía Personal y Atención a las personas en situación de dependencia*, henceforth LAPAD), which is a state social service law, common for all regions (*Comunidades Autónomas*). Its main objective was to improve living conditions of dependent people of all ages, including people with physical or mental disabilities and for frail older adults dependent on help in doing Activities of Daily Life (ADL) (Deusdad et al., 2016b; see Deusdad, Javornik et al., in this volume; Hidalgo-Lavié and Fernández-Sanz, 2010; Vilà, 2011).

LAPAD provides a choice between three benefits:

- Cash transfers to purchase services, with a choice among Telecare, day centres, residential and home care.
- An anticipated service-linked benefit (*Prestación vinculada al servicio*) for people assessed as having a degree of dependence and wanting to be in a care home. The regional administration gives a cash transfer to enable the advance payment of residential care. This measure was suspended during the peak of the 2008 crisis. Other cash transfers for buying technical equipment and adapting homes are also granted.
- An allowance for family care (*Prestación económica para cuidados en el entorno familiar*), or for hiring a personal assistant. This last option has almost never been implemented, except in the case of the Basque Country (Deusdad et al., 2016b).

Overall, though LAPAD was not intended to be a de-institutionalisation policy, it indirectly affected the way ageing in place played out in Spain. However, *the implementation of LAPAD fell victim of the economic crisis*. Major austerity measures were implemented: two Royal Decrees, 20/2011 and 20/2012, imposed cutbacks on LTC at the State level, whereby the full implementation of this law was postponed and the benefits for family care reduced (see Deusdad, Javornik et al., in this volume).

Even though the law considered the allowance for family care an 'exceptional measure', it has been implemented since 2007 in ways that gave it a deep nationwide presence. Older adults with extensive care needs have remained at home under the supervision of family carers, instead of being institutionalised. This was especially reinforced due to the economic crisis. Families could not afford assisted living facilities solely relying on retirement pensions. Moreover, in situations of unemployment and mortgage debt, living under the same roof as older adults became a way of saving money, enabling relatives to use the older adults' pensions as a source of income (Deusdad et al., 2016b). Added to this there were long waiting lists due to increasing delays between applying for and receiving these benefits, often taking years, by which time the applicant might have died. All this intensified reliance on family care.

Concluding, LAPAD, which introduced the allowance for family care, was not aimed at promoting 'ageing in place' as such, but at reducing public spending and at meeting users' and their families' preferences. However, due to both the actions of implementing administrators and people's agency, the law ended up leading to a *false ageing in place/de-institutionalisation policy* and reinforcing *re-familisation* (Deusdad et al.,

2016b; see the notion of 'passive' re-familisation in Leibetseder et al., in this volume). Ageing in place in Spain is, then, not a clear and intended social policy goal but mainly the unintended result of scarcity of resources and of high rates of female and male unemployment, which have pushed different generations back to living together and to relying on family care.

## 5.  DISCUSSION, COMPARISON AND CONCLUSIONS

In this section we shall examine the three country cases in the light of the three questions that encapsulated our evaluation.

First, we asked, 'how far were discourses of de-institutionalisation and ageing in place embraced in actual policy strategies?' In Malta, the policy of ageing in place, declared since the late 1980s, started with a short-lived hope to actually return older people from a mega institution back to community living. In fact, institutional and residential beds for older adults have still risen constantly since then. In contrast, Israel, which initiated its strategy at an earlier stage in the demographic ageing process when demand was weaker, succeeded in reducing residential beds occupied by older persons. In Spain, LAPAD aimed to provide support for dependent people to improve their quality of life and autonomy. While LAPAD did not particularly mention the greater or lesser use of institutions, it offered services like home support, daycare and assisted-living residential care. Without being an explicit goal of the law, de-institutionalisation became a clear effect (Mesa-Raya and Gracia-Romero, 2010). In the end, the benefit most implemented was the Allowance for Family Care – as a way of reducing costs, but also as a response to the growing demand (Deusdad et al., 2016b). The effect was a reduced dependence on institutions along with a *re-familisation* process involving an increasing care burden on female family members. In Israel, in fact, although the state provides resources for ageing, the de-institutionalisation process is partial, because not enough benefits are allocated at the community and household levels to adequately allow older adults to 'age in place' when they have no family support. No legislation aimed at de-institutionalisation has been launched in Spain or Malta, and while there is a good supply of residential beds, not all of them are publicly subsidised. While institutional care is highly valued in both countries, waiting lists severely limit the availability of such care.

The above takes us to the second question, that is, 'which older adults are given access to institutional care?' Older adults seek institutional care due to frailty, poor health and lack of family support. Our question is whether institutional care is a preferred option or, rather, a last resort amidst a rise in care needs and a fall in the supply of care traditionally provided by the family (see Deusdad, Javornik et al., in this volume) in the Mediterranean. We have seen that, in the three countries, inadequate resources and limited legal entitlement result in limited formal community service. In Spain this was further worsened by stringent budgets due to economic crisis, while institutionalisation is publicly funded only when older adults are severely dependent. In Malta, the growth of community resources has been slow and at times stagnant. The answer to our second question would therefore seem to be that it is not strictly only those adults who are most frail or in poorest health who enter institutional care, but largely those without adequate support for ageing in place. Lack of adequate community resources makes it impossible to ensure that institutionalisation only occurs as a matter of true need or personal choice.

The third question concerns 'to what extent have policy discourse and strategies corresponded to reality?' It is worth noting that although in all three countries we see a reduction in available family care due to rising female employment, times of crisis and austerity may sometimes reverse this order. For instance, a rise in unemployment in Spain may have led to the opposite phenomenon: an increased availability and expectation of family care, falling more often than not on women's shoulders. Thus, in the case of Spain, although institutionalisation is accepted and the different generations have become more reluctant to live together (Jensen and Møberg, 2011), austerity measures have seriously limited access to affordable residential care. As a consequence, ageing in place is made possible by the *re-familisation* of care (Deusdad et al., 2016b). This is less strong in the case of Malta or Israel, where no similar austerity measures followed the 2008 economic crisis. In fact, Israel differs markedly from the two other countries, in that more state resources are placed into the enabling of ageing in place.

While valued by the Charter of fundamental rights of the European Union (European Parliament, 2010), discouraging institutionalisation is not the best solution for every older adult. What is best depends on the range of services available in the community or at home, the degree of dependency and the kind of services required for the older adult. Ideally, selecting appropriate services for the older adult should derive from considerations of the best interest of that older adult (Grabowski, 2006; Mansell et al., 2007; Wysocki et al., 2015). Yet, as we can see in the three countries, issues of availability and affordability mean that it is often not the interests of the older adult upon which such selection is eventually made.

Such insufficient responses by the state to implement a de-institutionalisation process of care for older people have facilitated the privatisation of institutional care services, even in countries with significant state funding, like Israel. Marketisation in these three Mediterranean countries varies from quasi-markets in Israel, through outsourcing mechanisms in all the three countries, to private–public partnerships and greater reliance on irregular employment in Spain and Malta. Where privatisation and marketisation processes result in cream-skimming of the more affluent elderly clients, this can exacerbate the social exclusion of less well-off older adults. Another result of inadequate community resources is the growing reliance in all three countries on home-based migrant care workers, mostly women, who substitute or complement family care. This bottom-up development, not initiated by policy-makers, merits further research.

Overall, as Gal (2010) indicated, regional similarities do exist. The three countries clearly share common values and approaches. While traditionally valorising a male breadwinner–female carer family model, rising female employment rates have – in the absence of adequate state resources for ageing in place – contributed to a dearth of care for older adults. Those unable to afford private care solutions, or to employ migrant carers under the counter, often enter last-resort government-subsidised institutional care after long waiting lists not by choice but for want of an alternative. These common threads suggest the existence of a common Mediterranean regime for the care of older adults.

Nevertheless, each country does have specific features. In Israel there has been a de-institutionalisation process during the last three decades, reflected in LTCIP. Yet this process is limited due to the partial assistance the LTCIP provides. In contrast to the community care provided by LTCIP, full funding by the government for institutional care is available, subject to an income test. Thus, where more supervision or assistance is required due to severe disability or illness, and the older adult and his or her family cannot afford the assistance required in the community, institutionalisation becomes the only solution.

In Malta, widespread public support for institutional care has perhaps facilitated the delayed, sketchy and somewhat stagnant development of community care alternatives. Institutionalisation might be more acceptable in Malta because, within its compact population, frequent – even daily – visiting by relatives is made easy by proximity. While innovative measures are now being taken to reduce waiting lists for institutions through a public wage subsidy for carers, it will be interesting to find out whether this pilot scheme will manage to be both effective and sustainable to help meet the accelerating challenges of ageing and of female employment.

In the case of Spain, institutionalisation of older people is lower than in the two other cases, and can also be considered a *false de-institutionalisation* because ageing in place happens with almost no resources, which increases the care burden on the family and, above all, on women. In fact, paradoxically, de-institutionalisation in Spain is often the result of not having enough resources to go into care institutions, in other words, families being unable to afford it. In such circumstances, it seems that whether or not an older adult chooses to enter (or indeed to leave) an institution depends far less on his or her choice or needs, but more on the time and financial resources of relatives and the availability of adequate and affordable community services. The LTC law only helps cases assessed as higher degrees of dependence, and then only through co-payment schemes and after having been on a waiting list for a long period, so as to obtain a place on an assisted-living care home, which is publicly funded.

Though more research is needed, there is enough evidence that de-institutionalisation, though cited as a goal in EU policy, has not been fully embraced by these three Mediterranean states. It may be argued that the three countries manifest an illusory policy of de-institutionalisation, because not enough public and community resources are invested to assure desirable and adequate conditions for ageing in place in the face of decreased autonomy in the activities of daily living or of additional challenges like dementia.

To conclude, while all three countries have attempted, to different degrees, to move away from institutional care and towards ageing in place, the reduction of the family care burden has been limited. Israel was the only country to achieve what could be called *numerical de-institutionalisation* – a reduction of residential populations, and possibly also the most notable degree of individual *de-institutionalisation* – the actual move of persons back to the community. All three countries achieved a certain amount of *preventive de-institutionalisation*, that is, the diversion of individuals from institutional care by maintaining them in the community. In Spain, the planned growth of community support was stopped in its tracks by the economic crisis, resulting in a *re-familisation process, a forced ageing in place* and a *false de-institutionalisation*, in which the responsibility for care was not transferred to formal community services as planned, but largely back to family care – a resource that paradoxically increased due to the crisis.

## REFERENCES

Angelelli, J. (2006), 'Promising models for transforming long-term care', *The Gerontologist*, **46** (4), 428–30.

Asiskovitch, S. (2013), 'The long-term care insurance program in Israel: solidarity with the elderly in a changing society', *Israel Journal of Health Policy Research*, **2** (1), 3.

Azary-Viesel, S. and H. Stier (2014), 'Welfare budgets for Israel's elderly population', in D. Ben-David (ed.), *State of the Nation Report: Society, Economy and Policy in Israel*, accessed 1 November 2016 at http://taubcenter.org.il/wp-cont ent/files_mf/e2014.15welfarebudgetsfortheelderly70.pdf.

Bachrach, L.L. (1976), 'De-institutionalisation: an analytical review and sociological perspective', *DHEW Publication No. (ADM)376-51*, Washington: US Government Printing Office.

Ben-Zvi, B. (1990), 'The contribution of the long-term care insurance law to the welfare of severely dependent elderly', *Social Security*, 2, 100–16.

Borowski, A. (2015), 'Israel's long-term care social insurance scheme after a quarter of a century', *Journal of Aging and Social Policy*, 27 (3), 195–14.

Borowski, A. and H. Schmid (2001), 'Israel's long-term care insurance law after a decade of implementation', *Journal of Aging and Social Policy*, 12 (1), 49–71.

Brodsky, J., J. Habib and M. Hirschfeld (2003), 'Long-term care strategies in industrialised countries: case studies of insurance based and non-insurance based long-term care systems', Jerusalem: Myers-JDC-Brookdale Institute and WHO NMH/CCL, accessed 28 March 2016 at http://brookdale.jdc.org.il/_Uploads/ PublicationsFiles/123-03-longtermcare-new-ES-ENG.pdf.

Brodsky, G., Y. Snoor and S. Beer (2015), 'Elderly in Israel: facts and figures', Jerusalem: Myers-JDC-Brookdale Institute.

Central Bureau of Statistics – Israel (2016a), 'Population 2015, by population group, religion, sex, age', accessed 26 October 2016 at http://www.cbs.gov.il/rea der/shnaton/templ_shnaton_e.html?num_tab=st02_03&CYear=2016.

Central Bureau of Statistics – Israel (2016b), 'GDP data', accessed 28 March 2016 at http://cbs.gov.il/publications16/1633/pdf/t17.pdf.

Central Bureau of Statistics – Israel (2016c), 'Social protection expenditure', accessed 28 March 2016 at http://cbs.gov.il/shnaton66/st10_08.pdf.

Damiani, G., V. Farelli, A. Anselmi, L. Sicuro, A. Solipaca, A. Burgio, D. Iezzi and W. Ricciardi (2011), 'Patterns of long term care in 29 European countries: evidence from an exploratory study', *BMC Health Services Research*, 11 (316), accessed 28 February 2016 at https://www.ncbi.nlm.nih.gov/pmc/articles/ PMC3228675/.

Davey, J., G. Nana, V. de Joux and M. Arcus (2004), 'Accommodation options for older people in Aotearoa/New Zealand', Report prepared for the Centre for Housing Research Aotearoa/New Zealand (CHRANZ), Wellington, Aotearoa/ New Zealand: NZ Institute for Research on Ageing/Business & Economic Research Ltd, accessed 28 February 2016 at https://www.beehive.govt.nz/sites/ all/files/Accomodation%20Options%20for%20Older%20People.pdf.

Deusdad, B., C. Pace and A. Anttonen (2016a), 'Facing the challenges in the development of long-term care for older people in Europe in the context of an economic crisis', *Journal of Social Service Research*, 42 (2), 144–50.

Deusdad, B., D. Comas-D'Argemir and S. Dziegielewski (2016b), 'Restructuring long-term care in Spain: the impact of the economic crisis on social policies and social work practice', *Journal of Social Service Research*, 42 (2), 246–62.

Doron, A. (ed.) (2007), *Formulating Welfare Policy In Israel, 2000–2005*, Jerusalem: Taub Center, accessed 1 March 2016 at http://taubcenter.org.il/for mulating-welfare-policy-israel-2000-2005/.

Doyle, M. and V. Timonen (2007), *Home Care for Ageing Populations: A Comparative Analysis of Domiciliary Care in Denmark, the United States and Germany*, Cheltenham, UK and Northampton, MA, USA: Edward Elgar Publishing.

EC – European Commission, DG for Employment, Social Affairs and Equal Opportunities (2008), *Report of the Ad Hoc Expert Group on the Transition from Institutional to Community-based Care*, Brussels: European Commission.

EEGTICC – European Expert Group on the Transition from Institutional to Community-based Care (2012), 'Common European guidelines on the transition from institutional to community-based care', accessed 30 March 2016 at http://www.deinstitutionalisationguide.eu/wp-content/uploads/2016/04/GUIDELINES-Final-English.pdf.

European Commission (2007), *Special Barometer 283 – Health and Long-Term Care in the European Union*, accessed 30 March 2016 at https://data.europa.eu/euodp/en/data/dataset/S657_67_3_EBS283.

European Commission (2012), *Long-Term Care: Need, Use and Expenditure in The EU27*, accessed 30 March 2016 at http://ec.europa.eu/economy_finance/publications/economic_paper/2012/ecp469_en.htm.

European Commission (2015), *The 2015 Ageing Report*, accessed 20 November 2016 at http://ec.europa.eu/economy_finance/publications/european_economy/2015/pdf/ee3_en.pdf.

European Parliament (2010), *Charter of Fundamental Rights of The European Union*, accessed 15 April 2016 at http://ec.europa.eu/justice/fundamental-rights/charter/index_en.htm.

Eurostat (2016a), *Population by Five Year Age Groups and Sex*, accessed 16 October 2016 at http://appsso.eurostat.ec.europa.eu/nui/show.do?dataset=demo_pjangroup&lang=en.

Eurostat (2016b), *Life Expectancy at Age 60 Data Set*, accessed 28 March 2016 at http://appsso.eurostat.ec.europa.eu/nui/submitViewTableAction.do.

Eurostat (2016c), *Social Protection Data Set*, accessed 27 March 2016 at http://ec.europa.eu/eurostat/web/social-protection/data/database.

Eurostat (2016d), *Long-Term Care Beds in Nursing and Residential Care Facilities by NUTS 2 Regions Dataset*, accessed 25 October 2016 at http://appsso.eurostat.ec.europa.eu/nui/show.do?dataset=hlth_rs_bdsns&lang=en.

Fakhoury, W. and S. Priebe (2007), 'De-institutionalisation and reinstitutionalisation: major changes in the provision of mental healthcare', *Psychiatry*, **6** (8), 313–16.

Ferrera, M. (1996), 'The Southern model of welfare in social Europe', *Journal of European Social Policy*, **6**, 17–37.

Gal, J. (2009), 'Is there an extended family of Mediterranean welfare states, or did Beveridge and Bismarck take the Mediterranean cruise together?', paper presented at the SPA Annual Conference, University of Edinburgh.

Gal, J. (2010), 'Is there an extended family of Mediterranean welfare states?', *Journal of European Social Policy*, **20** (4), 283–300.

Gal, J. and R. Pesach (2002), 'The development of the social security system for the aged in Israel and its implications', *Social Security*, **62**, 114–41.

Goffman, E. (1968), *Asylums: Essays on the Social Situation of Mental Patients and Other Inmates*, New York: Doubleday.

Grabowski, D.C. (2006), 'The cost-effectiveness of noninstitutional long-term care services: review and synthesis of the most recent evidence', *Medical Care Research and Review*, **63** (1), 3–28.

Guillén, A.M. and M. León (ed.) (2011), *The Spanish Welfare State in European Context*, Farnham, UK and Burlington, USA: Ashgate.

Harnett, T. (2010), 'Seeking exemptions from nursing home routines: residents' everyday influence attempts and institutional order', *Journal of Aging Studies*, **24** (4), 292–301.

Hidalgo-Lavié, A. and M. Fernández-Sanz (2010), *Trabajo social en el Ámbito de la Ley de Dependencia: Reflexiones y Sugerencias*, Oleiros La Coruña: Netbiblo.

Iecovich, E. (ed.) (2003), *The System of Community and Institutional Services for the Elderly*, Jerusalem: JDC-ESHEL.

Iecovich, E. (2012), 'The long-term care insurance law in Israel: present and future', *Journal of Aging and Social Policy*, **24** (1), 77–92.

Ilinca, S., K. Leichsenring and R. Rodrigues (2015), 'From care in homes to care at home: European experiences with (de) institutionalisation in long-term care', Vienna: European Centre for Social Welfare Policy and Research, accessed 15 December 2016 at www.euro.centre.org/data/1449741582_83911.pdf.

Imserso (2014), *Informe 2014. Las personas mayores en España*, accessed 1 November 2016 at http://www.imserso.es/InterPresent1/groups/imserso/docu ments/binario/22029_info2014pm.pdf.

Jensen, P. and R.J. Møberg (2011), 'Tensions related to the transition of elderly care from an unpaid to a paid activity', in B. Pfau-Effinger and T. Rostgaard (eds), *Care Between Work and Welfare in European Societies*, Basingstoke: Palgrave Macmillan, pp. 98–114.

Kane, R.L. and R.A. Kane (2001), 'What older people want from long-term care, and how they can get it', *Health Affairs*, **20** (6), 114–27.

Koren, M.J. (2010), 'Person-centered care for nursing home residents: the culture-change movement', *Health Affairs*, **29** (2), 312–17.

Lang, G., B. Löger and A. Amann (2007), 'Well-being in the nursing home – a methodological approach towards the quality of life', *Journal of Public Health*, **15** (2), 109–20.

Lavee, Y. and R. Katz (2003), 'The family in Israel: between tradition and modernity', *Marriage and Family Review*, **35** (1–2), 193–217.

Lehmann, S. and J. Havlíková (2014), 'Predictors of the availability and variety of social care services for older adults: comparison of Central European countries', *Journal of Social Service Research*, **41** (1), 113–32.

Leibfried, S. (1992), 'Towards a European welfare state', in C. Jones (ed.), *New Perspectives on the Welfare State in Europe*, London: Routledge, pp. 133–56.

Lerman, P. (1985), 'De-institutionalisation and welfare policies', *The ANNALS of the American Academy of Political and Social Science*, **479** (1), 132–55.

Mansell, J., M. Knapp, J. Beadle-Brown and J. Beecham (2007), 'Deinstitutionalisation and community living – outcomes and costs: report of a European Study', *Executive Summary*, no. 1, accessed 30 May 2016 at https://www.kent.ac.uk/tizard/research/research_projects/DECLOC_Volume_1_Exec_Summary.pdf.

Mathew-Puthenparambil, J. and T. Kröger (2016), 'Using private social care services in Finland: free or forced choices for older people?', *Journal of Social Service Research*, **42** (2), 167–79.

Mesa-Raya, C. and F. Gracia-Romero (2010), 'Mujer y atención a la dependencia en Aragón: una aportación para la consecución de la igualdad entre hombres y mujeres', *Aequalitas: Revista Jurídica de Igualdad de Oportunidades entre Mujeres y Hombres*, **27**, 62–70.

Moise, P., M. Schwarzinger, M.-Y. Um and the Dementia Experts Group (2004), 'Dementia care in 9 OECD countries: a comparative analysis', *OECD Health, Working Papers* no. 13, accessed 30 September 2015 at http://www.oecd.org/health/health-systems/33661491.pdf.

Moreno, L. (2000), *Cuidados precarios: la 'Última Red' de Protección Social*, Barcelona: Ariel.

Moreno-Fuentes, F.J. and P. Mari Klose (2015), *The Mediterranean Welfare Regime and the Economic Crisis*, London: Routledge.

Naon, D. and N. Strosberg (1996), *Changes in the Pattern of Institutionalisation of Disabled Elderly Following the Implementation of the Community Long-term Care Insurance Law*, Jerusalem: The Brookdale Institute.

OECD (2016a), 'Health statistics', accessed 28 March 2016 at http://stats.oecd.org/index.aspx?DataSetCode=HEALTH_STAT.

OECD (2016b), 'Long-term care public expenditure', accessed 28 March 2016 at http://www.oecd-ilibrary.org/social-issues-migration-health/health-at-a-glance-2015/long-term-care-public-expenditure-health-and-social-components-as-share-of-gdp-2013-or-nearest-year_health_glance-2015-graph201-en.

Pace, C. (2002), 'Remodelling service for new context – a response to community mental health need in Malta', PhD thesis, University of Leicester, accessible at https://www.um.edu.mt/library/oar//handle/123456789/944.

Pace, C. (2009), 'The Maltese welfare state: hybrid wine in Rightist bottles (with Leftist labels)?', in K. Schubert, S. Hegelich and K. Bazant (eds), *The Handbook of European Welfare Systems*, London: Routledge, pp. 344–62.

Pace, C., S. Vella and S.F. Dziegielewski (2016), 'Long-term care of older adults in Malta: influencing factors and their social impacts amid the international financial crisis', *Journal of Social Services Research*, **42** (2), 263–79.

Petmesidou, M. (1996), 'Solidaridad y protección social en Grecia', *Cuaderno de Trabajo*, **9**, 291–301.

Rabig, J., W. Thomas, R.A. Kane, L.J. Cutler and S. McAlilly (2006), 'Radical redesign of nursing homes: applying the Green House concept in Tupelo, Mississippi', *The Gerontologist*, **46** (4), 533–9.

Rhodes, M. (1996), 'Southern European welfare states: identity, problems and prospects for reform', *South European Society and Politics*, **1** (3), 1–22.

Schmid, H. (2009), 'Israel's long-term care insurance scheme', paper presented at the International Expert Meeting on Monitoring Long-Term Care for the Elderly, Hebrew University of Jerusalem, accessed 15 December 2016 at www.euro.centre.org/data/1254227500_87459.pdf.

Schmid, H. and A. Borowski (2004), 'Selected issues in the delivery of home care services to the elderly after a decade of implementing Israel's long-term care insurance law', *Social Security*, **7**, 87–114.

Solomon, R. (2004), 'The role of the social worker in long-term care', *Journal of Gerontological Social Work*, **43** (2–3), 187–202.

Thomas, W.H. (2004), *What are Old People for? How Elders Will Save the World*, Acton: Vander Wyk & Burnham.

Toren, N. (2003), 'Tradition and transition: family change in Israel', *Gender Issues*, **21** (2), 60–76.

Torrens-Bonet, R. (2012), 'La contratación de mujeres inmigrantes ¿Una alternativa a la crisis del cuidado de las personas?', *Portularia*, **XII** (extra), 221–30.

Vara, M.J. (2014), 'Long-term care for elder women in Spain: advances and limitations', *Journal of Aging and Social Policy*, **26** (4), 347–69.

Vilà, A. (2011), *Serveis Socials. Aspectes Històrics, Institucionals i Legislatius*, Barcelona: UOC.

WHO – World Health Organization (2007), 'Global age-friendly cities: a guide', accessed 20 January 2017 at http://www.who.int/ageing/publications/Global_age_friendly_cities_Guide_English.pdf?ua=1.

Wysocki, A., M. Butler, R.L. Kane, R.A. Kane, T. Shippee and F. Sainfort (2015), 'Long-term services and supports for older adults: A review of home and community-based services versus institutional care', *Journal of Aging & Social Policy*, **27** (3), 255–79.

PART IV

Local Initiatives, Social Innovation and Social
Inclusion

# 13. The Janus face of social innovation in local welfare initiatives

**Liisa Häikiö, Laurent Fraisse, Sofia Adam, Outi Jolanki and Marcus Knutagård**

## INTRODUCTION

The aim of this chapter is to understand the relationship between local welfare initiatives and social innovation and how it varies across places. Since welfare policies must tackle increasing needs with scarcer resources, the topic of social innovation has become relevant. Social innovation expresses a shared hope for making things better in the future (Evers, 2015). It is a semantic magnet that attracts many different meanings and is charged with many positive connotations (Bergmark et al., 2011). As Martinelli (Chapter 1, in this volume) suggests, social innovation is an important dimension of the restructuring of social services and must be integrated into the analysis.

To explore the role of social innovations in the restructuring of social services, we analyse four local welfare initiatives in health and social services. By 'local welfare initiatives', we refer to collective practices that arise at the municipal or neighbourhood level for creating or sustaining the welfare of individuals, groups or communities through the provision of services. The local initiatives under study take place in four municipalities in different European countries and aim to renew social policy practices and services in neighbourhoods or for particular groups of people. Our focus is on the variations in the way social innovation is created and sustained in these local welfare systems, which we define as 'dynamic arrangements in which the specific local socioeconomic and cultural conditions give rise to different mixes of formal and informal actors, public or not, involved in the provision of welfare resources' (Andreotti et al., 2012, p. 1925). As a result, new local combinations of social activities emerge in the welfare diamond (Martinelli, Chapter 1, as well as Leibetseder et al., in this volume), i.e. among state and municipal services, social entrepreneurs, third sector organisations, and community and family networks (Evers and Ewert, 2015).

By combining theoretical discussions on social innovation with empirical evidence from the cases, we argue that social innovation has an ambivalent character in local welfare initiatives. Different streams of theoretical and political discussion outline social innovation differently. The case studies highlight how local welfare initiatives combine different versions of social innovation, social practices and societal aims. The manner in which the notion of social innovation is mobilised is flexible and varies according to opportunities and context in a pragmatic way. Accordingly, we argue that socially innovative urban and local initiatives and experiments, and their consequences for local welfare systems, are decidedly Janus-faced (Swyngedouw, 2005).

In what follows, we first discuss the varieties of social innovation in the relevant literature and present the four case studies on local welfare initiatives. Subsequently, we analyse these local welfare initiatives from the perspectives of value orientation and institutionalisation. To conclude, we briefly summarise our findings and discuss the ambivalent nature of social innovation as part of local welfare solutions.

## 1.   SOCIAL INNOVATION AS A CONTINUUM BETWEEN TWO APPROACHES

Thinking about social innovation has progressively emerged during the 2000s, first in the academic sphere (Moulaert et al., 2010) and then on the political agenda. The historical roots of social innovation have been related to the self-organised political and economic experimentations that emerged within the first worker's associations and movements, i.e. the utopian, mutual aid and cooperative experiences of the early period of industrialisation in the nineteenth century (Martinelli, 2010). However, social innovation as an explicit concept was first used to describe the wave of new practices and strategies that evolved in the late 1970s and early 1980s from new social and urban movements (Touraine, 1981; Chambon et al., 1982; Castells, 1983; Lévesque, 2007). Grassroots initiatives based on protest and activism were aimed at meeting unsatisfied local welfare needs and improving living conditions. These community initiatives providing new social services often presented themselves as emancipatory practices compared to existing bureaucratic and paternalistic social services, inspiring academic discussion on social innovation.

Compared to this first period, one of the major shifts in the last fifteen years has been the end of the monopoly held by the civil society and the academic world over social innovation discourse and actions. During the last decade, social innovation has also received political attention in the context of economic austerity. It has become a new EU-sponsored policy agenda for responding to the financial crisis. The idea has become subject to some forms of regulation and funding, not only at the EU level but also at national and local levels (Fraisse, 2013). At the EU level, one of the main objectives of the Europe 2020 strategy is to promote economically efficient social innovations that facilitate smart, sustainable and inclusive growth and address the needs of the most vulnerable groups in society (see Gómez-Barroso et al., in this volume). Socially innovative strategies aim to mobilise the entire society to meet welfare needs and to provide social services. However, the EU innovation agenda, supported by dedicated social programmes and research funding, coexists with strong recommendations for austerity measures and cuts in public spending in the Eurozone. Austerity policies have accelerated welfare retrenchment, especially in Southern European countries (León et al., 2015), and have weakened the ability to invest in social services. In this context, there is a risk that national and local governments can interpret social innovations as substitutes or default solutions under the pressure to cut social spending.

The multiple roots of social innovation reveal different types of thinking. With reference to the political and academic discussion on social innovation, two main perspectives can be identified: a more mainstream discourse and a more radical view. Despite the similarities of these two perspectives with the two 'schools' of social innovation – one technocratic, the other democratic – as recently characterised by Montgomery (2016), we do not consider the mainstream policy discourse and the radical view as being fully alternative paradigms but rather as reference points in the intellectual discussion on the varieties of social innovation. In other words, distinguishing between these two lines of thinking is a heuristic device for positioning the varied meanings that social innovation can take in the restructuring of local welfare and service systems. The zone between these two poles is populated by highly variegated academic conceptualisations, political discourses and social practices (for example, see Gallouj and Djellah, 2010; Nicholls et al., 2015).

In our simplified dichotomy, the EU policy agenda (BEPA, 2010; European Commission, 2013) can be placed within the mainstream discourse, which focuses on the development and implementation of 'new ideas (products, services and models) to meet socially recognised needs and create new social relationships or collaborations' (Mulgan, 2012, p. 22). Having a functionalist logic, this definition understands social innovations as *local strategies to preserve social cohesion in times of crisis* and tends to stress *cost-efficient solutions from the social entrepreneurship perspective as well as social experimentations by local authorities*. In our opinion, it reinforces the neo-liberal agenda by introducing business methods and resources in the management of social services, extending the rules of competition to the delivery of social services and prioritising cost-efficiency within restricted public budgets. Social innovations are viewed as responses to the failure of the state to provide public goods and to the failure of the civil society to provide effective goods and services to their beneficiaries (Nicholls et al., 2015).

The more radical view refers to Moulaert's definition of social innovation (Moulaert et al., 2005; also see Klein et al., 2014) as grassroots initiatives that develop *to satisfy unmet basic human needs, to empower excluded social groups and communities to access social and citizenship rights, to change power relations and to transform governance practices*. It includes the potential for resistance to welfare dismantlement and the neo-liberal agenda. Social innovations that emerge from such grassroots movements implementing social change strategies are a potential source for counter-hegemonic projects (Moulaert et al., 2007). This notion of social innovation provides an alternative perspective on society and the reform of services.

In practice, the abovementioned differences are not always that sharp. The use of the social innovation concept is often flexible and varies according to opportunities and context in a pragmatic manner. Both the mainstream policy discourse and the radical view on social innovation integrate a normative dimension and, hence, a value orientation. From both perspectives, social innovation is a positive social phenomenon, either for incremental improvement or transformative social change, 'progressing toward something better' (Brandsen et al., 2016, p. 6). They both value bottom-up initiatives as the drivers of social innovation (Manzini, 2014; Rønning and Knutagård, 2015), thereby emphasising the importance of the local scale as the appropriate locus for effective governance. Social innovation emerges when people or 'the final recipients' are directly involved in the local decision-making process and the co-production of social services (Moulaert et al., 2007).

However, the two views on social innovation differ in their understandings of the social dimension. For the mainstream policy discourse, the social is a resource. Consumer involvement or mutual-help practices among ordinary people become a key instrument for cost-effective strategies in the restructuring of social services. Citizens participate in order to solve common problems, deliver care, form communities of mutual help, innovate and, most importantly, save public money (Häikiö, 2010; Manzini, 2014). Although their outcomes have great importance for the individuals and their well-being, these initiatives do not challenge or change social relations since social resources are not mobilised beyond the everyday life of the actors involved. The mainstream approach prioritises social stability and the maintenance of the social order. Therefore, the changes expected from the institutional support for innovative welfare services are limited to strengthening social cohesion.

For the radical view on social innovation, the social has a relational dimension, including power relations, and social innovations emerge from empowering processes that restructure social relations. Changes in social relations are regarded as a precondition for addressing major social problems. In addition to improving the well-being of the specific context in which they are developed, the new processes of service provision challenge the existing power relations, empower people and promote equality. This occurs through the engagement of civil society associations and/or social movements in socially innovative practices (Gerometta et al., 2005). Through their potential to identify and address the unmet needs of local people, socially innovative practices are related to collective actions and social transformations from the bottom up (Moulaert et al., 2013). Such socially innovative services have the potential to mobilise social resources and empower social groups that are excluded from or dissatisfied with certain social services. From this perspective, social innovation relates to the emancipatory agenda of social policies, as analysed by Mätzke et al. (in this volume).

To summarise, the mainstream and radical policy discourses on social innovation diverge in regard to:

- their intention and capability to challenge disempowering social relations;
- the societal reach of the changes involved;
- their standing with regard to the neo-liberal restructuring of social policies and services.

As stressed above, the aforementioned distinctions do not feature clear-cut models but highlight how social innovation in local welfare initiatives has a Janus face (see Swyngedouw, 2005). The varied forms of social innovation in the restructuring of local welfare systems relate to multifaceted value orientations and institutionalisation strategies.

In our interpretation, *value orientation* relates to the understanding of social innovation itself and to people's impetus to participate in creating and establishing social innovation. In the radical approach, social innovation has 'a value orientation in conflict with mainstream hegemonic values', encompassing the quest for progressive social change including social justice, environmental protection, gender equality, empowerment and so on (Vicari Haddock and Tornaghi, 2013, p. 265). In mainstream policy discourse, social innovation has a value orientation that is in line with the retrenchment, re-commodification and re-familisation of social services. The controversial aspects of these definitions are a source of the ambivalent interpretations of social innovation and also shape local welfare initiatives for providing and reforming social services. Value orientation is thus vocal for analysing not only the normative dimensions of social innovation but also the interplay between different actors and organisational forms of new initiatives, 'raising locally hopes and expectations within the sociopolitical and socioeconomic context of their emergence' (Brandsen et al., 2016, p. 6).

*Institutionalisation*, in turn, refers to the capability of local initiatives to have an influence on the public discourse and their potential to be sustained and transformed from experiments at the local scale into new social-political practices in the delivery of social services. The ability of local welfare initiatives to be integrated within governance arrangements and to consolidate institutional change means going beyond the pragmatic and local benefits achieved through the diffusion of a new social practice. It requires taking into account the strategic links between 'micro' social innovation and 'macro' institutional and social changes (Jessop et al., 2013). This multiscalar dimension is crucial for assessing the sustainability and institutionalisation of innovative practices. The long-term sustainability of socially innovative services depends on their ability to influence and be integrated into the regulatory and financial frameworks of social policies.

## 2.   THE CASE STUDIES ON LOCAL WELFARE INITIATIVES

The four case studies selected for our analysis of social innovation include local welfare initiatives in health and social services from different welfare models and regulatory systems. These different sociopolitical contexts also embed different sociocultural contexts with specific local norms and social relations. These contextual characteristics create distinct circumstances and environments for social innovation (Grimm et al., 2013).

Three of the four cases were studied in the course of the COST Action IS1102 *SO.S. COHESION – Social services, welfare states and places –* two from Nordic countries (Helsinki, Finland and Helsingborg, Sweden) and one from Southern Europe (Thessaloniki, Greece) (see CAP Knutagård, 2014; CAP Adam and Papatheodorou, 2014; CAP Jolanki, 2014). Another was added from Continental Europe (Lille Metropole, France) (Fraisse, 2016). These countries have different welfare frameworks. In Finland and Sweden, public social services play an important role in welfare provisions for all citizens. Public participation has been integrated into the services through civil society activities and the legislative rights of service users (together with municipal democracy, councils and so on). France and Greece are characterised by greater differences among regions and social groups. Moreover, in France, the long tradition of the welfare state and the provision of social services have been affected by a lengthy deindustrialisation process and structural long-term unemployment. In Greece, the financial crisis and the European austerity agenda have involved dramatic cuts in social spending, with relevant impacts on society.

**The Cases from the Nordic Countries**

Housing First in Helsingborg (Sweden) is based on a global idea developed in New York in 1992 by the Pathways to Housing non-profit organisation (Tsemberis, 2010) that diffused to other countries and was also adopted in a context representing the Nordic model. In 2009, the Director of Social Services in Helsingborg embarked on the implementation of this model in an attempt to combine the independent model of the service user with the tradition of the Nordic welfare state. The principles of Housing First significantly differ from the traditional 'treatment first model', with the latter emphasising abstinence from alcohol or drugs as a precondition for access to housing (Knutagård and Kristiansen, 2013; CAP Knutagård, 2014). By contrast, Housing First considers housing to be a prerequisite for the individual to accomplish other changes in life, makes a clear distinction between housing and treatment, and prioritises the active participation of homeless people in the design and provision of services. Recovery and harm reduction are also key ingredients in this approach.

The other case from Nordic countries, a senior co-housing unit in Helsinki (Finland), is an endeavour by a group of older women to create co-housing for their old age. The social and cultural context in which the process of building senior co-housing occurred is connected to the development and changes in Finnish services for older people. For a long period of time, public discussion and government reports on older people's housing and care have revolved around the problems in the availability and quality of both home-based care services and residential services. The discussion created an image of helpless people abandoned in their homes or mistreated in institutional care structures. The co-housing unit arose as an antidote to the prevailing image and practices of housing services for older people (Jolanki and Vilkko, 2015). The co-housing initiative represents an attempt to create housing and care alternatives *by* older people *for* older people (CAP Jolanki, 2014). In 2006, the residents moved into this multi-storey house with privately owned apartments and a common space, but the building process had begun much earlier, in 2000. A civil association was created to co-operate and negotiate with banks, builders and city professionals. The senior co-housing unit of Helsinki is the first of its kind in Finland. The core principles of the co-housing initiative revolve around the self-management and collective decision-making of the residents. It functions in a non-hierarchical manner, without paid care workers. Therefore, it differs from the tradition and practices of ordinary senior housing and services organised by other formal actors, such as NGOs, municipalities, or the private for-profit sector, which offer limited channels of influence to residents. The overall intention is not only to create an active social life, mutual help and meaningful activities for old age but also to have an influence on the housing and services that are offered for older people.

**The Case from Continental Europe**

The urban co-planning initiative in Lille Metropole (more specifically in the Roubaix-Tourcoing-Wattrelot district; Ilot Stephenson) can be considered a pilot project to test an alternative approach to urban renewal. The architect Patrick Bouchain and his colleagues launched the *Construisons ensemble, le grand ensemble* (Working together to build the neighbourhood) concept, which was applied between 2009 and 2012. The socially innovative local initiative in urban co-planning was initiated as a protest by inhabitants against the demolition of their housing and living area in a remote district of a larger urban renewal project, in the context of a deindustrialised area of a country within a Continental welfare state.

The conflict was transformed into a co-operative resource for renewal, and the protest evolved into a housing co-production action involving architects, local authorities and the residents' organisation. The architects located part of their office in the area, and the daily presence changed the relationships with the inhabitants and other stakeholders as well as the architects' perception of their initial architectural scheme by setting it against the backdrop of the habits and needs of everyday life. The project office was transformed into a public space where participation and communication between residents and architects occurred. The co-production addressed the reduced costs of housing, living possibilities for vulnerable groups, employment and education as well as new architectural models, encouraging the residents' participation in the self-rehabilitation of their neighbourhood.

**The Case from Southern Europe**

The Solidarity Clinic in Thessaloniki stems from the initiative of a group of health professionals and activists in solidarity with the hunger strike of 50 migrants in Thessaloniki in 2011. Universal public health care was never fully implemented in Greece, despite the introduction of a National Health System in 1983, due to a number of flaws in the policy design and implementation. After the introduction of the austerity measures following the 2008 financial crisis, the Greek government opted for dramatic cuts in public health expenditure (Kentikelenis et al., 2014). The budget for public hospitals was reduced by 40 per cent as admissions simultaneously increased by 30 per cent (Ifanti et al., 2013). The Solidarity Clinic was a response to this situation, and particularly to the demand of the Ministry of Health to exclude undocumented migrants from public health care as a fiscal cost containment strategy.

The core operating principles make it different from traditional public health care provision and other social clinics initiated by other formal agents (NGOs, municipalities, the church). These principles include an anti-racist orientation, the provision of service to all persons in need, a non-hierarchical structure, self-management and collective decision-making, rigid criteria for accepting funding and donations (i.e. not from political parties, EU programmes, private for-profit companies), and exclusive dependence on voluntary and unpaid staff. This initiative inspired other similarly minded solidarity groups across the country, and they eventually formed a network to better channel their political demands. However, they are reluctant to collaborate with the state and to become institutionalised for fear of losing their autonomy and resistance strategy. The Solidarity Clinic in Thessaloniki displays innovative aspects that are mostly related to the operational model it follows (non-hierarchical management, non-screening of potential beneficiaries) and the political advocacy role that it plays through public events.

## The Analytical Perspectives on the Cases

Next, we turn to the analysis of social innovation in the four local welfare initiatives in health and social services above. We build on the methodological approach proposed by Vicari Haddock and Tornaghi (2013) and mobilise the following parameters for our assessment: value orientation and institutionalisation.

As stressed above, the value orientation dimension of social innovation encompasses not only the normative dimensions for social change but also the relations between different actors and organisational forms of new initiatives. Social innovation stems from the interplay of a multiplicity of actors, ranging from civil society and everyday life actors to public services and local governments, which all hold diverse values. Moreover, the diversity of actors and social relations means differences in the resources and capabilities to which these actors have access. This relates to material conditions, but equally important is the articulation of identities and interests (Häikiö, 2007; Moulaert et al., 2007). Therefore, intertwined material and discursive circumstances shape the value orientations that define the meaning and practices of social innovation.

Institutionalisation refers to the capability of local initiatives to sustain broader changes by being replicated, reproduced over time, and embedded in formal institutions in two main ways: by triggering changes in the public discourse and broadening the spectrum of models and practices, and by being formalised beyond the local scale through linkages with state authorities (Vicari Haddock and Tornaghi, 2013). Therefore, the fulfilment of the socially innovative potential of local initiatives in social services is significantly articulated with scale. Local initiatives inherently refer to local social relations, resources and needs. Social innovation may be locally based, but its real potential unfolds when it bypasses the local and affects the broader society (see Manzini, 2014). In particular, social innovation in urban governance relations signifies the establishment of new inclusive social practices for participation (Gerometta et al., 2005). In addition, sustained changes may occur through the replication of local initiatives in new places and at other scales.

## 3.   THE JANUS FACE OF SOCIAL INNOVATION

### Value Orientation: Mobilising Co-operation

Value orientation is related to the contexts in which local welfare initiatives are created and established. The Housing First initiative in Helsingborg and senior co-housing in Helsinki represent local initiatives that engaged with the mainstream policy discourse on social innovation and, by doing so, challenged the established local welfare practices and social services by considering people as contributors and active participants. This, in turn, contributed to the diversification of welfare provision. Although these local welfare initiatives challenged the dominant sociocultural context of 'normal procedures', they improved welfare practices *within* the existing welfare systems and sociopolitical contexts. They aimed to improve welfare practices with new ideas on methods of providing services to meet the welfare needs of particular groups of citizens. In line with the EU approach to social innovation, they stress cost-efficient solutions for social services and social experiments for renewing local practices.

The two other cases, urban co-planning in Ilot Stephenson in Lille Metropole and the Solidarity Clinic in Thessaloniki, relate to the ideas represented by the radical view on social innovation, which aim to empower excluded social groups and to transform power relations. Both of these local initiatives aim at resisting welfare dismantlement in the realms of housing and health care, respectively. In the case of the co-planning initiative in Ilot Stephenson, the context of deindustrialisation is a long-term regional process, and the innovative practice is a local reaction to a vast national and regional urban renewal programme. However, the promotion of the inhabitants' participation in the production or rehabilitation of social housing is an urban planning alternative that has not been considered a priority in the national demolition-reconstruction programme in France.

The emergence of the Solidarity Clinic is strongly related to the financial crisis and the European austerity agenda. The value orientation of solidarity and a horizontal decision-making process as a resistance strategy to neo-liberalism and racism correspond to the willingness to transform users into active participants in the social struggle for universal public health care.

Despite these contextual differences in value orientations, all four local welfare initiatives perform co-production practices that include horizontal co-operation among actors and vertical integration between local and national welfare institutions. All involve the participation of civil servants, professionals and people in a co-operative manner, with the aim of creating material and cultural resources for socially innovative activities. All show how the commitment of these diverse actors mobilises resources and capacities for local initiatives to establish and sustain socially innovative practices.

All of the initiatives start with a small group of actors. Social service professionals initiated the Housing First pilot project, seeking to make policies for homelessness more effective. A group of health professionals took action with the Solidarity Clinic as an answer to the lack of health care. The co-housing unit arose from the initiative of a group of citizens who joined together to prepare themselves for future housing and care needs. The urban co-planning initiative emerged from the activities of working-class inhabitants who organised and protested against the demolition of their houses. However, these groups were also able to attract and mobilise other actors. For example, the Ilot Stephenson co-planning initiative started as a conflict between inhabitants and authorities but, after several years, opened a new space for co-operation among inhabitants, planning authorities and professionals. The demolition project was stopped, and the Lille Metropolis authorities decided to transfer the management of the urban renewal development to a semi-public company with an obligation to properly integrate sustainable development and participatory approaches in the planning process. The architect Patrick Bouchain and his team were invited to rethink the urban project with the inhabitants of the neighbourhood.

Another important aspect is the potential of a local initiative to build a contextually shared value orientation and cultural capacity for defining and articulating new identities and interests. Although all of the cases contribute to the cultural capabilities of citizens and professionals to engage with the socially innovative co-production of welfare, in the local initiative of Housing First, social innovation was precisely about creating a space for identity politics that increased the cultural capabilities of the homeless. This was not the key intention when the local initiative was taken, but the implementation of the pilot opened a space for the engagement of a group of tenants with a long history of homelessness. These tenants could not join established service user organisations if they were on medication-assisted treatment. Therefore, they formed their own peer-support organisation to share their experiences and to address their particular social needs for housing. The social services offered a place where the Housing First tenants could meet, and later on they took charge of the facilities themselves. The co-production of the different activities between the Housing First tenants and the social workers has led to an increased trusting relationship between the two parties (CAP Knutagård, 2014; Sanders and Stappers, 2008).

The trajectories of social innovations studied from the value orientation perspective differ depending on whether their practices include a contentious aspect in their relationship with local authorities and established institutions. A 'conflictual co-operation' dynamic is present in local initiatives that articulate a radical view on social innovation. Those that are in line with the mainstream policy discourses on social innovation generally aim to establish co-operation by negotiation and dialogue with authorities.

All of the cases, however, articulate social relations in a similar manner. They construct social relations that simultaneously address local problems and take action for a better future. Doing so creates a space for public participation and co-operation. For example, in the Lille Metropole area, the co-planning initiative articulated social relations so that the inhabitants' participation in the production of social housing and the rehabilitation of the area became a key principle for improving co-habitation in the city. In turn, the co-housing initiative in Helsinki emphasised the right of older people to be treated as individuals, ensuring their own choices with collective practices of co-operation, social interaction, mutual help and support. At a very practical level, the rationale for senior co-housing integrated individualistic and collective understandings of better ageing. To date, the socially innovative potential of the co-housing initiative has been more cultural than political in nature.

## Institutionalisation: Moving Across Scales

The institutionalisation perspective can be assessed at different levels. First, social innovations travel from place to place. Our cases demonstrate how local welfare initiatives are not limited to the local. Since the first experiments in the United States at the turn of the 1990s, the Housing First initiative has progressively become a global policy concept that has been replicated in different places. In Sweden, the example from Helsingborg has made the model more attractive to other local authorities. The senior co-housing unit in Helsinki followed the example of the 'Färdknäppen' Swedish collective housing unit, founded in the 1970s. The co-housing unit has also received major attention in Finnish public discussion, giving birth to other initiatives. The Ilot Stephenson co-planning initiative in the Lille Metropole area was not developed in a vacuum but had its roots in the idea of participatory urban planning and developed into a showcase for these types of practices with local and regional publicity. The Solidarity Clinic in Thessaloniki relates to the anti-austerity solidarity movement in Greece. The practices developed there have influenced other clinics. It has offered technical expertise to other Solidarity Clinics across Greece.

Second, all local welfare initiatives are connected to more or less institutionalised networks, processes and resources from other scales. In all four cases, the co-production of services depends on the capability of the actors involved to build multi-stakeholder and multilevel coalitions. Professionally driven initiatives needed to open spaces for the participation of citizens. Citizen-driven initiatives needed to engage with professionals and civil servants in co-operative ways to transform their modes of working and to promote social innovation. For example, many of the residents in the senior co-housing initiative in Helsinki were people with higher education, such as former journalists and doctors, with good educational, financial and social resources, but they also required support and resources during the process from various institutional actors. City officials and funding agencies provided advice concerning rules and regulations as well as on how to organise the funding of the construction. Small grants were given by the city of Helsinki and the Ministry of Social Affairs and Health for the preparation of the project. Similarly, the success of the Solidarity Clinic must be attributed to the engagement of a large number of other health and non-health professionals, apart from the founding team. In terms of financial support, the Solidarity Clinic relied on trade unions and individual citizens from within Greece and abroad.

Third, institutionalisation and up-scaling are a major challenge for local welfare initiatives and highlight the political character of social innovation. Shifts between governance scales from the local level to the national or international level illustrate the potential of socially innovative initiatives for societal change. All four cases show how the up-scaling of social innovation largely depends on the ability of local initiatives to become visible at other scales and to affect the public discourse on social policy.

The success of the Ilot Stephenson housing renewal has been possible because of the mediation of a well-known architect and his team at the national level, which accelerated local innovation processes and overcame resistance at the local level. The impact of the project went far beyond the local community. Many architecture professors and students, delegations of technicians from other cities and even international visitors have been visiting the building site and meeting the urban planning team. The architects have conceptualised and communicated the new urban approach to social housing construction and urban rehabilitation through publications, conferences and videos. One of the architects who worked in the Stephenson neighbourhood throughout the entire project even won a prize for young urban planners in 2012.

The senior co-housing in Helsinki has also received national attention through widespread media coverage, which has enabled public discussion and the dissemination of the idea and experience among citizens and institutional actors. Over the years, countless articles have been published in newspapers and magazines. The residents have taken an active role in spreading the idea through a book (Dahlström and Minkkinen, 2009), a website and various blogs. The place itself has been visited by a large number of visitors. Although the idea of senior co-housing has taken some time to take root and foster new initiatives, currently the National Development Programme for Housing for Older People 2013–2017 (*Ikääntyneiden asumisen kehittämisohjelma 2013–2017*) includes the goal of increasing alternative housing options for older people, particularly those that enhance community participation, reciprocity, mutual help and support, thus feeding into a sense of community. Recently, new funding has been reserved to study the possibilities of facilitating similar types of innovative solutions and implementing them in the future.

The Solidarity Clinic of Thessaloniki was one of the initiators of a broader network of autonomous Solidarity Clinics all over Greece, which collaborate both in practical aspects (for example, in the circulation of prescription drugs) and the organisation of public events (demonstrations for universal public health care). It has also managed to garner attention from international audiences through international field visits of activists and the participation of the Solidarity Clinic's members in campaigns abroad.

However, despite this movement among implementation scales, the institutionalisation of local welfare initiatives and social innovations in urban or national governance seems to be rare. Local initiatives relying on the mainstream policy discourse on social innovation are not targeting governance arrangements or aiming at direct institutional change. They connect with upper scale institutions and actors for practical reasons. For these local initiatives, governance is a context for their activities, not a site of transformation, and their inherent aspects of identity politics that promote new cultural capacities do not transform into struggles for social change. For example, when the city of Helsinki did not seriously consider that the senior co-housing unit would be a stakeholder in organising health care services for a wider community, the residents pragmatically turned to private providers to organise those services. Despite all the public interest, no institutionalisation process has taken place in relation to senior co-housing in Finland or Helsinki. On the other hand, the ideas that underlie the co-housing model have been reinterpreted, and new examples of communal types of housing are being developed with the assistance of institutional actors. To date, they offer a complementary example to the mainstream welfare model and housing options. Similarly, the scaling-up of the Housing First pilot initiative – as with other Housing First programmes in Sweden – continues to face many barriers in the prevailing institutional order (Knutagård, 2015). Although the pilot was a success in making all ends meet, it has not yet affected the overall structure of the social housing programme or local governance.

Local initiatives that embrace a more radical view of social innovation do bring about some forms of institutional changes. However, even these differ with regard to conflict and/or collaboration. The Ilot Stephenson co-planning initiative was a local political process for the first ten years. The struggle against the dominant sociopolitical context then turned into the development of practices to better meet the particular housing needs of excluded groups. And yet, despite the interest expressed by professionals, students and activists, national urban planning policies have not been changed because of this initiative. The influence of such co-planning experimentations on the dominant national and urban revitalisation programmes seems to be limited in a national context where quantitative aims (build more) prevail over qualitative and innovative actions (participation and co-production). In the case of the Solidarity Clinic of Thessaloniki, relations with the state authorities have been adversarial because of the austerity-imposed policies in health care and the social struggle orientation of the initiative. Although similarly minded initiatives across the country have jointly formed a network of autonomous Solidarity Clinics to better channel their political demands, they have mostly engaged in public events and demonstrations. Relations with the national scale have been difficult, given the potential danger that solidarity health care provision may actually facilitate the further retrenchment of national health services. For this reason, they seem reluctant to collaborate with the state and to become institutionalised for fear of losing their autonomy and resistance dimension.

## 4.  CONCLUSIONS

In this chapter we have analysed the socially innovative character of four local welfare initiatives in health and social services, that is, collective practices for developing new solutions or sustaining the welfare of individuals, groups and communities at the local level. The initiatives addressed were similar in terms of being grassroots endeavours that were developed as solutions to local social problems. All of them included local co-operation and, to some extent, integration among local and national welfare actors and institutions. Therefore, they represent new local combinations of actors in the welfare providers' 'diamond' (Leibetseder et al., in this volume). However, the four initiatives differed in terms of how they articulated social innovation, who the central actors involved were and what the level of institutionalisation was (see Table 13.1).

In a time of austerity, social innovations have become a focus of interest for local, national and EU social policies. Although local initiatives often represent citizens' solutions to failing or lacking public services and may be inspired by the goal to challenge the institutional order, regulatory and funding measures have been taken at national and EU levels to support social innovations as cost-effective methods of organising public services without altering the existing social order. Local initiatives are often grassroots solutions that may or may not develop into social innovations that last over time and can be transferred to other contexts. Social innovations have the potential to serve not only as a solution to local problems but also as a medium for social change; however, not all social innovations incorporate both of these aspects.

One central argument made in this chapter is that social innovations have a Janus face (Swyngedouw, 2005), which was illustrated in the analysis of the case studies. In assessing the value orientation of social innovations, as suggested by Vicari Haddock and Tornaghi (2013), the drive to act in the mainstream version of social innovation is to find a local remedy for the ills of failing social services and to mobilise local resources to find solutions that do not challenge the established power relations or the social order itself. By contrast, the value orientation inherent in the more radical

*Table 13.1  Value orientation and institutionalisation of social innovation in the four case studies*

| Local welfare initiative | Housing First, Helsingborg, Sweden | Senior co-housing, Helsinki, Finland | Co-planning urban renewal, Lille Metropole, France | Solidarity Clinic, Thessaloniki, Greece |
|---|---|---|---|---|
| Value orientation | Combining independence and involvement of the service users with cost-effective service provision | New housing and care solutions by integrating ideas on active ageing, autonomous living, self-management and collective decision-making | Renewing sectoral and professional activities in urban planning through co-planning with residents | Collective identity based on resistance against neo-liberalism and racism Promotion of universal health care |
| Institutionalisation | Transfer of a global idea to local authorities Implementation also in other municipalities No institutionalisation in national policies | Follows an example from Sweden, triggering other localities in Finland No institutionalisation in national or local policies | Applies general ideas of participatory planning Source of inspiration for similar initiatives No institutionalisation in national housing and urban policies | Replication by imitation, network of autonomous clinics No institutionalisation in national or local policies |

socially innovative initiatives encompasses a quest for social change by reorganising power relations and strengthening the participatory role of citizens as co-planners in welfare practices. Therefore, social innovations can be distinguished on the basis of who the key actors are and what the role (and power) of citizens is in relation to institutional actors and the dominant social order.

A key question concerning the opportunity to transform local initiatives into social innovations is their degree of institutionalisation. Some initiatives, such as the Solidarity Clinic in Greece and the co-planning initiative in Lille, France, stem from local social problems, whereas others, such as the Housing First initiative, are inspired by a global policy concept and applied in a local context. The co-housing initiative in Helsinki represents a local solution to the quest for finding alternative housing options for older people based on a co-housing model adopted from a neighbouring country. All of these initiatives have stood the test of time and have not died out, but their level and form of institutionalisation vary.

Housing First in Sweden and co-housing in Finland have involved a close collaboration among local citizens, communities and institutional actors, and they seem to have the potential to be applied beyond a local context and to be further developed in collaboration with different actors. The likely reason for their sustainability is the co-operation among different actors and the fact that, to some extent, they complement formal welfare services without seriously questioning the existing order. In contrast, the co-planning urban project in Lille, France and the Solidarity Clinic in Greece seek to question the dominant sociopolitical order and to develop local solutions that challenge its legitimacy. They too have endured, but to date none of these initiatives has managed to truly alter governance arrangements or national welfare policies. However, they have managed to introduce the ideas of the participation of citizens and the co-production of services at the local level and to offer solutions to local problems. In this regard, they have managed to create new local combinations among public actors, third sector organisations and community networks (Evers and Ewert, 2015) in organising welfare services and developing new solutions to local social problems. The Solidarity Clinic, in particular, stands out for its commitment to work outside established formal structures.

To some extent, all four initiatives addressed in this chapter share the goal of spreading social innovation beyond the local level and establishing new practices that could engender more permanent social change. However, a closer examination gives reason to argue that the promise of local initiatives to develop into social innovations that challenge and reorganise the existing power relations among institutional actors, local communities and citizens (Moulaert et al., 2005) is, to date, unfulfilled. Whether they will do so in the future or whether they will further strengthen the complementary role of local initiatives as part of mainstream welfare solutions remains to be seen.

# REFERENCES

Adam, S. and C. Papatheodorou (2014), 'Social medical centers of solidarity in turbulent times', unpublished paper presented at the COST Action IS1102 Workshop, University of Tampere, Tampere, 2–6 June.

Andreotti, A., E. Mingione and E. Polizzi (2012), 'Local welfare systems: a challenge for social cohesion', *Urban Studies*, **49** (9), 1925–40.

BEPA – Bureau of European Policy Advisers (2010), 'Empowering people, driving change: social innovation in the European Union', accessed 28 June 2016 at http://ec.europa.eu/DocsRoom/documents/13402/attachments/1/translations/en/renditions/native.

Bergmark, A., Å. Bergmark and T. Lundström (2011), *Evidensbaserat Socialt Arbete: Teori, Kritik, Praktik*, Stockholm: Natur och Kultur.

Brandsen, T., A. Evers, S. Cattacin and A. Zimmer (2016), 'Social innovation: a systematic and critical interpretation', in T. Brandsen, A. Evers, S. Cattacin and A. Zimmer (eds), *Social Innovations in the Urban Context*, London: Springer Open, pp. 3–21.

Castells, M. (1983), *The City and the Grassroots. A Cross-cultural Theory of Urban Social Movements*, Berkeley: University of California Press.

Chambon, J.-L., A. David and J.-M. Devevey (eds) (1982), *Les Innovations Sociales*, Paris: Presses Universitaires de France.

Dahlström, M. and S. Minkkinen (2009), *Loppukiri. Vaihtoehtoista Asumista Seniori-iässä*, Helsinki: WSOY.

European Commission (2013), *Guide to Social Innovation*, accessed 28 June 2016 at http://s3platform.jrc.ec.europa.eu/documents/20182/84453/Guide_to_Social_Innovation.pdf.

Evers, A. (2015), 'Analyser en contexte la dimension normative de l'innovation sociale', interview conducted by Laurent Fraisse, *Sociologies Pratiques*, **31** (2), 15–21.

Evers, A. and B. Ewert (2015), 'Social innovation for social cohesion', in A. Nicholls, J. Simon and M. Gabriel (eds), *New Frontiers in Social Innovation Research*, New York: Palgrave Macmillan, pp. 107–28.

Fraisse, L. (2013), 'The social and solidarity-based economy as a new field of public action: a policy and method for promoting social innovation', in F. Moulaert, D. MacCallum, A. Mehmood and A. Hamdouch (eds), *The International Handbook on Social Innovation. Collective Action, Social Learning and Transdisciplinary Research*, Cheltenham, UK and Northampton, MA, USA: Edward Elgar Publishing, pp. 361–71.

Fraisse, L. (2016), 'Lille Metropolis: co-production of housing in a major urban renewal district', in T. Brandsen, S. Cattacin, A. Evers and A. Zimmer (eds), *Social Innovations in the Urban Context*, London: Springer Open, pp. 205–13.

Gallouj, F. and F. Djellah (2010), *The Handbook of Innovation and Services. A*

*Multi-disciplinary Perspective*, Cheltenham, UK and Northampton, MA, USA: Edward Elgar Publishing.

Gerometta, J., H. Häussermann and G. Longo (2005), 'Social innovation and civil society in urban governance: strategies for an inclusive city', *Urban Studies*, **42** (11), 2007–21.

Grimm, R., C. Fox, S. Baines and K. Albertson (2013), 'Social innovation, an answer to contemporary societal challenges? Locating the concept in theory and practice', *Innovation: The European Journal of Social Science Research*, **26** (4), 436–55.

Häikiö, L. (2007), 'Expertise, representation and the common good: grounds for legitimacy in the urban governance network', *Urban Studies*, **44** (11), 2147–62.

Häikiö, L. (2010), 'The diversity of citizenship and democracy in local public management reform', *Public Management Review*, **12** (3), 363–84.

Ifanti, A., A. Argyriou, F. Kalofonou and H. Kalofonos (2013), 'Financial crisis and austerity measures in Greece: their impact on health promotion policies and public health care', *Health Policy*, **113** (1–2), 8–12.

Jessop, B., F. Moulaert, L. Hulgård and A. Hamdouch (2013), 'Social innovation research: a new stage in innovation analysis?', in F. Moulaert, D. MacCallum, A. Mehmood and A. Hamdouch (eds), *The International Handbook on Social Innovation. Collective Action, Social Learning and Transdisciplinary Research*, Cheltenham, UK and Northampton, MA, USA: Edward Elgar Publishing, pp. 110–30.

Jolanki, O. (2014), 'Senior cohousing community as a way to organize help and support for older people', unpublished paper presented at the COST Action IS1102 Workshop, University of Tampere, Tampere, 2–6 June.

Jolanki, O. and A. Vilkko (2015), 'The meaning of a "sense of community" in a Finnish senior cohousing community', *Journal of Housing for the Elderly. Special Issue: Nordic Housing Research*, **29** (1–2), 111–25.

Kentikelenis, A., M. Karanikolos, A. Reeves, M. McKee and D. Stuckler (2014), 'Greece's health crisis: from austerity to denialism', *The Lancet*, **383** (9918), 748–53.

Klein, J.-L., J.-L. Laville and F. Moulaert (2014), *L'innovation Sociale*, Toulouse: Erès.

Knutagård, M. (2014), 'The moral geography of homelessness', unpublished paper presented at the COST Action IS1102 Workshop, University of Tampere, Tampere, 2–6 June.

Knutagård, M. (2015), 'Bostad först som strategi eller strategisk strimma', *Alkohol and Narkotika*, no. 4, 12–15.

Knutagård, M. and A. Kristiansen (2013), 'Not by the book: the emergence and translation of Housing First in Sweden', *European Journal of Homelessness*, **7** (1), 93–115.

León, M., E. Pavolini and A.M. Guillén (2015), 'Welfare rescaling in Italy and Spain: political strategies to deal with harsh austerity', *European Journal of Social Security*, **17** (2), 182–201.

Lévesque, B. (2007), 'L'innovation dans le développement économique et le développement social', in J.-L. Klein and D. Harrisson (eds), *L'innovation Sociale. Emergence et Effets sur la Transformation de la Société*, Quebec: Presses de l'Université du Québec, pp. 43–68.

Manzini, E. (2014), 'Making things happen. Social innovation and design', *Design Issues*, **30** (1), 57–66.

Martinelli, F. (2010), 'Historical roots of social change: philosophies and movements', in F. Moulaert, E. Swyngedouw, F. Martinelli and S. Gonzalez (eds), *Can Neighbourhoods Save the City? Community Development and Social Innovation*, London: Routledge, pp. 17–48.

Montgomery, T. (2016), 'Are social innovation paradigms incommensurable?', *Voluntas: International Journal of Voluntary and Nonprofit Organizations*, **27** (4), 1979–2000.

Moulaert, F., D. MacCallum, A. Mehmood and A. Hamdouch (eds) (2013), *The International Handbook on Social Innovation: Collective Action, Social Learning and Transdisciplinary Research*, Cheltenham, UK and Northampton, MA, USA: Edward Elgar Publishing.

Moulaert, F., F. Martinelli, S. González and E. Swyngedouw (2007), 'Introduction: social innovation and governance in European cities. Urban development between path dependency and radical innovation', *European Urban and Regional Studies*, **14** (3), 195–209.

Moulaert, F., F. Martinelli, E. Swyngedouw and S. González (2005), 'Towards alternative model(s) of local innovation', *Urban Studies*, **42** (11), 1969–90.

Moulaert F., E. Swyngedouw, F. Martinelli and S. Gonzalez (eds) (2010), *Can Neighbourhoods Save the City? Community Development and Social Innovation*, London: Routledge.

Mulgan, G. (2012), 'Social innovation theories: can theory catch up with practices?', in F. Hans-Werner, J. Hochgerner and J. Howaldt (eds), *Challenge Social Innovation. Potentials for Business, Entrepreneurship, Welfare and Civil Society*, Berlin and Heidelberg: Springer, pp. 19–43.

Nicholls, A., J. Simon and M. Gabriel (eds) (2015), *New Frontiers in Social Innovation Research*, New York: Palgrave Macmillan.

Rønning, R. and M. Knutagård (2015), *Innovation in Social Welfare and Human Services*, Abingdon, UK and New York, USA: Routledge.

Sanders, E.B.N. and P.J. Stappers (2008), 'Co-creation and the new landscapes of design', *CoDesign*, **4** (1), 5–18.

Swyngedouw, E. (2005), 'Governance, innovation and the citizen: the Janus face of governance-beyond-the-state', *Urban Studies*, **42** (11), 1991–2006.

Touraine, A. (1981), *The Voice and the Eye: An Analysis of Social Movements*, Cambridge: Cambridge University Press.

Tsemberis, S. (2010), *Housing First: the Pathways Model to End Homelessness for People with Mental Illness and Addiction*, Center City: Hazelden.

Vicari Haddock, S. and C. Tornaghi (2013), 'A transversal reading of social innovation in European cities', in F. Moulaert, D. MacCallum, A. Mehmood and A. Hamdouch (eds), *The International Handbook on Social Innovation. Collective Action, Social Learning and Transdisciplinary Research*, Cheltenham, UK and Northampton, MA, USA: Edward Elgar Publishing, pp. 264–73.

# 14. Social innovation in the field of Roma inclusion in Hungary and Austria: lessons to foster social cohesion from *Thara* and *Tanodas*

**Carla Weinzierl, Andreas Novy, Anikó Bernát, Florian Wukovitsch and Zsuzsanna Vercseg**

## INTRODUCTION

Be it the increase in poverty and unemployment, 'Brexit', or the current refugee tragedy – there is clear evidence that social and territorial cohesion is at stake in Europe. Historically, struggles for social cohesion were intended to repair the damages done by capitalist modernisation, such as the dissolution of traditional communities or widening class cleavages. Since the 1990s, social cohesion became a key European policy concern. While in line with the Lisbon Agenda the term has been de-politicised and framed as functional to competitiveness (Maloutas et al., 2008, p. 260), social cohesion has to be understood as the contradictory and contested quasi concept with different definitions in different policy fields (Jenson, 1998). From a socioeconomic perspective, it deals with the exclusionary dynamics of social inequality and poverty. While equality was never achieved in centralised welfare regimes, there has been a uniformisation in the access to social services and infrastructure which was often not very attentive to diversity. From a political perspective, social cohesion includes participation, representation and mobilisation, questioning an understanding of citizenship based on nationality. From a culturalist perspective, some stress the right to difference as well as recognition, dignity and belonging, while others focus on essentialist identity-building based on 'outsiders' and 'insiders'.

Due to this complexity, we define social cohesion as a *problématique* of enabling people to live together and yet to have the opportunity to be different (Novy et al., 2012, p. 1874). It is a complex, multilayered challenge that can only be tackled in a transdisciplinary, multiscalar and multidimensional way. Therefore, in line with Patsy Healey, the policy challenge consists in finding context-sensitive ways of 'living together differently' (Novy et al., 2012, p. 1874), that means an ongoing negotiation between the right to be equal and to belong and the right to be different. It is characterised by the tensions between claims for the recognition and respect for cultural, gender, age and other forms of diversity, on the one hand, and the more traditional socioeconomic claims for universal social protection and civic and social rights on the other hand. The adoption of the EU's motto 'United in Diversity' in 2000 synthesises this *problématique*. But the heated discussions on refugees show that intercultural conviviality remains an unresolved challenge in fostering social cohesion, which is currently increasingly solved in a reductionist way: defending identities at the expense of appreciating diversity.

Sociocultural and ethnic discrimination has long been perceived as a key weakness of European welfare models. Assimilationist tendencies of European welfare states, which discriminate against ethnic minorities, are especially strong in the conservative Central European countries. Even if Hungary has been considered a 'transition' economy, a persistent path-dependency can be detected in its welfare model due to its historical roots in the nineteenth-century authoritarian-paternalistic Austro-Hungarian empire (Aspalter et al., 2009). Although the separation in the twentieth century has led to different pathways, there remain several structural similarities, as Hungary – despite its communist legacy – shows governance structures that can also be classified as conservative-corporatist, rather than under the broad category of Eastern or 'transitional' welfare state models. In the conservative welfare model, the *problématique* of social cohesion is facing structural 'insider–outsider' dynamics: the middle and lower classes remain protected (as long as they remain employed), but the specific social needs of newcomers (e.g. immigrants, refugees) or 'outsiders' (e.g. homeless people, Roma) are hardly dealt with. In light of these 'insider–outsider' dynamics, which entails that 'outsiders' are more affected by austerity policies than insiders, new creative solutions and broad alliances are required to contribute to Roma inclusion and to foster social cohesion. The European Commission, for example, has undertaken efforts to foster social inclusion of Roma, the largest European ethnic minority, via financial incentives and agenda setting.

This chapter explores the potential and limits of modifying and broadening the conservative-corporatist governance model in what concerns increasing social cohesion. More specifically, it presents an analysis of the socially innovative potential of two projects in the domain of Roma inclusion, focusing on their governance structures and approach to social cohesion: *Thara* in Austria and *Tanoda(s)* in Hungary. We investigate to what extent these two initiatives are laboratories of social innovation to tackle the *problématique* of social cohesion. In the context of austerity, welfare state retrenchment and the re-organisation of social services in particular, social innovation has become a key issue of European policy discourse. As social cohesion, it is a contested term, which has increasingly been instrumentalised in a neo-liberal agenda as a policy to compensate for welfare state retrenchment – fostering markets and entrepreneurship (Jenson, 2015). However, this undermines the innovative potential of social innovations as transforming social relations and empowering disadvantaged social groups (Oosterlynck et al., forthcoming). Therefore, we conceptualise social innovation as defined by Moulaert et al. (2005; 2010) and further developed in the ImPRovE research framework[1] (Oosterlynck et al., 2013a; 2013b): successful social innovation has to fight social exclusion and contribute to empowerment by addressing both the material and the process dimension of social cohesion. First, social innovation contributes to addressing social needs hitherto neglected by the welfare state (material dimension); secondly, it contributes to a change of social relations among local actors and among these and institutions, as well as to empowering excluded groups (process dimension).

Our case study analysis (Wukovitsch et al., 2015; Bernát and Vercseg, 2015) is rooted in a critical realist philosophy and is transdisciplinary, i.e. attempts to foster a dialogue with practitioners to improve respective agency (e.g. Cassinari et al., 2011; Novy et al., 2013). In both initiatives, interviews were conducted with stakeholders, including staff members of the implementing organisations, policy-makers or representatives of the respective administrative institutions and funding bodies. Preliminary results were discussed in focus groups and further feedback was used to refine the arguments. The focus of this multi-method approach was on mapping the policy field in terms of relevant actors and their governance relations, identifying innovative aspects and governance challenges such as striking the balance between diversity and equality (ImPRovE Social Innovation Team, 2013).

In the remainder of this chapter, first we briefly present the historical and institutional context of Roma exclusion in Austria and Hungary. Subsequently we describe the two initiatives and elaborate on their socially innovative potential with a focus on their contributions to Roma empowerment and the creation of social cohesion. In the last section we reflect on the strengths and limitations of these innovative initiatives in the context of their respective welfare regimes.

# 1.  ROMA EXCLUSION IN AUSTRIA AND HUNGARY

Roma are the largest ethnic minority in Europe. While they are a small and heterogeneous group in Austria (approximately 0.3 per cent of the total population), they are an important minority in Hungary (more than 7 per cent of total population) (Bernát and Mosuela, 2014).

In the case of Austria, Roma settled in the country centuries ago. These autochthonous Roma – amounting to roughly 10000 people – suffered terribly from the genocide during the Nazi regime (Baumgartner and Freund, 2007a; 2007b), as less than 10 per cent survived. They were given official status as an ethnic minority group in 1993 (Fink, 2011, pp. 4–5). The group of allochthonous Roma – amounting to about 45000 to 60000 people – consists of immigrants from the 1960s and 1970s, their descendants, as well as more recent flows who migrated due to push factors in their home countries. Many of them do not come from within the EU (i.e. from Serbia, Kosovo, Bosnia and Macedonia) and lack any official status. Some are asylum seekers. They are hardly seen as Roma in public as well as in political debates, since much public attention is given to 'poverty' migration, i.e. short-term commuters from South-Eastern European countries, who come to Austria and beg in the streets. They suffer severe prejudices, discriminatory treatment by the police and negative press reports. Apart from constitutionally codified minority policies, more systematic Roma policies have only been implemented due to incentives from the policy frameworks of the EU. A common feature of autochthonous Roma is low educational attainment (irrespective of gradual improvements made during the last two decades), resulting in above-average labour market problems for young people of Roma origin (Fink, 2011, pp. 4–5). Although the Public Employment Service (*Arbeitsmarktservice*) offers qualification measures, supports employment and provides financial support, language barriers exclude part of the minorities from welfare services, despite the relatively high rate of unemployment in this population group (13 per cent) when compared with the Austrian average (about 5 per cent) (ETC Graz, 2012; Riesenfelder et al., 2011).

In the case of Hungary, the aforementioned 'insider–outsider' dynamics regarding Roma becomes apparent when looking at the school system, as there is a tendency to marginalise children from less educated and poor families (Kertesi and Kézdi, 2012). According to a 2014 survey on school segregation, 'the distribution of Roma and non-Roma students across schools has become considerably more unequal in Hungary since the 1980's' (Kertesi and Kézdi, 2013, p. 5). The study from Corvinus University and the Hungarian Academy of Science identifies as the decisive factor for segregation that most municipal educational bodies fail to maintain the representation of Roma students in mostly non-Roma schools (whether municipal or non-municipal schools). Distributing students according to residence would result in a more mixed composition of classrooms. However, students' 'free school choice and [low commuting costs] diminish the role of residential distribution because many students commute to schools of their choice' (Kertesi and Kézdi, 2013, p.40). Quite a few municipalities let their higher status ('elite') schools practise admission policies that tend to further segregate, and many allow segregated Roma schools to exist. All this undermines equal chances to quality education. Moreover, complementary support services are not widespread and disadvantages are not dealt with systematically. Another survey in 2014 showed that one of the main reasons behind poor school results was the lack of stimuli at home (Kertesi and Kézdi, 2014, p.3). The survey was based on the comparison between Roma and non-Roma children of similar social circumstances of income, wealth and parental education in the same class, and pointed out that ethnicity was of minor importance in children's performance, whereas the home environment and financial status of parents made the real difference. The two surveys highlight the fact that unequal opportunities of Roma and/or poor children derive from the inaccessibility of quality education through segregation and poorer social environment affecting their cognitive skills.

In conclusion, Roma communities suffer discrimination and social exclusion in both countries. EU member states have since 2011 been obliged to prepare national Roma inclusion strategies within the broader framework of national social inclusion policies (Austrian Federal Chancellery, 2011, p.5). In Austria, the Roma strategy has received a prominent place in the National Action Plan against discrimination. The Federal Chancellery has committed itself to involving an advisory council as well as civil society organisations in its implementation (Austrian Federal Chancellery, 2011, p.22). Furthermore, it has become the national contact point for the 'Austrian Roma Strategy' (Bundeskanzleramt, 2013). In Hungary, in contrast, the focus is not on Roma, but on vulnerable social groups in general. The strategy seeks to reduce poverty and social exclusion, with special regard to the Roma population. The document entitled 'National social inclusion strategy (extreme poverty, child poverty, the Roma) 2011–2020' provides a framework for implementing the social inclusion objectives defined in the government programme. In line with the Europe 2020 agenda, it aims to tackle the barriers to Roma inclusion in a broader way, rather than only as a poverty policy.

## 2.  THE *THARA* AND *TANODA* INITIATIVES' APPROACH TO SOCIAL COHESION

In this section, first, the two case studies are described. Then, the innovative potential of both initiatives is explored in terms of their contribution to (1) addressing social needs; (2) transforming social relationships; (3) empowerment; and (4) their contribution to social cohesion. Although both initiatives address the Roma minority, *Thara* is a single initiative located in Vienna, which coordinates several projects and associations to improve Roma access to the labour market, whereas the Hungarian 'study halls' (*Tanodas*) are spread all over the country – but particularly in cities – and address the improvement of school performance of Roma pupils.

### The *Thara* Initiative in Vienna

*Thara* means 'tomorrow' or 'future' in Romanes. The chief aim of this initiative is improving Romas' access to the labour market and relevant national institutions. Although organised as a project and financed on an annual basis, *Thara* has become institutionalised as a cornerstone in the Austrian national Roma policy. It tries to compensate for a long history of discrimination and stigmatisation by means of occupational advice for the Roma as well as sensitisation workshops and information events for members of mainstream society.

*Thara* started in the form of a number of labour market projects funded by the EU community initiative EQUAL from 2005 to 2007, and has received annual project support from the Federal Ministry of Labour and Social Affairs ever since. From the very beginning, issues of labour market integration and ethnic identity were addressed in tandem. This has allowed Roma poverty to be dealt with as a multidimensional issue – focusing on low income, poor housing, low educational attainment – while also acknowledging it as the outcome of secular discrimination due to legacies of past deprivation. The first education and activation programme, for instance, consisted of a broad variety of elements, reaching from personal tutoring on career opportunities, computer and media workshops, social counselling, career and business start-up counselling and business behaviour training, complemented by workshops on theatre, music, dance and Roma history as well as language courses in Romanes. Later projects also included internships, with financial contributions from the Public Employment Service. Currently, four women are employed in *Thara*, two belonging to the Roma community. One of them is working as project leader, one as project coordinator and two as educational and occupational consultants.

The first project was based on a close collaboration between *Romanodrom*, a strong community player, and *Volkshilfe*, a large non-profit organisation that is non-partisan. This co-operation was difficult because there were about 20 to 25 associations with different targets. The lack of a clear umbrella organisation in such a fragmented and hetero-geneous field increased tensions within the community. In the evaluation of the EQUAL project, a key conclusion was that the dependence on one strong community player – *Romanodrom* – resulted in one player holding the interpretational authority over all Roma affairs. This led to the decision to have one neutral player – *Volkshilfe* – doing the organisation in order to facilitate networking with all interested parties (Gneisz, 2010). Therefore, *Volkshilfe* has had sole responsibility from the second, nationally funded *Thara* project onwards. It turned out that the embedding of *Thara* in a large organisation has been a big advantage in the corporatist setting of the Austrian welfare state. *Volkshilfe* is well established and recognised for its capacity to manage complex projects. However, the specific way in which *Volkshilfe* manages *Thara* is in part due to the personal commitment of the organisation's managing director. In contrast to most other services of *Volkshilfe*, *Thara* is managed by the umbrella organisation at the federal level and not by the provincial departments. Community members have continued to be involved in decision-making and to be part of the project team. *Volkshilfe* facilitates networking with other stakeholders, one of them being Romano Centro, one of the biggest NGOs for Roma empow-erment in Austria. However, the decision was also criticised, as non-Roma ('Gadje') would benefit from funding that was in principle reserved for members of the Roma community (Gneisz, 2010).

In the coming years, the governance of labour market projects is expected to change, as the European level has become important again in the new European social fund (ESF) programme period. With a funding opportunity of ten times the original budget, more Roma associations – also in other parts of Austria – might get involved in *Thara*, in order to make the project more participatory. They have already been invited to present their ideas for improving the position of Roma in the labour market. But since there will not be a classical call for proposals, small asso-ciations will depend on the participation of a big player such as *Volkshilfe* to get involved in an EU project, as barriers of liquidity and administrative capacity remain.

**Addressing Social Needs**

Innovative practices introduced by *Thara* are new in the Austrian context, as they refer to different types of affirmative action for marginal socioethnic populations. These activities emerged as a consequence of a mix of circumstances: new opportunities offered by EU policies on anti-discrimination, proactive action by key persons working in the labour market section of the national government, competent civil society organisations and the increasing pressures exerted by Roma associations.

Formally, the main social need that *Thara* addresses is labour market access for Roma. Right from the beginning, there was broad agreement that employability is not a single issue, but a problem rooted in multiple forms of discrimination and uneven access to mainstream institutions in general. Roma suffer from discrimination in job selection, but also from lower levels of education and formal skills. Improved access to the labour market often requires prerequisites with respect to education, health, self-esteem or networks. To identify relevant needs, the participation of individuals and organisations from the target group was encouraged.

**Transforming Social Relationships (Building Trust)**

Community work has been crucial in the project's day-to-day business. Networking and close contacts with the community enabled activists to recognise diverse needs and to formulate strategies to deal with them. Awareness in mainstream circles has also been raised as a consequence of the general shift brought about by EU initiatives and their implementation in the form of national strategies. This changing public attitude has contributed to more openness and greater consciousness about the problems of Roma.

There were many conflicts between Roma and non-Roma in the first *Thara* project. Among others, there was criticism that Austrians would receive money that should be reserved for the needs of Roma. As one stakeholder explained, this perception was in part due to the top-down approach of the project and the fact that money was allegedly not spent in the most efficient way. This clearly illustrates the lack of understanding of the functioning of institutions and international funding schemes on the part of Roma associations; it also reflects the unequal power relations that exist in these types of projects. Small grassroots initiatives are disadvantaged and target groups are often beneficiaries without being involved in decision-making. Just one indication of the technocratic approach of the first project is the fact that the proposal was written by a civil servant with a clear commitment to anti-discrimination policies but little experience in Roma affairs. The original proposal had the merit to problematise the situation of Roma and argue for public action. But there was still little understanding of Roma issues and how to build an open and representative, but working consortium.

Many stakeholders justify targeted measures for Roma with reference to the long history of stigmatisation and discrimination and the requirement to build up trust between the institutions of the mainstream society and the Roma. But Roma are often very sceptical of public institutions and hesitate to ask for services or to apply for financial support. Therefore, despite anti-discrimination legislation, discrimination is still an issue in job applications and everyday life. Changing social relationships is a secular challenge requiring a proactive approach to build trust among Roma and non-Roma communities and public institutions. In the case of *Thara*, this was achieved by intercultural mediation, active involvement of community members and easier access to public institutions. Thus, several aspects of the *Thara* experience are innovative: not only the mediation between Roma and the institutions of the labour market as well as potential employers, but also the mediation among different groups and associations within the Roma community and their increased networking.

Indeed, there has been some success in raising awareness and changing behaviour of key stakeholders. Although Austrian welfare state actors usually defend mainstream approaches to welfare policies, *Thara* shows that they also recognise the value of having targeted measures as well. A clear indication of this is the fact that the Public Employment Service sends job seekers from the Roma community to *Thara* when they ask for support, since they have accumulated expertise. A long-term, more structural change of attitudes would, however, require the implementation of larger programmes instead of small projects funded on a year-to-year basis.

**Empowerment**

Empowerment and participation were key issues in the first EQUAL project. Individual empowerment happened rather informally. A number of Roma women who work(ed) for *Thara* have even become leading actors in the community and started a career in delivering social services or raising awareness in the media. Individual empowerment in this case has contributed to creating a cognitive framework to handle the *problématique* of diversity and belonging. It has strengthened the pride in belonging to a special ethnic group as well as being a full member of the Austrian society. At the same time, it has not excluded personal choices to keep one's ethnic identity in private. To strike the balance between these diverging aspirations and life choices, the project actively integrated Roma associations and individual persons from the community.

In Austria, ethnic community funding is only provided for a small part of ethnic minorities, with rather limited resources (which, in addition, have not been augmented in nominal terms for years). Projects such as *Thara*, that receive a relevant amount of publicity, can provide an essential contribution to framing discourses and fostering networking. The open governance model that was established in *Thara* has fostered in itself the collective empowerment of an ethnic community hitherto weakly organised, with hardly any relationship with the public administration.

**Contributions to Social Cohesion**

It is assumed that social cohesion in Austria is obtained by providing universal services of high quality to all ethnic and social groups. Policy areas such as education, housing and health are allegedly open to the broad majority of the population, the key argument being that a well-functioning welfare state protects all citizens against social risks, thus making social targeting unnecessary. This is the justification of public bodies for being reluctant in implementing affirmative action for disadvantaged groups. There is a lack of experience as well as low intercultural diversity in existing personnel to target measures according to specific needs and contexts. The multidimensional approach used in *Thara* aims at tackling this weakness in administrative skills and public awareness. Proponents of *Thara* argue for proper support structures by Roma and non-Roma professionals to access public institutions, of which Roma are often frightened and thus try to avoid contacting as much as possible due to secular historic discrimination.

**The *Tanoda* Initiatives in Hungary**

In Hungary, a *Tanoda*, meaning 'after-school' or 'study hall',[2] is a community space with its own independent infrastructure, typically operated by a non-governmental organisation, providing after-school services. But in the recent past, study halls operated by state schools have also been entitled to provide such services after compulsory classes. Study halls offer extra-curricular education tailored to each student to improve their skills and school performance. *Tanodas* mainly operate in disadvantaged areas and small settlements, as their target group consists predominantly of students aged 6 to 18 coming from low educated and poor families – many of them Roma.

The *Tanoda* movement in Hungary consists of bottom-up initiatives that involve a wide range of civil society actors and Roma organisations, in order to satisfy the basic needs of socially excluded children. The first *Tanoda* started in the early 1990s in Józsefváros, one of the poorest districts of Budapest with a significant Roma population. It was funded by two foundations and later with EU resources. This pioneering study hall had to downsize its activities and eventually close down a couple of years ago, due to lack of funding.

In 2015 there were 189 *Tanodas* in Hungary, as they have become part of the national educational policy, and EU funds have also been allocated to expand the study hall system. They are very diverse in their aims, methods and current situations. Their origin, their institutionalisation, as well as their mainstreaming rely heavily on EU funding. A number of study halls collaborate under the informal umbrella organisation, *Tanodaplatform*, organised by educational experts and civil actors who all work in study halls and have several years of pedagogical and project management experience.

Study halls typically offer a set of services dealing with personal development in a holistic way. According to experts, poor school results have primarily been the outcome of poorly developed skills due to families' low socioeconomic status. Therefore, the study halls have intended to promote and develop basic competences holistically. However, these ambitious objectives often suffer from inadequate funding. In reality, activities are often concentrated on 'catching up' tutoring, i.e. on filling the gaps in basic school requirements. Study halls are envisioned to be innovative and autonomous professional workshops, independent of the public educational system. Ideally, the work is carried out by a 'self-help' local peer group, supported by teachers, social workers, parents and the local school, all working together democratically. The initiatives concentrate on disadvantaged and multiply disadvantaged pupils and students and on children of Roma origin, whose needs are inadequately met in the public education system.

The majority of the study halls we focused on do not work with full-time employees. In most cases, employees are on temporary contracts or work on a voluntary basis, which highlights that the most pressing problem is the lack of professional teachers due to funding deficiencies. Pedagogical approaches are diverse across study halls. In terms of the organisation of learning, pupils in general work in small groups, which makes it possible for them to get actively involved. But besides group work, individual tutoring is also widely used, and in some places this method is the most important teaching tool. There are even some tutors who practise traditional teaching methods, i.e. lecturing *ex cathedra*, although there is a systematic effort to use innovative pedagogical methods. In many study halls there is even an explicit mobilisation against traditional pedagogical practice. A group of study hall leaders have recognised that poor school results of children often derive from the incomplete acquisition of basic competences and so they strive to offer services that complement school education. Thus, in these study halls an improvement of basic skills has become the most important pedagogical target – to provide long-lasting results and promote social cohesion.

## Addressing Social Needs

Study halls pursue three main goals in order to enhance social integration of vulnerable children via extracurricular education with a proper pedagogical approach: (1) providing catch-up activities and preparation for the secondary school graduation exam through a wide range of activities and pedagogical initiatives that conform to the needs of the broad target group; (2) to support the most disadvantaged students and pupils with the worst school results; and (3) to develop the talents of disadvantaged pupils in order to support their further training. All three goals address both general and individual-level social needs directly or indirectly, either in the short or the long term, thereby breaking the poverty cycle of vulnerable families.

Besides these immediate goals the after-school programmes also create an environment in which values of solidarity can thrive, along with a focus on the principles of democracy, equality and impartiality. In this respect, each initiative operates as a self-governing, informal institution serving social purposes: above all, they seek to ease educational disparities and the inadequacy of schools to provide opportunities for social mobility. Last but not least, study halls reduce the cost of social exclusion for the government.

## Transforming Social Relationships (Building Trust)

Study halls challenge the commodification of life chances and provide a complementary service to the official school system. By enabling children to access quality educational services, study halls contribute to the empowerment and sociopolitical mobilisation of socially excluded groups. Moreover, the principles of solidarity and equality practised in *Tanodas* can re-build and strengthen communities and enhance the process of integration of the entire community, both indirectly by spreading these values and directly by involving parents and families in some of the activities and programmes. Although small settlements are not always cohesive local communities, fragmentation can be tackled with community-focused initiatives such as the extracurricular programmes of study halls that cross the borders of generations, ethnicities and social groups.

At the institutional level, many study halls have established links with other educational bodies and have featured in the ESF-funded social renewal operational programmes since 2004. EU funds are directly allocated to extend the *Tanoda* system, thereby building up a system of compensation for the lack of institutions in the mainstream school system that deals with the latter's deficiencies. While EU funds have made the *Tanoda* system possible, there are clear indications of passive subsidiarity due to a lack of funding by the Hungarian welfare state, as the aims and intended services of *Tanodas* do not totally correlate with the public school system.

## Empowerment

The main pedagogical aim of study halls is to develop the basic compe-tences of children, assuming that poor school results are primarily due to the lack of numeracy, literacy and cognitive skills. Accordingly, innova-tive pedagogical tools have been developed, such as non-formal teaching methods, alternative evaluation techniques, the rewarding of pedagogical endeavour, and the provision of greater autonomy for children in how they want to learn.

Apart from an emphasis on individual development, study halls aim to improve communities and strive to establish heterogeneous spaces, so that study hall users can step out of its physical location and social boundaries. Also, study halls contribute to the empowerment of impoverished families by providing children with quality tutoring and extracurricular educa-tional programmes.

Overall, however, empowerment is generally accomplished at the level of individual capacity development, whereas the projects' contribution to empowerment as collective emancipation is more limited.

## Contributions to Social Cohesion

Unequal opportunities for Roma people in Hungary derive from the lack of access to quality education due to segregation and exclusion, which hampers the development of their cognitive skills. *Tanodas'* social services, therefore, complement the mainstream educational system with an inde-pendent set of activities and idiosyncratic measuring and evaluation with long-term objectives. According to the interviewees, study halls recognise that the improvement of basic and broad competences is the most impor-tant goal that can provide long-lasting results and contribute to social cohesion. But remaining at the margin of the public education system, this long-term goal of empowerment has often been replaced with short-term concerns of direct tutoring in order to keep children's results at a level suf-ficient to pass the grades.

There is a deliberate effort at affirmative action to empower marginalised groups. These efforts are undertaken in a context-sensitive way, respecting local specificities and the diverse needs of different age, migratory background and socioeconomic deprivation categories. However, study halls are sometimes seen as segregated institutions where different social dynamics embroil low-performing and Roma students and exclude children with higher social status who might be equally in need of the study hall services. These dynamics then create a segregated environment where poor children do not meet either Roma or non-Roma children of other social status. These mechanisms exclude children who might need support but are not allowed in the study hall because of its stereotypical position in the community. As a result, study halls are sometimes seen as a place where 'the poorly performing Roma children go so they are not on the street', where even other Roma children cannot attend because of the low social status of such after-school programmes. If study halls are segregated through such social dynamics, then, it becomes questionable to think of the concept of integration at all in these settings. To sum it up, due to lack of public support, the limited extent of the system and burning short-term requirement does not permit study halls to attain the critical mass for large-scale social cohesion. Furthermore, they tend to deal inadequately with rural areas, where problems of social exclusion tend to be greater.

## 3.   SYNTHESIS AND OUTLOOK

The two socially innovative initiatives presented in this chapter offer rich insights for fostering social cohesion in Europe, as they strike the balance between equality and diversity in a creative way. Neither *Tanodas* nor *Thara* question the existing welfare system. Both aim at improving its functioning by introducing adequate solutions to unanswered social needs of the Roma minorities emerging out of sociocultural discrimination. Thereby they aim at complementing universal service provisioning with affirmative action, but not at substituting existing services with more targeted ones. Yet they take on a role of compensating shortcomings in the traditional welfare regime, a situation the initiatives are not happy about.

   First, we have looked into the socially innovative potential of these two initiatives in terms of empowering socially excluded groups. The *Thara* initiative responds to social needs by improving access to the labour market in a multidimensional way (by fostering education, self-esteem, social networks, etc.). *Tanodas* offer complementary educational services to improve equality in educational opportunities in a public school system that is significantly segregated. Both focus on individual capacity building and support the participants' pride in their ethnicity, while at the same time fostering their perception of being a full member of the broader society. In both initiatives, social relations have been changed, and trust has been built between the Roma and the non-Roma communities and institutions. In these respects, they can both be considered as social innovation laboratories, experimenting with striking a balance between the respect for diversity and the rights and obligations of being part of a civic community.

Second, stakeholders in both *Thara* and *Tanodas* agree on the need for targeted national support measures for Roma, due to their long history of oppression, stigmatisation and discrimination. In Austria, however, there is fear among public authorities and funding institutions that stronger cultural identity as Roma – via the increase in non-German language skills and knowledge of Roma culture – might strengthen a culturally homogeneous 'parallel society'. The same occurs in Hungary, where there is no political support for affirmative actions. Therefore, the study halls initiatives have remained entirely dependent on EU funding and several *Tanodas* have had to close down or curtail their activities due to irregular funding.

Third, *Thara* and *Tanodas* are initiatives dealing with the special needs of a disadvantaged segment of the population, aiming at fostering social cohesion as the capacity to 'live together differently' (Novy et al., 2012, p. 1874). But they focus on awareness raising and individual capacity development to increase employability and to empower the target group individually.

Third, a key insight from *Thara* and *Tanodas* is that achieving social cohesion goes well beyond easing the material deprivation of poor households. Social cohesion is attained when a society is able to tackle the tensions between 'us' and 'them', 'insider' and 'outsider'. Promoting empowerment as collective emancipation in the sense of sociopolitical mobilisation would imply problematising the 'insider–outsider' dichotomy and would allow a focus on the necessary institutional and structural changes in favour of 'insiders' as well as 'outsiders'. 'We Europeans' have witnessed the recent erosion of the huge civilisational progress of welfare institutions after World War II due to neo-liberalisation (Judt, 2010; Streeck, 2013), a process very remote from the problems and possibilities related to intercultural conviviality. Increased social insecurity persists with and without scapegoats. It is a key sociocultural challenge to overcome the perception of the 'outsider' as potentially problematic: how to live together differently in a continent which has always been a melting pot of cultures and peoples? What are the common norms, laws and rules to be obeyed by all; and how to organise a governance system so that all inhabitants 'have the opportunity to be different and yet be able to live together' (Novy et al., 2012, p. 1874)?

Finally, collective empowerment in the sense of sociopolitical mobilisation capable of triggering lasting societal transformations has never been on the agenda. This has limited the scope of the achievements of these two initiatives. In both countries, social services specifically targeted at Roma, by social workers, pedagogues and other professionals, are constantly under threat due to political pressure. Two factors are of prime importance – austerity and increasing xenophobia.

Austerity – strongly supported by the European Commission – has long undermined solidarity in Europe, up to becoming a real threat to European integration. In a context of welfare state retrenchment the complementary potential of *Thara* and *Tanoda* – and especially their innovative aspects in terms of multidimensionality – cannot be fully realised. As long as there is increasing pressure on socially innovative initiatives to compensate in a short-term logic for weaknesses of welfare regimes, there are limited resources available to focus on exploring their full potential for social cohesion.

Institutionalising social cohesion would require affirmative action and a firm political commitment to increasing the capabilities of the Roma population. As the current refugee crisis shows, to tackle this challenge constructively will be of crucial importance for the future of European societies, which have become increasingly intercultural. Unfortunately, it seems as if the current crisis is reinforcing path dependencies, thereby deepening secular deficiencies and reinforcing essentialist concepts of identity, ethnic homogeneity and enforced assimilation. Not even the arguments by economists – especially in Germany and Austria – who insist on the long-term beneficial effects of immigration in general and the current refugees in particular (Aiyar et al., 2016), seem to influence a diversity-adverse attitude. A young immigrant population could be an asset and an opportunity, if the political framework is well structured. But the public debate – dominated by mass media and right-wing discourses – reinforces a 'fortress Europe' perspective, spurring ethnic–cultural cleavages. Avoiding 'parallel societies' at all costs leads to an embrace of assimilationist policies, which have long been discredited in pedagogy as well as policy-making. All this blatantly contradicts the aspiration of 'unity in diversity'. Given a clear political commitment, the multidimensional and long-term support for ethnic minorities could have become a decisive investment in building a Europe 'united in diversity'. The many initiatives of empowering Roma, which have been supported by the European Commission over recent years, had exactly these intentions. The Commission promoted laboratories like the ones we have presented. Although the current political climate is most adverse, these initiatives contain long-term lessons for social cohesion by bridging communities and building trust. But when will they be learned?

## NOTES

1. *Thara* and *Tanodas* are two of 31 case studies conducted in the context of the research project *ImPRovE – Poverty Reduction in Europe: Social Policy and Innovation* (www. improve-research.eu) funded by the Seventh Framework Programme of the European Union. Individual case study reports can be found at: http://improve-research.eu/?page_ id=170. The comparison of the *Thara* and *Tanodas* cases was developed in the context of the COST Action IS1102 *SO.S. COHESION – Social services, welfare states and places*.
2. The terms 'Tanoda', 'study hall' and 'after-school programme' are used interchangeably in the remainder of the chapter.

## REFERENCES

Aiyar, S., B. Barkbu, N. Batini, H. Berger, E. Detragiache, A. Dizioli, C. Ebeke et al. (eds) (2016), *The Refugee Surge in Europe: Economic Challenges*, Washington: IMF.

Aspalter, C., K. Jinsoo and P. Sojeung (2009), 'Analysing the welfare state in Poland, the Czech Republic, Hungary and Slovenia: an ideal-typical perspective', *Social Policy and Administration*, **42** (2), 170–85.

Austrian Federal Chancellery – Legal and Constitutional Service (2011), 'An EU framework for national Roma integration strategies up to 2020. Political and legal measures', presentation of integrated packages of political and legal measures in the context of a broader social inclusion policy in accordance with the Council's conclusions of 19 May 2011 on the EU Framework for National Roma Integration Strategies up to 2020, as endorsed by the European Council of 23–24 June 2011.

Baumgartner, G. and F. Freund (2007a), 'Der Holocaust an den österreichischen Roma und Sinti', in M. Zimmermann (ed.), *Zwischen Erziehung und Vernichtung. Zigeunerpolitik und Zigeunerforschung im Europa des 20. Jahrhunderts*, Stuttgart: Franz Steiner Verlag, pp. 203–25.

Baumgartner, G. and F. Freund (2007b), *Roma Politik in Österreich*, Vienna: Kulturverein Österreichischer Roma.

Bernát, A. and C. Mosuela (2014), 'Overview of the situation of Roma in the EU', ImPRovE Milestone 15, accessed 5 October 2016 at http://improve-research. eu/.

Bernát, A. and Z. Vercseg (2015), 'Study halls (Tanoda) for Roma and vulnerable children in Hungary', ImPRovE case study, accessed 5 October 2016 at http://im prove-research.eu/.

Bundeskanzleramt – Verfassungsdienst (2013), 'EU-Rahmen für nationale Strategien zur Integration der Roma bis 2020', Vienna: Fortschrittsbericht zur Umsetzung der Österreichischen Roma Strategie.

Cassinari, D., J. Hillier, K. Miciukiewicz, A. Novy, S. Habersack, D. MacCallum and F. Moulaert (2011), 'Transdisciplinary research in Social Polis', Social Polis Discussion paper, accessed 5 October 2016 at http://www.socialpolis.eu/uploads/ tx_sp/Trans_final_web_double_page.pdf.

ETC Graz – European Training and Research Centre for Human Rights and Democracy Gratz (2012), 'Austria – FRANET national focal point. Social thematic study. The situation of Roma 2012', accessed 5 October 2016 at http://

www.etc-graz.at/typo3/fileadmin/user_upload/ETC-Hauptseite/publikationen/ Occasional_papers/situation-of-roma-2012-at.pdf.

Fink, M. (2011), 'Austria – promoting social inclusion of Roma. A study of national policies', Report on behalf of the European Commission, Brussels: DG Employment, Social Affairs and Inclusion.

Gneisz, E. (2010), 'Arbeitsmarktpolitische Projekte für Romnja und Roma in Österreich. Eine sozialanthropologische Untersuchung der Projekte "Thara. Amarotrajo" und "Mri Buti"', Diploma-Thesis, University of Vienna, accessed 5 October 2016 at http://othes.univie.ac.at/11133/1/2010-06-03_8301114.pdf.

ImPRovE Social Innovation Team (2013), 'Governance challenges for successful local forms of social innovation', ImPRovE Milestone 42, accessed 5 October 2016 at http://improve-research.eu/.

Jenson, J. (1998), *Mapping Social Cohesion: The State of Canadian Research*, Ottawa: Renouf Publishing.

Jenson, J. (2015), 'Social innovation: redesigning the welfare diamond', in A. Nicholls, J. Simon, M. Gabriel and C. Whelan (eds), *New Frontiers in Social Innovation Research*, Basingstoke: Palgrave Macmillan, pp. 89–106.

Judt, T. (2010), *Ill Fares the Land*, London: Penguin Group.

Kertesi, G. and G. Kézdi (2012), 'Ethnic segregation between Hungarian schools: long-run trends and geographic distribution', *Budapest Working Papers on the Labour Market*, no. 8, accessed 5 October 2016 at http://www.econ.core.hu/file/ download/bwp/bwp1208.pdf.

Kertesi, G. and G. Kézdi (2013), 'School segregation, school choice and educational policies in 100 Hungarian towns', *Budapest Working Papers on the Labour Market*, no. 12, accessed 5 October 2016 at http://www.econ.core.hu/file/down load/bwp/bwp1312.pdf.

Kertesi, G. and G. Kézdi (2014), 'On the test score gap between Roma and non-Roma students in Hungary and its potential causes', *Budapest Working Papers on the Labour Market*, no. 1, accessed 5 October 2016 at http://www.econ.core. hu/file/download/bwp/bwp1401.pdf.

Maloutas, T., M. Raco and T. Tasan-Kok (2008), 'Conclusion. Competitiveness and cohesion: one discourse, multiple realities and new challenges for policy and research', in P. Ache, H.T. Andersen, T. Maloutas, M. Raco and T. Tasan-Kok (eds), *Cities Between Competitiveness and Cohesion. Discourses, Realities and Implementation*, Rotterdam: Springer, pp. 259–73.

Moulaert, F., F. Martinelli, E. Swyngedouw and S. González (2005), 'Towards alternative model(s) of local innovation', *Urban Studies*, **42** (11), 1969–90.

Moulaert, F., F. Martinelli, E. Swyngedouw and S. Gonzalez (eds) (2010), *Can Neighbourhoods Save the City? Community Development and Social Innovation*, Oxford, UK and New York, USA: Routledge.

Novy, A., D. Coimbra Swiatek and F. Moulaert (2012), 'Social cohesion: a conceptual and political elucidation', *Urban Studies*, **49** (9), 1873–89.

Novy, A., S. Habersack and B. Schaller (2013), 'Innovative forms of knowledge production: transdisciplinarity and knowledge alliances', in F. Moulaert, D. MacCallum, A. Mehmood and A. Hamdouch (eds), *The International Handbook on Social Innovation. Collective Action, Social Learning and Transdisciplinary Research*, Cheltenham, UK and Northampton, MA, USA: Edward Elgar Publishing, pp. 430–41.

Oosterlynck, S., Y. Kazepov, A. Novy, P. Cools, E. Barberis, F. Wukovitsch, T. Saruis et al. (2013a), 'The butterfly and the elephant: local social innovation, the welfare state and new poverty dynamics', *ImPRovE Discussion Paper*, no. 3, accessed 5 October 2016 at http://improve-research.eu/.

Oosterlynck, S., Y. Kazepov, A. Novy, P. Cools, E. Barberis, F. Wukovitsch, T. Saruis et al. (2013b), 'Exploring the multi-level of welfare provision and social innovation: welfare mix, welfare models and rescaling', *ImPRovE Discussion Paper*, no. 12, accessed 5 October 2016 at http://improve-research.eu/.

Oosterlynck, S., A. Novy, Y. Kazepov, P. Cools, T. Saruis, B. Leubolt and F. Wukovitsch (forthcoming), 'Improving poverty reduction: lessons from the social innovation perspective', in B. Cantillon, T. Goedemé and J. Hills (eds), *Improving Poverty Reduction in Europe. Lessons from the Past, Scenarios for the Future*, Oxford: Oxford University Press.

Riesenfelder, A., S. Schelepa and P. Wetzel (2011), 'Beschäftigungssituation von Personen mit Migrationshintergrund in Wien', Vienna: Endbericht von L&R Sozialforschung im Auftrag der Kammer für Arbeiter und Angestellte für Wien.

Streeck, W. (2013), *Gekaufte Zeit. Die vertagte Krise des Demokratischen Kapitalismus*, Berlin: Suhrkamp.

Wukovitsch, F., A. Novy and C. Weinzierl (2015), 'Thara – improving labor market access for Roma', ImPRovE case study, accessed 5 October 2016 at http://improve-research.eu/.

# 15. The social inclusion of immigrants in the United Kingdom and Italy: different but converging trajectories?

**Rosa Mas Giralt and Antonella Sarlo***

## INTRODUCTION

Over the last 25 years, immigration flows in Europe have significantly increased, both from outside the continent and within the European Union (EU). Traditional countries of destination in Northern Europe have been joined by Southern European ones – such as Italy and Spain – in receiving growing immigrant populations. More recently the dramatic increase in the number of asylum seekers coming from war zones, although still relatively low compared to other categories, has brought the issue of immigration to the centre of political discussions. Old and new demands for social services coming from immigrant populations are seen to compete with other social needs, in a context of generalised austerity measures, contributing to a radicalisation of political discourses about the social inclusion of immigrants.

Few data suffice to illustrate the changed geography of immigration. According to Eurostat (2016), the number of people born in a non-EU country that were resident in the EU-28 on 1 January 2014 amounted to 33.5 million, with the highest numbers in Germany (7.0 million), the United Kingdom (henceforth UK) (5.0), Italy (4.9), Spain (4.7) and France (4.2). As a percentage of the total resident population, the share of foreign residents was highest in Spain (10.1 per cent), followed by Germany (8.7 per cent), Italy (8.1 per cent) and the UK (7.8 per cent). Although the latter figures reflect different immigration histories and citizenship-granting regimes, it is unquestionable that the five countries mentioned above now concentrate the large majority of foreign residents, to an extent that is higher than their share of the overall population: 76 per cent of all foreign residents in the EU-28, compared to 63 per cent of total residents (Eurostat, 2016).

The distance between established countries of immigration and 'latecomers' has also shrunk in relation to immigration policies. As stressed by several scholars (Caponio, 2004; Zincone, 2009; Ambrosini, 2008), the different 'immigration models' identified in Europe in the second half of the last century are now outdated, as the original strategies – assimilationist, multiculturalist, pluralist – have become increasingly muddled and stratified, as a consequence of evolving national preoccupations and aims. Different categories of immigrants are granted different social rights, especially in what concerns access to social services. Moreover, a growing divergence is observed between national regulations and local policies, together with a greater diversification among local practices for the social inclusion of immigrants (Ambrosini, 2008).

Against this general background and in tune with Ambrosini's reading, the key aim of this chapter is to explore to what extent two countries that were initially very different with regard to origin and timing of immigration, management of their integration, and structure of the welfare state, such as the 'pluralist' UK and the 'latecomer' Italy, have come to converge in the last 15 years and reduce their differences in relation to the social inclusion of immigrants and their access to social services. To do so, we will make a distinction between *immigration policy* – legislation dealing with the 'entry' of immigrants, and *immigrant (integration) policy* – legislation and programmes dealing with the social inclusion of immigrants, i.e. the granting of social rights and services (Hammar, 1989). In what concerns the latter, we shall distinguish among three main categories of social services, which exhibit different degrees of 'right' (Busso et al., 2013):

- 'Universalistic' social services, such as health or education, the access to which is generally regulated at the national level and depends on the legal status of immigrants. In many countries the regional and/or municipal government levels have substantial discretionary power in applying such regulation in more or less restrictive terms.
- 'Migrant-specific' social services, such as legal aid, counselling, job search or housing assistance, which are specifically targeted at the foreign population, exhibit a weaker national regulation and are generally organised and provided at the regional or local scale.
- 'Ethnic-sensitive' social services, such as language assistance or dedicated counselling, which are targeted at specific ethnic groups to facilitate their access to 'universalistic' services, the regulation and supply of which is highly differentiated among EU countries, as they are generally organised and provided exclusively at the local level.

In what follows we shall first provide some theoretical background to the understanding of welfare, immigration and immigrant policies.

Subsequently we will summarise the national trajectories and current policy approaches to immigration in the UK and Italy, with particular attention to the access of documented or regular immigrants[1] to social services. In the last section of the chapter we will draw some conclusions and highlight similarities and differences between the two models.

## 1. IMMIGRANTS AND WELFARE: CONCEPTUAL PERSPECTIVES

Given the relevance that immigration has acquired in welfare debates, a growing comparative social policy scholarship has highlighted the need to develop better understandings of immigrants' social rights and their 'actual' (not only formal) inclusion/exclusion from welfare systems (Sainsbury, 2006, 2012; Wilkinson and Craig, 2011). Depending on their overall attributes, different welfare systems incorporate the social rights of resident non-citizens to a greater or lesser extent, for instance, in relation to base of entitlement (need, work and/or citizenship), type of benefits (flat rate or earnings-related) or type of funding (taxation normally being more inclusive) (Sainsbury, 2012). Different combinations of these attributes mean different levels of inclusivity for newcomers in relation to universalistic policies and social services addressed to the general population.

As Sainsbury (2006; 2012) has suggested, immigrants' social rights in any given country are also mediated by specific immigration and immigrant policies that regulate the conditions whereby newcomers are able to enter and become members of their receiving societies. Immigration policy regulates the range of entry categories in any given country: asylum seekers, economic immigrants according to types of visas, family members, etc. (Sainsbury, 2006). Each of these entry categories is normally granted more or less restrictive entitlements to accessing social benefits – whether cash benefits or in-kind services (Hammar, 1989). These differential entitlements are related to immigrant policy, by regulating the level of access to public services granted to newcomers. A related wider dimension of immigrant policy is the overall 'incorporation or integration' regime, which determines newcomers' possibilities to acquire permanent residency or citizenship (Sainsbury, 2006).

In this chapter, we build on Sainsbury's (2006; 2012) analytical approach to studying the social rights of immigrants by considering the intersection of these policy domains (welfare, immigration and immigrant policies) with the systems of government and governance that manage and implement them. Although commonly understood as concerning federal or multinational states, multilevel systems of government also apply to the relations between central, regional and local authorities in unitary states (Hepburn and Zapata-Barrero, 2014). These multilevel systems may also include multilevel policies for a particular social area as is often the case with immigrant incorporation. The governance apparatuses which are responsible for implementing these multilevel policies can be considered 'Type II Multi-level governance' systems (Hooghe and Marks, 2003, p. 237), as they incorporate a significant number of jurisdictions, operate at multiple territorial scales and have task-specific (immigrant integration) and flexible approaches. As has been noted, processes of immigrant integration take place primarily at the local level (Scholten, 2014). It is at this level that immigrants lead their lives in the receiving society, need to enrol their children in school, find jobs and housing, and interact with social and health services. It is also at this level that their social needs become apparent, and intersecting levels of policy and implementation respond or fail to respond to these needs.

As Scholten (2014, p. 151) has highlighted, the recognition that 'migrant integration is a multilevel policy field [. . .] does not mean that policy processes and policy efforts at the various levels are necessarily harmonious and congruent'. Taking into account the multilevel nature of immigrant integration policy, and according to the theoretical and analytical framework that informed the COST Action IS1102 *SO.S. COHESION – Social services, welfare states and places* and the present book, we propose that to understand fully the social rights of immigrants in a given country, we need to interrogate: (a) the 'vertical' division of authority within the state with regard to immigration and immigrant policies and the tensions between central and regional/local government; (b) the 'horizontal' division of responsibility, that is the enlarged local governance of immigrant policies and services, including a range of non-governmental organisations, more or less supported by the national and local governments; (c) the actual role of such organisations in complementing and/or substituting for public social services. In the next two sections, we analyse the trajectories of the UK and Italy in the last decades in relation to these different dimensions.

## 2.   IMMIGRATION AND SOCIAL CITIZENSHIP IN THE UNITED KINGDOM

The UK has a longer history of immigration than many other European nations, and its modern period is normally traced back to the end of the Second World War, when a significant shortage of labour in the country transformed colonies and ex-colonies in main sources of immigrant workers (Spencer, 2011a). For instance, the number of people born in India residing in England and Wales nearly doubled between 1961 and 1971 – from 157 000 to 313 000 (Office for National Statistics, 2013). Gradually immigration to the UK has grown and diversified and the UK-born minority ethnic population has increased. Census data highlights that in 2011, 20 per cent of the population identified with an ethnic group other than White British in contrast to 3 per cent in 2001 (Jivraj, 2012). Since the early 2000s, the heterogeneity in country of origin has been accompanied by other types of immigration and diversification along the lines of gender, age, religion, language, migration channel and status; a situation which Vertovec (2007) has conceptualised as 'super-diversity' and which has significant consequences for the range of social needs of immigrants.

Since the 1950s, immigration policy in the UK has followed an increasingly 'restrictive' trajectory, although also responding to economic requirements for labour and to public pressures in different periods (Spencer, 2011a). For instance, the economic prosperity of the late 1990s and early 2000s led successive Labour governments (1997–2010) to shift to policies committed to economic immigration but with stricter security controls ('secure borders' after the 9/11 and 7/7 terrorist attacks). In addition, British authorities have increasingly adopted measures of 'exclusion from the welfare state' as tools of immigration control (Spencer, 2011a, p. 45). As entitlement to most public services and benefits in the UK is determined by 'residence and need', this has long raised concerns that immigrants would 'take advantage' of the welfare and health systems (The Migration Observatory, 2014). Consequently, successive UK governments have introduced welfare restrictions and/or 'tests of eligibility' to delay 'immediate' social rights for immigrants (Spencer, 2011a). Irregular migrants have actually been stripped of nearly all social rights and can only access compulsory education and emergency healthcare.

For regular migrants, a main restrictive mechanism has been the application of the principle of 'no recourse to public funds' (introduced by the *Immigration Act 1971*) to an increasing number of immigrants from third countries, non-EU/EEA[2] (Wilkinson and Craig, 2011; Sainsbury, 2012). Since the 1980s, an expanding range of benefits, tax credits and allowances have been classified as 'public funds' (social housing, means-tested jobseeker's allowance and so on), thus effectively excluding newcomers from these provisions (Sainsbury, 2012). Immigrant policies related to naturalisation have also become stricter, as the residence period for 'new' immigrants to qualify for settlement status and thus rights of access to 'public funds' has been gradually extended and normally requires five years' legal residence (Sainsbury, 2012).

Following the 2004 and 2007 EU enlargements, the increase of EU/EEA immigration to the UK has come to dominate governmental and public attention, renewing populist discourses of 'benefit and health tourism' in the country. Despite little evidence that the welfare system works as an attraction for EU/EEA migrants – fewer than 5 per cent were claiming jobseeker's allowance in 2013 (The Migration Observatory, 2014) – consecutive British governments have introduced measures to restrict (mainly delay) EU/EEA immigrants' access to welfare assistance (Kennedy, 2015). Effectively the 'no recourse to public funds' and eligibility tests have created a mosaic of differentiated social rights for newcomers in the UK, which, together with a shortage of funding and resources at the local level, are making delivery of social services for immigrants increasingly difficult.

## The Vertical Division of Authority Within the State: The Shift of Social Inclusion Responsibilities from the National to Lower Levels of Government

In the UK responsibility for immigration policy and related regulations regarding welfare entitlements for different types of immigrants has remained the prerogative of the central government. However, this has not been accompanied by the development of a national policy framework on immigrant integration (Spencer, 2011b). Instead, from the 1960s, the UK's integration approach has generally had a mainstreaming character; that is, by making 'an effort to reach people with a migration background through needs-based social programming and policies that also target the general population' (Ali and Gidley, 2014, p. 1). Examples of this approach are found in the significant anti-discrimination legislation which has been passed since the 1970s or the 'community cohesion' policies first introduced in the 2000s in response to the 'segregation fears' prevalent after the 9/11 and 7/7 terrorist attacks.

In the year 2000, the UK saw the deployment of its only formal national immigrant integration policy, which made exclusive reference to refugees; this policy, expanded in 2005, set out a clear framework to manage the integration process of refugees across the country (Home Office, 2005). During the third term of the Labour government (2005–10), responsibility for immigrant integration (except for refugees) was transferred from the Home Office (national level) to the Department of Communities and Local Government. The Conservative–Liberal Democrat or Coalition Government (2010–15) embraced a 'community cohesion' approach (through its policy paper 'Creating the conditions for integration') based on shared values, social responsibility, active participation, social mobility and rejection of extremism, thus not 'targeting' immigrants exclusively, but communities as a whole (Ali and Gidley, 2014).

In the devolved and multi-tiered government system of the UK, integration approaches have varied across England, Scotland, Wales and Northern Ireland, and within them. In this system, a range of areas of service provision are devolved to local authorities (education, housing), who have considerable freedom to develop their own goals in integration policy and related migrant-specific or ethnic-sensitive services (Ali and Gidley, 2014). For instance, in 2009 the Mayor of London implemented an integration strategy for refugees and migrants in the city (updated in 2013), establishing key priorities such as increasing access to English courses for speakers of other languages and tackling housing, employment, education and health inequalities (Greater London Authority, 2013). However, not all local authorities have developed such strategies and there have been different levels of engagement with the integration of immigrants across the country (Ali and Gidley, 2014).

In the UK, the local provision of social and health services involves a range of public and sub-contracted actors. Some services and provisions are the responsibility of the local authority (education, housing, social care, council tax benefit), but in-/out-of-work benefits are managed nationally by the Department of Work and Pensions through local delivery offices (Department for Work and Pensions, 2016). In addition, primary healthcare is provided through practices of general practitioners or dentists for local catchment areas who are contracted by the National Health Service (National Health Service, 2013). Overall, the complex system of immigrant categories and differentiated social rights makes it difficult for front line staff in this range of 'local' services to establish immigrants' entitlements, which may lead to discrimination when access is refused (CAP Mas Giralt, 2014). In some instances, welfare restrictions also prevent local authorities from assisting vulnerable immigrants (with 'no recourse' to public funds) and may jeopardise public services' duty of care towards victims of trafficking and exploitation.

There is an additional constraint to local authorities' ability to develop or fund 'migrant-specific' or 'ethnic-sensitive' social services in support of immigrants' integration in their localities. Alongside its transfer of responsibility to the local level, the Coalition Government (2010–15) implemented a political programme intended to reduce the country's fiscal debt and scale down public expenditure. Financial cuts were applied across government and local authorities; for instance, from 2011 and over a five-year period, there were plans to reduce 43 per cent of funding from central government to local authorities (Local Government Association, 2013). The measures implemented have also affected the taxes that local authorities can collect, including a cap on Council Tax (the most substantial local tax). Thus, financial constraints further jeopardise the activities of local authorities and, in the last few years, services or initiatives addressing the social needs of immigrants have been curtailed. A recent study, conducted with Latin American immigrants (with EU citizenship) in London, identified that since 2010 cuts in public funding have translated into a retrenchment of 'ethnic-sensitive' social services (outreach and interpreting services) provided by local authorities for newly arrived immigrants, in turn leading to difficulties in accessing 'universalistic' services (CAP Mas Giralt, 2014).

### The Horizontal Division of Responsibility: The Relevant Role of Third-Sector Organisations

The multi-tiered governance systems of the UK are characterised by a strong reliance on cross-sectoral partnerships, which incorporate non-statutory actors and coordinate different statutory agencies. In the early 2000s, the Home Office funded 12 regional 'Strategic partnerships for asylum and refugee support' across the UK, which in 2007 widened their remit to incorporate all types of immigrants (Ali and Gidley, 2014). The subsequent shift of the Coalition Government (2010–15) towards localism stripped many of these partnerships of their 'regional' identity (and some ceased to exist), but many continue to play a significant role in coordinating integration initiatives in their regions.

These partnerships are funded by the central government and include representatives from local authorities and a range of statutory agencies (health, police and education services), migrant and refugee organisations and the Home Office; they may also include representation from the private sector (Ali and Gidley, 2014). They fulfil a strategic role by facilitating collaboration among public, non-governmental and private actors; monitoring trends to inform policy and minimise adverse local impacts; working with local delivery partners to design and oversee services that respond to immigrants' needs; and acting as a point of contact between the Home Office, other government departments and regional partners (Migration Yorkshire, 2015).

However, in recent years, local statutory and non-statutory actors have faced increasing difficulties to access state funds to address the local impacts of immigration. For instance, the Labour government introduced a GBP 50 million Migration impact fund (MIF) in 2009, financed through a GBP 50 levy on the visas of non-EU/EEA immigrants entering the UK (Tonkiss, 2013). The MIF sought to support the local integration of immigrants and assist with the costs of the transitional impacts of immigration on public services. Applications to the funds were open to councils, police, health trusts and third-sector organisations. In 2010, however, the Coalition Government axed the fund, alleging that 'the impacts of migration [were] better addressed though controlling immigration' (Tonkiss, 2013). Without funding streams such as MIF, local authorities have struggled to cope with increases on service demand.

**Third Organisations at the Local Level: Agents of Change or Substitute Providers?**

As the previous section implies, third-sector actors play an important role in supporting the integration of immigrants in the UK. Although this sector involves all types of voluntary, community and charity organisations with a remit in social inclusion and welfare, it also includes distinctive minority ethnic and immigrant groups (Black and minority ethnic voluntary and community sector – BMEVCS). Starting in the 1960s to 1980s, a range of grassroots initiatives were developed, including self-help strategies such as educational activities, co-ethnic financial assistance or savings committees in the South Asian and Caribbean communities, or even more formal forms of organisation such as the black housing movement created to address the discrimination that BME residents faced in mainstream housing (Craig, 2011). Thus, a semi-formal BMEVCS began to emerge in the 1980s and was consolidated and diversified in the 1990s, reflecting a tradition of pluralist approaches at the local level (Craig, 2011). Many of their activities were initially funded through community resources but as associations established themselves more formally, state support became available if they provided specialised services to minority groups ('migrant-specific' or 'ethnic-sensitive' social services). For instance, some BME groups have been entrusted by mainstream welfare services to deliver specialist provision, such as care for older people (Craig, 2011). These organisations have also played prominent roles in advocating and lobbying for the social rights of immigrants (Craig, 2011; Ware, 2013).

However, during the last few years, this sector's resources have been depleted by the loss of financial support from central and local government and the difficult fundraising and economic climate post-2008 (Ware, 2013). Thus, the horizontal subsidiarity that had long characterised the delivery of 'migrant-specific' and 'ethnic-sensitive' social services for immigrants and minority ethnic residents in Britain has been increasingly disrupted (Craig, 2011). At the same time, within the transition from diverse to super-diverse immigrant populations, third-sector organisations have experienced a significant increase in the demand for advisory and support services due to a shortage of appropriate statutory provision (Craig, 2011; CAP Mas Giralt, 2014).

The Coalition Government (2010–15) and current Conservative Government (2015 onwards) and their agenda of 'devolution' to 'the local level' has had a significant impact on the type of expectations placed on third-sector actors in the delivery of social services. The Coalition Government introduced the so-called 'Big society' ideology based on the premise of 'reduc[ing] the state's role and empower[ing] [. . .] civil society to deliver services' (Ali and Gidley, 2014, p. 8). Although not formally adopted in legislation (and subsequently abandoned), the philosophy of the 'Big society' is implicit in the *Localism Act 2011* and its view of voluntary and community groups as conducting 'the most innovative and effective work in public services' and the benefits of involving these groups and individuals further in 'tackl[ing] problems in the way they want' (Department for Communities and Local Government, 2011, p. 8). Despite this, in February 2016, the Conservative Government announced that it would insert a new clause into all its grant agreements to prevent such funds being used by charities and other voluntary organisations to lobby government (Ricketts, 2016). The National Council for Voluntary Organisations has highlighted that this move is 'tantamount to making charities take a vow of silence' and it potentially disrupts the historic role of this sector in promoting policy change and social inclusion (Ricketts, 2016).

## 3.   IMMIGRATION AND SOCIAL CITIZENSHIP IN ITALY

Italy is generally included in the so-called 'Southern European immigration model' (Pugliese, 2002). Some scholars actually consider it a 'paradigmatic case' (King and Ribas-Mateos, 2002), characterised by a late and rapid increase of immigration flows – mostly generated on the supply side and informally inserted into the local labour markets – and by a late and reluctant acknowledgement and regulation by public actors (Pugliese, 2002).

According to Mantovan (2007), the specific features of what she calls the 'implicit' Italian integration model include: (a) a weak national regulatory framework, as witnessed by the repeated use of amnesties and ad hoc decrees to regularise immigrants and deal with emergency issues; (b) the limited action of central government institutions and, in contrast, the relevant role of regional and local actors – both public and private – in addressing the economic and social inclusion of immigrants; (c) the initially informal and casual forms of insertion in the labour market and the local socioeconomic context, only subsequently and progressively institutionalised; and (d) the predominance of employment in manual and unskilled tasks, often with no regular contract (especially in the South). Two more specific traits can be added: (e) the great heterogeneity of origin, which stems from the absence of a strong colonial past; and (f) the great regional differentiation in socioeconomic structures and immigrant inclusion practices (Ambrosini, 2005; Balbo, 2015). The latter features make Italy eligible for the concept of 'super-diversity' originally coined by Vertovec (2007) to describe the UK immigration model, underscoring the possible convergence between Southern and Northern European immigration models.

Recent trends have further complicated the picture. The financial crisis of 2008 and the ensuing industrial closures in Northern Italy have triggered a territorial diffusion of immigrants, as employment has shifted from industry to agriculture and from Northern to Southern regions, where opportunities to find casual work in agriculture are greater (Pugliese, 2013; Sarlo, 2015). Settlement preferences have also shifted from large metropolitan areas to small municipalities and rural places, in search of cheaper housing (Balbo, 2015; Sarlo et al., 2014). At the same time, the political crises and the new conflicts arising in the Southern and Eastern shores of the Mediterranean have generated new daily humanitarian emergencies.

In this evolving context Italian immigration policies, which have remained a prerogative of the central state, have been swinging – in a sort of 'bipolar' mode – between 'opening' and 'closing' stances (Sarlo et al., 2014), a fact that aggravated the unclear division of labour between different levels of the state and the possibility to implement a coherent strategy. At the same time, immigrant policies, which were already characterised by inadequate regulation, have witnessed a progressive pulling out of the central state and a shift of responsibility onto local governments. Local welfare systems are thus forced to address added demands for services, which magnify already existing structural inadequacies (Zincone, 2009). In this context, the relevant role played by the EU, through its Cohesion policy, in the implementation of local immigrant policies and practices must be stressed. In fact, many local projects for the social inclusion of immigrants throughout Italy were financed with resources from the European structural funds.

## The Vertical Division of Authority Within the State: The Shift of Social Inclusion Policies from the Central State to Regional and Local Governments

In the last fifteen years, there has been a paradigmatic change in national immigration policies in Italy: from an approach based on the 'certainty of social security rights' to an approach based on the 'right to security' (Baratta, 2000), which, while attempting to control immigration flows, also tended indirectly to undermine immigrants' social rights. Three legislative acts mark this evolution.

The National law 40/1998 (aka 'Turco-Napolitano law', later transformed into the Legislative decree 286/1998) was approved by a centre-left government and marked the transition from a piecemeal approach to a more coherent regulatory framework. For the first time the notion of immigrant policy was introduced and a 'reasonable integration model' was posited (Zincone, 2000), which established a clear distinction between 'regular' and 'irregular' immigrants. The former were granted social rights and access to 'universalistic' social services such as public health care, social security benefits, social housing; the latter were only granted access to compulsory public education and emergency health services. The law established a dedicated National fund for immigrant policies (*Fondo nazionale per le politiche migratorie*), i.e. for the implementation of plans for the social inclusion of immigrants, a Committee for integration policies (*Commissione per le politiche di integrazione*) and a Council for immigration (*Consulta per l'immigrazione*), made up of representatives from the regional governments, municipalities and civil society organisations. It also defined the vertical division of responsibility among the different levels of the state: while immigration policies (entry procedures and quotas) remained firmly with the central state, the responsibility for immigrant policies was transferred to regional governments and municipalities, albeit still within a national regulatory and funding framework (Caponio, 2004) – thereby anticipating the Constitutional reform of 2001, which would transfer to regional governments the exclusive responsibility on all social services.

The subsequent National law 189/2002 (aka 'Bossi-Fini law'), approved by a centre-right government, did not alter the general structure of the previous legislation, but introduced more rigid requirements for entry and permanence. More importantly, although ostensibly maintaining the 'reasonable integration' approach, the central government initiated an indirect strategy of disengagement from immigrant policy, by progressively dismantling both the funds and the committees established to support the early multiscalar approach to immigrant policies, thereby transferring onto regional and local governments the financial burden of supporting the social inclusion of immigrants.

With the National Law 94/2009 (aka 'Maroni law' or 'Security package'), also approved by a centre-right government, the 'reasonable integration' strategy was explicitly abandoned and a straightforward 'security-oriented' approach was adopted. The new law made it very difficult for immigrants to maintain a 'regular' status, by 'designing the legal position of foreigners as guests, on perpetual trial, for whom the test never ends' (Bascherini, 2010, p. 462, translated from Italian). Indirectly, the new legislation also made access to social rights more difficult, further undermining the initial fragile attempt at establishing an inclusive policy framework. Moreover, it granted greater power to mayors and municipal councils in the domain of public order and security, thereby opening the possibility for veritable 'exclusionary' actions at the local level, via municipal decrees and warrants allegedly pursuing public order (Ambrosini and Caneva, 2012).

The existence of national, regional or local regulation in Italy does not necessarily mean that they are consistently applied. The increased discretionary power given to local authorities to interpret and mediate between, on the one hand, the national policies oriented to 'control', and, on the other hand, the necessity to address the needs of immigrants locally, has contributed to amplify the distance between discourses, legislation and practices, and the already existing territorial differentiation in the way Italian regions and localities deal with the social inclusion of immigrants (Ambrosini and Caneva, 2012; Balbo, 2015). These contradictions and differences are particularly evident in relation to, for example, the granting of 'legal' residence, which is the key step for accessing 'universalistic' social rights; or the application of means-tested fees in certain social services such as daycare. Strange paradoxes can be found between formal entitlements and 'actual' access to services. For instance, in some North-Eastern regions and municipalities governed by centre-right coalitions – where political discourses are outright exclusionary and where municipal decrees allegedly oriented to maintain 'public order' have been enacted which limit the access of immigrants to certain public facilities – immigrants actually do enjoy access to most social services (Cancellieri et al., 2014; Semprebon, 2014). In contrast, in some Southern regions, where inclusive discourses are showcased and dedicated policies are promoted (see, for example, the Appulia Regional Plan for Immigrants 2013–15), dramatic situations of social exclusion and exploitation of seasonal immigrant workers in agriculture are still found (Galossi, 2011).

## The Horizontal Division of Responsibility: The Relevant Role of Third-Sector Organisations

The local is thus the key government level in Italy to deal with the needs of the varying and increasingly complex social universe of immigrants. As early as the late 1980s, in the absence of any specific regulatory framework, forms of 'horizontal subsidiarity' had developed. With the more recent retrenchment of the national government in what concerns both immigrant policy and social services in general, local collective actors – often of quite diverse origin, ranging from business associations to trade unions, from Catholic organisations to lay voluntary groups, from philanthropic foundations to community organisations – have become invaluable providers of social services to immigrants (Ambrosini, 2005; Barberis, 2009), complementing or even substituting for local authorities.

These 'organised solidarity' actors (Ambrosini, 2005) – associated in varying networking configurations, local and national – provide both 'migrant-specific' services such as legal aid, orientation services, housing or job application procedures and 'ethnic sensitive' services such as language classes or cultural mediation. They also perform a key role in building awareness and information about the immigration phenomenon (Ambrosini, 2005), and a lobbying and advocacy role, at both central and local levels (Zincone and Di Gregorio, 2002). For example, business associations have at times put pressure on the central government for less restrictive entry policies, while advocating more inclusive social policies at the local level (Barberis, 2009, p. 236); trade unions have played a key role in advocating for better integration policies and access to social services; and Catholic organisations have played a double role as service providers and pressure groups for more inclusive immigrant policies (Barberis, 2009).

The recent territorial diffusion of immigrants and the intensifying landings of asylum seekers, especially in the South, have further triggered local 'organised solidarity' initiatives, in which 'short-range' community networks interact with 'long-range' solidarity networks such as Caritas, Médecins sans Frontières or national trade union organisations, generating answers to the social needs of immigrants, in different forms and with different degrees of institutionalisation – also depending on the local social capital, welfare system and political traditions. As stressed by Barberis (2010, p. 47, translated from Italian), a 'micro-regulation model, without a central state paradigm and largely based on residualism and local networks' has thus taken shape in Italy.

### Bottom-up Initiatives at the Local Level: Agents of Change or Substitute Providers?

In Italy, many bottom-up local initiatives have developed in relation to pressures created by immigration since the very beginning of the phenomenon. It is actually possible to identify a 'thread' running across different initiatives, in different urban contexts, with different origins and aims, through three main phases.

The first phase started in the late 1980s and was characterised by the absolute centrality of local authorities, in the absence of any national regulatory framework. Initiatives mostly concerned the social inclusion of 'economic' migrants in the large cities of the North and influenced the national legislation to a significant extent (Caponio, 2004). In Milan, for example, a Municipal council for immigration (*Consulta cittadina per l'immigrazione*) was created in 1986, a Centre for foreigners (*Centro per gli stranieri*) was opened in 1989, and literacy classes for adults and initiatives to help children settle at school were launched (Zincone, 2009). Similar educational, hospitality and mediating services to facilitate access to social services as well as formal immigrant organisations were created in Turin and Bologna in the late 1980s and early 1990s (Caponio, 2004).

The second phase started in the late 1990s and was more emergency-driven, prompted by the recurring arrival of immigrants from war zones, especially in the South. Particularly interesting in this phase were the initiatives that unfolded from 1997 in a few small municipalities of Calabria (Badolato and Riace), which linked the humanitarian reception of asylum seekers with an urban regeneration strategy, through projects that mobilised the immigrants themselves in rehabilitating the abandoned housing stock in old depopulated boroughs (Sarlo, 2015; CAP Sarlo and Martinelli, 2016). This practice was later institutionalised with a dedicated regional law and even influenced the national 'Bossi-Fini law', which established the Protection system for asylum seekers and refugees (*Sistema protezione richiedenti asilo e rifugiati – SPRAR*).

The third phase was triggered by the onset of the economic crisis in 2008 and the 'Maroni law' of 2009, with the ensuing cuts in national funding and the curtailment of immigrants' social rights. It is characterised by a further proliferation of local practices, answering a variety of local needs, sometimes – again – with truly innovative features: from those deployed in Lombardy, such as the housing and service activities developed with and for immigrants in the small municipality of Breno or the participatory processes developed in the province of Brescia to promote a vision of integration as a common good (Semprebon, 2014), to those experimented within Latium, such as the XI Comunità Montana '*Castelli romani e prenestini*', which promoted initiatives to support the employment of immigrants in the hotel and tourism sector (Cremaschi and Fioretti, 2015).

What brings together this quite variegated range of initiatives is that they basically act as surrogates for a missing national policy, supporting Barberis' notion of an Italian 'micro-regulation model' (2010). This fact in turn raises two relevant questions. First, are immigrants in the end the most expendable among vulnerable social groups and hence the target of a more or less explicit disengagement of the central state from providing social inclusion services? Second, how far can local innovative initiatives go if their role is no longer to challenge – and contribute to change – the way social services are provided, but only to substitute for them in the context of an increasingly exclusionary national agenda? Bottom-up practices cannot be expected to 'work miracles' (Mingione and Vicari, 2015, p. 100, translated from Italian). They are not sustainable 'in the absence of a stable policy and normative framework and, most importantly, of a defined social project' (Barberis, 2010, p. 47, translated from Italian), as well as in the absence of stable funding mechanisms (Martinelli, 2012). Moreover, precisely because of the lack of national regulation and funding and their dependence on bottom-up local initiatives, the social rights of immigrants are widely uneven among places, a fact that mirrors the Italian territorial differentiation in the supply of social services in general, but is certainly aggravated in the case of services for immigrants.

## 4. CONCLUDING REMARKS

This chapter sought to contribute to understanding immigrants' social rights and their inclusion/exclusion from social service provisions in the UK and Italy. To conclude this endeavour, we reflect on the similarities and differences observed in our analysis of the two countries' trajectories, in relation to the 'vertical' and 'horizontal' divisions of responsibility for immigration/immigrant policies and services and to the role of non-governmental organisations in complementing or substituting retrenching public provisions.

In terms of the 'vertical' division of authority, our review shows that, despite different histories and timings of immigration, the central state in both countries is pulling out of immigrant 'integration' policy and concerning itself prevailingly with immigration policy, while explicitly or implicitly curtailing newcomers' social rights. In both cases, the responsibility for immigrant policy, particularly in relation to developing migrant-specific and ethnic-sensitive social services, has been shifted to local governments, but with increasingly limited financial resources and support. Tensions between state-led welfare regulations and the needs of immigrants, which are manifest at the local level, expose contradictions. In the UK, a growing diversity of immigrant categories with differential social rights regulated by central government may translate into further exclusion in practice when difficulties in establishing immigrants' entitlement lead to barred access to local services. In Italy, particular local manifestations of the crossing between national immigration policies and local integration initiatives result in inconsistent levels of access to services in different localities. Despite synergies, there are still significant differences in the overall approach to vertical coordination across different government levels in both cases. Although eroded during the Coalition (2010–15) and Conservative (current) administrations, cross-sectoral regional migration partnerships in the UK play a key role in acting as a 'point of contact' between lower levels of government and the Home Office. In contrast, Italy shows a greater level of 'formal' disconnection between different levels of government.

There are also significant parallels between the two countries in terms of their 'horizontal' division of responsibility at the regional/local levels. In both cases, 'horizontal subsidiarity' has developed, involving a wide range of local actors who provide both 'migrant-specific' and 'ethnic-sensitive' services and often lobby for the social rights of immigrants. Differences remain in the formal recognition of cross-sectoral partnerships. In Italy, these types of partnerships seem to have been developed through particular bottom-up initiatives in particular localities and regions, while the UK has a long history of cross-sectoral collaborations across all types of social services. Nonetheless, the 'withdrawal' of the British central government in providing 'leadership' in the immigrant integration policy area and its curtailment of funding streams both at national and local levels has deeply disrupted the traditional horizontal subsidiarity which had characterised the delivery of services for immigrants.

In both countries, third-sector and other solidarity actors are thus 'compensating' for retrenching or nonexistent public provision at local level, especially in relation to 'migrant-specific' and 'ethnic-sensitive' social services.[3] In the UK, both the former Coalition and the current Conservative governments have explicitly recognised the key role third-sector actors can play in the delivery of 'locally appropriate' social services, but without proper resourcing this sector cannot perform the tasks entrusted to them and cannot respond to the growing and diversifying needs of immigrants. In Italy, the recognition of third-sector organisations is less explicit and, in the absence of stable normative frameworks or funding mechanisms, services for the social inclusion of immigrants increasingly depend on bottom-up local solidarity initiatives which have no means to transform into sustainable solutions. In both countries, the augmented role of the local level and the varied nature of micro-approaches are contributing to a growing territorial differentiation in the provision of services for the social inclusion of immigrants.

## NOTES

\*   This chapter is the joint product of a close collaboration between the two authors. However, the Introduction and section 3 should be attributed to Antonella Sarlo and sections 1 and 2 to Rosa Mas Giralt, whereas the Conclusions are obviously shared.
1.   Undocumented or irregular immigrants in both countries have limited social rights – i.e. access only to basic compulsory education and emergency healthcare.
2.   Non-European Union/European Economic Area immigrants.
3.   In the case of undocumented or irregular immigrants, these organisations play a key role in filling a structural gap, by providing services to people who would otherwise be completely excluded from social services.

# REFERENCES

Ali, S. and B. Gidley (2014), *Advancing Outcomes for All Minorities: Experiences of Mainstreaming Immigrant Integration Policy in the United Kingdom*, Brussels: Migration Policy Institute Europe.

Ambrosini, M. (2005), *Sociologia delle migrazioni*, Bologna: Il Mulino.

Ambrosini, M. (2008), *Un'altra globalizzazione. La sfida delle migrazioni transnazionali*, Bologna: Il Mulino.

Ambrosini, M. and E. Caneva (2012), *Local Policies of Exclusion: the Italian Case*, Technical Report ACCEPT-PLURALISM; 2012/07, 4, Seventh EU Framework Programme, European University Institute, accessed 12 June 2016 at http://cadmus.eui.eu/handle/1814/22317.

Balbo, M. (ed.) (2015), *Migrazioni e piccoli comuni*, Milan: F. Angeli.

Baratta, A. (2000), 'Diritto alla sicurezza o sicurezza dei diritti?', *Democrazia e Diritto*, no. 2, 19–36.

Barberis, E. (2009), 'La dimensione territoriale delle politiche per gli immigrati', in Y. Kazepov (ed.), *La dimensione territoriale delle politiche sociali*, Roma: Carocci, pp. 223–46.

Barberis, E. (2010), 'Il ruolo degli operatori sociali dell'immigrazione nel welfare locale', *La Rivista delle Politiche Sociali*, **XXIV** (1), 45–60.

Bascherini, G. (2010), 'Immigrazione e nuovi paradigmi della sicurezza. Note sulla penalizzazione delle irregolarità migratorie', in S. Gambino and G. D'Ignazio (eds), *Immigrazione e diritti fondamentali*, Milan: Giuffrè Editore, pp. 461–80.

Busso, S., E. Gargiulo and M. Mannocchi (2013), *Multiwelfare. Le trasformazioni dei welfare territoriali nella società dell'immigrazione*, Turin: FIERI Rapporti di Ricerca, accessed 12 June 2016 at http://fieri.it/wp-content/uploads/2013/09/RAPPORTO-Multiwelfare_SETTEMBRE-2013.pdf.

Cancellieri, A., G. Marconi and S. Tonin (2014), *Migrazioni, politiche e territorio in Veneto*, Venice: Cattedra Unesco SSIIM, Università Iuav di Venezia, accessed 12 June 2016 at http://www.unescochair-iuav.it/blog/rapporti-di-ricerca/.

Caponio, T. (2004), 'Governo locale e immigrazione in Italia. Tra servizi di welfare e politiche di sviluppo', *Le istituzioni del federalismo*, **25** (5), 789–812.

Craig, G. (2011), 'Forward to the past: can the UK black and minority ethnic third sector survive?', *Voluntary Sector Review*, **2** (3), 367–89.

Cremaschi, M. and C. Fioretti (2015), 'Il Lazio e l'area metropolitana', in Balbo M. (ed.), *Migrazioni e piccoli comuni*, Milan: F. Angeli.

Department for Communities and Local Government (2011), *A Plain English Guide to the Localism Act*, London: Department for Communities and Local Government.

Department for Work and Pensions (2016), *About Us*, London: Gov.uk, accessed 12 June 2016 at https://www.gov.uk/government/organisations/department-for-work-pensions/about.

Eurostat (2016), *Migration and Migrant Population Statistics*, Brussels: European Commission, accessed 21 April 2016 at http://ec.europa.eu/eurostat/statistics-explained/index.php?title=Migration_and_migrant_population_statistics&oldid=228736.

Galossi, E. (ed.) (2011) *Immigrazione, sfruttamento e conflitto sociale. Una mappatura delle aree a rischio e quattro studi di caso territoriali*, Research Report,

Rome: IRES-Istituto di Ricerche Economiche e Sociali, accessed 15 June 2016 at users2.unimi.it/escapes/wp-content/uploads/Indagine_territori_a_rischio.pdf.

Greater London Authority (2013), *London Enriched: Update*, London: Greater London Authority, accessed 12 June 2016 at https://www.london.gov.uk/sites/default/files/london_enriched_update.pdf.

Hammar, T. (1989), 'State, nation and dual citizenship', in W.R. Brubaker (ed.), *Immigration and The Politics of Citizenship in Europe and North America*, Lanham: University Press of America.

Hepburn, E. and R. Zapata-Barrero (eds) (2014), *The Politics of Migration in Multilevel States: Governance and Political Parties*, Basingstoke, UK and New York, USA: Palgrave Macmillan.

Home Office (2005), *Integration Matters: A National Refugee Strategy*, London: Home Office.

Hooghe, L. and G. Marks (2003), 'Unraveling the central state, but how? Types of multi-level governance', *The American Political Science Review*, **97** (2), 233–43.

Jivraj, S. (2012), 'How has ethnic diversity grown 1991–2001–2011?', *Dynamics of Diversity: Evidence from the 2011 Census Series*, Manchester: Centre on Dynamics of Ethnicity (CoDE), University of Manchester, accessed 12 June 2016 at www.ethnicity.ac.uk/medialibrary/briefings/dynamicsofdiversity/how-has-ethnic-diversity-grown-1991-2001-2011.pdf.

Kennedy, S. (2015), 'Measures to limit migrants' access to benefits', *Briefing Paper*, 06889, London: House of Commons Library, accessed 21 February 2016 at http://researchbriefings.files.parliament.uk/documents/SN06889/SN06889.pdf.

King, R. and N. Ribas-Mateos (2002), 'Towards a diversity of migratory types and contexts in Southern Europe', *Studi Emigrazione/International Journal of Migration Studies*, **XXXIX** (145), 5–25.

Local Government Association (2013), 'No more cuts councils tell Chancellor ahead of Autumn statement – LGA press release 5 November 2013', Local Government Association, accessed 12 April 2014 at http://www.local.gov.uk/media-releases/-/journal_content/56/10180/5636691/NEWS.

Mantovan, C. (2007), *Immigrazione e cittadinanza. Auto-organizzazione e partecipazione dei migranti in Italia*, Milan: F. Angeli.

Martinelli, F. (2012), 'Social innovation or social exclusion? Innovating social services in the context of a retrenching welfare state', in H.-W. Franz, J. Hochgerner and J. Howaldt (eds), *Challenge Social Innovation. Potentials for Business, Social Entrepreneurship, Welfare and Civil Society*, Berlin: Springer, pp. 169–80.

Mas Giralt, R. (2014), 'Access to social protection for Latin American migrants with EU citizenship and their families in London: the exclusionary dynamics of migration and welfare policy change in the UK post-2008', unpublished paper presented at the COST Action IS1102 Workshop, University of Tampere, Tampere, 2–6 June.

Migration Yorkshire (2015), 'Strategic Migration Group [SMG]', Leeds: Migration Yorkshire, accessed 14 April 2016 at http://www.migrationyorkshire.org.uk/?page=strategicmigrationgroup.

Mingione, T. and S. Vicari (2015), 'Politiche urbane e innovazione sociale', in A. Calafati (ed.), *Città tra sviluppo e declino: un'agenda urbana per l'Italia*, Rome: Donzelli, pp. 97–108.

National Health Service (2013), 'The NHS structure explained', *NHS Choices*, accessed 12 April 2014 at http://www.nhs.uk/NHSEngland/thenhs/about/Pages/nhsstructure.aspx.

Office for National Statistics (2013), 'Immigration patterns of non-UK born populations in England and Wales in 2011', London: Office for National Statistics, accessed 11 October 2015 at www.ons.gov.uk.

Pugliese, E. (2002), *L'Italia tra migrazioni internazionali e migrazioni interne*, Bologna: Il Mulino.

Pugliese, E. (ed.) (2013), *Immigrazione e diritti violati. I lavoratori immigrati nell'agricoltura del mezzogiorno*, Rome: Ediesse.

Ricketts, A. (2016), 'Government to introduce new clause preventing the use of grant funding for lobbying', *Third Sector*, accessed 8 April 2016 at http://www.thirdsector.co.uk/government-introduce-new-clause-preventing-use-grant-funding-lobbying/policy-and-politics/article/1382553.

Sainsbury, D. (2006), 'Immigrants' social rights in comparative perspective: welfare regimes, forms in immigration and immigration policy regimes', *Journal of European Social Policy*, **16** (3), 229–44.

Sainsbury, D. (2012), *Welfare States and Immigrant Rights: The Politics of Inclusion and Exclusion*, Oxford: Oxford University Press.

Sarlo, A. (2015), 'L'immigrazione nella Calabria dall'economia fragile', in M. Balbo (ed.), *Migrazioni e piccoli comuni*, Milan: F. Angeli.

Sarlo, A. and F. Martinelli (2016), 'Housing and the social inclusion of immigrants in Calabria. The case of Riace and the "Dorsal of hospitality"', *COST Action IS1102 Working Papers*, no. 13, accessed 12 June 2016 at http://www.cost-is1102-cohesion.unirc.it/docs/working-papers/wg2.italy-calabria-housing-and-social-inclusion-immigrants-sarlo-and-martinelli.pdf.

Sarlo, A., F. Martinelli and M. Imperio (2014), *Immigrazione e politiche di inclusione in Calabria*, Venice: Cattedra Unesco SSIIM – Università Iuav di Venezia, accessed 12 June 2016 at http://www.unescochair-iuav.it/blog/rapporti-di-ricerca/.

Scholten, P. (2014), 'The multilevel dynamics of migrant integration policies in unitary states: the Netherlands and the United Kingdom', in E. Hepburn and R. Zapata-Barrero (eds), *The Politics of Migration in Multilevel States: Governance and Political Parties*, Basingstoke, UK and New York, USA: Palgrave Macmillan, pp. 150–74.

Semprebon, M. (2014), *Le politiche di inclusione degli immigrati in Lombardia: tra discorsi escludenti, ordinanze securitarie e sperimentazioni innovative*, Venice: Cattedra Unesco SSIIM – Università Iuav di Venezia, accessed 12 June 2016 at http://www.unescochair-iuav.it/blog/rapporti-di-ricerca/.

Spencer, S. (2011a), *The Migration Debate*, Bristol: Policy Press.

Spencer, S. (2011b), *Policy Primer: Integration*, Oxford: Centre on Migration, Policy and Society.

The Migration Observatory (2014), 'Commentary. Costs and "benefits": benefits tourism, what does it mean?', Oxford: COMPAS, accessed 12 May 2014 at http://www.migrationobservatory.ox.ac.uk/commentary/costs-and-%E2%80%98benefits%E2%80%99-benefits-tourism-what-does-it-mean.

Tonkiss, K. (2013), 'Migration and integration are now policy challenges too far for many local authorities', Migrants' Rights Network, Migration Pulse blog, 27 September, accessed 16 May 2016 at http://www.migrantsrights.org.uk/migration-pulse/2013/migration-and-integration-are-now-policy-challenges-too-far-many-local-authorit.

Vertovec, S. (2007), 'Super-diversity and its implications', *Ethnic and Racial Studies*, **30** (6), 1024–54.

Ware, P. (2013), '*Very Small, Very Quiet, a Whisper . . .*' – *Black and Minority*

*Ethnic Groups: Voice and Influence*, Birmingham: Third Sector Research Centre.

Wilkinson, M. and G. Craig (2011), 'Wilful negligence: migration policy, migrants' work and the absence of social protection in the UK', in E. Carmel, A. Cerami and T. Papadopoulos (eds), *Migration and Welfare in the New Europe*, Bristol: Policy Press, pp. 177–94.

Zincone, G. (ed.) (2000), *Primo rapporto sull'integrazione degli immigrati in Italia*, Commissione per le Politiche di Integrazione degli Immigrati, Bologna: Il Mulino.

Zincone, G. (2009), *Immigrazione: segnali di integrazione. Sanità, scuola e casa*, Bologna: Il Mulino.

Zincone, G. and L. Di Gregorio (2002), 'Il processo delle politiche di immigrazione in Italia: uno schema interpretativo integrato', *Stato e Mercato*, no. 3, 433–66.

# 16. Housing and neighbourhood: basic needs, governance and social innovation

**Peter Brokking, Marisol García, Dina Vaiou and Serena Vicari Haddock**

## INTRODUCTION

The financial crisis that began in 2008 has profoundly reorganised existing welfare state trajectories, affecting social services provision all over Europe (Martinelli, Chapter 1, in this volume). Earlier retrenchment of the State from public provision of social services and investment in public infrastructures had already modified these trajectories, also in countries not (or less) affected by the crisis. In this context, the provision of, and access to, housing is not an exception. This chapter focuses on initiatives and practices to meet needs in the area of housing and neighbourhood services that emerged from the restructuring of welfare systems and the recent, ongoing financial crisis.

There is widespread agreement among contemporary scholars that housing and neighbourhoods are under particular stress as the logic of the market becomes increasingly pervasive and that the area of need has grown, affecting different social groups who are bearing the brunt of the crisis. Following Cassiers and Kesteloot (2012), there are four processes that have brought about the expansion of unmet social needs. First, there is *globalisation*, which directed investment toward the economic competitiveness of cities and territories in preference to the welfare of their citizens. Secondly, there is *financialisation*, the process of global expansion of credit, which has brought about increasing investment in real estate and an unprecedented rise in housing prices. These two processes have driven the transformation of low-cost housing areas into primary real estate developments and have induced the growth of speculative housing markets. The third process is *flexibilisation* of the labour market, which has led to unstable and unprotected work arrangements, temporary employment, involuntary part-time work and low-paid employment and thus to an increase in numbers of the working poor as well as high levels of unemployment. Finally, there is *restructuring of the State* and the privatisation of public services, which has engendered further dynamics of exclusion and deprivation. To these four processes, we add two demographic factors (see Martinelli, Chapter 1). First, migration involving increasing numbers of migrants seeking safety and new opportunities, who, faced with discrimination and potential exclusion, give rise to a differentiated demand for social assistance and housing. The second demographic factor is the ageing population, which results in large groups of older people who, with reduced pensions and assets in the form of housing property, are potentially less able to buy health and assistance services in the market.

The four processes and the demographic factors manifest the intimate relationship between housing and welfare services, which becomes even more evident when housing is interpreted to be more than a shelter. Housing in a broader perspective is associated with access to basic services such as potable water, sanitation, healthcare and education, as well as protection against forced evictions and natural threats to health and life (Rolnik, 2014). This understanding of housing as a gateway to other rights is based on Lefebvre's notion of the city as *oeuvre*, which refers to the right to belong to and the right to co-produce urban spaces (Lefebvre, 1968). Although Lefebvre's ideas are in contrast with the neoliberal developments of recent decades, his understanding of the inclusive city and citizenship are still pertinent for today's policy-making. Moreover, the perception that housing and neighbourhoods are interlinked entities in the welfare state remains topical, as local amenities of neighbourhoods, for example schools and health services, contribute to the capitalised value of homes in the housing market (Cheshire and Sheppard, 2004).

The reforms of welfare and housing systems in the last two decades have changed the relation between housing and the welfare state. The recent financial and economic crisis accentuated housing privatisation and marketisation in different European countries. The impacts are evident in a large number of major European cities, which have experienced severe housing crises, with the result that housing access and affordability have become increasingly difficult for large groups of people. The pending resettlement of large numbers of refugees in the EU is adding new pressure to rethink the housing question as part of the welfare of citizens. The housing emergency includes not only highly visible phenomena like the increase in homelessness and in the squatting component of urban movements, but also manifests itself in other developments such as the rise in the number of house evictions or the re-entry of young people into their parents' home. Moreover, the crisis is affecting sections of society previously not regarded as 'vulnerable'. This includes mainly, but not only, the young and the sectors of the middle classes affected by unemployment and underemployment. Under the pressure of fiscal austerity, the reduction and privatisation of public services such as social assistance, education and community amenities, cities are proving unable to respond to social needs. To counter these deficiencies, a wide range of bottom-up initiatives has emerged to cope with urgent housing needs and the lack of public support to people in need at different geographical scales, including the local/neighbourhood level. These socially innovative practices fill, to some extent, the gaps in neighbourhoods of cities where the welfare state no longer provides services related to, for example, housing, education and health care or where households can no longer afford to buy these services from private service providers.

The present chapter offers an analysis of these developments. First, we examine the role of housing provision and production as a key redistributive domain of traditional welfare states, highlighting the trends towards marketisation and stressing the importance of initiatives to cope with what has been denounced globally as a 'housing emergency'. Here we also examine the rise of the neighbourhood as a relevant scale of analysis in the current circumstances. Second, we discuss social innovation as an umbrella theoretical reference under which a wealth of responses to the retrenchment of the State and the resulting reduction in the provision of public services and urban amenities has been produced. Here we make use of cases taken from the COST Action IS1102 *SO.S. COHESION – Social services, welfare states and places*, as illustrations of our argument, rather than as 'background material' upon which to make conceptual claims. The cases address socially innovative responses from civil society or grassroots movements to particular unmet needs and exclusionary dynamics in housing and neighbourhood services in cities.[1] Third, in the concluding section, we summarise our main points and propose a new take on them, underlining the challenges that socially innovative practices in the areas of housing and neighbourhood present for governance at various levels of policy-making.

## 1.  COPING WITH UNMET NEEDS AT TIMES OF CRISIS: HOUSING AND NEIGHBOURHOOD

The financial and economic crisis of 2008 follows a long process of restructuring and withdrawal of the State from public provision of social services, social housing and investment in public infrastructures. The shrinking of social housing and/or publicly protected housing has led to increasingly unmet housing needs, to ever larger numbers of families on waiting lists and often to more socially excluded people and deprived and dilapidated neighbourhoods (CECODHAS, 2012). In these dire conditions, further aggravated by austerity policies, many initiatives have sprung up in different places to cope with unmet needs and to contribute to the development of social inclusion mechanisms (Maloutas and Malouta, 2004; Witten et al., 2003). Such initiatives have functioned as 'seedbeds of experimentation and social innovation' (Rodriguez, 2009, p. 86), putting forward an extraordinary variety of socially innovative practices to meet housing needs and enhancing patterns of inclusion and belonging in which the neighbourhood has acquired a renewed importance. This section will address both issues, the growth of precarious housing conditions and the emergence of local solidarity initiatives, in turn.

**Understanding the Housing Question Today**

The right to housing, recognised in international documents, for example the UN Declaration of human rights and the European social charter, has meant for several decades that housing was considered an area for welfare policy (Bengtsson, 2001). This justified the need for state intervention in welfare societies to secure the provision of housing to households with lesser means, for example through systems for social housing. However, since the 1990s an increasing share of households acquire their housing on the market, with only limited government intervention. At the same time, the number of people who have access to social housing is decreasing due to the reduction of public investment in public housing programmes in all European countries except France, Austria and Denmark (García and Vicari Haddock, 2016). As a result of the dominance of home ownership and the residualisation of social housing, housing holds an ambiguous and shifting position in the margins of the welfare state (Harloe, 1995).

Transformations in housing systems have been part of a larger restructuring of welfare relations, based on ideas such as individual responsibility and choice which are also embedded in the housing policy discourse (Malpass, 2008). The changes in housing systems have been supported by a process of deregulation and liberalisation, which began in the early 1980s and accelerated in the 1990s. Initially, the measures focused on deregulation of the rental sector designed to stimulate investments (Clapham, 2006), and on changes in housing subsidy systems (Holmqvist and Magnusson Turner, 2014). A further withdrawal of the state took place in the 1990s by privileging owner occupation, for example through 'right to buy' programmes (Doherty, 2004) and the liberalisation of the mortgage market to enhance financial assets for financing home ownership (Rolnik, 2013).

These market-oriented regulatory reforms have contributed to the commodification of urban housing provision (Kadi and Ronald, 2014), in which the logic of the market has become increasingly pervasive. Hence, housing is increasingly considered as a commodity for individual consumption (as first and second residences) but also as capital investment in a context of more or less constant housing price increases. Ultimately, home ownership has become a source to meet income needs in old age, where the owners consume the value of the property through equity release (Doling and Elsinga, 2012). In terms of housing need satisfaction, housing has turned into a conditional right constrained by financial commitments and risks, which has affected the prospects and conditions of urban households. The implications of this transformation vary, as they depend on local economic, political and cultural circumstances and require a detailed understanding of prevailing housing situations. As for home ownership, a significant expansion can be noted among all income groups in almost all EU-15 countries during the last three decades (Norris and Winston, 2012), but aggregate home ownership figures conceal differences among countries. For example, in Southern European countries high home ownership rates are widespread even among lower income groups as a result of strong family support either in cash or in-kind (land or labour). Yet, low-income households have burdensome housing costs and poor housing standards (Norris and Winston, 2012), which means that a certain amount of housing needs remain unmet even within the high percentage of home ownership.

The commodification of urban housing markets is central to an understanding of the marginalisation or exclusion of lower-income groups (Kadi and Ronald, 2014) and the diluted right to decent accommodation and living environments. Urban transformations and, in particular, policies of urban regeneration during the 1990s and 2000s to upgrade deprived neighbourhoods, triggered dynamics of displacement of low-income people, exclusion from newly developed places and the loss of a sense of belonging and identity. This displacement is not the result of individual household preferences, but rather of institutional factors behind these preferences, such as the state of the housing market and public policy (Slater, 2009), which reflect the neo-liberal state transformations towards commodification of urban housing markets.

The commodification of housing in combination with the liberalisation of the mortgage market fuelled housing markets worldwide, which resulted in an upswing of house prices. Increasing prices with diminishing state subsidies place an 'unreasonable burden' on household income (Edgar et al., 2002). In many countries house prices rose rapidly in the early 2000s, but after the financial crisis house prices declined dramatically in many (for example Spain, Denmark, Ireland and the Netherlands), but not all, European countries (Whitehead et al., 2014). This has affected a large number of families, even those that were not in vulnerable circumstances before the crisis. Since then housing affordability has become a major problem in many European cities, especially for young people but also for the unemployed, for some migrants and for the poor. The financial crisis has brought about an increase in arrears on mortgage payments, in mortgage defaults, in the numbers of housing repossessions and in evictions for failing to pay mortgages and monthly rent. To protect households from arrears and foreclosures, governments have adopted stricter mortgage regulations, which ultimately mean that particular groups and areas are excluded from the market for housing mortgage (Zwiers et al., 2016). Housing affordability problems following the financial crisis have resulted in the exclusion of large numbers of households. These exclusionary processes have stronger effects in societies where other features of the welfare state are missing or had historically been minimal. In these societies 'the symbolic and socioeconomic status of the home and its role in an implicit welfare economy has been enhanced' (Ronald, 2012, p. 3). In Southern European countries, for example, housing ownership is a fundamental capital good as well as a family source for inter-generational solidarity. It has been essential to family welfare because of the low level of protection provided by the welfare state, but it gradually becomes a burden when households depend on mortgages they cannot pay back.

The overall vulnerability of individual households has increased as a consequence of the regulatory reforms of the last three decades and the resulting increased reliance on the market, which, in combination with the decrease in the provision of social housing, in effect means that the right to housing is no longer guaranteed in contemporary welfare states. It is a vulnerability which affects not only lower-income groups but also middle-income households who suffer from the consequences of the housing market collapse and the economic recession. Besides losing their homes, these groups risk being excluded from access to basic services, partly as a result of austerity measures that aim to reduce public spending. In response to these developments many movements and (local) initiatives have arisen to cope with increasingly unmet housing needs, thus linking the patterns of access to housing to broader processes of urban restructuring at different scales, including the neighbourhood. One could thus argue that the global crisis of 2008 has contributed to reviving the relevance of the neighbourhood as a spatial scale at which demands left unanswered are expected to find satisfaction.

**Re-discovering the Neighbourhood**

It can be said that the local level, and the neighbourhood as part of it, have recently been 're-discovered' as an analytical and policy scale in many cities. This chapter follows one strand of analysis, which has associated the neighbourhood with innovative approaches to urban restructuring and regeneration and as a privileged locus for social innovation. As Moulaert (2009) explains, at the neighbourhood scale problems of decline and restructuring are more immediately experienced and agents responsible for them more readily identifiable, while it is at this level too that alternatives are constituted, often in the cracks of the system, and become known/shared. Urban neighbourhoods thus emerge as a focus of research on often innovative coping and/or resisting practices and as a place of experimentation with new forms of governance. In many Southern European cities, in particular, solidarity initiatives have sprung up, especially after the 2011 'indignados' movements, with diverse targets, varying actors and outcomes, as an arena for claims to the city and as a set of resources upon which (local) initiatives rely (Vaiou and Kalandides, 2016).

In the post-1989 literature, many urban scholars emphasise the importance of ever broader scales of reference, mobility, speed and time–space compression associated with processes of globalisation (Harvey, 2012). However, the majority of people continue to live 'local lives' in particular places and neighbourhoods with different local geographies and role/s in social cohesion. In these local lives the neighbourhood often functions as a set of resources (Witten et al., 2003), which can be material (for example buildings, public spaces), institutional (for example schools or other welfare services), relational (for example support networks among people in the neighbourhood, 'neighbouring') or immaterial (aspirations, dreams, images, reputation and so on).

The current multi-faceted crisis and the austerity policies implemented as 'remedies' have already severely impacted most of the above resources, for example through cuts in wages and services and reduced maintenance of infrastructures and public spaces. Urban neighbourhoods emerge as an important, though not unique, scale in the process of coping with the crisis, a scale at which alternative bottom-up (or bottom-linked) everyday routines and practices develop. These practices range from mutual assistance to complex solidarity networks and acquire a renewed importance in the present situation, as even minimal acts of reciprocity and mutual support may be crucial for survival and may mobilise processes of inclusion or at least allow residents to benefit from a certain conviviality. They may also lead to important connections and attachments to place, particularly for those residents who spend most of their time at the local setting. It must be emphasised, however, that people's time geographies differ significantly, as do practices and processes for social inclusion.[2]

Solidarity initiatives and alternative ways to access services that have been curtailed or completely cut, including housing, share many of the features that are analysed as social innovation and conceptualised as part of social mobilisation intended to counteract the exclusion of entire social groups and the dismantling of the welfare state while attempting, at the same time, to forge social ties in a fragmented society. In many ways, the actors involved in these practices go beyond common principles of the universalistic welfare state and become directly involved in the production and mutual practices of assistance and services. In these solidarity initiatives, different forms of governance are produced, including complex mixes of formal/institutional involvement and intervention (for example in the domain of social services) with informal 'ways of doing'.[3] Such mixes help to put in context the importance of formal rights along with the significance of informal practices, both of which are closely linked and mobilise mechanisms of inclusion and feelings of belonging (Kalandides and Vaiou, 2012). Such processes resonate with a conception of neighbourhood as changing, open and contingent rather than bounded, permanent and static, as a place constituted by a particular set of social relations which interact in a given location, by movement and contacts which may be local but also extend beyond it (Massey, 2005).

## 2. SOCIAL INNOVATION: HOUSING AND NEIGHBOURHOOD RESPONSES IN TIMES OF AUSTERITY

### Different Shades of Social Innovation

Ongoing restructurings of European welfare states, in both their 'strong' Scandinavian and their 'weaker' Southern European versions (see Martinelli, Chapter 1, in this volume), have resulted in unmet needs and difficulties of access to housing and neighbourhood services, particularly for the most vulnerable groups in European societies. At the same time, these difficulties have contributed to the emergence of alternative projects and bottom-up initiatives, studied as social innovation in a wide-ranging body of literature which has been developing since the early 2000s in many fields and disciplines (for reviews see Klein et al., 2014; Moulaert et al., 2013; Mulgan et al., 2007).

In this section a reading of a number of such initiatives is provided, through the lens of social innovation and particularly its strand concerned with local development. The cases illustrate the main argument of the present chapter, which stresses the societal responses at neighbourhood and city level to the negative effects of the (re-)commodification of housing and the impacts of the financial and economic crisis, which threaten the overall welfare of neighbourhoods. Some are examples of direct responses to the retrenchment of the State as part of the reformation of housing systems and austerity policies, and emerge as micro solutions to immediate needs of vulnerable sectors of the population (the cases of Calabria, Athens, Sweden, Slovakia and Milan). In other instances, they occur as bottom-up movements that contest the effects of privatisation and have a more political orientation in that they pose a challenge to the institutional level (the cases of Barcelona and Vienna). The main differences between the two types of initiatives are the visibility of the actors' innovative actions, their open confrontation with private and public institutions in the public sphere and the level of institutionalisation of the innovative practices.

Our analysis is informed by a specific reading of the concept of social innovation that emphasises three constitutive elements. First, practices are considered socially innovative if they contribute to satisfying basic human needs that remain unmet by the State or the market. Second, satisfaction of these needs occurs thanks to a change taking place in the governance system that steers and regulates the allocation of goods and services meant to satisfy them; third, the change in the governance system is the result of a process of individual and collective empowerment. Therefore, social innovation closely relates to the socio-spatial context and has to be assessed with reference to local social, economic, cultural and political structures.

Our analysis of specific innovative practices concerning housing and neighbourhood services starts with their identification in terms of the specific need they address and the social exclusion dynamics that can be said to produce that need; it then identifies the actors that are mobilised at different institutional levels and examines the extent of re-distribution of material and immaterial resources. We then assess social innovation along two dimensions: the degree of institutionalisation of innovative practices and the value orientation. The process of institutionalisation concerns the mutual recognition between the State and civil society associations and organisations achieving a certain degree of stability; this process induces innovation in public policies and influences public discourse relating to agenda-setting and to the finding of solutions. We analyse innovative practices and policies together, because what is interesting is, above all, the process of bringing new or alternative values into the public sphere, independently of the level of (formal) institutionalisation. The value orientation, which is the foundation of the actors' motivation, the 'fuel', so to speak, of social innovation (Vicari Haddock and Tornaghi, 2013), concerns the degree to which the action is oriented toward progressive social change, that is social justice, equality, democracy and empowerment. This value orientation signals the presence of alternative models vis-à-vis those that privilege the market economy, representative democracy, traditional cultural values, etc.; instead, socially innovative initiatives are centred on non-profit economic activities, the empowerment of people and their direct involvement in decision-making processes, the pursuit of social justice, equal opportunities and gender equality and the appreciation of diversity.

**Examples of Social Innovation Practices**

With regard to practices and services responding to housing needs, we see a somewhat renewed commitment and/or mobilisation for housing rights along with attention focused on excluded populations in housing provision, such as homeless and Roma groups. Our first illustration is the cross-national programme of Housing First, a programme for homeless people that started in the USA, in which some elements of co-production, self-determination and empowerment are present (Tsemberis et al., 2004). Introduced with different levels of institutionalisation in several countries, this policy promotes social inclusion by giving priority to housing access. This policy involves a re-organisation of welfare provision where there is a mutual accommodation between a public responsibility still strongly felt and the opening of the field of social services to not-for-profit providers. Housing First is thus understood as a way of quick re-integration into a completely self-determined but assisted life for a broad group of homeless people.

In Sweden, for example, Housing First has been implemented in a number of municipalities as a possible solution to combat growing homelessness, in the context of the dismantling of the Swedish housing system, the devolution of responsibility to municipalities and the activation of NGOs in the field (CAP Knutagård, 2014). The Housing First project is a research-driven initiative and a response to demand for access to housing for those who cannot afford to rent a place to live temporarily or permanently and do not qualify for institutionalised housing services. As Knutagård and Kristiansen (2013, p. 102) argue, Housing First in Sweden challenges institutional practice within the 'staircase' model, which is a multistage approach where individuals move through a number of steps and where independent living is only for those who finally qualify. Thus, introducing Housing First has involved a breakthrough in the governance of housing for the homeless and people in need of decent and affordable housing. From a governance perspective, the Swedish version of Housing First involves coordination with other social services, although Housing First services do not require compliance with treatment. This case illustrates two processes characteristic of the transformation of welfare systems, with the help of innovative approaches: changing institutional practice in response to unmet needs and the involvement of diverse actors.

Earlier in the chapter we looked closely at the contextual dimension of social innovation. This aspect becomes clearer when looking closely at how specific innovative projects cause changes in governance relations between national and local welfare institutions and civil society groups. A pilot project of Housing First in Vienna shows a strong role of both the municipal government as financing institution and regulator and of Neunerhaus, an organisation born out of a civic movement. The latter runs several emergency accommodations and houses for temporary living and provides social assistance and medical services for homeless people. The co-operation between the local institutions and the civic organisations has enabled a new governance principle to emerge concerning the participation and self-determination of homeless people. It has also promoted debates about housing accessibility criteria for targeted groups as well as a proposal to develop a more coordinated approach among providers of social housing for homeless people. In a national context in which social dwellings represent 23 per cent of the total housing stock, the Vienna case speaks also to the limits of a policy narrowed down to the small target group of the currently homeless while failing to address the structural conditions that increase the risks of becoming homeless. However, this social innovation showed multiple strengths: the empowerment of the target group, the growing public awareness of the structural links between homelessness and dynamics of the housing market and the changes in governance relations towards a more open and deliberative form (Weinzierl et al., 2016).

A contrasting case was found in an Eastern European context. The privatisation of housing has been particularly striking in post-communist countries. In these societies housing as a social right and welfare has been strongly challenged by market forces, resulting in the marginalisation or exclusion of lower-income groups, many of whose members often belong to cultural or ethnic minorities. For example, the proportion of social dwellings in Slovakia has been reduced to less than 10 per cent of the total housing stock. In these circumstances, the emergence of innovative strategies becomes an illustration of what a more generalised policy of social innovation could entail. In Slovakia where the Roma people have been hardest hit by the post-1989 changes and the dismantling of social housing, the project Building Hope, which combined self-construction with a microloan programme, offered the Roma better living conditions by integrating housing issues with other policies related to social empowerment. In order to implement the project, a broad coalition of public and private sector actors was established, which was able to change the perception of the Roma in the community and influence local policy-making processes (Szüdi and Kovácová, 2016). This case is particularly interesting because it illustrates the relevance of political empowerment. As the Roma community got a local mayor to represent them in the small Eastern Slovak municipality of Rankovce he was able to gather local, national and international financial resources and support in order to implement an inclusionary housing programme for the Roma minority. We argue, then, that the social innovation content here is strong, as the project empowers people with new, marketable skills while forging new partnerships in the governance system.

In Southern European countries, where austerity programmes have been implemented forcefully, a variety of responses have appeared as alternative solutions to the exclusionary potential of housing developments. In Italy, where social dwellings have become only 4 per cent of total housing stock, the recent economic crisis has dramatically decreased house affordability, as housing prices for purchase and renting have increased by 100 per cent and 70 per cent respectively in the decade prior to the financial crisis, while income levels have stagnated since 2008. The economic crisis and the growth of unemployment have resulted in the worsening of the situation for foreign immigrants. In this context, the associated and assisted self-building projects Paderno Dugnano (2005–12) and Casalmaggiore (2007–11) in which local residents were directly involved in the construction of the houses with their labour and organisational capacity, lowering housing production costs, implicated both user empowerment and the production of social capital in the process. Self-building projects have also been implemented, with the specific aim of fostering integration between migrants and the local population. The most successful cases are located in the metropolitan area of Milan, where volunteers and/or families built their own houses in their free time/outside working hours. Semprebon and Vicari Haddock (2016) show also the governance constraints in the implementation of otherwise innovative solutions, in line with the current trend of giving civil society and citizens in general more responsibility in the provision of 'active community welfare' (Annette and Mayo, 2010). These and other Italian cases exemplify mixed governance between public institutions (the Lombardy Region, the Province of Milan, municipalities) and local actors. Although the dialogue between civil society actors and the public administration appears fraught with difficulty and thus unable to ensure the sustainability of programmes, the Milan cases show possible choices in a more flexible governance context that can serve as a model for other countries. In general, it can be argued that the social innovation content is quite strong in all cases of self-building projects as they empower people with new, marketable skills and forge new partnerships in the governance system.

In Calabria, in the South of Italy, the emergency landing of asylum seekers starting in the late 1990s triggered renewed attention to unused housing stock as a resource to be exploited for socially innovative forms of responses to housing needs and local development. Among the most interesting instances are the projects by the municipalities of the so-called '*Dorsale dell'ospitalità*' where building-rehabilitation projects to provide accommodation for refugees were integrated into a broader strategy of urban regeneration and re-population of old boroughs, which included the re-modelling of public spaces, the revitalisation of old trades and crafts, the recovery and re-launching of cultural activities, in the context of an alternative tourism model, called 'solidarity tourism'. The hosting of refugees was taken as an opportunity to achieve the more ambitious aim of local redevelopment (CAP Sarlo and Martinelli, 2016).

In the case of Athens, the practices of survival, solidarity and resistance in the city seem ultimately to have reshaped the public sphere during the crisis years. The fields of action range from educational facilities to communal cooking, free clinics and neighbourhood assemblies, exemplifying what community needs and community support involve. Solidarity networks after 2011, such as Myrmigi, are examples of organised citizens operating as welfare providers with material resources collected from other citizens. Another example is the Hellinikon Social Medical Ward and Social Pharmacy (MKIE) network of doctors who provide healthcare on a voluntary basis. The actors involved in these practices are redefining the concept of the public sphere, going beyond political participation to include welfare socialisation. From a governance perspective, these cases show challenging situations for institutional policy implementation and for developing instruments with the input of bottom-up collective action (Vaiou and Kalandides, 2016).

A final example can be taken from specific instances of mobilisation and civic groups' activation. These instances are part of the development and the increasing articulation of movements for emancipation and democratisation opposing traditional and novel forms of oppression and domination (Fraser, 2011). The values of these movements nourish contemporary mobilisation in its multiple forms as well as civil society organisations motivated to work for social change with a progressive and inclusive orientation. With reference to housing issues, there is the example of the Stop evictions campaign and the PAH – *Plataforma d'afectats per la hipoteca* (Platform of mortgage victims) movement in Barcelona in 2009, following the bursting of the housing bubble in Barcelona and other big cities in Spain which left large numbers of households in precarious housing conditions. The socially innovative initiative transformed itself into a social movement and demonstrated organisational capacities that produced a creative bottom-up governance process in sequential stages. After achieving support at the neighbourhood level, it managed to scale up to city, regional, national and European public spheres. The movement reached European institutions, which forced the Spanish government to revise legislation and take policy action (De Weerdt and García, 2016). Partly in response to the PAH's effective campaigns, financial institutions and public institutions modified some governance regulations concerning mortgage payment conditions. The combination of a grassroots protest movement with bottom-linked dialogue and co-operation with local and regional public administrations has proved an effective way to deal with the housing needs of the affected population. Positive outcomes have been the relocation of hundreds of families in social dwellings and new investment in social housing by municipalities in a country where social dwellings accounts for less than 2 per cent of total housing stock. The impact of this case has reached beyond those described previously because of the consequent changes in governance. Actors involved in social innovation carried their mobilisation from the local to the national public sphere and the organisational strategy of the social movement used political confrontation as a resource. This strategy has been instrumental in bringing about changes in governance and in legislative outcomes.

## 3. CONCLUSIONS

In this chapter we have argued that the fundamental needs relating to housing and neighbourhood life have been increasingly unanswered in the last two decades. Particularly since the beginning of the 2008 financial crisis, the imposition of fiscal austerity has reduced the provision of social housing and social benefits to the detriment of the most vulnerable social groups, old and new. At the same time, national responses to increasing social needs have been slow or deficient. Instead, responses to the needs for housing and community services have appeared at the neighbourhood and municipal levels (Moulaert et al., 2013). This means that local governments, in order to cope with housing and neighbourhood needs, have to continue to develop responses to avoid further social exclusion while at the same time negotiating financial arrangements with regional and national governments. Moreover, local governments are increasingly relying on the contribution of other actors such as NGOs, for-profit associations or active citizens organised for specific social needs. As a result, in addition to negotiations developed vertically, new horizontal governance configurations develop among diverse actors attending to housing and neighbourhood service needs. This is especially the case in Southern European countries where social solidarity from below has emerged at the neighbourhood level to complement diminished state investment.

We see in the cases examined in the COST Action that innovative practices in housing and neighbourhood that are able to restore a sense of belonging in cities have been implemented through co-operation between civil society, public institutions and market actors in order to achieve the objectives of social and housing inclusion. Should policy instruments be redesigned according to the emerging scenarios? What can be learned from these cases in terms of policy?

All innovative initiatives and projects examined in the COST Action show that it is the interaction of citizens working with formal and informal organisations, in civil society and in the public sector, which is the most important driver of social innovation. Not all such initiatives, however, are conducive to the development of cohesive and inclusive territorial systems: crucial to the full development of social innovation along all the dimensions outlined in this chapter is the ability of the organisations involved (civil society, resident groups and administrations) themselves to be innovative and creative, to have the flexibility and openness to engage fully with residents and to look beyond existing institutional arrangements to find opportunities for collaboration and co-production. It is up to these organisations to provide both the opportunity for residents to exercise a high degree of control over the future of their housing and neighbourhood and the supportive framework to help them to achieve it. Important as these bottom-up actions may be as responses to social needs, to achieve lasting results they need institutional support. It is arguable from the evidence of the cases presented in this chapter and from other cases (see Moulaert et al., 2013) that a renewed welfare-state framework may provide the best environment for the active participation of the most marginal; short of this there are only processes of 'expulsion' from society (Sassen, 2014). In other words, we maintain that bottom-up action works best when seen as a complement, rather than an alternative, to the welfare state.

Perhaps the first question that needs to be addressed by a renewed welfare state is a conceptual one. There is a case for changing the emphasis in housing debates from a market concept – affordability – to the social concept of accessibility. By calling for housing accessibility, social movements are putting forward (again) the notion of housing as a social right to be guaranteed for every human being (Sendi, 2011). We have seen that the trend towards home ownership and market-based rents implies that access and affordability of housing become difficult for many households. There is an implicit danger of 'blaming the victim' for not being able to afford what the market provides. Even if governments provide programmes to help pay for accommodation under specific circumstances, the notion of help falls short of the notion of a social right.

The second question refers to the limited power of local administrations. The crisis that began in 2008 has shown that in many cities local authorities have increasing difficulties in meeting housing and collective needs. In some countries, local administrations have limited financial capacity to address housing problems, partly because local policy in relation to housing continues to play only a marginal role. As a result, local housing policies are unable to respond to growing social problems, made worse by added responsibilities that are shifted to the local community and the neighbourhoods (Zwiers et al., 2016). The crisis has shown that the central state continues to be the key player regulating the housing market. Governments in countries that were strongly affected by the financial crisis have resorted to stricter mortgage regulations and capital requirements to avoid high-risk loans to households; this may exclude low-income households from buying their own house (Whitehead et al., 2014). This exclusion makes some analysts recommend focusing on social innovation in seeking solutions (Costa et al., 2014).

The third question that requires attention is the neighbourhood as a particular form of non-bounded spatial scale, a place, in the sense of Doreen Massey's formulation, constituted by far-reaching relations, as well as by everyday practices (1994). The neighbourhood is a privileged place of everyday life and an arena for claims to the city, including claims to do with things as 'mundane' as the provision of social services, whose curtailing destabilises processes of social inclusion. Indeed, urban neighbourhoods in many European cities become the medium in struggles for inclusion and belonging (for a discussion, see Kalandides and Vaiou, 2012). From such a perspective, even if social innovation practices originate in or are identified with a particular place/neighbourhood, the links with different spatial scales and levels of governance constitute an essential component of an analytical and policy framework.

## NOTES

1.  It has to be kept in mind that the COST Action IS1102 *SO.S. COHESION* was not a research project with a structured theoretical and methodological framework. Cases are presented in this chapter as examples or illustrations of the trends discussed and of specific, collective ways of meeting social needs.
2.  As examples from crisis-ridden neighbourhoods indicate, it is not uncommon to experience conflicts and aggression on the basis of different forms of 'otherness' (e.g. ethnicity, religion, gender, sexuality). The current refugee crisis in the EU is a bitter example.

3. The PAH movement in Barcelona and in Spain more generally exemplifies, among other things, this complexity (De Weerdt and García, 2016).

# REFERENCES

Annette, J. and M. Mayo (2010), *Taking Part: Active Learning for Active Citizenship, and Beyond*, Leicester: NIACE – The National Institute of Adult Continuing Education.

Bengtsson, B. (2001), 'Housing as a social right: implications for welfare state theory', *Scandinavian Political Studies*, **24** (4), 255–75.

Cassiers, T. and C. Kesteloot (2012), 'Socio-spatial inequalities and social cohesion in European cities', *Urban Studies*, **49** (9), 1909–24.

CECODHAS – European Social Housing Observatory (2012), 'Impact of the crisis and austerity measures on the social housing sector', *CECODHAS Housing Europe's Observatory Research Briefing*, **5** (2), accessed at www.housingeurope.eu/resource-127/impact-of-the-crisis-and-austerity.

Cheshire, P. and S. Sheppard (2004), 'Introduction to feature: the price of access to better neighbourhoods', *The Economic Journal*, **114** (November), F391–F396.

Clapham, D. (2006), 'Housing policy and the discourse of globalization', *International Journal of Housing Policy*, **6** (1), 55–76.

Costa, G., G. Bezovan, P. Palvarini and T. Brandsen (2014), 'Urban housing systems in times of crisis', in C. Ranci, T. Brandsen and S. Sabatinelli (eds), *Social Vulnerability in European Cities: The Role of Local Welfare in Times of Crisis*, London: Palgrave Macmillan, pp. 161–86.

De Weerdt, J. and M. García (2016), 'Housing crisis: the Platform of Mortgage Victims (PAH) movement in Barcelona and innovations in governance', *Journal of Housing and the Built Environment*, **31** (3), 471–93.

Doherty, J. (2004), 'European housing policies: bringing the state back in?', *European Journal of Housing Policy*, **4** (3), 253–60.

Doling, J. and M. Elsinga (2012), 'Housing as income in old age', *International Journal of Housing Policy*, **12** (1), 13–26.

Edgar, W.M., J.M. Doherty and H. Meert (2002), *Access to Housing: Homelessness and Vulnerability in Europe*, Bristol: Policy Press.

Fraser, N. (2011), 'Marketization, social protection, emancipation: towards a neo-Polanyan conception of the capitalist crisis', in C. Calhoun and G. Derluguian (eds), *Business as Usual: The Roots of the Global Financial Meltdown*, New York: New York University Press, pp. 138–59.

García, M. and S. Vicari Haddock (2016), 'Special issue: housing and community needs and social innovation responses in times of crisis', *Journal of Housing and the Built Environment*, **31** (3), 393–407.

Harloe, M. (1995), *The People's Home? Social Rented Housing in Europe and America*, Oxford: Blackwell.

Harvey, D. (2012), *Rebel Cities: From the Right to the City to the Urban Revolution*, London: Verso.

Holmqvist, E. and L. Magnusson Turner (2014), 'Swedish welfare state and housing markets: under economic and political pressure', *Journal of Housing and the Built Environment*, **29** (2), 237–54.

Kadi, J. and R. Ronald (2014), 'Market-based housing reforms and the "right to the city": the variegated experiences of New York, Amsterdam and Tokyo', *International Journal of Housing Policy*, **14** (3), 268–92.

Kalandides, A. and D. Vaiou (2012), '"Ethnic" neighbourhoods? Practices of belonging and claims to the city', *European Urban and Regional Studies*, **19** (3), 254–66.

Klein, J.L., J.L. Laville and F. Moulaert (2014), *L' Innovation Sociale*, Paris: Editions Erès.

Knutagård, M. (2014), 'The moral geography of homelessness', unpublished paper presented at the COST Action IS1102 Workshop, University of Tampere, Tampere, 2–6 June.

Knutagård, M. and A. Kristiansen (2013), 'Not by the book: the emergence and translation of Housing First in Sweden', *European Journal of Homelessness*, **7** (1), 93–115.

Lefebvre, H. (1968), *Le Droit à la Ville*, Paris: Anthropos.

Maloutas, T. and M.P. Malouta (2004), 'The glass menagerie of urban governance and social cohesion: concepts and stakes/concepts as stakes', *International Journal of Urban and Regional Research*, **28** (2), 449–65.

Malpass, P. (2008), 'Housing and the new welfare state: wobbly pillar or cornerstone?', *Housing Studies*, **23** (1), 1–19.

Massey, D. (1994), *Space, Place and Gender*, Oxford: Polity.

Massey, D. (2005), *For Space*, London: Sage.

Moulaert, F. (2009), 'Social innovation: institutionally embedded, territorially (re)produced', in D. MacCallum, F. Moulaert, J. Hillier and S. Vicari Haddock (eds) *Social Innovation and Territorial Development*, Abingdon: Ashgate, pp. 11–24.

Moulaert, F., D. MacCallum, A. Mehmood and A. Hamdouch (eds) (2013), *The International Handbook of Social Innovation. Collective Action, Social Learning and Transdisciplinary Research*, Cheltenham, UK and Northampton, MA, USA: Edward Elgar Publishing.

Mulgan, G., S. Tucker, A. Rushanara and B. Sanders (2007), *Social Innovation: What it is, Why it Matters and How it Can be Accelerated*, Working Paper, Skoll Centre for Social Entrepreneurship, Saïd Business School, Oxford: The Basingstoke Press, accessed at www.sbs.ox.ac.uk/sites/default/files/Skoll_Centre/ Docs/Social%20Innovation%20-%20What%20it%20is,%20why%20it%20matters %20%26%20how%20it%20can%20be%20accelerated.pdf.

Norris, M. and N. Winston (2012), 'Home-ownership, housing regimes and income inequalities in Western Europe', *International Journal of Social Welfare*, **21** (2), 127–38.

Rodriguez, A. (2009), 'Social innovation for neighbourhood revitalization: a case of empowered participation and integrative dynamics in Spain', in D. MacCallum, F. Moulaert, J. Hillier and S. Vicari Haddock (eds), *Social Innovation and Territorial Development*, Abingdon: Ashgate, pp. 81–100.

Rolnik, R. (2013), 'Late neoliberalism: the financialization of homeownership and housing rights', *International Journal of Urban and Regional Research*, **37** (3), 1058–66.

Rolnik, R. (2014), 'Afterword: place, inhabitance and citizenship: the right to housing and the right to the city in the contemporary urban world', *International Journal of Housing Policy*, **14** (3), 293–300.

Ronald, R. (2012), 'Family property wealth and the new welfare state', Houwel

Working Paper Series, Working Paper no. 1, Centre for Urban Studies, University of Amsterdam.

Sarlo, A. and F. Martinelli (2016), 'Housing and the social inclusion of immigrants in Calabria. The case of Riace and the "dorsal of hospitality"', *COST Action IS1102 Working Papers*, no. 13, accessed at http://www.cost-is1102-cohesion. unirc.it/docs/working-papers/wg2.italy-calabria-housing-and-social-inclusion-im migrants-sarlo-and-martinelli.pdf.

Sassen, S. (2014), *Expulsions: Brutality and Complexity in the Global Economy*, Cambridge: Harvard University Press/Belknap.

Semprebon, M. and S. Vicari Haddock (2016), 'Innovative housing practices involving immigrants: the case of self-building in Italy', *Journal of Housing and the Built Environment*, **31** (3), 439–55.

Sendi, R. (2011), 'Housing accessibility versus housing affordability: introducing universal housing care', paper presented at the Enhr Conference, Toulouse.

Slater, T. (2009), 'Missing Marcuse. On gentrification and displacement', *City*, **13** (2–3), 293–311.

Szüdi, G and J. Kovácová (2016), '"Building hope: from a shack to 3E house" – innovative housing approach in the provision of affordable housing for Roma in Slovakia', *Journal of Housing and the Built Environment*, **31** (3), 423–38.

Tsemberis, S., L. Gulcur and M. Nakae (2004), 'Housing First, consumer choice and harm reduction for homeless individuals with a dual diagnosis, *American Journal of Public Health*, no. 94, 651–6.

Vaiou, D. and A. Kalandides (2016), 'Practices of collective action and solidarity: reconfigurations of public space in crisis-ridden Athens – Greece', *Journal of Housing and the Built Environment*, **31** (3), 457–70.

Vicari Haddock, S. and C. Tornaghi (2013), 'A transversal reading of social innovation in European cities', in F. Moulaert, D. MacCallum, A. Mehmood and A. Hamdouch (eds), *The International Handbook on Social Innovation. Collective Action, Social Learning and Transdisciplinary Research*, Cheltenham, UK and Northampton, MA, USA: Edward Elgar Publishing, pp. 264–74.

Weinzierl, C., F. Wukovitsch and A. Novy (2016), 'Housing first in Vienna: a socially innovative initiative to foster social cohesion', *Journal of Housing and the Built Environment*, **31** (3), 409–22.

Whitehead, C., K. Scanlon and J. Lunde (2014), *The Impact of the Financial Crisis in European Housing Systems: A Review*, Stockholm: Swedish Institute for European Policy Studies.

Witten, K., T. McCreanor and R. Kearns (2003), 'The place of neighbourhood in social cohesion: insights from Massey, West Auckland', *Urban Policy and Research*, **21** (4), 321–38.

Zwiers, M., G. Bolt, M. van Ham and R. van Kempen (2016), 'The global financial crisis and neighbourhood decline', *Urban Geography*, **37** (5), 664–84.

PART V

Social Services Disrupted: Challenges and Scenarios

# 17. Challenges and dilemmas in the provision of social services

**Anneli Anttonen**

## INTRODUCTION: THE GROWING IMPORTANCE OF SOCIAL SERVICES

'Social services' are a social policy field with a rapidly growing political and theoretical importance. They belong to a larger family of welfare services comprising care, health, housing, education, employment and personal social services. These services enhance human welfare and the overall well-being of people, but in different ways and through different mechanisms. Some welfare services are universal in the sense that they are designed for all people, such as primary education, and there are no needs tests used. Other services are universal but granted only after an individual assessment of needs, such as healthcare and certain care services for older people. Other social services still are strictly means-tested (Anttonen et al., 2012).

Social services provide immaterial and material resources for citizens to cope with changed life situations, such as becoming disabled or chronically ill, the parent of a child or a family caregiver. They constitute a very heterogeneous cluster of publicly funded and regulated services and benefits that are closely linked to the life-cycle risks people encounter during their life course from the cradle to the grave (Jensen, 2010). Care services for older people are typically needed to cope with frailty or disability in old age. They cover a wide range of functions, from home help to transportation and personal bodily services.

Care services differ from mainstream welfare services – those of universal childcare, education and healthcare services (Bode, in this volume) – in one important dimension: they are often unfocused and many-sided. They might include practical, emotional and physical help. Care services for older people are thus necessarily complex by definition. There is often also a complementarity dimension to be taken into account: a person needing care and help might receive services from municipal providers and informal help from his/her family; such an individual might additionally use his/her own money to purchase help. These different sources of help usually complement each other, but they can also be regarded as substitutes. Formal services have partly become a substitute for families in providing help, but there is also a strong trend in many countries towards re-familiarisation (e.g. Leibetseder et al., in this volume).

Another difference with mainstream welfare services is a lack of universality: social care services for older people are in practice always needs-tested, and often means tests are also used. As a result, access to these services is limited to poor, older people and those whose care needs are very extensive and who have no other available sources of aid.

Diversity and complexity mean that although in this context the notion of social services refers only to publicly funded and regulated services, the producer of the service might vary across policy fields and countries: there are service providers from local/regional/central governments, as well as from civil society associations, voluntary agencies and large and small private for-profit companies. In some countries, caregivers within the household have also become publicly subsidised care providers.

There are a number of reasons why care services for older people in their variety and diversity serve as a very good object to evaluate the development, dynamics and dilemmas of social services in contemporary European welfare states. There also is a need to better understand the main characteristics of social services in contemporary European societies.

In this book, broad attention is paid to trends and changes, transformations and tensions in social service policies and practices. Some chapters paint a broad picture of recent changes in social service landscapes and rationalities (Martinelli, Chapter 1, in this volume; Bode, in this volume), while others concentrate on a more limited aspect of change, for instance de-institutionalisation (Kröger and Bagnato; Kubalčíková et al; Deusdad, Lev et al., in this volume) and marketisation (Anttonen and Karsio, in this volume). This chapter, in turn, approaches social services – with specific reference to care for older people – from three angles. First, social services are discussed as benefits that are linked to 'life-course' welfare, as opposed to 'occupational welfare'. Second, care service provisions for older people are put into perspective with regard to universalism or the lack of it. Third, complexity and complementarity are taken into consideration as attributes that might influence the overall value and status of these services. Finally, conclusions are drawn on the basis of this examination.

# 1. SOCIAL SERVICES, LIFE-COURSE WELFARE AND THE LOW STATUS OF CARE SERVICES FOR OLDER PEOPLE

Social services enhance the human welfare of citizens (residents within one country) irrespective of their position in the labour market. They are needed during the entire life course and are closely linked to life-cycle risks (Jensen, 2010). There are social risks more directly attached to the individual's position in the labour market, such as retirement. These life-cycle risks are typically covered by more or less compulsory social insurance schemes paid for by employers and/or by employees and protected by national or federal legislation. Typically, beneficiaries have clearly defined social rights to occupational welfare benefits that are often earnings-related or income-tested. Life-cycle risks touch however the individual's and/or household's welfare also in cases of maternity, childhood, disability, old age, and other vulnerabilities related, for example, to ethnicity. These risks are something people meet both as insiders and outsiders in their relation to the labour market. Services and benefits attached to life-course welfare are typically covered by tax revenues and are provided by local governments, even in the absence of explicit social rights.

Unrecognised life-cycle risks increase vulnerabilities and might lead to severe neglect in meeting very basic needs, such as nutrition or shelter, and a loss of autonomy. This is currently the case with migrants in many European countries, as even the very basic social needs of many asylum seekers are not presently met. Social services are needed in very different life situations to safeguard a decent standard of living, to integrate people into society and to compensate for losses or shortages in capabilities and resources.

Earlier in history and even today, social services were and are needed by the most vulnerable groups of a society; the historical trend has, however, been towards the generalisation and normalisation (Anttonen et al., 2003; Bode, in this volume) of access to these services. Life-cycle risks involve all people and families, but only a few households have the capacity to arrange or purchase all the aid and help needed for instance in old age on the market if care needs are very extensive and 24-hour care and attendance is required for long periods. This example helps to clarify the universalisation of life-cycle risks. It can be argued that today, vulnerabilities touch the masses instead of just the marginal groups in society.

Although social services have become more 'normal' and they are used by much larger parts of the population than before, there still are hierarchies between different sets of welfare services and between occupational and life-course welfare. In the social policy literature, there is much more attention paid to 'occupational welfare', for instance, pensions and labour protection legislation. However, 'life-course welfare' is becoming more important due to the ageing of societies, prolonged and high youth unemployment, increased poverty among children and huge increases in immigration into Europe. A considerable proportion of people stay outside the (formal) labour market for shorter or longer periods, and not only because they are children or old, disabled or chronically ill. There are benefits of the first tier and benefits of the second tier: 'occupational welfare' tends to have a higher status compared to 'life-course welfare', and mainstream welfare services are more highly valued than most care services. Nonetheless, new polarisations are emerging not only between occupational and life-course benefits, but also within occupational welfare policies, since labour markets have become precarious and unpredictable (Seeleib-Kaiser, 2008). This development could mean that social services will gain a much stronger foothold in Europe. Already now, social risks covering unemployment, poverty, ill-health and old age in Europe add up to roughly 50 per cent of government spending (Hemerijck, 2013, p. 1).

Jensen (2010, p. 404) talks about a 'forgotten half' in the sense that occupational welfare is much more extensively studied compared to social services. The volume of social services has however significantly expanded in the last twenty years in Europe. Between 1990 and 2010 there was a steady increase in family services (Ferragina and Seeleib-Kaiser, 2015). Even after the financial crisis of 2008, spending most particularly on childcare has continued to increase in many European countries, while for instance the Netherlands and Southern and Eastern European countries have seen cuts (Bode, in this volume; Bouget et al., 2015). Expenditure on care for older people is reported to have remained fairly stable over this period after two preceding decades of fairly strong growth (Bouget et al., 2015). However, the situation of care services for older people differs greatly from that for children because the starting point was much lower and the share of the oldest older people has grown rapidly. Therefore, this stability means that on a per capita basis, expenditure may have diminished. Some social services, particularly childcare services, are now regarded by politicians as benefits that are expected to increase human capital in the same way as school and healthcare might do. The 'social investment' turn in welfare theorising and European Union policies has actually helped to recognise the productive and active role of social policies (Jenson, 2011). All this means that social services have gained a stronger foothold in research.

Hemerijck (2013, p. 33), however, argues that although the volume of social services has expanded in Europe, the average commitment to the 'social service state' is still weak. If the status of a social risk or of the service attached to that risk is weak and steady political backing is lacking, social services easily become subject to cuts and austerity policies when resources for welfare spending are reduced. It is often the case – as shown in this book – that care for older people and other social services are at the top of the list when publicly funded services must be cut. In this respect, the notion of the 'forgotten half' or 'forgotten part' of welfare services is true. The status hierarchies are there, despite the overall expansion of social services.

Care-based life-cycle risks are covered very differently in different European countries, and this is most particularly the case with care services for older people. At one end of the spectrum are some Southern and Central-Eastern European countries such as Greece and Poland, where care is understood strictly as a family responsibility. At the other end of the spectrum are the Nordic welfare states and Germany, where care for older people is recognised as a social right of citizens. Ultimately, satisfying the social, medical or cultural needs of citizens by means of social services is always based on the political recognition of the risks people might encounter during their life course. Before a service is made available for individuals, there has to be a political decision about the institutional design through which these services are made accessible and affordable to those needing them.

## 2. UNIVERSALISM IN CARE SERVICE PROVISION

'Universalism' means slightly different things in social services compared to pensions, for instance (Holmlund, 2016). The term refers first of all to inclusion: all are potentially included and all have the right at least to needs assessment. Second, there has to be public funding for service provision and also a public system of regulation and delivery. Third, services should be affordable to all, which means that they have to be subsidised for users by the state or local government. Fourth, the services should be of such a high quality that people in need want to use them.

International comparisons of care service provisions for older people (Anttonen and Sipilä, 1996; Ranci and Pavolini, 2013; Stoy, 2014) reveal that there are surprisingly large national-level differences in the funding, scale, scope and targeting of care services between European countries. The same is true when support for informal care, such as payments to caregivers and recipients, have been compared (Pfau-Effinger and Geissler, 2005). In some countries, for instance in Germany and Austria, there is a national care insurance scheme that covers adults. However, in these countries there are also some conditions that are taken into consideration before benefits are granted. The introduction of care insurance is nonetheless an important step taken in the longer history of the modernisation and universalisation of social services (CAP Bode, 2013).

In Northern European countries, service universalism is more advanced than elsewhere, as argued by Vabø and Szebehely (2012). They suggest that service universalism rests on four pillars: accessibility, affordability, attractiveness and flexibility. They also remind us that universal access to services does not automatically guarantee high rates of uptake. Publicly supported social services should be of a high quality so that people are willing and happy to use these services, otherwise they easily become residual, stigmatising or selective services. This is one reason why raw figures (e.g. coverage rates) do not provide enough information. Residential care services, if arranged in large, hospital-like institutions, might carry the labels of stigma and even shame, while places in small, home-like environments are viewed – at least in principle – as attractive and non-stigmatising for service users (Verbeek et al., 2009). Both quality and quantity matter for the evolution of service universalism.

In most European countries, care services for older people are strictly targeted at those who need them the most and have no other means or resources at their disposal. In nearly all countries, these services are granted only after professional assessment procedures, meaning that a needs test is used. Often a means test is also part of the evaluation process, so that only persons with a low income eventually receive care services. This is the case for instance in Greece or Southern Italy, where public care services for older people have remained residual, means-tested and lean: public home care service provisions there are both insufficient and inadequate, and the recent crises have worsened the situation (CAP Vaiou and Siatitsa, 2013; CAP Bagnato et al., 2014).

Southern European countries have had a strong commitment to the family as the primary provider of care, especially for adults. Even so, the 1990s and early 2000s saw some important steps taken towards more extensive public responsibility. In Spain, new social service legislation that could have paved the way towards a Nordic kind of service model was passed in 2006, but due to the 2008 crisis, the reforms were not implemented as planned (CAP Deusdad, 2013). In Greece and Southern Italy, the family model had already entered into crisis in the 1990s, but care remained individualised and within the family sphere due to the availability of informal migrant care workers that families could turn to (CAP Vaiou and Siatitsa, 2013; CAP Bagnato et al., 2014). This again has been a barrier to the development of public services – and vice versa: if there are services for only the most vulnerable and poor people, families are forced to find non-state-based solutions (CAP Pace and Bezzina, 2012). Thus, although care services for older people have become more extensive in the last thirty years, contradictory developments have also taken place. The differences between countries are still extensive, which somehow reflects the ambiguous and unstable status of social (care) services.

These examples indicate that while in some countries the development of care services is characterised by increasing universalisation, in some others universalism is still a very weak principle and a distant goal. However, the Nordic care model is also going through some major reorganisations due to the intensive marketisation of service provision (Anttonen and Karsio, in this volume), which has also framed and shaped the restructuring of social services in the United Kingdom (CAP Yeandle, 2014). Some countries that had a strong commitment to family care twenty years ago (Anttonen and Sipilä, 1996) have not redefined this commitment, but there are exceptions. Both some Southern European and post-socialist Central and Eastern European countries have only recently passed social service legislation similar to other European countries. Consequently, these countries are only now taking major steps towards some level of normalisation in their social service systems. A good example in the latter group is the Czech Republic (CAP Kubalčíková and Havlíková, 2013).

Care services at best should reduce the differences in meeting life-cycle risks, irrespective of social class, gender and place of residence. Although legally guaranteed or universal access to services is crucial in social service development, this does not automatically lead to high rates of uptake: services should be of high quality and free-of-charge or strongly subsidised so that everyone can and will want to use them. In some countries, rising service fees and new types of co-funding mechanisms have weakened universalism, despite equal access and assessment. If services can be purchased out of the citizen's own pocket and reimbursed via tax deductions, there is not necessarily an assessment taking place. Thus, people with better economic resources have access to subsidised services even if they are not entitled to municipally governed services. This is the case, for example, in Finland and Sweden. By contrast, low-income households do not benefit from tax deductions, and must thus turn to informal networks if the services provided by formal provision do not meet their needs.

Universalism can be weakened in many different ways. If subsidised service fees are too high for users, universalism starts to lose its significance as a mechanism for the redistribution of collective resources, and exits from the public service system increase. Universalism is not a stand-alone principle but it needs to be protected by other principles such as sufficient funding and quality control (Anttonen et al., 2012). When service systems start to differentiate and there are new mechanisms emerging alongside the old ones, it might become difficult to maintain universalism. There are some signs that marketisation weakens the principle of universalism

(Béland et al., 2014). In this respect, European countries might be coming together in a sort of 'downward convergence' (see the concluding chapter by Martinelli, in this volume).

## 3.  COMPLEXITY AND COMPLEMENTARITY: STRENGTH AND WEAKNESS

Life-course welfare benefits such as social services influence people's lives and choices in many ways and have manifold consequences. Childcare services, which might be educational or social by definition, exemplify this multiplicity very well. The ability of women to enter the labour market depends on the availability of care services, be they formal or informal, publicly or privately produced. Access to these services makes it possible for women to make very important life-course choices, promotes gender equality and provides children opportunities for learning and socialising. The same applies to care services for older people. They are important for working-age adults, most particularly working women, but they also make it possible for older people to continue independent living at home instead of moving into institutions or relying on their partners or family members when needing care. Services also create new jobs, both well-paid and low-paid, primarily for women and immigrants – this again has many consequences for the overall economy and the employment rate (see Martinelli, Chapter 19, in this volume). To sum up, within democracy social services encourage 'human development, not least in the capacity for exercising self-determination, moral autonomy, and responsibility for one's choices' (Dahl, 1989, p. 311).

While most social services relate to life-cycle risks, they should be defined in a broad and flexible way that takes into account the complexity of needs when we talk about care. *Complexity* means that there is a large *variety of needs* to be met: some people need house cleaning and help with personal hygiene once a week, while others need daily help in using the toilet and getting out of bed; there are tasks related to mobility, to eating and to the basic administration of medicines. This is a major challenge to service institutions and easily leads to differentiation. One option is to start from the ground up – to look at individuals and what they need. If we start from people and everyday life situations, it is not possible to draw strict demarcation lines between health and social services or between personal care and housing chores, as is increasingly done due to the profession-alisation, specialisation and fragmentation of service systems (to achieve greater cost efficiency and effectiveness).

The *complementarity* argument refers to a slightly different aspect.

There are usually strong *interdependencies*, for instance between informal and formal care, unpaid and paid care, municipal and voluntary work, and so on. Social services often function as mechanisms that foster interdependencies between social policy systems, different welfare agencies and sectors, and make it possible for people to obtain different sources of help and to move between them in a flexible way. This kind of plasticity should be taken as a major strength of care and other social services. There is a need for social policy measures and mechanisms that *integrate separate policy fields* and everyday sectors and combine different 'capitals' to be mobilised in meeting life-course risks. To some extent this is self-evident: parents take care of children part of the time, even though children are in organised daycare. Partners and spouses still have a more or less significant responsibility for caring activities, even if there are services provided at home for the person who needs care. There is, however, a big difference if these intersections are understood as complementary instead of *substituting* each other (see 'policy options' by Martinelli, Chapter 19, in this volume).

Complexity and complementarity are features that make social services vulnerable in political terms and the object of continuous redefinitions, rescaling and cuts. As already stated, care services for older people are often the first targets of cuts. The diminishing of these services can be done through tightening access criteria (to reduce coverage rates), increasing co-payments and user fees (to lower costs) or lowering the quality of service (to accelerate exit or non-use). As long as the overall status of social services is much weaker than the status of mainstream welfare services like schools and hospitals, they remain at the margin of social policies. Flexibility, plasticity and the everydayness of social services – however important they are as value markers – can easily be turned against these services. Politicians often use the language of the subsidiarity and exchangeability of social service functions when 'justifying their lower status' among welfare services. The status also remains low because some elements of care services can be produced by households: cleaning, food preparation, shopping and socialising. Decision-makers readily think that these functions belong to the sphere of relatives or charities and not public authorities.

Social services should thus be defined as broadly as possible to bring unity and integration to the diversity of meeting people's care needs. Social services need to remain somewhat unspecified and flexible in the same way that our daily lives are a little chaotic. There are highly professionalised and specialised segments of social services, for instance, services for disabled people or the young unemployed. But despite this specialisation, it is important to underline the 'integrative' dimension of service provision. This relates to the complementary role of social policy functions in responding to life-course risks. Unemployment benefits are necessary for daily living, but they do not get a person back into work or offer a decent life. Pensions may increase the independence of older people if their level is high enough, but they do not guarantee that care needs are met.

# 4.  CONCLUSIONS

This book provides ample evidence for the argument that social services are a social policy field with a growing academic and political importance. It also raises many important questions about how the social service system should be developed further, what can be learned from the experiences of other countries, and what the main similarities and differences are in social service provision. It is extremely important to know where we come from, where we are now and where we are possibly heading. The main aim of this chapter was to look at some common features typical of social (care) services, on the basis of the very rich empirical evidence gathered in the course of the COST Action IS1102 *SO.S. COHESION – Social services, welfare states and places*, with particular attention to services for older people.

Care services are a fairly recent concept, referring to such personal social services that aim at meeting care needs that are most extensive at the beginning and at the end of an individual's life course (Anttonen and Zechner, 2011). The ageing populations in the developed world have brought care services for older people to the fore in social research and social politics. The overall developments of modernisation and individualisation have accelerated the socialisation of care. The entry of women into paid labour has more or less radically changed the norm that families should bear the main responsibility for caring for older people. Indeed, the degree of universality of care services is a good indicator of both gender equality and strength of commitment to the social service state in different countries.

Our main conclusions are that social services are closely related to life-cycle risks. We can expect that 'life-course welfare' will become increasingly important due to the ageing of societies and other transformations, such as extensive youth unemployment, the social investment turn in social policies and the increase in social service research and knowledge. To some extent, it is possible to agree that 'social services' currently still lie at the margin of welfare state research, but they are moving towards the centre. Social service systems have followed some general trends in their development, but they also are rooted more or less deeply in specific national histories and circumstances. Thus, we cannot underestimate the diversity of social service systems, the different degree to which formal social services are accessible and affordable for citizens in different countries or the amount of choice that people can exercise in opting in or out of publicly funded service systems or informal dependencies. There are different regimes or models that seem to be fairly path-dependent: (1) the family-centric model in Southern and partly also in Eastern European countries; (2) the marketised welfare mix model in the UK; (3) the social insurance model of Germany and Austria; and (4) the public service model in the Nordic countries. These models can still be identified, but there is also a blurring of boundaries (see Martinelli, Chapter 19, in this volume).

Care services for older people are rarely universal entitlements when it comes to the coverage, access and funding of these benefits. This is connected to the fact that care services are not focused strictly on health or housing, for instance, but the range is very broad. Therefore, these services and their outcomes are necessarily to some extent multi-positioned. This explains the complexity and complementarity of these services. They are closely related to other welfare services and are thus 'integrative' by nature. Complementarity means that caring is often based on multiple sources of help and this should be a strength, but it is also a weakness, as complementarity easily turns into substitution, whereby families must take on more responsibility when services are curtailed. In conclusion, social services form a very interesting object of research: their specificities represent a strength, but also a major weakness. This dilemma cannot easily be solved until the ambiguity of caring situations is unravelled.

# REFERENCES

Anttonen, A. and J. Sipilä (1996), 'European social care services: is it possible to identify models?', *European Journal of Social Policy*, **6** (2), 87–100.

Anttonen, A. and M. Zechner (2011), 'Theorising care and care work', in B. Pfau-Effinger and T. Rostgaard (eds), *Care, Work and Welfare in Europe*, Basingstoke: Palgrave Macmillan, pp. 15–34.

Anttonen, A., J. Baldock and J. Sipilä (eds) (2003), *The Young, the Old and the State. Social Care in Five Industrial Nations*, Cheltenham, UK and Northampton, MA, USA: Edward Elgar Publishing.

Anttonen, A., L. Häikiö and K. Stefánsson (eds) (2012), *Welfare State, Universalism and Diversity*, Cheltenham, UK and Northampton, MA, USA: Edward Elgar Publishing.

Anttonen, A., L. Häikiö, K. Stefánsson and J. Sipilä (2012), 'Universalism and the challenge of diversity', in A. Anttonen, L. Häikiö and K. Stefánsson (eds), *Welfare State, Universalism and Diversity*, Cheltenham, UK and Northampton, MA, USA: Edward Elgar Publishing, pp. 1–15.

Bagnato, A., S. Barillà and F. Martinelli (2014), 'The public supply of care for older people in Reggio Calabria. The impact of the crisis on a long-standing deficit', presentation at the COST Action IS1102 Workshop, Ekonomickà Univerzita, Bratislava, 3–7 November.

Béland, D., P. Blomqvist, J. Goul Andersen, J. Palme and A. Waddan (2014), 'The universal decline of universality? Social policy change in Canada, Denmark, Sweden and the UK', *Social Policy & Administration*, **48** (7), 739–56.

Bode, I. (2013), 'The changing governance of domiciliary elderly care in Germany', unpublished paper presented at the COST Action IS1102 Workshop, Dunarea de Jos University, Galati, 5–8 November.

Bouget, D., H. Frazer, E. Marlier, S. Sabato and B. Vanhercke (2015), *Social Investment in Europe. A Study of National Policies*, Brussels: European Commission.

Dahl, R. (1989), *Democracy and its Critics*, New Haven: Yale University Press.

Deusdad, B. (2013), 'Regulatory trajectory and current organisational framework of social services and social care', *COST Action IS1102 Working Papers*, no. 1, accessed at http://www.cost-is1102-cohesion.unirc.it/docs/working-papers/wg1.spain-catalonia-social-services-b.deusdad.pdf.

Ferragina, E. and M. Seeleib-Kaiser (2015), 'Determinants of a silent (r)evolution: understanding the expansion of family policy in rich OECD countries', *Social Politics*, **22** (1), 1–37.

Hemerijck, A. (2013), *Changing Welfare States*, Oxford: Oxford University Press.

Holmlund, P. (2016), 'NPM I välfärdsstaten: hotas universalism?', *Statsvetenskpalig Tidskrift*, **111** (1), 39–67.

Jensen, C. (2010), 'The forgotten half: analysing the politics of welfare services', *International Journal of Social Welfare*, **20** (4), 404–12.

Jenson, J. (2011), 'Diffusing ideas for after neoliberalism. The social investment perspective in Europe and Latin America', *Global Social Policy*, **10** (1), 59–84.

Kubalčíková, K. and J. Havlíková (2013), 'The current development of social services in the care of the older people: deinstitutionalization and/or marketization?', unpublished paper presented at the COST Action IS1102 Workshop, Dunarea de Jos University, Galati, 5–8 November.

Pace, C. and D. Bezzina (2012), 'Trends in the provision and financing of long term care in residence and in the community in Malta for elderly, persons with mental health problems and with disability: a case study and a theoretical exploration', unpublished paper presented at the COST Action IS1102 Workshop, Rovira i Virgili University, Tarragona, 17–19 October.

Pfau-Effinger, B. and B. Geissler (eds) (2005), *Care and Social Integration in European Societies*, Bristol: Policy Press.

Ranci, C. and E. Pavolini (eds) (2013), *Reforms in Long-Term Care Policies in Europe. Investigating Institutional Change and Social Impacts*, New York: Springer.

Seeleib-Kaiser, M. (ed.) (2008), *Welfare State Transformations. Comparative Perspective*, Basingstoke: Palgrave Macmillan.

Stoy, V. (2014), 'Worlds of welfare services: from discovery to exploration', *Social Policy & Administration*, **48** (3), 343–60.

Vabø, M. and M. Szebehely (2012), 'A caring state for all older people', in A. Anttonen, L. Häikiö and K. Stefansson (eds), *Welfare State, Universalism and Diversity*, Cheltenham, UK and Northampton, MA, USA: Edward Elgar Publishing, pp. 121–43.

Vaiou, D. and D. Siatitsa (2013), 'Current organisational framework of elderly care services', *COST Action IS1102 Working Papers*, no. 2, accessed at http://www.cost-is1102-cohesion.unirc.it/docs/working-papers/wg1.greece-care-for-older-peo ple-d.vaiou-and-d.siatitsa.pdf.

Verbeek, H., E. van Rossum, S.M.G. Zwakhalen, G.I.J.M. Kempen and J.P.H. Hamers (2009), 'Small, homelike care environments for older people with dementia: a literature review', *International Psychogeriatrics*, **21** (2), 252–64.

Yeandle, S. (2014), 'Reconfiguring services for older people living at home in Leeds, UK: how have services changed?', unpublished paper presented at the COST Action IS1102 Workshop, University of Tampere, Tampere, 2–6 June; now published as S. Yeandle (2016), 'From provider to enabler of care? Reconfiguring local authority support for older people and carers in Leeds, 2008 to 2013', *Journal of Social Service Research*, **42** (2), 218–32.

# 18. The role of the state in the development of social services

**Margitta Mätzke**

## INTRODUCTION

This book has explored the current situation and ongoing developments in a number of publicly funded social service fields and in several European countries, regions and cities. Discursively an element of social investment strategies (see the opening chapters by Martinelli and by Gómez-Barroso et al., in this volume), social services are gaining importance, as social needs are multiplying and resources for informal family care are becoming increasingly scarce. Austerity policies in the large cash transfer schemes of many European welfare states add to the burden that has to be shouldered by social services (Sirovátka, 2016). With their highly individualised in-kind benefits, social services often address needs that have fallen through the cracks of more mainstream, often insurance-based cash transfer schemes (Spicker, 2013; Sachße, 2011). At the same time, much of that enhanced role is wishful thinking more than reality (see Bode, in this volume), as many public social services are under siege. While called on to respond to growing and increasingly diverse needs, they have to do so under conditions of more precarious resource bases and working conditions.

Together the chapters in this volume have presented a vivid picture of the changing landscape of social services in Europe. The analyses are based on case studies that were shared in the course of the COST Action IS1102 *SO.S. COHESION – Social services, welfare states and places.* They compare and synthesise the insights gained from these case studies from a variety of different substantive angles and theoretical perspectives. The emerging picture is thus necessarily variegated – a mosaic of images and interpretations, based on observations from a variety of different social service fields, countries, initiatives, actors involved in social service provision, or institutional characteristics of social service infrastructures.

Nonetheless, a shared theme has emerged from this mosaic. All chapters in this volume are aware of significant changes in the role of the public sector in social services, and they are all keenly attentive to the potential drawbacks and problematic aspects of the changing outlook of public policy engagement. This chapter seeks to understand the underlying commitments and building blocks of this critical assessment. To do so, it will first highlight the dominant tendency and policy development as it was observed in many of the preceding chapters. It will then think through the implications of this trend for the interpretation of the overall character of social services and pinpoint the criteria motivating the problematising and wary outlook on the changing social service landscape that is often expressed throughout the book. The concluding section revisits the question of how to think about public sector involvement in social services and points out how important it is to consider the details of implementation and the specific institutional settings and contextual factors of social service design when appraising the role of the state in social services.

## 1. SOCIAL SERVICE DEVELOPMENT DESCRIBED: A SHARED THEME WITH VARIED MANIFESTATIONS

As highlighted above, this book has embraced diversity: the chapters have different theoretical angles and thematic perspectives, and they cover a range of different social service fields and national contexts. As in many institutionally complex settings, path dependence is inherent in the trajectories (Pierson, 2000), so that diverse observations about policy developments come as no surprise. Notwithstanding this variety, however, the chapters have identified a main trend that is shared across contexts and thematic fields, and this is a tendency of central governments to turn their back on their traditional commitments to providing a social service infrastructure for all citizens in need. In fact, universal access to social services has been a *desideratum* rather than a reality in most countries, but access to publicly provided social care for those in need has been widely shared as a policy goal and moral ambition. It has inspired institutional development, since social services, with their focus on individualised needs at given points in people's life course, have been considered a catalyst of social integration and by that token an aspect of social citizenship in many countries and with regard to many areas of social care. It is this *social citizenship rights-based commitment to public social services* that governments in Western democracies are abandoning to a certain extent.

There is no universal tendency toward 'state withdrawal' from social policy, however. Changes in the role of the state vary in pace and form; there are no 'strong' or 'weak' states in terms of their role as welfare producers, only different *manifestations* of welfare state interventionism, which have evolved over time (Mätzke, 2011). We are not witnessing the 'decline of the state', but we do observe changing priorities of public policy intervention (Baldwin, 2005a) as well changing policy approaches (Baldwin, 2005b). Policy changes in the social service field are pointing in roughly similar directions, however: the activist role of the public sector as provider, organiser and financer of social services is increasingly contested, as are ideas of comprehensive public responsibility for ensuring citizens' well-being and social security. Instead, central government policy-making is relegated to its indirect and regulatory role, while social service provision and governance are often devolved to decentralised agencies or non-state organisations. It is in that sense, and as we will see below with reference to a specific set of norms, that the chapters in this book diagnose something that we like to call *'public sector disengagement'*. This 'public sector disengagement' and the shifts in tasks and responsibilities are manifest in 'vertical' and in 'horizontal' directions, and there are several public policy changes to fuel the tendencies (see also Martinelli, Chapter 1, in this volume).

### Disengagement of Central Governments as Decentralisation in a Setting of Chronic Underfunding

Responsibility for not only providing, but to an increasing extent also planning and financing social services has been shifting back to the local level. Hence, innovative local initiatives have become increasingly important and counted on by central government policy-makers, as there is often no additional national funding for the increasing scale of local activity, only the pressure of needs and responsibilities. Depending on the field of social services, central governments may continue to play a central role enacting framework legislation about availability of, sometimes even entitlement to, certain social services, regulating the supply and monitoring quality. But this is not always the case, and making social services available, funding them, providing the infrastructure and employing the staff is often (and increasingly so) declared a responsibility of municipalities (see Sabatinelli and Semprebon and Mas Giralt and Sarlo, in this volume). Developing and testing innovative forms of care service provision is also left to municipalities (see Kubalčíková et al.; Häikiö et.al. and Brokking et al., in this volume), and more often than not there is little more than rhetorical support for such local initiatives. In a sense social services have come full circle in their development, as almost all fields of social care have historically started at the municipal level (Sachße, 2011; Rathmayr, 2014), often as third-sector initiatives, in the context of local poor relief programmes. During the twentieth century, social policy had moved beyond isolated local initiatives and welfare state expansion in the social service field took the form of upward rescaling (see Sabatinelli and Semprebon, in this volume). There is now, therefore, an expectation of national standards for local social services and the definition of some minimal provisos helping local governments to live up to these standards. If this is not forthcoming, the impression that decentralisation is a form of retrenchment is not too far-fetched.

A process closely related to this trend toward decentralised service provision is de-institutionalisation. De-institutionalisation involves moving social care out of specialised organisations such as nursing homes or formal childcare facilities and back into informal settings. It may also merely entail the reduction of the size of organisations that provide care (see Anttonen and Karsio; Deusdad, Lev et al. and Kubalčíková et al., in this volume). It usually goes along with a greater role of private providers, and generally social service systems that are more complex and opaque in their structures of governance and supply (see Anttonen, in this volume). But de-institutionalisation is also the tendency that is least generalisable across different social service fields: it is rather pronounced in social care for older people, where the goal of 'ageing in place' has become an important objective in social service design, whereas in the field of childcare, or in social assistance services (see Raeymaeckers et al., in this volume), policy developments have been pointing in the opposite direction of a greater amount of institutionalisation (and even public involvement).

### Disengagement of the Public Sector and the Growing Importance of Non-state Actors

Three processes account for a growing importance of non-state actors in social service fields (see also Leibetseder et al., in particular Table 6.2, in this volume). The first is the growing importance of social care services provided by for-profit, private sector providers that can be observed in some policy fields and some countries (see Anttonen and Karsio, in this volume). Sometimes this takes the form of semi-formal 'grey' markets (see Kubalčíková et al., in this volume); some other times the private sector is explicitly endorsed by the state as institutional structure for supplying and governing social care services, amounting to what some observers call 'combining' public and private resources (Sirovátka and Greve, 2016a). The second process through which governments transfer responsibilities to non-state actors involves third-sector organisations (non-profit providers) or actors of organised civil society, such as private welfare associations or charities. This also entails quite explicit expectations of volunteer work and local initiatives of social innovation (see Häikiö et al.; Weinzierl et al. and

Brokking et al., in this volume), but overall within institutional frameworks that are much more volatile and complex than third-sector social service provision has traditionally been (see Bode, in this volume and Bode, 2006). Thirdly, families and informal care arrangements are explicitly enlisted as providers of social care. While large parts of social care have always been provided in informal settings and by private actors of various description (Sachße, 1994; 2011), in the second half of the twentieth century the social service systems of many countries had been moving away from an exclusive reliance on families and other non-state actors. Recent developments in many areas of social care have been pointing in the opposite direction, of (re-) endorsing informal care arrangements and counting on families in meeting the needs for social care in contexts of shrinking public resources and involvement, either intentionally or by default.

The chapters in this volume diagnose disengagement of the state mainly with regard to the provision and financing of social services, much less so with regard to legislation setting up general goals and regulatory frameworks concerning access and quality (see also Klenk and Pavolini, 2015). Attempts at state disengagement were at times driven by ideological convictions, being part of a 'neo-liberal turn' and an agenda that pictures a smaller role of public policy in economic and social affairs; more often than not there was not much of a political agenda involved, and the driving force was budgetary strain and the mere wish to cut costs by shedding responsibility for expensive and expanding tasks.

Given the diversity of settings, countries and thematic fields in which social services are delivered, the shared theme of 'public sector disengagement' manifests itself in different forms (see Kröger and Bagnato, in this volume, for a description of the ranges of policy approaches in a number of substantive dimensions). Even when disregarding the detailed substantive issues and searching for generalised trends, the shared themes are hidden behind diversity. In many countries and policy fields fiscal austerity in the wake of the 2008 financial crisis accelerated developments that had already evolved in the directions described above. This is certainly the case for some of the Nordic countries (Finland especially; see Anttonen and Karsio, in this volume). Some other countries, such as Germany or Austria, experienced much less fiscal strain to begin with, yet the regime of fiscal discipline that was installed in response to the euro-crisis provided the justification for intensifying older agendas of public sector retrenchment. In yet another geographic setting, the Mediterranean countries, the euro-crisis and its aftermath interrupted developments in which these southern European countries were in a process of 'catching up' – at least in legislative terms – with their richer northern European neighbours. With regard to this process one could argue that the euro-crisis has led to a resurgence of the old North–South divide that Europe was in the process of slowly closing before the crisis hit (see the concluding chapter by Martinelli, in this volume).

In some social service fields and countries, such as care for older people, the social inclusion of immigrants or other vulnerable groups, the tendencies toward state disengagement through underfunding or devolution of tasks can be observed very clearly, and the chapters in this volume describe the complex settings of informal and/or private sector delivery that result from these trends. In other fields, such as childcare and, perhaps, social assistance services or healthcare, the dominant trend in many countries has been one of *greater* public sector involvement, at times even greater central government intervention (Greer and Mätzke, 2015; Sirovátka and Greve, 2016b; Hora and Sirovátka, 2016). However, even here direct public sector provision takes second place behind outsourcing, and sometimes cash vouchers, albeit within a growing regulatory framework set by public authorities (Klenk and Pavolini, 2015; Pierson, 2007).

## 2.   EXPLORING POLICY IMPLICATIONS: SOCIAL SERVICES DISRUPTED

If policy development takes different forms in different settings, then the heterogeneity of socioeconomic contexts, specific social service needs and resources to address these needs will also produce a great variety of *specific impacts* on service quality and access, with the emergence of relevant patterns of inequality across these different settings. Rather than portraying all these differences, the following remarks will think through the implications of the developments described above for *the general character of social services* in the European polities and societies. In this respect, I submit, the chapters of this volume paint a picture that is surprisingly consistent across the many specific findings and interpretations.

We refer to this consistent theme as '*disruption*'. In our context disruption pertains to an erosion of the traditional commitment of public social policy, including social services. Even if this was nowhere fully realised, it still postulates something like the normative core of a 'New Liberal' (Katznelson, 1996), or social citizenship-based, progressive agenda in welfare state and more specifically social service development. Many social policy observers or practitioners subscribe to such an agenda, and from the perspective of *this* agenda discern undesirable traits in recent developments of social service fields. Following Thomas H. Marshall's (1950) lead, the agenda stipulates entitlement to a minimum standard of social care, if needed, as a privilege that comes with citizenship – a membership right,

not contingent on a quid pro quo (Somers, 2008). This citizenship conception of social rights insists on the important role of the public sector in
supplying and financing social services. It holds that membership rights
and recognition are complementary features, not alternatives, to a notion
of social rights that would focus on redistribution and income transfers
(Fraser, 2001; Fraser and Gordon, 1994). In terms of policy implications,
this citizenship idea of social service provision informs our authors' keen
understanding of the disruption caused by public sector disengagement
and the recent tendency to adopt market elements and commercial logics
in the design and distribution of social services (Cox, 2000; Katz, 2001).

There is a lot of trust in the professionalism and expertise of public sector
employees (Hood, 1995) and an overall positive appraisal of the long-term
historical trajectory of publicly provided service infrastructures and social
benefits (see Steinmetz, 1993, who labels this perception of social policy
improvement a 'whig narrative' of the welfare state). In historical perspective, the 'darker' side of early social policy intervention has not gone unno-
ticed and many historiographic accounts have pointed out the repressive
traditions of local poor relief (Sachße, 2011; Rathmayr, 2014; Sachße and
Tennstedt, 1986). Emancipation and professional development, along with
broadened access and dropping many of the old poor-relief lineages are
the building blocks of a story of social service modernisation often told. It
forms the backdrop against which the recent transformation – from public
service to public management (Gray and Jenkins, 1995) – is often eyed
with reservation. Some observers are worried about a decline of professional norms and public service ethos (Schimank, 2015; more moderately:
Noordegraaf, 2015), others are critical of possible repercussions of market
logics for quality and availability of social services, and still others fear new
forms of exclusion or a new 'welfare paternalism' (Soss, 2005; Evers, 2008)
to result from marketisation and managerialism.

The citizenship concept of social rights has not only informed much of
the scholarly debate about social services in welfare state development and
public policy more generally (see Mätzke et al., in this volume; Rothstein,
1998; Somers, 2008); it has also defined normative guidelines and a benchmark for evaluating the observations about specific social services, which
this volume's authors have all subscribed to in one way or another. This
benchmark comprises a combination of three core objectives, and we talk
about '*social services disrupted*' when one or more of these core objectives are severely compromised. In those cases, social service systems can
still serve beneficial ends, there may still be promising developments and
many good justifications for new approaches in the design and governance of social services, but they are not inspired by the idea of providing
social services as aspects of social citizenship rights. Evaluating such new

approaches becomes more volatile and potentially more arbitrary, because it lacks the clear normative reference point that the citizenship conception of social rights has provided. The citizenship conception is defined by the combination of three core commitments:

1.  *Inclusiveness* (as shaped by access and affordability). Entitlement to use certain services is determined by need; it does not have to be earned (Somers, 2008; Katz, 2001). There may be needs tests, and there may be targeting and positive discrimination, but access to social services is not based on privilege, certain behaviours or preconditions, and in that sense an egalitarian spirit almost always informs (citizenship-based) social service provision (Anttonen et al., 2012).
2.  *Equal entitlement* in terms of the substantive content of what is provided. Quality and the scope of services should not be contingent on who needs them and where persons in need live. Professionalism among providers is to secure ensure quality (Noordegraaf, 2015; Hood, 1995); central government coordination seeks to install territorial cohesion.

Taken together, these first two points amount to what Anttonen (Chapter 17, in this volume) defines as universalistic social service design.

3.  *Users' self-determination and empowerment.* These are important goals in social service design (Spicker, 2013) and social policy at large. Esping-Andersen (1990) has emphasised the emancipatory potential of the welfare state, while with regard to social services, autonomy (as independence of market income as well as family support) is a central evaluative category. In a citizenship conception of social rights, services are there to assist people (to avoid dependence and allow users to lead the lives that they choose as much as possible); their purpose is not to discipline them. Many service institutions do just that, however, so instrumentalist and paternalistic traits are entrenched in many social services (Anttonen et al., 2012), and autonomy is often a myth. But from the perspective of a citizenship-based conception of social rights it is a myth and a moral ambition, and as such has informed the way the authors in this volume have judged the policies and the developments that they have observed.

Together this set of core commitments echoes salient themes in scholarly debates about welfare state development (Rothstein, 1998; Somers, 2008), such as the role of social benefits, including social services, in defining patterns of inequality and exclusion (Esping-Andersen, 1990;

Ingram and Schneider, 2005) as well as the emancipatory role that social policy may or may not play, depending on how it is designed (see Mätzke et al., in this volume). It also reflects an agenda that motivates actors and decision-makers in particular social service fields and fuels their attempts at promoting social inclusion and equal social rights by providing highly individualised in-kind services and social work, especially for vulnerable groups that tend to fall through the cracks of insurance-based cash-transfer systems. It finally expresses a third major aspiration of many practitioners and analysts of social policy, namely the commitment to autonomy, in which (public) social services help people to lead the lives they want (Anttonen and Sipilä, 1996), rather than the lives that fit into some organisational logic conveniently.

To thrive as progressive agenda, the citizenship-based conception needs all three core commitments to be largely intact: a country can have universalistic systems of services and include everyone on equal footing, but still fall short on the commitment to autonomy, so that its public social services are hardly emancipatory and may even increase the number of limitations and arbitrary rules that users may be confronted with when they use social services. Likewise, countries may have social services systems strongly committed to preventing dependency and promoting autonomy, and these systems may even be open to everyone. If the quality and the scope of services offered vary wildly across who needs help and where they live, then entitlement is a matter of chance at best and a matter of privilege at worst. Finally, countries can design benefit schemes intended to enhance autonomy and empower all users on equal footing, but if access is contingent on long lists of preconditions that especially vulnerable groups in society often find difficult to fulfil, then much of the empowering and egalitarian thrust will run aground, and social service fields become just another structure of social exclusion.

What the chapters in this volume show is that disengagement of central government commitment to social services very often entails one or two of the dimensions falling short. Social service sectors could then still evolve on relatively stable trajectories; they may even enjoy increasing amounts of public resources and attention. Yet one would need to regard these trends with suspicion nevertheless, and more often than not diagnose troublesome trends: 'tragic moments', 'illiberal' service designs, Potemkin villages in which empowerment, equality and social inclusion reside in political rhetoric, not reality, and social service sectors that promise more than they can deliver by way of citizenship-based entitlement. In these instances, this book speaks of *disruption* – not necessarily because organisations, regulatory structures or funding sources are in total disarray, but because core normative commitments of social service supply are compromised: access to social services is losing its character as a facet of social citizenship rights and in that sense it is disrupted. Against the backdrop of this citizenship conception of social rights the authors in this volume have a hard time painting an unequivocally benign picture of social service development and instead point to a range of pitfalls and potential dangers of ongoing trends.

- The loss of stable public funding guarantees produces volatile and ultimately unreliable project-forms of social service provision that are often at odds with the nature and time frame of needs, prove unsustainable over time and may evolve into highly uneven and unequal patterns of access (Bode, 2006).
- Decentralisation along the territorial axis and excessive reliance on non-public provision has similar fragmenting effects, likewise producing both selective access and conditional entitlement. They have also the potential to produce and reproduce inequality and exclusion.
- Competition and quasi-market elements in the governance systems of care services (both public and privatised) are often at odds with the capabilities of providers and, more gravely, users, potentially generating patterns of unequal access and exclusion among users, as well as barriers to access and favouritism among providers.
- The same holds for de-institutionalisation of social care, especially if this strategy is implemented without providing adequate financial resources and institutional support for the evolving structures of domiciliary care.
- Disengagement from public commitments in the provision and financing of social services, if they are split off from regulation and provision (Sirovátka and Greve, 2016a), finally bears the risk of losing control over the qualitative aspects of social care delivery as well. The tasks of regulating service provision and monitoring service quality tend to become harder when public authorities are not involved in social service delivery and when they are up against a set of non-state actors who may not share an agenda of social inclusion, equality and empowerment.

Most of the analyses in this volume have therefore ended on a critical note when assessing the implications of the social service developments they analysed. All the cases studies of policy development point out the potential dangers of the trends they have observed; all reports of local initiatives and instances of social innovation point out the difficulties in generalising and institutionalising the innovative and successful practices in times of fiscal austerity. One reason for this problematising undertone has been given here: it is the surrender of one or several of the traditional core commitments of social service policies that has often bothered the authors in this volume, because that signals a kind of disruption that has to be acknowledged and weighed against the good arguments and actual advantages of policy changes.

## 3. CONCLUDING REMARKS: THE IMPORTANCE OF CONTEXT AND INSTITUTIONAL DETAIL

A lesser amount of direct public delivery and, overall, a smaller presence of state guarantees, state intervention or state guidance in the provision of services is a major tendency that the contributions in this volume have identified. There are many arguments that suggest why this tendency is attractive from a policy perspective. Policies such as de-institutionalisation, decentralisation, or cooperation across the public–private divide hold the promise of promoting structures of social care delivery that can leave behind some of the cost driving and sometimes patronising aspects of the former public social service designs. Decentralised and non-state provided social care is often favoured by policy-makers, because it is seen as a form of social service organisation that allows users to exercise consumer choice. This, the argument goes, not only installs an element of market discipline, it also promotes autonomy and self-determination and thus contributes to the classical emancipatory agenda. A varied mix of service providers – municipal service providers or ones run by third-sector organisations, for-profit or not-for-profit, formal or informal ones – allows for the diversity that makes choice meaningful and generates the expectation that providers are more responsive to people's needs, while allowing for social innovation and giving people in need of care the chance to define the kind of care arrangement they prefer (Sirovátka and Greve, 2016a).

When we take a closer look at all the preconditions that would be required for a scenario of 'public sector disengagement' to deliver such beneficial effects and become indeed the guarantor of autonomy and empowerment while preserving inclusiveness and equal entitlement, we become much more uncertain and wary of wholeheartedly embracing state disengagement. A 'progressive agenda' for citizenship-based social services would require the two dimensions of universalism – inclusive availability and equal entitlement – to be crucial elements in the assessment of social service designs. With regard to these two facets of universalism the problematic aspects of state disengagement stand out. Equality and access appear to be better served by retaining public involvement in what concerns both regulation and public financial support. Public control – in regulating and coordinating the delivery of social service infrastructures, in monitoring the quality of the services rendered and overseeing the training, professionalism and working conditions of care workers – is critically important for ensuring that social services are adequate and roughly equal for all citizens who need them. There must be substantive content to the definition of what should be available for all in need. Protecting that substance and its equitable distribution is a key function of public involvement. Only public funding and some measure of central government control over it can ensure the interregional transfers necessary to mitigate territorial disparities (see Sabatinelli and Semprebon; Martinelli, Chapter 19, in this volume). Public financial support is also needed to keep social service systems broadly accessible and evenly available in the face of fiscal constraints, demographic strain and competitive pressures in a globalised economy.

Now public involvement does not necessarily mean public sector delivery. But public involvement does not mean a preference for non-state actors as providers, financers and regulators of social care either. As the detailed analyses of social service developments, initiatives in social innovation or policy alternatives throughout this book have demonstrated, institutional forms of social service fields *alone* do not determine the success or failure of progressive agendas. Contextual factors also matter, and what is needed as well is regulatory and administrative capacity on the part of central governments for implementing universalistic policies. Moreover, for a citizenship rights approach to social service design to become a reality one would also need governments intent on implementing universalistic and emancipatory agendas, rather than favouring social protection systems that enhance existing structures of privilege and social exclusion. Public sector involvement and influence of a democratically elected political centre is most valuable where democratic values and social citizenship norms are not completely lost on the people controlling that political centre (Somers, 2008). Sometimes it is indeed better to have decentralised governance structures, potent third-sector players and diversified structures of social service delivery, because those may serve as protective institutional layers and safeguards against reckless and injurious tampering with successful institutional designs.

Contextual factors, therefore, not only define the institutional preconditions that set policy development in motion on distinct trajectories. Their role is not merely to generate the resources and administrative capacities for enacting and implementing social policy agendas. Besides path dependence and political feasibility, contextual factors also shape *intentions*. Assessing policy alternatives, therefore, not only requires us to have a set of guidelines at our disposal that allow us to distinguish beneficial policy developments from the harmful ones. It also needs contextual knowledge of the kind that the contributions in this volume have supplied.

# REFERENCES

Anttonen, A. and J. Sipilä (1996), 'European social care services: is it possible to identify models?', *Journal of European Social Policy*, **6** (2), 87–100.

Anttonen, A., L. Häikiö and J. Sipilä (2012), 'Universalism and the challenge of diversity', in A. Anttonen, L. Häikiö and K. Stefánsson (eds), *Welfare State, Universalism and Diversity*, Cheltenham, UK and Northampton, MA, USA: Edward Elgar Publishing, pp. 1–15.

Baldwin, P. (2005a), 'Beyond weak and strong: rethinking the state in comparative policy history', *The Journal of Policy History*, **17** (1), 12–33.

Baldwin, P. (2005b), *Contagion and the State in Europe, 1830–1930*, Cambridge: Cambridge University Press.

Bode, I. (2006), 'Disorganized welfare mixes: voluntary agencies and new governance regimes in Western Europe', *Journal of European Social Policy*, **16** (4), 346–59.

Cox, R.H. (2000), 'The consequences of welfare reform: how conceptions of social rights are changing', *Journal of Social Policy*, **27** (01), 1–16.

Esping-Andersen, G. (1990), *The Three Worlds of Welfare Capitalism*, Princeton: Princeton University Press.

Evers, A. (2008), 'Investiv und aktivierend oder ökonomistisch und bevormundend? Zur Auseinandersetzung mit einer neuen Generation von Sozialpolitiken', in A. Evers and R.G. Heinze (eds), *Sozialpolitik: Ökonomisierung und Entgrenzung*, Wiesbaden: VS-Verlag für Sozialwissenschaften, pp. 229–50.

Fraser, N. (2001), 'Recognition without ethics?', *Theory, Culture and Society*, **18** (2–3), 21–42.

Fraser, N. and L. Gordon (1994), 'Civil citizenship against social citizenship? On the ideology of contract-versus-charity', in B. van Steenbergen (ed.), *The Condition of Citizenship*, London, UK, Thousand Oaks, USA and New Delhi, India: Sage Publications, pp. 90–107.

Gray, A. and B. Jenkins (1995), 'From public administration to public management: reassessing a revolution?', *Public Administration*, **73** (Spring 1995), 75–99.

Greer, S.L. and M. Mätzke (2015), 'Health systems in the European Union', in E. Kuhlmann, R.H. Blank, I.L. Bourgeault and C. Wendt (eds), *The Palgrave International Handbook of Healthcare Policy and Governance*, Basingstoke: Palgrave Macmillan, pp. 245–69.

Hood, C. (1995), 'Emerging issues in public administration', *Public Administration*, **73** (Spring), 165–83.

Hora, O. and T. Sirovátka (2016), 'Employment in the health and social services: evidence and problems', in T. Sirovátka and B. Greve (eds), *Innovation in Social Services. The Public–Private Mix in Service Provision, Fiscal Policy and Employment*, London, UK and New York, USA: Routledge, pp. 21–54.

Ingram, H.M. and A.L. Schneider (2005), 'Public policy and the social construction of deservedness', in A.L. Schneider and H.M. Ingram (eds), *Deserving and Entitled. Social Constructions and Public Policy*, Albany: SUNY Press, pp. 1–28.

Katz, M.B. (2001), *The Price of Citizenship. Redefining the American Welfare State*, New York: Metropolitan Books.

Katznelson, I. (1996), 'Knowledge about what? Policy intellectuals and the New Liberalism', in D. Rueschemeyer and T. Skocpol (eds), *States, Social Knowledge, and the Origins of Modern Social Policies*, Princeton: Princeton University Press, pp. 17–47.

Klenk, T. and E. Pavolini (2015), 'Conclusions', in T. Klenk and E. Pavolini (eds), *Restructuring Welfare Governance. Marketization, Managerialism and Welfare State Professionalism*, Cheltenham, UK and Northampton, MA, USA: Edward Elgar Publishing, pp. 253–66.

Marshall, T.H. (1950), *Citizenship and Social Class*, London: Pluto Press.

Mätzke, M. (2011), 'Staatsbürger als Wirtschaftssubjekte und als demografische Ressource. Die Ziele staatlicher Akteure in der Sozialpolitik', *Leviathan*, **39** (3), 385–406.

Noordegraaf, M. (2015), 'New governance and professionalism', in T. Klenk and E. Pavolini (eds), *Restructuring Welfare Governance. Marketization, Managerialism and Welfare State Professionalism*, Cheltenham, UK and Northampton, MA, USA: Edward Elgar Publishing, pp. 121–44.

Pierson, P. (2000), 'Increasing returns, path dependence, and the study of politics', *American Political Science Review*, **94** (2), 251–68.

Pierson, P. (2007), 'The rise and reconfiguration of activist government', in P. Pierson and T. Skocpol (eds), *The Transformation of American Politics. Activist Government and the Rise of Conservatism*, Princeton: Princeton University Press, pp. 19–38.

Rathmayr, B. (2014), *Armut und Fürsorge. Einführung in die Geschichte der Sozialen Arbeit von der Antike bis zur Gegenwart*, Opladen and Berlin, Germany and Toronto, Canada: Verlang Barbara Budrich.

Rothstein, B. (1998), *Just Institutions Matter: The Moral and Political Logic of the Universal Welfare State*, Cambridge, UK and New York, USA: Cambridge University Press.

Sachße, C. (1994), 'Subsidiarität: Zur Karriere eines sozialpolitischen Ordnungsbegriffs', *Zeitschrift für Sozialreform*, **40** (11), 717–38.

Sachße, C. (2011), 'Zur Geschichte Sozialer Dienste in Deutschland', in A. Evers (ed.), *Handbuch Soziale Dienste*, Wiesbaden: VS Verlag für Sozialwissenschaften/Springer Fachmedien, pp. 94–116.

Sachße, C. and F. Tennstedt (1986), 'Sicherheit und Disziplin: Eine Skizze zur Einführung', in C. Sachße and F. Tennstedt (eds), *Soziale Sicherheit und Soziale Disziplinierung. Beiträge zu einer Historischen Theorie der Sozialpolitik*, Frankfurt am Mein: Suhrkamp, pp. 11–44.

Schimank, U. (2015), '"New public management" as de-professionalization – conceptual reflections with some applications to school teachers', in T. Klenk and E. Pavolini (eds), *Restructuring Welfare Governance. Marketization, Managerialism and Welfare State Professionalism*, Cheltenham, UK and Northampton, MA, USA: Edward Elgar Publishing, pp. 183–99.

Sirovátka, T. (2016), 'Factors shaping employment in social services', in T. Sirovátka and B. Greve (eds), *Innovation in Social Services. The Public–Private Mix in Service Provision, Fiscal Policy and Employment*, London, UK and New York, USA: Routledge, pp. 91–112.

Sirovátka, T. and B. Greve (2016a), 'Comparing the national cases', in T. Sirovátka and B. Greve (eds), *Innovation in Social Services. The Public–Private Mix in*

*Service Provision, Fiscal Policy and Employment*, London, UK and New York, USA: Routledge, pp. 201–26.

Sirovátka, T. and B. Greve (2016b), 'Social services and the public sector', in T. Sirovátka and B. Greve (eds), *Innovation in Social Services. The Public–Private Mix in Service Provision, Fiscal Policy and Employment*, London, UK and New York, USA: Routledge, pp. 9–20.

Somers, M. (2008), *Genealogies of Citizenship. Markets, Statelessness, and the Right to Have Rights*, Cambridge, UK and New York, USA: Cambridge University Press.

Soss, J. (2005), 'Making clients and citizens: welfare policy as a source of status, belief, and action', in A.L. Schneider and H.M. Ingram (eds), *Deserving and Entitled. Social Constructions and Public Policy*, Albany: SUNY Press, pp. 291–328.

Spicker, P. (2013), *Reclaiming Individualism. Perspectives on Public Policy*, Bristol: Policy Press.

Steinmetz, G. (1993), *Regulating the Social. The Welfare State and Local Politics in Imperial Germany*, Princeton: Princeton University Press.

# 19. Social services disrupted: changing supply landscapes, impacts and policy options

**Flavia Martinelli**

## INTRODUCTION

The aim of the COST Action IS1102 *SO.S. COHESION – Social services, welfare states and places* and this book was to gain a better understanding of the restructuring processes that have invested social services throughout Europe over the last thirty years. As pointed out by Anttonen (Chapter 17, in this volume), although social services may have acquired – at least in principle – a stronger foothold in national legislation and social policy agendas, their status has remained weak compared to other welfare benefits and to services such as education and health, a feature that has made them particularly vulnerable to recent processes of re-definition, re-scaling and cuts. Despite the great diversity observed in the restructuring of different services, in different countries and regions as covered in this book, a number of common trends do emerge, which in turn point to a number of similar consequences, albeit with different intensities depending on context. We – the editors and contributors of this book – contend that this restructuring has brought about a generalised 'disruption' in the public provision of social services as we knew it, in its norms, relations and actors.

In this last chapter, I briefly recapitulate the main changes in the public provision of social services as highlighted in this book, stressing continuities and discontinuities in national trajectories, as well as convergence and divergence among countries. I then focus on the main impacts of changes and their 'disruptive' character, which represent key challenges for the goal of a socially inclusive Europe. Finally, I address the policy implications of these challenges.

# 1.   A DIVERSE LANDSCAPE OF CHANGES

Over the last thirty years, the supply landscape of social services in Europe has changed. As the literature suggests and the illustrations presented in this book confirm, there is still enormous diversity in features and processes among countries and social service fields, owing to different welfare state traditions, policy designs and restructuring emphases. And yet, the chapters in this book also highlight a number of common trends across places and services. As stressed by Mätzke (Chapter 18, in this volume), three partly overlapping trends stand out, confirming the hypotheses raised earlier in the book (Martinelli, Chapter 1, in this volume).

First, a generalised *disengagement* of the state from the provision of in-kind services has taken place, both in quantitative and qualitative terms. In some countries, the quantitative retrenchment has generally occurred in a 'hidden' form, i.e. through reduced coverage, increased targeting, greater co-payments and/or reduced amounts of services per user. In the countries most hit by the financial crisis of 2008, austerity measures have meant an actual withdrawal of public support in many services. These trends are especially observed in care for older people (Kröger and Bagnato; Kubalčíková et al.; Deusdad, Lev et al., in this volume) and in services for the social inclusion of other vulnerable groups (Häikiö et al.; Mas Giralt and Sarlo; Brokking et al., in this volume), although with different intensity across places. In some countries, e.g. Spain, this withdrawal has even occurred in services such as childcare (Deusdad, Javornik et al., in this volume), which are generally expanding in Europe. In qualitative terms, there has been a generalised disengagement of the state from the *direct provision of services,* in favour of both outsourcing and cash transfers (Leibetseder et al.; Kröger and Bagnato, in this volume).

Secondly, there has been a *vertical re-articulation of responsibility* within the state, generally in the direction of a greater responsibilisation of local governments. Again, this process has occurred with varying intensity and timing, depending on contexts. Some places (such as the Nordic countries or the UK) had a longer tradition of local autonomy, whereas others (such as some Southern or Eastern European countries) experienced decentralisation of authority over social services more recently (Sabatinelli and Semprebon; Kubalčíková et al., in this volume). A key aspect for understanding the consequences of these (new) multilevel governance arrangements is the degree of funding and regulation retained by the central level. As many cases presented in this volume witness, in the absence of financial redistribution mechanisms and centralised regulation, local responsibility can easily turn into highly differentiated 'local welfare systems' (Sabatinelli and Semprebon, in this volume), thereby undermining the universalistic principle of equal access to services, independently of place (Martinelli, Chapter 1, in this volume). In many places where local governments were unable – or ceased – to respond to social needs, bottom-up initiatives came about, involving third sector and civil society organisations and attempting to compensate for the void left by the state (Häikiö et al.; Mas Giralt and Sarlo; Brokking et al., in this volume).

Thirdly, and strongly related to the above processes, there has been a *horizontal re-shuffling of responsibility*, with a reduction of the direct involvement of the state and an increase in the role of private service providers, both non-profit and for-profit, often but not always with some form of public support and regulation (subcontracting, accreditation). In many countries, the introduction of market principles in public services and the opening to for-profit suppliers – the 'marketisation' process described by Meagher and Szebehely (2013) and Anttonen and Karsio (in this volume) – have significantly altered the traditional role of the state. In some of these countries, an important role has been conferred to non-profit providers, leading in some instances to a 're-communitarisation' of services (Leibetseder et al., in this volume). In many places, especially Southern countries, the retrenchment of public provision has also triggered forms of 're-familisation' (Kröger and Bagnato; Deusad, Lev et al.; Deusdad, Javornik et al., in this volume). Overall, a complexification – and often fragmentation – of the supply landscapes has been observed (Bode; Leibetseder et al., in this volume).

Among the questions we raised at the beginning of our COST Action and in this book, were whether continuities or discontinuities could be observed in national and regional trajectories and whether some sort of convergence is occurring among European social service systems. We have no clear-cut answers, but many chapters in this book have provided salient indications. With regard to national trajectories, evidence from the Action confirms that in the 1990s all welfare systems have been affected by the so-called neo-liberal 'turn', although the timing and extent of this change of tack, away from state monopoly and in the direction of a greater reliance on the market, were conditioned by pre-existing welfare models. This shift marks a clear discontinuity with the preceding Keynesian 'regime' (Martinelli, Chapter 1, in this volume), hence a path-breaking moment, albeit tempered by path-dependent resiliences. This discontinuity and path-dependence are quite evident in Nordic countries, where despite a significant marketisation process in the care for older people, the social democratic universalistic principles somewhat hold their ground (Anttonen and Karsio, in this volume). In Continental countries, the neo-liberal turn is also discernible in the 'complexification' of the supply structure, albeit this is the family of countries where discontinuities are less evident and path-dependency stronger (Bode, in this volume). The neo-liberal restructuring of social services is less of a discontinuity in the liberal UK, albeit here too, many 'Beveridgean' social services that had been established in the Keynesian period had already been discontinued or re-sized in the 1980s and 1990s (Newman, 2001; Clarke, 2010). For both the Mediterranean and the Central and Eastern European countries the neo-liberal turn does not really represent a discontinuity, since these 'latecomer' countries (Martinelli, Chapter 1) began establishing or enlarging their public provision of social services already during the neo-liberal regime in the 1990s, adopting New public management (NPM), outsourcing and cash transfers as preferential mechanisms from the start (CAP Martinelli and Sarlo, 2012; Kröger and Bagnato; Deusdad, Javornik et al., in this volume).

Whether the financial crisis of 2008 represents a discontinuity is less clear. In some cases, the crisis only accelerated restructuring trends that were already in motion (retrenchment, marketisation), such as in the Nordic countries (Anttonen and Karsio, in this volume) or in the Liberal ones (CAP Yeandle, 2014). In other cases, it has determined a veritable path-breaking 'shock', dramatically interrupting pre-existing trends. This is certainly the case of Southern European countries, where the 'catching up' process observed with the establishment of many social services in the 1990s and early 2000s was abruptly interrupted by the crisis and the subsequent austerity measures. In many instances, such measures involved a reduction or even discontinuation of newly established universalistic programmes and services – an 'end of illusion' (Leon and Pavolini, 2014, p. 13) which brought the state back to a somewhat residual role.

Thus, in what concerns convergence and divergence, the picture appears contradictory. On the one hand, until 2008, there has definitely been a convergence among European countries, which blurred their national and regional specificities and their positioning in one welfare family or other. This convergence was made of two different but complementary trends: an 'upward' convergence, whereby Southern European countries such as Italy, Spain, Portugal or Greece had 'caught-up' with the Nordic universalistic ideal-type by enlarging their public supply of social services; and a 'downward' convergence, characterised by a weakening of that universalistic ideal-type, precisely in the Nordic countries that first had pursued it. On the other hand, after the financial crisis of 2008 a new divergence trend is taking shape. After decades of relative convergence among European social models, a new North–South divide is growing as a consequence of the hardship and cuts in social spending brought about by the crisis in Southern European countries and the austerity measures imposed by the EU Fiscal compact, as confirmed also by recent comparisons of social justice and social spending indicators in Europe (SIM, 2014; 2015).

## 2. THE IMPACTS OF RESTRUCTURING AND THE 'DISRUPTION' OF SOCIAL SERVICES

Most of the analyses in this volume were rather negative when assessing the implications of the changes they observed in the organisation and delivery of social services (for a summary, see Mätzke, Chapter 18, in this volume). In what follows, these impacts are briefly summarised, according to the five perspectives our COST Action brought forward to analyse the restructuring of social services (Introduction, in this volume): (a) cost efficiency/ satisfaction for users; (b) democratic governance; (c) social and territorial cohesion; (d) labour market conditions for care workers; (e) gender.

In what concerns the *cost and quality of services*, a major goal of the top-down restructuring of social services implemented since the 1980s has been cutting down public expenditures, while at the same time also allegedly reducing bureaucracy, diversifying the service supply and enhancing users' choice and satisfaction (Martinelli, Chapter 1, in this volume). However, even though the introduction of NPM, the shift to outsourcing, and the liberalisation of the service 'market' might have reduced public expenditures in some social services,[1] the majority of the chapters in this book attest that these changes have seldom increased the quality of services and users' choice, and when this has occurred it has only concerned the richer users. This is certainly due to the fact that together with organisational changes many countries also had to cut services or curb their growth. But other reasons lie in the very new supply mechanisms. As stressed by Anttonen (Chapter 17, in this volume), care involves a range of diverse and complementary activities that need to be integrated and personalised. NPM, in contrast, has involved a sort of 'Taylorisation' of the care process, by subdividing, standardising and quantifying tasks. Many case studies highlight that recent trends in home care services – in Denmark as in Calabria – have involved a reduction in the *range* of services offered and in the *time* allotted to each task per user (Kröger and Bagnato, in this volume), with a loss of personalisation and human contact, which is not very different from the bureaucratic and undifferentiated provision the reforms wished to overcome. Moreover, as will be stressed in the next paragraph, the pluralisation of supply has not necessarily increased users' choice.

In what concerns *governance*, the restructuring of the last thirty years has significantly changed both the vertical and the horizontal governance of social services. Vertical and horizontal 'subsidiarity' (Kazepov, 2010) were meant to increase the accountability of the state and the involvement of users and civil society in the organisation and production of social services, thereby contributing to making them more responsive to local needs and users' demands. In reality, the impacts of both trends have not fulfilled these promises. Barring a few exceptions, far from empowering users and communities, the vertical subsidiarity or decentralisation process, coupled with the cutting of financial resources from the central level, as has happened in the UK, Italy or Spain (Sabatinelli and Semprebon; Deusdad, Javornik et al., in this volume), has featured a 'blame avoidance' strategy (Pierson, 1994) and has placed severe pressures on local governments, third-sector organisations and families to compensate for such cuts and keep up provision. The horizontal subsidiarity or 're-mix' process (see Leibetseder et al., in this volume) has created a fragmentation of authority in place of the old system that was prevailingly financed and produced by the state. This generalised 'complexification' of the supply structure has not necessarily reduced bureaucracy and increased choice. In many places – especially rural places or small cities – the state monopoly has simply been substituted by a private monopoly. Furthermore, complexity has often reduced accessibility (which depends on the efficacy of information) and accountability (which depends on the degree of transparency) (Diamond and Liddle, 2012). This is especially the case for the most vulnerable groups (older people, minorities) and those who do not have the support of a family or a tutor to actually make choices, change supplier and/or file claims. Finally, these complex systems are not necessarily efficient, as they require higher coordination capabilities, which are not always available (Rhodes, 2007; Bode, in this volume).

Under the rubric of *governance*, the role of (socially innovative) local initiatives should also be addressed. As several chapters in this book show (Häikiö et al.; Weinzierl et al.; Mas Giralt and Sarlo; Brokking et al., in this volume), a great variety of 'local welfare initiatives' have developed throughout Europe to face unanswered social needs, most often based on community and voluntary organisations, with very uneven levels of support from local, national and EU public institutions or no support at all. The problem with these bottom-up initiatives – all too easily labelled 'socially innovative' in mainstream literature – is that they mostly emerge to *substitute* for missing or retrenching public services, with limited empowering and transformative impacts, let alone a sustainable horizon (Martinelli, Chapter 1; Häikiö et al.; Brokking et al., in this volume). Only in the initiatives for the inclusion of Roma (Weinzierl et al., in this volume) has this transformative potential manifested itself, also because of the involvement and financial help from the state and the establishment of a multilevel governance.

In what concerns *social and territorial cohesion*, most Action case studies and chapters in this book are quite straightforward in their assessment. Although achieving an 'inclusive' Europe is a major aim of the European social policy agenda and the Europe 2020 strategy (Gómez-Barroso et al., in this volume), there is strong evidence of growing exclusionary processes throughout Europe, both social (i.e. based on income, age, gender or origin) and territorial (i.e. among neighbourhoods, cities, regions and nations) (see also SIM, 2014; 2015). These exclusionary processes – which undermine the very principle of universalism to which many social services aspired when they were established (Martinelli, Chapter 1, in this volume) – are a most direct result of the restructuring of social services and the cutbacks that have occurred in many places.

In what concerns *social* exclusion, the 'horizontal' opening of public provision to private suppliers, especially for-profit ones, together with the introduction of other market mechanisms such as co-payments and vouchers, is creating a *stratification* of (publicly supported) social services, whereby richer people can access more diversified and better quality services and poorer people only have access to basic ones or must resort to family support. In this regard, it is useful to recall what Scharpf predicted in 2002 (p. 657), should competition prevail over social cohesion in EU strategies and should the social service 'market' become fully open to commercial providers. In his forecast, even Nordic states would:

> evolve into a very 'American' future through a vicious circle: once well-to-do clients gravitated towards private, but publicly subsidised, 'premium' services, financial constraints would reduce the comparative attractiveness of public providers that would still need to serve the poorer neighbourhoods and 'unprofitable' rural areas [. . .]. Just as is true of education and health care in the United States, the result could then be a two-class system where tax-financed public institutions could provide no more than minimal services for those who cannot afford to pay for private day care, school, health insurance, or long-term care for the elderly.[2]

In what concerns *territorial* exclusion, this is mostly a consequence of the 'vertical' reorganisation of responsibility, which in many instances has attributed the production of social services to local authorities, without guaranteeing a parallel redistribution of resources, thereby giving rise to widely differentiated 'local welfare systems'. In other words, the new social service systems that are being implemented no longer seem to aspire to providing universal access. Access is instead becoming increasingly a function of users' ability to pay and local authorities' ability to mobilise sufficient resources.

In what concerns the *labour market* of care and social work, the disengagement of the state is in many countries indirectly contributing to lowering the level of professional training and contractual protection of the workers engaged in social services (especially care for older people),[3] which in turn reverberates on the quality of the services provided. The quality of services depends, in fact, very much on the training of service workers, their salary, working conditions, benefits and job security. The shift to a system with a plurality of service producers and the growing involvement of private providers – often not adequately regulated – has in many places led to a lowering of the training requirements and a worsening of the contractual conditions of private care workers (Cunningham, 2008), compared to public social workers. There has been, in other words, a process of deskilling, segmentation, 'casualisation' and, therefore, demotivation of such workers. This trend was observed in many case studies, especially in Southern European countries where labour regulation is weak and an informal labour market of caregivers has developed (Kröger and Bagnato; Deusdad, Lev et al., in this volume). It is also occurring in some Continental European countries (Bode, in this volume), although not (yet) in Nordic countries.

Finally, in what concerns *gender*, the restructuring of social services is deeply affecting the societal and labour market position of women, who are both users and providers of social services. In this regard, contradictory trends are observed across services and countries. On the one hand, strong forms of re-familisation are observed, especially in care for older people, which often imply an increased care burden on women. On the other hand, in some countries and places increased public responsibility and a relative expansion of services have been observed in what concerns early childhood education and care, especially after the Barcelona Council (Morgan, 2013; Ciccia and Bleijenbergh, 2014), which encourage de-familisation.

As already stressed by Mätzke (Chapter 18, in this volume), all these impacts configure a generalised 'disruption' in the established norms, relations among and roles of actors involved in providing social services. The key dimensions of this disruption can be summarised as follows:

- A de-alignment between aims and strategies (sometimes even legislation) concerning social services, on the one hand, and reality, on the other – or 'implementation gap' (SIM, 2015).
- A mismatch between (growing) demands – social needs – and a (shrinking) supply of public social services, which is eroding the principle of universal social rights and restoring social stratification and territorial differentiation.
- A fragmentation – often leading to disconnection and 'disorganisation' (Bode, in this volume) – in the service supply structure, which reduces quality, access and accountability.

- A disconnection in multilevel governance, especially between the central and the local government levels, which puts excessive pressures and expectations on the 'local' and on 'socially innovative' initiatives.
- A disruption of some national trajectories (especially in 'latecomer' countries) and an interruption in the convergence observed between Southern European countries and the rest of Europe.
- A displacement of the state, which is abdicating its historic mission, both in general and with regard to social services: from provider and guarantor of social rights and justice, thereby steering the market and supporting redistributive mechanisms, the state is transforming into a 'commissioner' or 'enabler' of market-led provision, with reduced compensatory power.

## 3.   ASSESSING POLICY OPTIONS

What does all this imply for policy? In this final section I explore the policy implications of the empirical evidence and analyses presented in the volume. Rather than set forth *policy recommendations*, which are liable to reproduce the customary calls for more resources, more recognition, more room for manoeuvre, more of everything that populate so many social policy debates, I will explore the potential effects – whether intended or unintended – of different concrete *policy options*, as they have emerged from the discussion in this book. Many such options can be construed as alternatives – 'either/or' – but in practice they are often complementary. The *effects* of each option, though, are quite different and it is these differences I wish to highlight. What does each of these policy options involve in terms of users' satisfaction, democracy, social and territorial cohesion, working conditions, gender, and/or role of the state? The agenda for inclusive, universalistic and empowering social service designs described by Mätzke (Chapter 18, in this volume) provides the normative benchmark against which this evaluation is performed.

### Central or Local Responsibility

A first key choice is which *government level* should be responsible for social services: the central (national or federal) or the local (generally municipal) level. This choice never features a pure alternative ('either/or'), since a 'vertical' division of responsibility has always existed among government levels for the four main *functions* (funding; regulation; coordination, planning and monitoring; production and delivery) involved in every social service system (Martinelli, Chapter 1, in this volume). Moreover, in many places responsibilities are also assigned to some meso-level, such as *Bundesländer*, regions, cantons or departments. In any case, depending on the configuration of the vertical division of authority, we can have more or less *centralised* or *decentralised* systems.

The actual *production and delivery* of social services occurs at the local level by necessity, usually at the municipal, county or district level, since services require close proximity to end users. The *coordination, planning and monitoring* function is generally either local, shared between the central and the local, such as for example in Sweden, or between the meso- (regional, departmental) and the local, as in Italy. But the two functions that really matter in the vertical division of responsibility within the state are *funding* and *regulation*, as they more directly bear on the state's universalistic commitments.

Theoretically, a fully decentralised system of social services, i.e. a system where each region or locality is responsible for all four functions, would inherently involve territorial differentiation in the availability of social services, since the extent to which regional or local governments would be able to invest in these services would depend on the wealth (tax base), legislative framework, planning, and production capabilities of the local institutions and actors of each place. Such a fully decentralised system would by default defeat the principle of universal social citizenship that is implied – albeit generically – in the constitution of many European countries, i.e. the principle of equal rights to social services *independently of place* within the boundaries of the national state. To mitigate territorial differences, national governments can deploy two mechanisms. First, they can ensure some degree of *financial redistribution*, whereby regions and localities can count on financial resources independently of their fiscal levying capacity and rich places subsidise poor places. Secondly, they can try to ensure basic levels of entitlements in all places by establishing a common *regulatory framework* that defines minimum quantity and quality standards for services, access criteria for users, minimum requirements for providers, etc. Both these 'equalising' mechanisms – in the funding and regulation of social services – can only be ensured by the *central* level, whatever is the division of responsibility in the other two functions.

The actual equalising impact of the above mechanisms, if in place, obviously depends on the capabilities of the central state to *implement* financial redistribution and *enforce* national regulation. But even in a context of equalised financial resources and homogeneous regulation, a relevant role is then played by the meso- and local governments in charge of organising and producing services. These governments may have *different levels of institutional capital* and/or make *different organisational choices*, thereby yielding different service outcomes. In other words, even within the same financial and regulatory context, the liberalisation and diversification that has been encouraged in organisational and delivery arrangements (see below), is bound to produce a differentiated social service landscape.

The empirical evidence gathered in the Action and in this book corroborates much of the above scenarios. The decentralisation or expansion of responsibility for the planning and delivery of social services at the local level has often occurred without ensuring either balanced or adequate resources – and in some cases even reducing central funding to municipalities, such as in Italy and England in the last ten years – thereby putting undue pressures on the poorest local governments and jeopardising their capability to provide services. In Italy, in particular, the full decentralisation of authority in what concerns the regulation, planning and production of social services that occurred in 2001, with little and decreasing central financial redistribution, has contributed to further accentuate the already existing regional differences (CAP Martinelli and Sarlo, 2012; Kazepov and Barberis, 2013).

### Cash or Services

Another major policy option concerns the choice between cash transfers (i.e. the strategy of 'cash-for-care')[4] and in-kind services. Cash-for-care transfers include a variety of tools such as cash *allowances* for users (e.g. people who are not self-sufficient) or caregivers (family members providing informal care) or *'personal budget'* or *vouchers*, more or less 'earmarked', to be spent for purchasing services, often from a range of more or less regulated/accredited providers. They have become quite fashionable among policy-makers for various reasons.

From the ideological point of view cash transfers neatly fit the goal of enhancing users' choice, since the beneficiaries of cash transfers can in principle choose among a variety of services and/or providers and find the solution that best responds to their needs. How far this freedom of choice reaches, however, depends on financial and regulatory conditions, such as the entity of the allowance; the number of suppliers among which it is possible to choose; the degree of differentiation among suppliers and customisation of services; the availability of information concerning suppliers and services. An important aspect is whether cash transfers are truly universalistic (a flat allowance for all), are means-tested and/or are targeted to specific needs/ groups. In the latter two cases, regulation and 'gate-keepers' play a major role in determining access.

Another key reason that explains policy-makers' preferences for cash transfers is the lower *operational* burden for the state: cash transfers require less organisational effort than providing in-kind services. In fact, the growth of cash transfers – in countries where no supply of public services existed – or the shift to cash transfers – in many places where a public provision already existed – most often aimed at lowering operational costs and/or direct public employment.

Cash transfers do not necessarily involve a reduction in public expenditures, since public support remains. They nonetheless involve a disengagement of the state from coordination and production, which are conferred to the market, the community or the family, within a more or less regulated framework. Thus, the preference for – or the shift to – cash transfers, might entail the dangers of social stratification and territorial differentiation (hence a loss of universalism as defined in Chapter 1), since access to the same quality of service will depend on the generosity of the benefit and the users' capability to top it up with their own resources, as well as on the characteristics of the local supply. Choice might be greater, but only for some users.

Moreover, cash transfers – especially when they are not targeted or 'earmarked' – tend to reproduce gender inequality, as gendered social norms prevail when families have a choice about how to spend cash transfers for the care of people who are not self-sufficient or small children. In many instances – such as in the case of unemployed women – cash transfers that are not earmarked end up supporting the household, rather than being used to purchase the needed services and support women's access to the labour market.

Finally, in many countries cash transfers have encouraged the development of a market of *privately hired caregivers*. The type of market and its social impacts depend very much on national regulation (see Van Hooren, 2012, for a comparison of Italy, the UK and the Netherlands). In Mediterranean countries – but increasingly also in other European ones – it is a rather unregulated and informal market, which thrives for the larger part on often undocumented immigrant women originating from both Eastern European and extra-European countries, who live with the family, are not specifically trained as caregivers and, because of their fragile legal status, often suffer exploitative working conditions.

Italy is a good illustration of the intended and unintended consequences of the choice of cash transfers. In the 1980s the national government established a cash allowance for non-self-sufficient adults (*Indennità di accompagnamento*), which ended up being the main form of support for older people. Being targeted to non-self-sufficiency, but not means-tested (the same monthly allowance of close to EUR 500 is granted to every qualifying person), it reinforces social stratification since richer beneficiaries can top up their allowance and purchase better services. Moreover, since the allowance is not earmarked, i.e. there is no control on how it is spent, it reproduces gendered roles as it is very often used to support the income of the family taking care of the beneficiary. Alternatively, it supports the expansion of the informal market of privately hired caregivers, i.e. immigrant – often undocumented – women (the so-called *badanti*) (Van Hooren, 2010; NNA, 2015).

**Outsourcing or Direct Public Provision**

The decision to provide in-kind public services – as opposed to cash transfers – can be implemented in two ways: mobilising public structures and personnel to produce services or paying private organisations – whether for-profit or non-profit – to do it.

The preference for *outsourcing* was ideologically inspired by the wish to introduce competition among providers, hence increasing the quality of services and – here as well – users' choice. In practice, the preference has also been driven by the more pragmatic goals of either 'slimming' the rather expensive and often bureaucratic public apparatuses (in places where direct public provision existed) or quickly setting up a publicly 'supported' service supply (in places where such a direct provision did not exist). The first goal has clearly been pursued in many Nordic countries and localities, which have moved from direct to outsourced public provision (Anttonen and Karsio; Kröger and Bagnato, in this volume). The second goal has been pursued in 'latecomer' countries and regions, such as in Southern and Eastern Europe, which did not have a tradition of – and the institutional capital necessary for – direct provision of services, or wished to get away from an inefficient and/or qualitatively inadequate state provision (CAP Martinelli et al., 2014; CAP Bagnato et al., 2014; Kubalčíková et al., in this volume).

The impacts of outsourcing depend, again, on the level of public funding, the degree of regulation, and the type of providers involved. The level of public support clearly affects the quality and the differentiation of services: in many cases the public component only covers basic services, whereas additional/optional services require the payment of user fees which are contingent on the purchasing power of users, thus opening the way to a stratification of supply. The regulation of outsourcing concerns the accreditation and selection of providers (e.g. via competitive tenders or direct conferment) and the level of public monitoring. Both strongly influence the quality of services and the extent of users' choice. Particularly important is whether providers are for-profit or non-profit. The former behave according to a profit-maximising logic, which is no guarantee of meeting users' needs. There is evidence that the drive to contain costs in order to remain competitive can lead to a standardisation of tasks and a reduction of the time allotted to each task, which lowers the quality of services and runs counter to the goal of providing better customised and integrated services (Kröger and Bagnato, in this volume). Non-profit organisations, which used to follow a more 'community' or 'user-centred' logic, are now increasingly pressured to adopt more competitive practices in order to remain on the 'market' (Bode, in this volume). This often means that to maintain their more integrated and user-friendly approach they must rely on unpaid voluntary work. In both types of organisations, especially in Southern countries, there is also evidence of a lowering of training and skill requirements and a worsening of contractual conditions for care workers (Kröger and Bagnato, in this volume). In the end, the strategy of outsourcing public services *can* actually enhance users' choice and improve the efficiency and diversification of services, provided they are sufficiently funded and firmly regulated by the state.

In places where *direct public provision* has resisted, the introduction of new public management (NPM) practices, as well as the 'activation turn', have also brought about changes. The quantification – and monetisation – of needs and services, the standardisation – and often separation – of tasks, the tightening of eligibility criteria and/or the increased conditionality of services, together with the increase in user fees, have in many places determined a fragmentation of the service system, a worsening of access, and a stratification of users. In some cases, there has also been an enhancement of the 'disciplining' dimension of services (Mätzke et al.; Raeymaeckers et al., in this volume).

### Institutional Care or Home-based Care

Another choice that policy-makers face is whether to organise the delivery of services within *specialised institutions* where users live permanently or for long stretches of time (nursing homes, older people residences, LTC centres) or where they come daily (daycare centres), or *at the home of the users* (domiciliary or home-based care).

The advantages of the first form include economies of scale and specialisation, as well as the possibility to integrate in one place several different services (practical care, social care, health care, education, counselling, socialisation, etc.). But, especially in what concerns care for older people, institutional or residential care has come to be questioned. In the wake of the de-institutionalisation movement against mental health institutions, nursing and retirement homes have also been criticised, often on accurate grounds, for their alienating and disempowering effects. As early as the 1980s strategies for developing domiciliary or home-based services were implemented in many countries. In the 1990s, prompted by the rapidly rising numbers of older people and the need to contain public expenditures, these strategies were further supported throughout Europe by official discourses about 'ageing in place', the assumption being that domiciliary care services are less expensive than residential care, while allowing older people to keep living in their own surroundings.

Once again, this is not a pure 'either/or' choice. As revealed in many of our COST Action case studies and stressed repeatedly in this volume, needs – and applications – for care in residential structures remain very high everywhere, since only a portion of the older population can keep living at home, provided they receive adequate domiciliary support. Moreover, as stressed by Anttonen (Chapter 17, in this volume), care presumes different types of complementary services, generally provided by different institutions/suppliers and/or workers – practical help, personal care, medical care, socialisation – which need to be integrated. But this integration proves difficult in the case of home-based care, since different specialised workers must reach a significant number of different users during the work day and do not necessarily interact. Therefore, integration and personalisation of services are not a natural outcome of the home-based strategy: in many cases both users and care workers lament the 'tyranny of the clock' and the fragmentation of the services provided (Kröger and Bagnato, in this volume).

In the end, both institutional and home care have advantages and disadvantages. In the case of users who have some degree of self-sufficiency, domiciliary services can definitely improve – at least in principle – their quality of life and their satisfaction. In reality, however, domiciliary services are often inadequate and very imperfect substitutes for care that in many cases should be institutional. Moreover, home-based services very often require complementary care or organisational support from family members, which is not always available. In the case of people with limited self-sufficiency and no family to rely on, institutional care remains the only option. Residential institutions are – in principle – more conducive to ensure greater integration of services and case management; but in reality, nursing homes, retirement homes and LTC structures remain more often than not vulnerable to mass production and disempowering routines. To overcome these problems, smaller – community-like – structures are encouraged, but in many places, especially where austerity measures are in force, there are no resources to implement them.

To conclude, home-based and institutional care for older people constitute a 'fake' alternative. They respond to different needs and should *both* be provided and expanded. In contrast, in many countries and regions, especially in Southern and Eastern Europe, the implementation of 'de-institutionalisation' and 'ageing in place' strategies means a reduction in the public supply or support of residential care institutions, despite swelling waiting lists, while at the same time inadequate financial resources are allocated to domiciliary services (Kröger and Bagnato; Kubalčíková et al.; Deusdad, Lev et al., in this volume).

## 4.   CONCLUSIONS

Beyond the different supply landscapes and policy tools highlighted in this book, the key issue underlying most of the observed restructuring processes is the scarcity of public financial resources available for social services in the face of growing social needs.

This is a structural problem, throughout Europe, driven by concurrent and cumulative processes (see Table 1.1 in Chapter 1 of this volume): the slowdown of growth rates since the 1980s, topped by the financial crisis of 2008, with the ensuing fiscal stress for central and local governments; changes in the industrial structure and labour markets, with rising unemployment, underemployment and 'casualisation' of work; demographic trends (ageing of the population, global migration) and sociocultural changes (rising female activity rates, dual-earning households, single parents). All these trends have broadened the platform of social risks. The neo-liberal austerity measures and deficit management recipes enacted to face these crises and changes, far from easing the problems, have intensified income polarisation, unemployment, poverty and social exclusion, thereby further amplifying social needs, in a perverse vicious circle. In other words, despite the very ambitious goals of 'Europe 2020' and related EU social policy frameworks, which place great emphasis on smart, sustainable and *inclusive* growth, there is a growing gap – an 'implementation gap' (SIM, 2015) – between discourses, strategies and reality, which comes down to the shortage of resources that national states are able or willing to mobilise for social policy and services.

While the EU 'Fiscal compact' conditions the ability of many a state to allocate national resources to social policy, especially in countries most hit by the crisis, the EU resources made available through its Cohesion policy and Structural and investment funds do not manage to make any real difference (Gómez-Barroso et al., in this volume). First, the amounts of resources mobilised are far from sufficient, especially in regions characterised by an accumulated deficit in social services. Secondly, these resources are mostly for investment in social infrastructure and not for operating costs. But most importantly, aid is couched in the same competitive ideology that permeates the overall restructuring of social services, as it is generally provided through the same bidding procedures that are implemented for the outsourcing of public services. In this system, institutions, providers and places are pitted against each other and the stronger bidders are implicitly favoured, independently of actual needs. Moreover, aid is granted on a 'project' basis, thereby providing only short-term financial support, which is out of sync with the structures and the time frame of needs.

In the face of the above apparently unsolvable conundrum, I will conclude making a double plea for a change of paradigm, i.e. for reversing the way we think about social services and especially about two seemingly unavoidable directions of social policy design. The first plea calls for a reversal of the idea that social services are a mere redistributive mechanism aiming to ensures social justice – hence a 'cost' – and for (re)considering them as key *economic activities*. Not only because they contribute to lowering the costs of reproduction of labour, thereby sustaining the accumulation process; not only because they represent a productive investment, as postulated by the 'social investment' strategy, which contributes to lowering future costs; but most importantly because they can act as a Keynesian mechanism and contribute to relaunching domestic demand and economic growth. This view is timidly supported in a number of academic and policy circles. An 'Opinion' of the European Economic and Social Committee (EESC, 2014), for example, in rejecting one-sided austerity policies, has recently called for a counter-cyclical 'stimulus' programme and for excluding social investment from the calculation of net governments' deficit under the EMU fiscal rule. It also underlines the enormous employment and stabilisation potential of such a programme.

The second plea calls for a reversal of the idea that the market is inherently better than the state. As is becoming increasingly evident, the current directions of change in social services are undermining two key dimensions of Mätzke's 'progressive agenda' (Chapter 18, in this volume): *universalism* and *empowerment*. But they are also falling short of achieving the very aim of many neo-liberal reforms, i.e. *efficiency* and *choice*. Market-inspired or market-led reforms do not seem to be able to ensure the greater efficiency of the service system that the market ideology promises (at least not in the long run), nor do they seem to increase users' choice (at least not for everybody). The idea of choice, which was promoted from below by a number of social movements in the 1980s, has been appropriated by the neo-liberal strategy which equates users' choice with 'customers' choice'. But the latter choice is inevitably confined to the richer users, while at the same time neo-liberal reforms are further reducing the already limited universalistic dimension some of these services had attained in the past. Neither do these reforms create spaces for real users' empowerment, except when they self-produce services that have been curtailed. This means that we have to re-think – 're-invent' (Martinelli, 2012) – the *role of the state* and creatively re-assert its *steering* role, not only to compensate for, but also to prevent market failures.

I should also stress that, despite the overall gloomy picture presented in this book, which focused on services for especially vulnerable groups in society, the last ten or fifteen years have also witnessed important progress in the public provision of some services, such as childcare, and the blooming of many instances of experimentation and social innovation – within the public realm and outside it. These practices have contributed to bring forward users' empowerment, user-centred provision, choice, and self-determination, although they have not always been able to deploy their full transformative potential in terms of upscaling and institutionalisation. This is one more reason why, rather than leaving free rein to the logic of profit, the state should recover its role of 'guardian' and 'enhancer' of social citizenship, innovation and accumulation, ensuring that the market does not undermine itself by creating social and territorial inequalities. It is only within a renewed state commitment – at all scales – to both welfare *and* development that choice can be granted *together with* universal access and that social innovation at the local level can fulfil its potential for empowerment and change, instead of improperly and inadequately substituting for retrenching public services.

This reversal of the way we should think about the role of the state apparently clashes with the globalisation imperatives, in the name of which national sovereignty has been sacrificed and a race to the bottom is being passively accepted. The question then become 'which' state. We certainly cannot go back to the old national welfare state. But this should not hold us back from exploring new regulatory architectures, at a supra-national scale but involving multilevel governance, that would not fully give in to market logics and would recover the goal of a more balanced distribution of wealth.

## NOTES

1. There are actually many examples to the contrary, such as in the case of childcare in the UK, the cost of which has skyrocketed with privatisation (Mätzke et al.; Deusdad, Javornik et al., in this volume).
2. In fact, marketisation also pre-empts Esping-Andersen's notion that in a universalistic public system all benefit and all feel obliged to pay (1990).
3. This especially applies to the social component of care for older people, whereas the training requirements and contractual conditions of the health component are still regulated to a greater extent.

4.  I am here considering only cash transfers geared to purchase services and not income support benefits, such as unemployment benefits or other.

# REFERENCES

Bagnato, A., S. Barillà and F. Martinelli (2014), 'The public supply of care for older people in Reggio Calabria. The impact of the crisis on a long-standing deficit', presentation at the COST Action IS1102 Workshop, Ekonomickà Univerzita, Bratislava, 3–7 November.

Ciccia, R. and I. Bleijenbergh (2014), 'After the male breadwinner model? Childcare services and the division of labor in European countries', *Social Politics*, **21** (1), 50–79.

Clarke, J. (2010), 'After neo-liberalism? Markets, states and the reinvention of public welfare', *Cultural Studies*, **24** (3), 375–94.

Cunningham, I. (2008), 'A race to the bottom? Exploring variations in employment conditions in the voluntary sector', *Public Administration*, **86** (4), 1033–53.

Diamond, P. and R. Liddle (2012), 'Aftershock: the post-crisis social investment welfare state in Europe', in N. Morel, B. Palier and J. Palme (eds), *Towards a Social Investment Welfare State? Ideas, Policies and Challenges*, Bristol: Policy Press, pp. 285–308.

EESC – European Economic and Social Committee (2014), 'Opinion of the European Economic and Social Committee on "The impact of social investment on employment and public budgets"', *Official Journal of the European Union*, C 226, 21–27.

Esping-Andersen, G. (1990), *The Three Worlds of Welfare Capitalism*, Princeton: Princeton University Press.

Kazepov, Y. (ed.) (2010), *Rescaling Social Policies towards Multilevel Governance in Europe*, Avebury: Ashgate.

Kazepov, Y. and E. Barberis (eds) (2013), *Il welfare frammentato*, Rome: Carocci.

Leon, M. and E. Pavolini (2014), '"Social investment" or back to "familism": the impact of the economic crisis on family and care policies in Italy and Spain', *South European Society and Politics*, **19** (3), 353–69.

Martinelli, F. (2012), 'Social innovation or social exclusion? Innovating social services in the context of a retrenching welfare state', in H.-W. Franz, J. Hochgerner and J. Howaldt (eds), *Challenge Social Innovation. Potentials for Business, Social Entrepreneurship, Welfare and Civil Society*, Berlin: Springer, pp. 169–80.

Martinelli, F. and A. Sarlo (2012), 'Regulatory trajectories and organisational frameworks of social services. Country profile of Italy', unpublished paper presented at the COST Action IS1102 Workshop, Oslo and Akershus University College, Oslo, 18 June.

Martinelli, F., S. Barillà and A. Sarlo (2014), 'Daycare services in the municipality of Reggio Calabria. The impact of the crisis on a long-standing deficit', *COST Action IS1102 Working Papers*, no. 7, accessed in December 2016 at http://www.cost-is1102-cohesion.unirc.it/docs/working-papers/wg2.italy-rc-childcare-martinelli-barilla-and-sarlo.pdf.

Meagher, G. and M. Szebehely (eds) (2013), *Marketization in Nordic Eldercare: A Research Report on Legislation, Oversight, Extent and Consequences*, Stockholm: Stockholm University.

Morgan, K.J. (2013), 'Path shifting of the welfare state: electoral competition and the expansion of work–family policies in Western Europe', *World Politics*, **65** (1), 73–115.

Newman, J. (2001), *Modernising Governance: New Labour, Policy and Society*, London: Sage.

NNA – Network Non Autosufficienza (ed.) (2015), *L'assistenza agli anziani non autosufficienti in Italia*, Fifth Report, Santarcangelo di Romagna: Maggioli Editore (RN), accessed in December 2016 at http://www.maggioli.it/rna/2015/pdf/V-rapporto-assistenza_anziani.pdf.

Pierson, P. (1994), *Dismantling the Welfare State? Reagan, Thatcher, and the Politics of Retrenchment*, Cambridge: Cambridge University Press.

Rhodes, R.A.W. (2007), 'Understanding governance: ten years on', *Organization Studies*, **28** (08), 1243–64.

Scharpf, F.W. (2002), 'The European social model: coping with the challenges of diversity', *Journal of Common Market Studies*, **40** (4), 645–70.

SIM – Social Inclusion Monitor Europe (2014), *Social Justice in the EU. Index Report*, Gütersloh, Germany and London, UK: Bertelsmann-Stiftung and London School of Economics.

SIM – Social Inclusion Monitor Europe (2015), *Social Policy Reforms in Europe. A Cross-National Comparison*, Gütersloh, Germany and London, UK: Bertelsmann-Stiftung and London School of Economics.

Van Hooren, F. (2010), 'When families need immigrants: the exceptional position of migrant domestic workers and care assistants in Italian immigration policy', *Bulletin of Italian Politics*, **2** (2), 21–38.

Van Hooren, F.J. (2012), 'Varieties of migrant care work: comparing patterns of migrant labour in social care', *Journal of European Social Policy*, **22** (2), 133–47.

Yeandle, S. (2014), 'Reconfiguring services for older people living at home in Leeds, UK: how have services changed?', unpublished paper presented at the COST Action IS1102 Workshop, University of Tampere, Tampere, 2–6 June; now published as S. Yeandle (2016), 'From provider to enabler of care? Reconfiguring local authority support for older people and carers in Leeds, 2008 to 2013', *Journal of Social Service Research*, **42** (2), 218–32.

# Index